Chinese Fiction
of the
Cultural
Revolution

Chinese Fiction
of the
Cultural Revolution

Lan Yang

香港大學出版社
HONG KONG UNIVERSITY PRESS

Hong Kong University Press
14/F Hing Wai Centre
7 Tin Wan Praya Road
Aberdeen, Hong Kong

© Hong Kong University Press 1998

ISBN 962 209 467 8

Printed in Hong Kong by Caritas Printing Training Centre.

Contents

List of Tables

Foreword

It is a great pleasure to be able to introduce Dr Yang's work to a wider audience. During the course of his study of Cultural Revolution fiction, I have been again and again impressed with the thoroughness of his research. Even more, I have been astonished and delighted at the results his painstaking work has yielded. Once and for all, the widespread misconception (repeated even by people who lived through that period) that in literature and the arts the Cultural Revolution produced no more than 'eight model operas' should be laid to rest. What is truly unexpected, and unique to Dr Yang's investigations, are such revelations as the artistic or poetic sides to the main heroes' temperaments in Cultural Revolution fiction, and the relative decline in vulgar and abusive expressions in the dialogue and narrative during this period.

Dr Yang was one of the original readers to whom these novels were addressed. Unlike many of those readers, he has retained a certain sympathy for the novels which has enabled him to dedicate several years of his life to the patient collection of their linguistic and literary data. His scrupulously objective methodology avoids any hint of bias, but, since few readers now are willing to read them, he has performed a great service for the scholarship of this period with his comprehensive and detailed analyses.

Dr Yang's study will find its natural audience among students and scholars of modern Chinese literature and intellectual history, but I should also like to commend it as absorbing reading for scholars of comparative literature. Too little is still known about those writers who braved quite extraordinary risks (given the swift and violent changes in political line during 1960s and 1970s China) to see their stories in print, although Dr Yang makes clear that despite the pressure of orthodoxy their individual contributions can still be discerned. Even less is understood about the condition of literature in modern totalitarian states. Dr Yang's work is an outstanding contribution towards our enlightenment.

Bonnie S. McDougall
Professor of Chinese
University of Edinburgh

Preface

In the history of literature it often seems that in periods of great vitality there was a sharp rejection of the immediate past. Official literature in the People's Republic of China may be divided into pre-Cultural Revolution (CR) literature (1949–65), CR literature (1966–76) and post-CR literature (1977–). It is generally taken for granted that post-CR literature, especially in the first ten years, is the most prosperous stage in contemporary Chinese literary history, and for this reason also there is an abundance of studies of post-CR literature.

In contrast, CR literature is undoubtedly the most bleak, and scholarly examinations of this literature are limited. Nevertheless, CR literature has its own position in the history of contemporary China. It tested the new CR literary theories and principles; it carried out the radical elements of pre-CR literary theories and principles; more importantly, it indirectly determined the deviation of post-CR literature from its predecessors. This book is a comprehensive study of CR fiction, with a particular focus on two aspects: characterization and language.

Since CR literature fundamentally aimed to serve ideology, my examination of the characters in CR fiction lays stress on the social and ideological significance of the characteristics shown in their personal background, physical qualities, temperamental and behavioural qualities, and so on. Because CR literary creation was designed to cut off relationships with traditional and foreign literature and art, and became an unprecedentedly closed system in contemporary Chinese literature, this analysis is mainly confined to CR and pre-CR fiction, although the framework of reference sometimes covers other fiction, such as traditional Chinese and Western novels, and Soviet novels.

My linguistic analysis of CR fiction focuses on vocabulary. Based on a number of sample works, twelve stylistic categories have been established through statistical analysis: vulgar expressions, ideological words and expressions, idioms, proverbs, *xiehouyu*, classical verses, 'bookish', 'colloquial' and dialectal words, military items in metaphorical use, meteorological items in metaphorical use, and inflated items. The investigation presents the density and distributions of the stylistic items concerning narrators and different types of characters, the general fictional language style, the relation between the general style and the authors' individual language style, and the similarities and differences between pre-CR novel language style and CR novel language style.

Help from many people was indispensable for the completion and publication of this book. First and foremost I wish to thank my supervisor, Professor Bonnie S. McDougall, for her guidance, criticism and encouragement during my three years of Ph.D. studies and my current post-doctoral research work.

I am also in particular grateful to the staff of Hong Kong University Press, and to the anonymous referee of my manuscript for their confidence, suggestions and efficiency in arranging the publication of this book.

Dr T. M. McClellan, Dr Po-Ching Yip and Dr Karin McPherson read and commented on the manuscript. Professor He Ande, Professor Li Anping and Professor Duan Zhongqiao helped me in collecting materials. Hu Xiaoming, Li Yelin, She Shenglin, Hu Xiaoyan, Hu Cen and Yang Qiming were helpful in the statistical evaluation of the linguistic analysis. Carol Rennie, Liliana Riga and Jane Elisabeth Rubino proofread the manuscript. Dr Bill Dolby gave me help in compiling the glossary. I wish to thank each of them. I also owe gratitude to my wife, Yu Jieling, for her untiring support of my work.

Finally, my visit to Britain was initially supported by the Sino-British Friendship Scholarship Scheme. My Ph.D. studies were assisted by an Overseas Research Students Award from the Universities of the United Kingdom, and a Vans Dunlop Scholarship from the University of Edinburgh, which are also warmly appreciated.

L.Y.
Department of East Asian Studies
at the University of Edinburgh
October 1997

Introduction

Both inside and outside China, the Great Proletarian Cultural Revolution ('CR' for short) was known as the most sensational political movement in contemporary China under the People's Republic. Some scholars prefer to date the Cultural Revolution from 1966 to 1969 and to define the period from 1969 to 1976 as a radical leftist phase. This book adopts the definition which dates the CR from 1966 to 1976 and divides the decade into two periods. The latter definition was the post-CR Chinese government's official definition, and it is also widely adopted by Western scholars. In his *China's Continuous Revolution: The Post-Liberation Epoch 1949–1981*, Lowell Dittmer states, the Cultural Revolution 'consisted of two distinct periods, the first of which was characterised by spontaneous mobilisation of disprivileged strata, lasting from the summer of 1966 through the fall of 1968; the second of which was characterised by elite attempts to sponsor and channel mass mobilisation, which lasted from late 1968 until the downfall of the Shanghai radicals in October 1976'.[1]

There is a multitude of books in the world which deal with the Cultural Revolution. Since the movement, in spite of its name, produced very little that can seriously be considered a contribution to China's cultural development, of those existing books referring to the Cultural Revolution, most concentrate on analysing its political aspects or describing its process.

This book is about the literature produced during the Cultural Revolution. It is well known that literature and art was one of the most prominent spheres with regard to the movement. On the one hand, the movement was initiated in this field which consequently was one primary target of the 'revolution'. On the other hand, literature and art was cultivated as one of the most important measures to carry out the movement. Actually, during the Cultural Revolution, literature and art was the only domain which was consistently under the control of Jiang Qing and her followers.[2]

In 1972, Cyril Birch pointed out, 'It is a commonplace observation that no regime in Chinese history has been more assiduous than the present one in cultivating the garden of letters . . .'[3] While criticizing literature and art from before the Cultural Revolution, the authorities headed by Jiang Qing vigorously attempted to create new literature and art. The following declaration of 1967 indicates their intention.

> Under the leadership of the Central Committee of the Party and Chairman Mao and under the guidance of Marxism-Leninism and Mao Tse-tung's thought, we must create a new socialist revolutionary literature and art worthy of our great country, our great Party, our great people and our great army. This will be a most brilliant new literature and art opening up a new era in human history . . . To create a fine work is an arduous process, and the comrades in charge of creative works must never adopt a bureaucratic or casual attitude but must work really hard and share the writers' and artists' joys and hardships . . . There should be no fear of failure or mistakes. Allowance should be made for them, and people must be permitted to correct their mistakes . . . so that a work may become better and better and achieve the unity of revolutionary political content and the best possible artistic form.[4]

What are the characteristics of the new literature and art? There are studies of CR poetry, fiction, drama and film, although they are scanty and usually on a small scale.[5]

Some genres consist of two sets of works, official and unofficial. For example, amounts of underground and exile fiction were produced and circulated during the CR decade, most of which are short stories and novellas. It is only natural that the underground and exile works are separate from the new literature and art although some of them unavoidably reflect certain styles of that period. Probably due to accessibility of materials or scholars' special interest, existing studies of CR fiction are mostly concerned with unofficial works. No substantial scholarly treatment of official CR fiction has appeared in Chinese or English. Sporadic critical discourse in Chinese on official CR fiction has often been strongly subjective.

The present study is of novels officially published during the Cultural Revolution. It aims to reveal characteristics of CR novels by analysing a number of sample works and comparing them with works published before the Cultural Revolution, with a view to determining the position of CR novels in the history of contemporary Chinese literature.

My study will be from a perspective of combining literature and linguistics (linguo-stylistics). On the one hand, the combining perspective is in accordance with the fact pointed out by Leo Ou-fan Lee that language and characterization are two emphasized aspects of pre-CR and CR literature.[6] On the other hand, the dual perspective complies with the tendency of literary criticism stated by J. H. Miller, that is, the aims of literary study had shifted from an élitist interest in aesthetic appreciation of poetic text to an egalitarian emphasis on the importance of the assessment of textual value in both literary and ordinary language.[7]

In view of the prominent position of portrayal of heroes in the then current literary aesthetic views and the importance of words and expressions in linguistic style, this book includes two main parts: the characterization of the main heroes, and the lexical style of the language. Generally, the study lays more stress on those collective or period literary and stylistic characteristics of CR novels than on individual or isolated features of specific authors or works.

CR NOVELS AND CR AGRICULTURAL NOVELS

In Chinese terms, fiction is sub-divided into *changpian xiaoshuo* [literally, long fiction or novels], *zhongpian xiaoshuo* [middle length fiction or novellas] and *duanpian xiaoshuo* [short fiction or short stories]. However, no established quantitative criterion can be found for these divisions. For example, with regard to the division between novels and novellas, according to different publishers' labelling, Zhou Jiajun's *Mountain Wind* [*Shan feng*] with 341 pages and Chen Dabin's *The Surging Dongliu River* [*Benteng de Dongliuhe*] with 363 pages are novellas, but Liu Qing's *Wall of Bronze* [*Tong qiang tie bi*] with 245 pages and Liu Huaizhang's *Turbulent Current* [*Jiliu*] with 294 pages belong to novels. In spite of the disagreement, nevertheless, according to my investigation into different publishers' labelling, the confusing length mainly exists between 200 pages and 350 pages, that is, no work with fewer than 200 pages was labelled a novel, and a work with over 350 pages was generally labelled a novel. In the present study, in order to avoid possible confusion with regard to statistics, only fiction of over 200 pages is taken into consideration, all of which I consider novels.

Next, for the sake of convenience of analysis, I need to define three terms which are frequently used in this presentation: CR novels, pre-CR novels and post-CR novels. CR novels are those first published during the Cultural Revolution, pre-CR novels are those first published between the foundation of the People's Republic and the initiation of the Cultural Revolution (October 1949 – May 1966); and post-CR novels are those first published after the Cultural Revolution. CR novels generally were written after 1969, with a few exceptions where the drafts were completed before the Cultural Revolution. As the large literary periodicals, which often serialized long novels, were discontinued during the Cultural Revolution, CR novels were generally published in book form.

CR Novels

According to my statistics, there are 126 CR novels in total, among which about 25 have 200–350 pages, and the others are all over 350 pages.[8] The statistics exclude reprints or revised editions of pre-CR works. For example, Liu Qing's *Wall of Bronze*, which was first published in 1951 but reissued in a revised form in 1976, is not included. On the other hand, a novel of more than one volume is counted as one unit even though the volumes were published in different years and the page numbers are not continuous. For example, Li Yunde's *Seething Mountains* [*Feiteng de qunshan*] is in three volumes, among which Volume 1 was published in 1972, Volume 2 in 1973, and Volume 3 in 1976.

The average number of CR novels produced per year is therefore about twelve. According to other statistics, the total number of pre-CR novels is about 170. The annual quantity produced during the seventeen-year period between 1949 and 1966 is therefore about ten. The number of post-CR novels produced between 1977 and 1986 is about 1,000. The annual quantity produced was about 100.[9] Thus, although the annual quantity of CR novels only accounts for about one-tenth of post-CR novels, it is not below the annual production of pre-CR novels. The distribution of CR novels according to year is as follows.

Year	Number of CR novels
1972	10
1973	11
1974	21
1975	36
1976	48
Total	126

The first CR novel is *Battle Chronicles of Hongnan* [*Hongnan zuozhan shi*], which was published in February 1972. No novels were published in the five years between the beginning of the Cultural Revolution and the publication of this novel. As pointed out by Cyril Birch, the production of literature and art works during the first five years was reduced to an unprecedentedly low level. In the later period, even Mao pointed out that the country was 'short of poetry, short of fiction, short of prose and short of literary comments'.[10] According to the above table, the annual quantity of CR novels increased by a big margin in 1975 and 1976. The change could reflect the adjustment of the relevant policies after Mao's criticism.

With respect to subject matter, the 126 CR novels cover different areas, including agriculture, industry, military affairs, counter-espionage, education, medicine, forestry, livestock husbandry, fishery, and so on. Some categories have unconventional meanings which reflect the times. For instance, novels on medicine are mainly about barefoot doctors in the countryside rather than medical workers in urban hospitals. In the decade from 1966 to 1976, new policies pursued by the government gave rise to a variety of 'socialist new things' [shehuizhuyi xinsheng shiwu]. The promotion of barefoot doctors is an example. Another example is the practice of assigning school-leavers [zhishi qingnian] to work in the countryside, which was considered 're-education'. These 'socialist new things' became an important part of the subject matter for CR novels.

The four largest categories of subject matter in the 126 CR novels and their distribution are shown in the table below.

Subject matter		Time-setting	
		1927–49	post-1949
Military affairs	32	17	15
Agriculture	24	–	24
Industry	18	2	16
'Re-education'	17	–	17

The total number of novels in the four categories is 91, which make up 72.2 percent of the total 126 CR novels. The three largest categories are military affairs, agriculture and industry, reflecting Mao's directives on serving workers, peasants and soldiers. In the novels of the fourth major category, main characters include school-leavers as students, who were then called 'new peasants' [xinshi nongmin], and local peasants as 'teachers'. Among the rest, some novels describe the construction of large infrastructure projects such as the harnessing of the Hai River, in which workers, peasants and soldiers cooperated. Other works, classified as children's stories, concentrate on children's contribution to agriculture, industry, counter-espionage and so on.

Among the 126 novels, except for Li Huixin's *Beside the Lancang River* [*Lancangjiang pan*], which describes a professional medical team working in the countryside, no others can be found which focus on professional intellectuals such as teachers, authors, artists, doctors (other than barefoot doctors) and scientists. Another characteristic of subject matter is that no CR novel has been found on historical themes ('historical' here refers to the time before the end of the imperial era in 1911). Although written evidence is hard to come by for this period, it was widely known that the CR authorities were highly suspicious of works set in traditional China. After Wu Han's historical play *Hai Rui's Dismissal from Office* [*Hai Rui ba guan*] was attacked by Yao Wenyuan as criticism of the authorities by innuendo, historical settings became a forbidden zone in literature and art. Furthermore, as pointed out by Jeffrey C. Kinkley, no CR novel 'about crimes committed by typical Chinese' ('crime fiction') can be found since 'socialist realist fiction was supposed "realistically" to reflect the brightness of the future in the society of the present'.[11] Moreover, no CR novel can be called 'science fiction' (the Chinese usually call it 'science-fantasy fiction' [*kexue huanxiang xiaoshuo*].[12]

The earliest time-setting in the 126 novels is the Second Civil War (1927–37), but only Li Ruqing's *Mountains in Red* [*Wan shan hong bian*] (Vol. 1) is set in this period. The other works are all set after 1937 when the Sino-Japanese War broke out. According to convention, I group time-settings into two categories: 1919–49 and post-1949. Among CR novels, those with a post-1949 time-setting make up the overwhelming majority. Such a distribution reflects the official promotion of subject matter concerning socialist revolution under the People's Republic and the disapproval or prohibition of historical subject matter.

I have not investigated in detail the distribution of pre-CR novels with regard to subject matter and time-setting. It is generally agreed that, among pre-CR novels, those with subject matter concerning industry, agriculture and military affairs also make up the majority. However, on the whole, pre-CR novels have a larger scope of subject matter by comparison with CR novels. For example, there were historical novels before the Cultural Revolution, such as Yao Xueyin's *Li Zicheng* (Vol. 1) (1963). Other novels, such as Yang Mo's *Song of Youth* [*Qingchun zhi ge*], Gao Yunlan's *Stories in a Small City* [*Xiao cheng chunqiu*] and Ouyang Shan's *Three Families in a Lane* [*San jia xiang*], focus on intellectuals in the underground movement rather than the struggles of workers, peasants and soldiers. Such novels were attacked in the Cultural Revolution for glorifying the petty bourgeoisie. Moreover, compared to CR novels, the greater proportion of pre-CR novels is set between 1919 and 1949.

According to the above table, military affairs rank first among the four major categories. There are several reasons for this. Firstly, during the Cultural Revolution, the campaign of learning from the Chinese People's Liberation Army (PLA), which was initiated in 1963, reached its highest stage,[13] and novelists who used military subjects were likely to win support. Secondly, military affairs had been prominent in contemporary Chinese literature and art before the Cultural Revolution. For example, of the eight model theatrical works (all based on pre-CR works), five focus on military subjects. Among pre-CR novels, the quantity of military novels is far ahead of others. This literary and artistic tradition necessarily had an impact on CR novel creation. Thirdly, the PLA had been active under different names before the foundation of the People's Republic and experienced numerous military events which offered a great quantity of material for plots and settings. This is the reason why, as shown in the above table, among the four major categories of subject matter, the distribution of 1919-49 time-setting in the military category ranks first. Finally, literary creativity in the PLA was especially encouraged by the authorities during the Cultural Revolution. For example, the authoritative official CR document with respect to literature and art was based on a forum convened in the Army (the 'Forum on the Work in Literature and Art in the Armed Force with which Comrade Lin Biao Entrusted Comrade Jiang Qiang').

CR Agricultural Novels

The quantity of CR agricultural novels ranks second. By agricultural novels we mean only those which focus on stories of farmers in the countryside. Therefore, novels also set in the countryside narrating stories about children, barefoot doctors, soldiers, school-leavers and so on are not included. Also, if the main story of a novel is not about agriculture, the novel does not belong to this category, although its main characters might be farmers. The 24 CR agricultural novels are listed in Appendix 1.

The present investigation focuses on the CR agricultural novels. Why should I choose agricultural novels rather than military novels which rank first according to the distribution of subject matter? Firstly, unlike military novels, agricultural novels all describe life in the People's Republic. This post-1949 time-setting reflects the main trend of CR novels. Secondly, unlike military novels, in which the main stories are about fighting against enemy troops, CR agricultural novels mainly reflect inner Party struggles. The inner Party struggles are the basic 'theme' of the Cultural Revolution and also the most important motif of CR literature. Thirdly, from the point of view of literary creation, agricultural novels represent a recognized higher level of technique in the realm of novel-writing during the CR period. It is obvious that not all the 126 CR novels can be on the same level with regard to their literary quality. Post-CR Chinese critics generally gave more praise to the following four works: Hao Ran's *The Golden Road* [*Jinguang da dao*], Ke Fei's *Swift is the Spring Tide* [*Chun chao ji*], Chen Rong's *Evergreen* [*Wan nian qing*] and Li Ruqing's *Mountains in Red*. Of the four, three are agricultural novels. Moreover, the authorship of CR agricultural novels includes not only professional writers such as Hao Ran, who was the most important writer in the CR period, but also young writers of potential such as Chen Rong and Gu Hua, who later became well-known post-CR novelists.

With sub-types of subject matter taken into consideration, the 24 CR novels all concern specific politicized campaigns in the countryside during the pre-CR and CR periods. Below are the sub-types of subject matter and their distribution in the 24 novels.

1. Cooperative transformation, six works: *The Surging Dongliu River* (Chen Dabin), *The Peacock Flies High* (Gao Zhongwu), *The Golden Road* (Hao Ran), *Swift is the Spring Tide* (Ke Fei), *Mountains Emblazoned with Crimson* (Sun Feng), and *Battle Chronicles of Hongnan* (Shanghai Xian Hongnan *zuozhan shi* Xiezuo Zu).
2. Opposition to quotas on a household basis, five works: *Evergreen* (Chen

Rong), *The Roaring Songhua River* (Lin Yu and Xie Shu), *Spring Comes to Zhang River* (Wang Dongman), *The Jumang River* (Yang Chuntian), and *Xiangshui Bend* (Zheng Wanlong).

3. Socialist Education, two works: *Violent Thunder* (Wang Zhongyu *et al.*) and *Qingshi Fort* (Zhu Jian).

4. Mechanization of agriculture, one work: *Billows and Waves* (Bi Fang and Zhong Tao).

5. Learning from Dazhai, ten works: *Zhangtian River* (Cheng Xianzhang), *Yinsha Beach* (Feng Yunan), *The Mountains and Rivers Roar* (Gu Hua), *Mountains Green after Rain* (Guangxi Zhuangzu Zizhiqu Baise Diqu Sanjiehe Chuangzuo Zu), *Dawn over Emerald Ridge* (anonymous, 'collective'), *Baizhang Ridge* (Shao Chuang), *The Long Rainbow* (Tian Dongzhao), *At the Foot of the Kezile Mountain* (Tuerdi Keyoumu), *The Daughter of Slaves* (Wang Zhijun), and *Mountain People* (Zhang Xue).

These sub-types of subject matter and their distribution are different from those of pre-CR and post-CR agricultural novels. In pre-CR agricultural novels, cooperative transformation (including consolidation of collectivization) is the sole subject matter. As for post-CR agricultural novels, only a few, which were published soon after the Cultural Revolution, primarily concern the two sub-types: cooperative transformation and learning from Dazhai. Soon after, the above five sub-types of subject matter generally disappeared from post-CR agricultural novels because such politicized campaigns were disapproved of. This situation does not mean that the campaigns have been banned from post-CR novels, but that they have not appeared as focal and glorified events as in the CR novels.

The CR novels about cooperative transformation were produced mainly in the early stage when CR novels appeared. The first two CR agricultural novels, *Battle Chronicles of Hongnan* and *The Golden Road* (Vol. 1), which are also the first two of all CR novels published in 1972, are about cooperative transformation. The former was written between June and December in 1971, and the latter between December of 1970 and November of 1971. The third CR agricultural novel is *Swift is the Spring Tide*, which also concerns cooperative transformation. These facts indicate that novelists still followed the example of pre-CR agricultural fiction on subject matter during the early period of the Cultural Revolution. In contrast, among the other 21 CR agricultural novels, which were mainly published between 1975 and 1976, only three deal with cooperative transformation. This situation indicates the changes in CR novelists' selection of sub-types of subject matter in agriculture in the late period of CR novel creation.

The other four sub-types of subject matter did not appear in CR agricultural novels until 1974. On the one hand, their appearance was related to the authorities' promotion of the Cultural Revolution. Even in the early CR period, the authorities in charge of literature and art began to call for works on the Cultural Revolution.[14] During the later CR period, writing about the Cultural Revolution was greatly promoted. The new literary magazine *Rosy Dawn* [*Zhaoxia*] (including the *congkan* [collection], started in 1973, and the *yuekan* [monthly], started in 1974), which was directly under the control of Jiang Qing, Zhang Chunqiao and Yao Wenyuan, played a leading role in encouraging writing about the Cultural Revolution. On the other hand, these new sub-types of subject matter about agriculture embodied the spirit of the Cultural Revolution and/or represented the current central tasks of the government.

The sub-type of 'opposition to quotas on a household basis' reflected the clashes between Mao and his Party opponents in the early 1960s, relating to the Party-line struggles of the Cultural Revolution.[15]

The Socialist Education movement was a nationwide political campaign carried out between 1964 and 1965. The purpose of the campaign was to struggle against the so-called capitalist-roaders ('Party persons in authority taking the capitalist road'), in accordance with the subsequent struggles of the Cultural Revolution.[16]

Ever since Mao's call to develop agricultural mechanization was issued in the 1950s with relation to the cooperative campaign, the goal of 'mechanization of agriculture' was periodically promoted. During the Cultural Revolution, the government once again attached importance to the problem while emphasizing the development of agriculture.[17] Bi Fang's CR novel *Billows and Waves* [*Qian chong lang*] is set in the Cultural Revolution. As indicated in the publishers' description [*neirong shuoming*] of the novel, the theme of the novel is 'to glorify with zeal the Great Proletarian Cultural Revolution' by describing the achievements of mechanization in agriculture.

Lastly, the sub-type of learning from Dazhai ranks first in distribution among the 24 CR agricultural novels. Mao issued the call 'in agriculture learn from Dazhai' in 1964, but the campaign did not reach its peak until the Cultural Revolution.[18] In 1975, a conference on learning from Dazhai was held by the government; the central task of the whole country was announced as being 'popularization of Dazhai-like counties' [*puji Dazhai xian*]. Of the ten novels about learning from Dazhai, eight were finalized and published after the congress although writing generally began in 1974. Moreover, the novels about learning from Dazhai are generally set during the Cultural Revolution.

The Authorship and Readership of CR Novels

The authorship of CR novels may be classified into four types: single, joint, collective and collective-individual. Joint authorship and collective authorship are understood here as defined in Bonnie S. McDougall's research into CR poetry.[19] That is, in the former case, two or more (only two for CR novels) authors have affixed their names to a work, and in the latter case, only the name of a writing group to which the work units are attached is given,. The term *saniehe* [three-in-one], which represents the collaboration of leaders, professionals and the masses, is sometimes noted alongside the name of collective writing group. Examples of a collective authorship are Shanghai Xian *Hongnan zuozhan shi* Xiezuo Zu [The Writing Group of *Battle Chronicles of Hongnan* of Shanghai County] (for the novel *Battle Chronicles of Hongnan*) and Guangxi Zhuangzu Zizhiqu Baise Diqu Sanjiehe Chuangzuo Zu [The Three-in-one Group of Baise Prefecture of the Guangxi Zhuang Autonomous Region] (for the novel *Yu hou qingshan* [*Mountains Green after Rain*]). By collective-individual authorship, I mean cases in which, apart from the name of a writing group, the individual(s) who did the actual writing is (are) identified. For example, in the novel *Jing lei* [*Violent Thunder*], the identification of 'Heilongjiang Sheng Shuangcheng Xian Geming Weiyuanhui, Zhongguo Renmin Jiefangjun Jing Zi 801 Budui Lianhe Chuangzuo Zu' [The Collaborative Writing Group of the Revolutionary Committee of Shuangcheng County in Heilongjiang Province and the PLA 801 Unit under the Beijing Command], is followed by recognition of the actual writers Wang Zhongyu, Chen Genxi and Xie Shu, although their individual contributions are not distinguished.

The distribution of the types of authorship of the total 126 CR novels is as follows:

Type of authorship	Number of novels	Percentage of the total 126
Single	107	84.92
Joint	8	6.35
Collective	9	7.14
Collective-individual	2	1.59

According to this table, single authorship still accounts for the overwhelming majority of CR novels. With respect to pre-CR novels, single authorship is even more prominent. Joint authorship also exists in pre-CR novels. However, I have so far found neither collective authorship nor collective-individual authorship in pre-CR novels although the data I have obtained is insufficient to exclude any occasional exception.

There are 122 individual authors in total. This number includes co-authors in joint authorship and actual writers in collective-individual authorship, but it excludes repetitive counting, i.e. an author who wrote more than one novel is counted only once. With a few exceptions, I do not know with precision the age, sex, social background, educational level, or family life of the individual authors. According to their writing experience, these 122 individual authors may be classified into two groups: Group One, which includes 13 individual authors who had literary publications before the Cultural Revolution, and Group Two, which includes 109 authors who had no publications before the Cultural Revolution. This classification is based on Meishi Tsai's *Contemporary Chinese Novels and Short Stories, 1949-1974: An Annotated Bibliography*, and Kam Louie and Louise Edwards's *Bibliography of English Translations and Critiques of Contemporary Chinese Literature 1945-1992*.

The authors in Group One were generally middle-aged or older during the Cultural Revolution. Most of them began to publish fiction (short stories, novellas or novels) in the 1950s, and some had become noted professional novelists before 1966, for example, Hao Ran,[20] Lin Yu, Zhou Jiajun, Zhang Changgong, Zhang Jun,[21] Mu Chongguang, Li Ruqing[22] and Li Yunde. Four authors from Group One, Hao Ran, Zhang Changgong, Li Yunde, and Ke Yang, published more than one novel during the Cultural Revolution. In Group Two, the authors were mainly young or middle-aged during the Cultural Revolution. Some were labelled 'spare-time writers' [*yeyu zuozhe*]. Spare-time writing was promoted and well-organized during the Cultural Revolution. The spare-time writers were mainly workers, peasants, soldiers, school-leavers, and school teachers. Usually, their occupations were labelled by presses, which indicates the authorities' promotion and encouragement of spare-time writing. For example, Guan Jianxun, the author of *Yun yan* [*The Swallow through Cloud*], is labelled 'a young peasant', and Wang Lei, the author of *Jianhe lang* [*Waves on the Jian River*], is labelled as 'a school-leaver'. The authors in Group Two generally referred to themselves as novices in literary creation. No author from this group published more than one novel during the decade except for Xie Shu who is the co-author of two CR novels.

In view of the strict ideological control over the literary and art world during the CR decade, the ideological standing of the authors of CR novels may be assumed to be beyond reproach by the authorities. However, the ideological standing does not always mean that the authors had a 'good' political status or family background. Furthermore, to a certain extent authors had freedom to write by themselves although revision and publication were under close guidance and censorship. For instance, in Laifong Leung's *Morning Sun: Interviews with Chinese Writers of the Lost Generation*, only Zhang Kangkang,[23] Ye Xin, and Zheng Wanlong[24] are CR writers. Of the three, Zhang and Ye had similar experiences during the Cultural Revolution. They were both born in big cities: Zhang was born in Hangzhou and Ye in Shanghai. According to their accounts, Zhang was not a member of the Communist Youth League and was from a 'bad' class background; Ye's family were classified as members of the 'Five Black Categories', and Ye was not allowed to join the Red Guards. In response to the government's call, they went to the countryside in the early stages of the Cultural Revolution. Zhang went to the Great Barren North (in northeast China), and Ye to Guizhou Province (in southwest China). Zhang began publishing in 1972 and Ye in 1974. In 1974 Zhang wrote her CR novel *Fenjie xian* [*Demarcation*], and Ye wrote his novel *Yan Ying* [*Stone Falcon*]. Coincidentally they both sent their manuscripts to Shanghai People's Press. They received replies from the press very soon, and were invited to the press to make revisions under the editors' guidance. Zhang's *Demarcation* was published in 1975. Ye's novel was under revision and was about to be published when the Cultural Revolution ended (the novel was eventually published in 1978). When they recalled their writing experience during the Cultural Revolution, both Zhang and Ye claimed that they wrote their fiction on their own initiative in the countryside, that the editors were willing to help them, and that their 'bad' family background did not hinder their writing and publication.

With regard to writing capability, a number of CR novelists did seem professionally competent. As regards the Group One novelists, they had been active in writing before the Cultural Revolution and their large numbers of literary publications showed their professional competence. As for the Group Two CR writers, apart from their experience in the CR period, many were still active in writing after the Cultural Revolution. A few of them, such as Chen Rong (Shen Rong),[25] Gu Hua,[26] Mo Yingfeng,[27] Li Huixin,[28] Zhang Kangkang and Zheng Wanlong have been recognized as talented novelists in the post-CR literary world. These facts indicate the potential of some of the young CR novelists. Moreover, according to the above stories of Zhang Kangkang and Ye Xin, the concerned departments and authorities mainly set store by the manuscripts themselves, which certainly showed the novice authors' potential.

In the CR period the authors of CR novels claimed to take a serious attitude towards their writing and showed themselves willing to talk about their intentions and motives. The following ideas are commonly found in their statements: Firstly, they claimed to be moved by real people and their deeds, which inspired their writing. Secondly, they attributed their works to the Party and Mao's line in literature and art. Lastly, they claimed to follow official literary and artistic principles and to strive for high quality both in content and in form. The following quotation from the postscript of *Shanchuan huxiao* [*The Mountains and Rivers Roar*] may be taken as a representative statement. The author, Gu Hua, later became famous for his post-CR novel *Furongzhen* [*Furong Town*] in 1981.

> I am an amateur in literary writing. I have worked and studied in the countryside for over ten years, during which I have met a lot of heroic people who did well in the movement of learning from Dazhai. . . Their heroic deeds have educated me, encouraged me and inspired me. So I take this novel as an ideological report which represents my progress in the Cultural Revolution . . . Under the guidance of Chairman Mao's revolutionary line of literature and art, I am determined to remould my world outlook and to learn conscientiously the creative experience of the model theatrical works . . . I shall try to write works of high quality loved by workers, peasants and soldiers.[29]

Some writers such as Gu Hua and Chen Rong kept silent about the period in retrospect in the 1980s. Some writers wrote about their anxieties in this connection after the Cultural Revolution. However, other writers do not take an entirely negative attitude towards certain of their writings in the period. For example, Hao Ran's CR novel *The Golden Road* was reprinted in 1994. He was unwilling to, and did not, make any revision because he did not regret the stand he took when writing this novel. While recalling her writing experience, Zhang Kangkang admitted in 1988 that in the CR period she treated Mao's 'Talks at the Yan'an Conference on Literature and Art' with an absolutely pious attitude. We thus have no grounds to conclude that the CR novelists' declamations during the Cultural Revolution about their writing were insincere although they acted in accordance with circumstances.

The readership of CR novels is open to question. No statistical survey was undertaken as far as is known. According to Chinese publishers' convention, the print-run of a book is usually indicated. Generally, the number of copies of the first printing of a CR novel was at least 100,000. A number of novels reach 500,000 copies or more in reprinting. By comparison with serious novels in the late 1980s and 1990s, of which the impression of a work usually has only about 10,000 copies, the print-runs of CR novels are certainly huge. However, the numbers are not substantively informative about the popularity of the novels. At most we may tentatively conclude that the first impression of a work mainly reflected the degree of positive evaluation by the authorities concerned, although, up to a point, the number of reprints indicated readers' attitude, apart from the authorities' judgement. Nevertheless, it is certain that CR novels published earlier had more readers. Works published in 1976 usually had little influence.

Perry Link pointed out, 'in contemporary China, as in other places and times, the place of fiction in society cannot be understood without at least some reference to levels and types of readership'.[30] He also analysed the difference between actual reader preferences and prescribed reader preferences, and observed a paradox, i.e. during the Cultural Revolution, 'literature became so politically bowdlerized that actual reader preferences were frightened almost entirely out of sight. Yet there was a sense in which enthusiastic Red Guards did enjoy such literature.'[31] Roughly speaking, according to our observation, the organizational censorship caused the literary authorities of different levels and some fellow-writers of the authors to become the most attentive readers. In addition to political content, the censorship covered the form of a work, which was required to conform to a number of rules and regulations concerning newly established creative technique. Another group of enthusiastic readers were people who aspired to learn to write. Having studied the fashionable literary policies and theories, they read novels not for entertainment but for understanding the literary principles and rules in practice. The real voluntary readers were primarily school students and students who had just left school. The prohibition of classical works, foreign works and pre-CR works made CR novels the main novels to which they had access. The school education and the ideological environment cultivated their preconceived amusement from reading such novels.

As described by Jeffrey C. Kinkley, 'untutored "popular" taste was also served by hand-copied romances and thrillers that circulated underground even during the Cultural Revolution'.[32] Moreover, in spite of official prohibition, classical Chinese works, foreign works and pre-CR Chinese works circulated underground among intentional readers during the Cultural Revolution. For instance, poets and novelists such as Bei Dao, Shu Ting, Mo Yan, Gu Hua, and Zhang Kangkang claimed that they read considerable foreign poetry and fiction and/or classical Chinese works during the CR decade.

LITERARY POLICY AND THEORY IN THE CULTURAL REVOLUTION

Mao Zedong's 'Talks at the Yan'an Conference on Literature and Art'

From its publication in 1942 until the late 1970s, Mao's 'Talks at the Yan'an Conference on Literature and Art' ('Yan'an Talks' or 'Talks' for short) dominated the literature and art of the Chinese Communist Party. After seven years' propagation and practice in Yan'an and other areas controlled by the Party, the principles of the 'Yan'an Talks' were announced to be the uniquely correct line of guidance for the literary and art world of the whole of China at the First National Congress of Chinese Literature and Art Workers convened in July 1949. According to Zhou Yang, every achievement in PRC literature and art must follow Mao's literary and artistic line, as represented in the 'Talks'.

During the Cultural Revolution, the literature and art of the previous seventeen years were fundamentally criticized. Although the previous literary and art authorities had consistently stressed carrying out the principles of the 'Yan'an Talks', the general charge against pre-CR literature and art during the Cultural Revolution was that they had opposed the 'Talks'. According to Li Chi's metaphor, the 'Yan'an Talks' was only a framework: 'A careful framework, then, was drawn for the literary workers and all that they had to do was to fill out that framework with particulars, each according to his ability, experience and understanding.'[33] The authorities in the Cultural Revolution tried to fill out the 'framework' in new ways, which they thought to be orthodox.

During the Cultural Revolution the 'Yan'an Talks' was given particular prominence among Mao's works. For example, between 1966 and 1967, the whole document was reprinted twice in *Hongqi [Red Flag]*, the authoritative journal of the Party in the Cultural Revolution. It was announced to be the 'revolutionary programme [*gangling*] of the Proletarian Cultural Revolution'.[34] The following comments on the 'Yan'an Talks', quoted from an editorial of *Red Flag*, reflected the new official understanding of Mao's document.

The *Talks* are a compass which, in complex and acute class struggle, gives us guidance in finding our direction, and in distinguishing between fragrant flowers and poisonous weeds, between revolution and counter-revolution and between true revolution and sham revolution.

The *Talks* are a "magic mirror" to detect demons, the sharpest weapon for thoroughly destroying all monsters. Facing it, all words and deeds which oppose the Party, oppose socialism and oppose Mao Tse-tung's thought will be shown up in their true form and will have no place to hide themselves.

The *Talks* are the clarion that sounds the advance. They call the broad masses of workers, peasants and soldiers to act as the main force, and on those who work in the field of literature and art to go among the workers, peasants and soldiers, to go into the heat of the struggle, to take an active part in this great proletarian cultural revolution, to repudiate thoroughly the reactionary culture of feudalism, capitalism and revisionism and to create an entirely new proletarian, socialist culture.[35]

According to the above statement, the role played by the 'Yan'an Talks' in the Cultural Revolution was first and foremost a 'weapon' used to attack the previous literature and art. On the one hand, the previous literary and art world was attacked for carrying out a line which ran counter the principles of the 'Talks'. On the other hand, the criticism in the 'Talks' of some negative views, which existed in the literary and art world of Yan'an in the 1930s and 1940s, was thought to be an example for attacks against the bourgeois and revisionist theories of literature and art.

With respect to literary and artistic creation, two propositions from the 'Talks' received particular attention in the CR period. Firstly, Mao had stated, 'Whether at a high level or a low level, our literature and art serve the popular masses, primarily workers, peasants, and soldiers; they are created for workers, peasants, and soldiers and are used by them.'[36] This was known as the 'direction of serving workers, peasants and soldiers'. It is evident that the 'workers, peasants and soldiers' in this proposition refer to the audience for the Party's literary and artistic works. During the Cultural Revolution, however, a new interpretation was added, i.e. 'to describe workers, peasants and soldiers, to sing the praises of workers, peasants and soldiers, and to create heroic images of workers, peasants and soldiers'.[37] The 'workers, peasants and soldiers' here exclusively refer to modern or contemporary workers, peasants and soldiers. It is obvious that this augmented directive became the theoretical basis for condemning subjects and imagery which were not directly related to modern or contemporary workers, peasants and soldiers. As mentioned before, no historical CR fiction can be found, and few CR works focused on the portrayal of modern professional intellectuals.

Secondly, according to Mao, 'Life as reflected in works of literature and art, compared with ordinary actual life, can and ought to be on a higher plane, more intense, more concentrated, more typical and more idealized, and therefore has greater universality' ('six mores' for short).[38] The 'six mores' had not been especially emphasized until 1958, when Mao proposed the Combination of Revolutionary Realism and Revolutionary Romanticism (2RR). In the discussion on the new creative method, some people pointed out that the spirit of 2RR was in accordance with Mao's 'six mores' in the 'Yan'an Talks'.[39] So along with the promotion of 2RR, the 'six mores' were given prominence. During the Cultural Revolution, the 'six mores' were further promoted, with a subtle change in use. Before the Cultural Revolution, the 'six mores' referred to life in general, whereas during the CR period, they were mostly concerned with the characterization of proletarian heroes.

The Combination of Revolutionary Realism and Revolutionary Romanticism

Along with his 'Yan'an Talks', Mao's slogan of 2RR was also further promoted in the Cultural Revolution. The authorities declared, 'As for creative method, we must adopt the Combination of Revolutionary Realism and Revolutionary Romanticism.'[40] During that decade, the highly unified propaganda and strict censorship undoubtedly intensified the practice of this slogan. The eight model theatrical works and all other officially promoted CR works were claimed as achievements in carrying out 2RR.

Since the method of 2RR developed from Socialist Realism (SR), a development seldom taken into account by scholars, it is necessary to put it into brief historical perspective here. SR was introduced to China not long after it was proposed in the Soviet Union in 1932. In November 1933, Zhou Yang, one of the main leaders of left-wing literary circles in Shanghai, published 'On "Socialist Realism and Revolutionary Romanticism": The Negation of the "Dialectical Materialist Method of Creation"', which was later taken to be the first published document to introduce SR in detail. However, the influence of SR was limited in China in the 1930s because no nationwide political force or literary organization was ready to popularize the new slogan. Leftist intellectuals shared reservations that SR had its foundations in the conditions of the Soviet Union and that conditions in China were not yet ripe for adopting SR. Actually, a series of competing slogans based on the formula 'X realism' was proposed in the late 1930s. They include 'revolutionary realism', 'realism of the Three People's Principles', 'realism of the resistance against Japan', 'democratic realism', 'extensive realism', and 'national revolutionary realism'.[41]

Reference to SR became more frequent during the 1940s, especially after the publication of Mao's 'Yan'an Talks', in which Mao affirmed SR. However, the authorities began to promote SR on a grand scale only after 1949. It was declared by the authorities that the socialist elements in politics, the economy and culture were increasing, providing a substantial and practical foundation for SR. The promotion of SR reached a peak at the Second National Conference of the Representatives of Literature and Art Workers (23 September – 7 October 1953). SR was officially confirmed as the criterion of literary creation and criticism in China, and a new evaluation of the recent past was officially put forward. According to the premier, Zhou Enlai, 'During the previous thirty years, the Communist Party and the proletariat held the leading position in the Chinese revolution, and so the dominant ideology in culture during the last thirty years was Socialist Realism.'[42] Lu Xun was hailed as 'the great pioneer and representative of Socialist Realism' in China. The situation is similar to the Soviet Union, in which SR was established in the 1930s, but Maxim Gorky's 1906 novel *Mother* was announced as the representative pioneering work of SR. As for definition of SR, Chinese literary circles had adopted the following formulation confirmed by the Congress of Soviet Writers in 1934.

> Socialist realism, being the basic method of Soviet imaginative literature and literary criticism, demands from the artist a truthful, historically concrete depiction of reality in its revolutionary development. At the same time this truthfulness and historical concreteness of the artistic depiction of reality must be combined with the task of the ideological moulding and education of the working people in the spirit of socialism.[43]

In 1956, following criticism of Stalin in the Soviet Union, SR was re-evaluated worldwide. In China, under the new policy of 'letting a hundred flowers blossom and a hundred schools of thought contend', the promotion of SR began to be questioned. The slogan was criticized for overemphasizing socialist ideology, excluding other creative methods and underestimating romanticism. In spite of some criticism, however, the attitude of Chinese literary intellectuals towards SR remained on the whole positive.

Later, as the political campaign against 'Rightists' developed, counter-criticism became dominant. One of the charges made against 'Rightist' critics and writers such as Qin Zhaoyang and Liu Shaotang was that they had opposed SR. Actually, from mid-1957 to late 1958, discussion of SR took the form of a massive reaffirmation. Just as the reaffirmation of SR in China reached its climax in 1958, the Combination of Revolutionary Realism and Revolutionary Romanticism came into being.

At a conference in March 1958, Mao Zedong discussed folk songs and new poetry:

> New poetry ought to develop on the basis of folk songs and classical poetry. The forms of new poetry ought to be national, and the contents ought to be the unity of opposites of realism and romanticism. Poems cannot be composed in a too realistic way.[44]

About two months later, in May, he said at another conference, 'Proletarian literature and art ought to adopt the creative method of the combination of revolutionary realism and revolutionary romanticism'.[45] In the same month, Zhou Yang published 'New Folk Songs Have Opened a New Path for Poetry' in the first issue of *Red Flag*, which was later taken to be the first official document to announce and expound the slogan.

Although we cannot be sure whether the final form of the slogan was invented by Mao personally, it can be shown that Mao had been consistently in favour of 'revolutionary romanticism'. As early as 1939, Mao had juxtaposed the 'Realism of Resistance against Japan' and 'Revolutionary Romanticism'.[46] In the 'Yan'an Talks', some of Mao's elaborations on literary creation embodied romantic ideals, which were quoted later by some critics as support for 'revolutionary romanticism' or even 2RR. Finally, Mao's own practice as a poet incorporated elements of romanticism. Under 2RR, his poems were acclaimed as 'perfect representations of revolutionary romanticism, and models of a perfect combination of revolutionary realism and revolutionary romanticism'.[47]

The slogan was welcomed by the Chinese literary world. In addition to individual inclinations, there were social reasons for the support of the new slogan. The government was then promoting the Great Leap Forward and the atmosphere was full of fanaticism and extravagant fantasies. Writers and critics agreed that the noble spirit of the heroic and new epoch needed romanticism.

Initially, 2RR and SR were not seen as mutually exclusive and they ran parallel to each other. However, SR soon began to decline. At the Third National Conference of Chinese Literature and Art Workers (1960), Zhou Yang stated, 'Our Combination of Revolutionary Realism and Revolutionary Romanticism critically carries forward the advanced tradition of realism and romanticism in literature and art of the past, . . . and becomes a completely new artistic method.'[48] The last appearance of the term SR in the *Literary Gazette* [*Wenyi bao*] of the 1960s was in No. 13-14 in 1960. The entire disappearance of SR was evidently related to the political opposition between China and the Soviet Union during the 1960 and 1970s, during which SR was still promoted in the Soviet Union.

Unlike SR, which had an official definition, 2RR has never been given an established definition. The principles and definitions of 2RR existed only as scattered comments in the discussions welcoming its proposal by Mao. Nevertheless, although it replaced SR, 2RR inherited and developed the tenets of SR. The following generalized tenets are significant.

1. 2RR emphazises idealism. Realism had been dominant in Chinese literature and art since the 1920s and 1930s. In the early 1950s, this tendency was intensified to the point where realism was taken to be 'the most revolutionary, the most advanced and the most ideal creative method in the history of human literature and art'.[49] Correspondingly, other literary and artistic methods and schools including romanticism were denigrated or excluded. In 2RR, however, romanticism was treated on equal terms with realism. 'Revolutionary romanticism' in 2RR was deemed consistent with idealism

[*lixiangzhuyi*]. Zhou Yang stated, 'The basic spirit of our revolutionary romanticism is revolutionary idealism, i.e. the manifestation of revolutionary idealism in artistic methods.'[50]

2. 2RR emphasizes the Marxist world outlook of writers and the ideological utilitarianism of literature and art. The main trend in literary and art circles before the promotion of 2RR had been to advocate Marxist ideology for writers and an ideological nature for literature and art. Nevertheless, disagreements grew out of conflicting interpretations of the principles of realism. For instance, a well-known argument in the name of adhering to the principles of realism was that a true and profound depiction of life by means of the realistic method was helpful in mastering dialectical materialism and expressing it in literature.[51] However, under 2RR, the dominance of a Marxist world outlook in literary and artistic creation and the political utility of literature and art was unconditional. Critics stated, 'When considering the meaning of 2RR, we should emphasize the attribute "revolutionary", which is the crux of the artistic method, rather than stressing the artistic concepts of realism and romanticism.'[52] 'In order to master 2RR, we have no method other than to plunge into the thick of life to build up a Marxist world outlook.'[53]

3. 2RR emphasizes tendentiousness in literary and artistic *zhenshi* [truth or truthfulness]. Before 2RR, there existed a contradictory double standard about *zhenshi*. On the one hand, many critics and writers held that literary *zhenshi* was subordinate to *qingxiangxing* [tendentiousness] of class and party. But, on the other hand, it was also claimed that, according to the principles of realism, literature and art should be true to life and avoid glossing over reality. Zhou Yang stated, 'In describing life, *zhenshi* is the highest principle of realistic art.'[54] More often than not, critics criticized individual works for being of poor artistic quality because they ignored the realistic *zhenshi* or the objectively descriptive *zhenshi*. However, after 2RR was promoted, the emphasis on tendentiousness in literary *zhenshi* reached a justifiably higher level because the status of revolutionary romanticism was raised. Thus, the previous rhetoric of advocating realistic *zhenshi* and objectively descriptive *zhenshi* was now taken to be revisionism.

4. 2RR emphasizes idealized heroic characters. Under the slogan of SR, an important task of socialist literature and art was thought to be the portrayal of new characters (heroic characters), showing their socialist or communist morality and ideology. After the advancement of 2RR, still more importance was attached to the portrayal of revolutionary heroes, and 2RR was taken to be the most effective way of fulfilling this task.

The above tenets of 2RR were established before the Cultural Revolution. During the CR period, the tenets of 2RR developed, under which the position of revolutionary romanticism was further advanced. In other words, the above tenets, which mainly grew out of the promotion of romanticism, were more emphasized and intensified. A fashionable expression indicating the principle of 2RR was *yuan yu shenghuo, gao yu shenghuo* [to be based on life, but on a higher plane than life]. The 'six mores' from Mao's 'Yan'an Talks' became the typical interpretation of 2RR. More particularly, new principles about the portrayal of heroic characters were established. According to the 'Summary of the Forum on the Work in Literature and Art in the Armed Forces with which Comrade Lin Biao Entrusted Comrade Jiang Qing',[55] the idealized heroes were to be endowed with the following new qualities: they had to be heroes following the correct Party line, capable of distinguishing the correct from the wrong line. Revolutionary optimism was the keynote of their heroic spirit. Sentimentalism, especially love between men and women, was taken to be bourgeois.

'Summary of the Forum on the Work in Literature and Art in the Armed Forces with which Comrade Lin Biao Entrusted Comrade Jiang Qing'

According to her own testimony, Jiang Qing began to oppose pre-CR literature and art in 1962. Her main accusation was that large numbers of literary and artistic works propagated bourgeois or feudal ideology, and misrepresented the images of workers, peasants and soldiers.[56] Mao himself was also dissatisfied with the current literature and art. In the same year, while talking about struggles in the ideological sphere, he warned, 'The use of the novel for anti-Party activities is quite an invention.'[57] In 1963 Mao pointed out, 'Problems abound in all forms of art such as the drama, ballads, music, the fine arts, the dance, the cinema, poetry and literature and the people involved are numerous; in many departments very little has been achieved so far in socialist transformation . . . Isn't it absurd that many Communists are enthusiastic about promoting feudal and capitalist art, but not socialist art?'[58] In 1964, Mao issued an even more severe comment on the previous years' literary and art world: 'In the last 15 years these associations, most of their publications (it is said that a few are good) and by and large the people in them (that is not everybody) have not carried out the policies of the Party . . . In recent years, they have slid right down to the brink of revisionism. Unless they remould themselves in real earnest, at some future date they are bound to become groups like the Hungarian Petofi Club.'[59] In 1965, with Mao's permission, Jiang Qing commissioned Zhang Chunqiao and Yao Wenyuan to write an article 'Views on *Hai Rui's Dismissal from Office*' ['Ping Hai Rui baguan'], published in November under Yao Wenyuan's authorship.[60] Its publication was the prelude to the Cultural Revolution.

From the 2nd to the 20th of February 1966, Jiang Qing organized the Forum on Work of Literature and Art in the Army in Shanghai, supported by Lin Biao. Under Jiang Qing's supervision, the content of the forum was summarized in a report, i.e. 'Summary of the Forum on the Work in Literature and Art in the Armed Forces with which Comrade Lin Biao Entrusted Comrade Jiang Qing' ('Forum Summary' or 'Summary' for short). Mao went over the manuscript three times in person. The main content of the 'Forum Summary' was published in a *PLA Daily [Jiefangjun Bao]* editorial on 18 April. The original was a restricted document until its publication in *Red Flag* in September 1967.

The 'Forum Summary' significantly influenced the literature and art of the Cultural Revolution. According to the 'Summary', traditional Chinese literature and art were generally denounced as feudalism. Moreover, it argued that the Chinese literary and art world from the foundation of the People's Republic to the Cultural Revolution had been controlled by a 'black line'. The 'black line' was defined as 'the combination of bourgeois ideas on literature and art, modern revisionist ideas on literature and art, and the literature and art of the thirties'.[61] Under this judgement, most Chinese writers, artists, and critics active in the left-wing literature and art movement in the 1930s (the only noted exception in the 'Forum Summary' is Lu Xun), and/or active between 1949 and 1965, were criticized personally and for their works.[62] The 'Summary' also listed a number of views on literary and artistic creation as 'typical expressions of this black line'. They are 'truthful writing', 'the broad path of realism', 'the deepening of realism', 'opposition to "subject-matter as the decisive factor"', 'middle characters', 'opposition to "the smell of gunpowder"', 'the spirit of the age as the merging of various trends"', and 'discarding the classics and rebelling against orthodoxy'. These expressions will be discussed in the coming section.

Foreign literature and art were also generally criticized by the 'Forum Summary'.[63] Western literature and art bore the brunt of this criticism. American classical films were in particular mentioned as exercising harmful effects on the Chinese literary and art world. However, the 'Summary' laid more stress on Russian and Soviet literature and art. It praised Stalin for his disapproval of modernist literature and art, but criticized him for his acceptance of Russian and European classics. Of all Soviet writers and critics, Maxim Gorky, who was claimed to be the founder of the Socialist Realism in the Soviet Union, had enjoyed the highest reputation in the Chinese literary world, and had frequently been quoted by Chinese literary authorities. However, Gorky was neither mentioned in the 'Forum Summary' nor quoted by literary authorities during the CR period.

The 'Summary' proposed to oppose the previous long-standing admiration of the Chinese literary world for Soviet literature and called for criticism of 'big figures'. Mikhail Alexandrovich Sholokhov was criticized as 'the father of revisionist literature and art'. His representative works *Quiet Flows the Don*, *Virgin Soil Upturned* and *The Fate of a Man* were specifically targeted for attack. Sholokhov was one of the most prominent writers of Soviet Socialist Realism, and his fiction was commended as representative of SR works in the Soviet Union after the Second World War. Sholokhov himself consistently declared to advocate SR, even in 1965 at the ceremony in which he was awarded the Nobel Prize. Criticism of Sholokhov and his works implied denial of Socialist Realism in spite of no explicit criticism. However, as SR was the foundation from which 2RR developed, the denial of SR did not mean that SR was on the whole opposite to the new Chinese literary trend during the CR period, only that it had not reached the characteristics of the new style of writing. For instance, in the later criticism against Sholokhov, one important argument put forward by Chinese critics was that his heroic characters often had 'shortcomings'. CR literature promoted perfection of heroic characters.

It needs to be noted that the general criticism of foreign literature in propaganda could not lead to the thorough elimination of any practical influence of individual foreign literary works on Chinese CR literature. Before the Cultural Revolution, Chinese translations of a considerable number of well-known foreign literary works had been published in China. They continued to be circulated underground among interested readers during the CR period. Some of the works were not criticized by name in the Cultural Revolution. In fact, the heroism of the protagonist in several foreign novels had some similarity to the promoted heroic quality in CR literary works. Generally, CR novelists had the chance to read a number of foreign works before and/or during the CR decade. Some young CR writers declared after the Cultural Revolution that the Soviet author Nikolay Ostrovsky's *How the Steel Was Tempered* had been their favourite foreign novel. Zhang Kangkang recalled in the late 1980s that this novel and Mao's 'Yan'an Talks' had had a great impact on her youth.[64] Likewise, British author E. Y. Voynich's novel *The Gadfly*, which was also commended in *How the Steel Was Tempered*, impressed some CR writers. Wendy Larson and Anne Wedell-Wedellsborg recapitulate the post-CR representative 'hazy' [*menglong*] poet Bei Dao's observation which indicates the availability of foreign literary works during the CR and their influence on young writers' writing: 'During the chaos of the Cultural Revolution, restricted books often became available to students and youth, opening to them the possibility of writing in an unofficial language and the eventual possibility of developing their own language.'[65] It thus stands to reason that CR novelists could consciously or unconsciously take certain elements from individual foreign works.

Nevertheless, in spite of the influence on individual authors and works, the holistic trend determined by the 'Forum Summary' in the prelude to the Cultural Revolution was certain. That is, apart from modernism which had consistently been attacked by communists, other styles of literature and art to which communists had once consented or even promoted, such as classicism and critical realism, were denied. Consequently, the literature and art of the Cultural Revolution were designed to cut off all relationships with traditional and foreign literature and art, and became an unprecedentedly closed system in the history of contemporary Chinese literature and art.

On the basis of denying previous theories and works of Chinese and foreign literature and art, the 'Forum Summary' established a set of propositions, of which the creation of heroic images as a fundamental task of socialist literature and art was the most important. Special consideration will be given to this proposition later.

The Eight Negative Expressions

From 1949 to 1965, the general tendency in Chinese literature and art was towards increasing radicalism. However, the policies of literature and art often changed within certain limits in accordance with changing political situations and ideological views. In response to those relatively mild policies of literature and art or purely out of their individual artistic awareness and bravery, literary intellectuals or leaders challenged the radical tendency. The above eight expressions listed in the 'Forum Summary' may be taken as examples of the challenging views. Criticism of these views in the CR period formed an important part of CR literary and artistic policies and theories. In order to reveal the connection between the pre-CR literary radicalism and CR literary policies and theories, based on the data obtained thus far, I place them into a brief historical perspective here.

Truthful writing

This was a long-standing controversial proposition and was subject to massive criticism three times during the pre-CR period. In 1954, Hu Feng wrote his 'Views on Literature and Art' ['Dui wenyi wenti de yijian'] and sent it to the CCP Central Committee.[66] In his presentation, Hu stressed the principle of 'describing factual life truthfully, deeply and resolutely'. In the subsequent campaign against Hu Feng launched in 1955, his view on 'truthful writing' was attacked along with his other claims. Next, during the period of 'letting a hundred flowers blossom and a hundred schools of thought contend' between 1956 and 1957, 'truthful writing' was put under discussion. Chen Yong, later thought to be the representative of those in favour of this view during that period, stated, 'If a work does not loyally reflect actual life but glosses over reality, it will lose artistic truthfulness and consequently have no artistic quality, even though it is very progressive politically. . . Truthfulness is the life of art. Without truthfulness, art will lose life.'[67] The views of Chen Yong and other literary intellectuals in favour of truthful writing were attacked in the Anti-Rightist Campaign. Later, in 1960, in view of the tendency towards untruthfulness in literature and art during the Great Leap Forward (1958 and 1959), Li Helin pointed out, 'The ideological quality of a work of literature or art depends on whether it reflects life truthfully; and its truthful reflection of life represents its artistic quality.'[68] Li Helin's point was soon criticized during the height of the campaign against 'revisionist ideology of literature and art' (1959-60). In the 'Forum Summary' 'truthful writing' was listed as the first negative expression.

The broad path of realism

In 1956 and 1957, the Soviet Union and East European communist countries began to criticize Stalin and orthodox policies in areas like literature and the arts. In China, Mao proposed 'letting a hundred flowers blossom and a hundred schools of thought contend'. During this relatively open period, writers and critics, such as He Zhi (Qin Zhaoyang), Zhou Bo and Chen Yong, expressed their views. One of the most important articles was He Zhi's 'Realism: the Broad Path' ['*Xianshizhuyi — guangkuo de daolu*']. This article criticized the dogmatism prevalent in the literary and art world by analysing the shortcomings of Socialist Realism. According to the author, literature and art should not serve current politics at the cost of sacrificing the laws and characteristics of literature and art. He emphasized that literature and art could only spring from a broad realistic life and should reflect this life truthfully. After initial endorsements, He Zhi's article was subject to severe attacks in the Anti-Rightist Campaign. In the 'Forum Summary', the title of this article was listed as a negative expression of the 'black line'.

The deepening of realism

The main trend in literature and art during the Great Leap Forward was an overwhelming emphasis on romanticism, which was thought to bear out the new slogan 2RR. Later, along with the Party's policies of modification in politics and economy due to the failure of the Great Leap Forward, the literary and art world began to readjust its policies. In August 1962, at 'the Forum on the Creation of Agricultural Short Stories', Shao Quanlin, Party Secretary of the Chinese Writers' Association, proposed the concept of 'deepening realism'. He pointed out, 'Realism is the foundation of our creation; there is no romanticism without realism. Our creation should be closer to reality and reflect reality in a down-to-earth manner. . . Deepening realism is the basis on which we create the forceful revolutionary romanticism and explore the path for the 'Combination of Revolutionary Realism and Revolutionary Romanticism'.[69] This is the source of 'the deepening of realism' in the 'Forum Summary'.

Opposition to 'subject-matter as the decisive factor'

In 1961 when the literary and art world began to readjust the prevailing radicalism of the Great Leap Forward, *Wenyi Bao* published an editorial titled 'The Problem of Subject Matter' ['*Ticai wenti*']. The editorial criticized the current promotion of important topics (mainly indicating sensational politicized events) only as subject matter. According to the editorial, 'It is necessary to do away with restrictions on subject-matter . . . Subject matter itself cannot be taken as the primary or decisive criterion, still less the unique criterion . . . Writers and artists have full freedom to choose their subject matter without any restriction.'[70] This article and its contentions became the source of the expression 'opposition to "subject-matter as the decisive factor"'.

Middle characters

At the same forum as mentioned in the section 'The deepening of realism' (page 24), along with the deepening of realism, Shao Quanlin proposed another point which challenged the pervasive emphasis on creating heroic characters, namely, the portrayal of 'middle' characters. According to him, 'Heroes and backward people are in the minority; people in the middle are in the majority . . . To portray heroes is to set examples, but we should also portray the people in the middle. If we only create heroic characters but do not portray characters who suffer from hesitation and contradiction, the fiction's realism will be insufficient . . .'[71] This view was later criticized along with the deepening of realism in 1964, and was listed in the 'Forum Summary'.

Opposition to 'the smell of gunpowder'

Once, in 1964, while seeing the dance drama *The White-haired Girl* [*Bai mao nü*], one official from the Ministry of Culture commented, 'The smell of gunpowder in this drama might be too strong and the armed struggle too prominent.'[72] This incidental statement with regard to a concrete work was the source of the expression 'opposition to "the smell of gunpowder"'.

The spirit of the age as the merging of various trends

In October 1962, Zhou Gucheng published his article 'The Historical Position of Artistic Creation' ['*Yishu chuangzuo de lishi diwei*'] in *New Construction* [*Xin Jianshe*], in which he gave an explanation of 'the spirit of the age'. According to him, 'the spirit of the age' is a merged unity of ideologies of different classes in a specific age. 'Although the spirit of an age is a unity, its expression from different classes or individual persons might be very different. Such differences reflected in artistic works become the characteristics or originality of the works . . .'[73] Zhou Gucheng's idea was generally dismissed in academic and literary circles soon after its publication. In the 'Forum Summary', it was generalized as 'the spirit of the age as the merging of various trends'.

Discarding the classics and rebelling against orthodoxy

In a conference on feature films convened in July 1959, a film official criticized current production for placing too much emphasis on military subjects. He said, 'Among the twelve planned feature films reported by the studios across the country, there are eight on military affairs. Film production today is characterised by such stereotypes as "classics of revolution" and "orthodoxy of war" . . . Today, my speech simply discards the "classics" and rebels against the "orthodoxy".'[74] In fact, 'discarding the classics and rebelling against orthodoxy' [*li jing pan dao*] is a Chinese idiom. The speaker used it in this context as a humorous metaphor to encourage the diversification of subject matter in film production. In 1964, this humorous and incidental remark was attacked by Zhang Chunqiao and others. In the 'Forum Summary', it was defined as 'discarding the classics of Marxism-Leninism, of Mao Tse-tung's thought, and rebelling against the orthodoxy of people's revolutionary war'.

Soon after they were listed in the 'Forum Summary' as representative negative views on literature and art, the above eight expressions were frequently named as targets in official publications. They were attacked as the theoretical basis on which numbers of so-called anti-Party and anti-socialist works were produced in the pre-CR period.[75]

Actually, according to the foregoing, the eight expressions appeared at different times before the Cultural Revolution. Criticized not long after they were proposed, they did not exert much influence on actual literary and artistic practice. The criticism of them in the Cultural Revolution exaggerated their influence on pre-CR literature and art. The 'Forum Summary' in effect dismissed all previous views on literature and art which challenged radical tendencies.

Portraying Heroic Characters: The Fundamental Task of Socialist Literature and Art

During the pre-CR and CR periods, official literary policies consistently emphasized the portrayal of new characters [*xin de renwu*], advanced characters [*xianjin renwu*] or heroic characters [*yingxiong renwu*] of workers, peasants and soldiers. Here the terms 'new character', 'advanced character' and 'heroic character' are synonymous. In the 1950s, before Mao proposed 2RR, the 'new character' and 'advanced character' were more frequently used in speeches or writings concerning literary and artistic theories and critics. While 2RR was in vogue, particularly during the Cultural Revolution, the term 'heroic character' was more frequently used. When the term 'heroic character' referred to a fictional character, the term 'heroic character' was often substituted with 'heroic image' [*yingxiong xingxiang*]. In addition, during the Cultural Revolution, 'heroic characters/images of workers, peasants and soldiers' and 'proletarian heroic characters/images' were equivalents.

The emphasis on creating heroic characters may be divided into three stages. First, before 2RR was proposed in 1958, and in spite of promoting the portrayal of new characters or advanced characters, no official opposition was found against careful portrayal of backward or middle characters. It was believed that the portrayal of backward characters was conducive to showing the contrast and contradiction between heroic and backward characters. In a speech of 1956, Zhou Yang openly encouraged writers to create backward or middle characters: 'It is as if to portray backward or middle characters has become unnecessary because of the stress given to new characters. This is a kind of partiality. Like the realistic world, the artistic world should have a range of different characters . . .'[76] Moreover, before 2RR, it was permissible to show the new characters' shortcomings and mistakes, although primary importance was attached to demonstrating their meritorious qualities and achievements. According to Zhou Yang, 'Shortcomings in the lives of heroes may be described . . . If a hero has no shortcomings in life nor mistakes in work, he would be a god.'[77] 'Certainly, we should not "deify" or "formularise" heroes . . . Heroic characters cannot be perfect in all aspects.'[78]

At the second stage, which covers the period under 2RR before the Cultural Revolution, the previous propositions regarding the careful portrayal of other categories of characters and the description of the shortcomings and mistakes of heroes were altered. Shao Quanlin's case for 'portraying middle characters' was such an example. Actually, his endorsement of middle characters rested on his prior endorsement of portraying heroic characters. He said, 'It is necessary to emphasize advanced characters or heroic characters because they embody the spirit of our age. On the whole, however, in our literature, the characters in the middle are relatively insufficient.'[79] As for the shortcomings of heroic characters, Shao did not directly endorse describing them at that time, but commented, 'Heroic characters may not have shortcomings, but their development through experience ought to be described. If only their merits are described, that means that one class has only one typical character.'[80] However, his mildly challenging views were attacked as bourgeois propositions during this stage.

During the third stage, i.e. during the Cultural Revolution itself, the promotion of the portrayal of heroes reached its height. The principle that 'to try to create heroic characters of workers, peasants and soldiers is the fundamental task of socialist literature and art' had consistently been dominant among a number of newly established ideas since it was first declared in the 'Forum Summary'. According to the authorities' arguments for this proposition, to create the heroic characters of workers, peasants and soldiers was one way of serving the workers, peasants and soldiers. Moreover, according to this view, every class tried to create its own heroic characters in literature and art in order to advance its own politics, ideology and morality. Proletarian literature and art should also create proletarian heroic characters, even taking it as the fundamental mission. Below is a quotation from *Red Flag*, which shows the officially proclaimed significance of the portrayal of heroic characters.

> To portray lofty, great, perfect and dazzlingly brilliant proletarian heroic characters is our most important political task, and also a new task in the proletarian revolution in literature and art. It is this which significantly distinguishes proletarian literature and art from the literature and art of the exploiting classes, which include the bourgeois literature and art of the Renaissance and the Enlightenment, and the literature and art of critical realism in the nineteenth century.[81]

In a comparative sense, in theory and practice regarding the creation of heroic characters, the difference between the third stage and the second stage includes two aspects. Firstly, during the second stage, the portrayal of other categories of characters was simply disapproved of in principle, while at the third stage, unlike the previous disapproval, the portrayal of other characters was prescribed to set off the heroic characters. Secondly, and also during the second stage, although the proposition of describing shortcomings of heroic characters was criticized by radicals, the opposite — the promotion of perfect images — had not been openly established as yet. At the third stage, however, not only was the description of shortcomings unambiguously excluded, but the perfection of heroic characters was also promoted as the desirable goal. General standards were then established, i.e. 'lofty, great and perfect' [*gaoda, wanmei*], to which were sometimes added 'brilliant' [*guanghui*] or 'dazzlingly brilliant' [*guangcai zhao ren*].

Around the claimed fundamental task of socialist literature and art to create 'lofty, great, perfect and brilliant' proletarian heroic characters, other new theories and policies were established. In brief, the proposition of the 'fundamental task', and accompanying principles and techniques designed to fulfil this task, constituted the critical feature of the literary and artistic theories and policies established in the Cultural Revolution.

The Experience of 'Yangban Xi' [the Model Theatrical Works] and the Principle of 'San Tuchu' [Three Prominences]

While strongly criticizing traditional Chinese literature and art, foreign literature and art, and most especially communist literature and art before the Cultural Revolution, the Cultural Revolution authorities declared eight theatrical works as models in 1967. These were five Peking operas: *The Red Lantern* [*Hong deng ji*], *Shajiabang* [*On the Shajia River*], *Taking Tiger Mountain by Strategy* [*Zhi qu Weihushan*], *Raid on the White Tiger Regiment* [*Qixi Baihutuan*] and *On the Docks* [*Haigang*]; two dance dramas: *Red Detachment of Women* [*Hongse niangzijun*] and *The White-haired Girl* [*Bai mao nü*]; and one symphony: *Shajiabang* [*On the Shajia River*].

Except for the dance drama, *The White-haired Girl*, which was based on an opera of the same name created in the Yan'an period, the other model works were revised or rearranged from a number of Peking operas shown in the National Festival of Modern Peking Operas [*Quanguo Jingju Xiandai Xi Guanmo Yanchu Dahui*] in June and July 1964 in Beijing. They were selected by the authorities headed by Jiang Qing after the festival, who intended to make them model works. The final revisions to these works were completed during the Cultural Revolution. It stands to reason that the former selection indicated that the original works had certain factors which complied with the selectors' literary and artistic views. Moreover, the later revision and finalization were made directly under the care and supervision of Jiang Qing. Therefore, although their original forms were made before the Cultural Revolution, these works represented the direction of literary and artistic theories and practice promoted during the Cultural Revolution.

After they were set as models, a nationwide campaign to popularize the theatrical works was launched, in which the experience [*jingyan*] of their creation was also promoted throughout the literary and art world. Of the eight works, the five modern Peking operas were the most popular. This could be because they were relatively easy to perform and more readily understood by the masses than the dance dramas and the symphony. Moreover, the creation of operatic images was more appropriate for imitation in other forms of literature and art, such as fiction and films, than in music or dance.

The central point of the model theatrical works was to fulfil the 'fundamental task' of creating lofty, great and perfect proletarian heroes. The following paragraph by Qian Haoliang in 1967, who played the part of Li Yuhe in *The Red Lantern*, describes Jiang Qing's directives.

> Comrade Jiang Qing asked us to create the proletarian heroic image of Li Yuhe through the use of magnificent things. That is, we must resort to the most beautiful music, the best arias, the most impressive movements, and the most important positions on the stage to make this heroic image more prominent, more ideal, and more lofty. [82]

The experience of the model theatrical works was summarized into a set of general principles, of which *san tuchu* [the 'three prominences'] is the most important. This delineates the relationship between the primary hero and other characters within a work. The formula first appeared in an article by Yu Huiyong, Minister of Culture during the Cultural Revolution, published in May 1968. His definition is as follows:

> Among all characters, give prominence to positive characters; among the positive characters, give prominence to main heroic characters; among the main heroic characters, give prominence to the central characters. [83]

The standard definition of the principle was made by Yao Wenyuan in November 1969:

> Among all characters, give prominence to the positive characters; among the positive characters, give prominence to the heroic characters; among the heroic characters, give prominence to the main heroic characters. [84]

The two definitions differ only in terminology, and the terminology in Yao's definition referring to the classification of characters was also commonly adopted.

After the principle of 'three prominences' was established, another parallel formula, 'three foilings' [*san peichen*], was proposed.

> Between the negative characters and the positive characters, make the negative characters serve as foils to the positive characters; between the positive characters and the heroic characters, make the positive characters serve as foils to the heroic characters; between the heroic characters and the main heroic characters, make the heroic characters serve as foils to the main heroic characters.[85]

The principle of 'three foilings' is evidently another expression of the 'three prominences', emphasizing ways of creating the prominences. The two principles formularized a hierarchical relationship among the categories of character. In short, characters are given a four-level ideological classification from the lowest to the highest: Negative Characters [*fanmian renwu*], Positive Characters [*zhengmian renwu*], Heroic Characters [*yingxiong renwu*] and Main Heroic Characters [*zhuyao yingxiong renwu*]. Each type sets off the next type on the higher level, but the ultimate aim is to make the first three types set off the main heroic characters.

The principle of the 'three prominences' continued to be promoted during the late 1960s and early 1970s. In late 1975, it was reformulated as the 'creative experience of the model theatrical works' in line with Mao's comments in 1975. According to Mao, regulations governing the model theatrical works were too strict: 'It is not enough to have only the model theatrical works. Literary works are blamed only for small shortcomings. The policy of letting a hundred flowers blossom has disappeared.'[86] Mao's comments discouraged formulaic expressions such as the 'three prominences', although the principles themselves were not under criticism.

The model theatrical works had a great impact on CR literature and art. Since its key principle focuses on the portrayal of proletarian heroic characters, the experience of the theatrical works is mainly applicable to those categories of works which have plots and characterization. For example, as McDougall pointed out in regard to poetry, 'The limits imposed by the Gang of Four — chiefly the requirement to learn from the *yangbanxi* — did not directly impinge on the poet's choice of compositional techniques.'[87] On the other hand, fiction is one of the most obvious genres in which the principles from the model theatrical works could be used. In fact, in the CR period novelists invariably claimed to be following the experience of the model theatrical works.

In 1968, Mark Schorer made the following remark on literary criticism, which was quoted by Leo Ou-fan Lee in his well-known essay 'The Politics of Technique: Perspectives of Literary Dissidence in Contemporary Chinese Fiction':

Modern criticism has shown us that to speak of content as such is not to speak of art at all, but of experience; and that it is only when we speak of the *achieved* content, the form, the work of art as a work of art, that we speak as critics.[88]

To sum up, however, put into a holistic perspective, CR literary policy and theory intensified the tradition of modern Chinese literary writing and criticism analysed by Leo Ou-fan Lee, i.e. the tradition to give prominence to content rather than to form — literary technique. Therefore, in the following analyses, we shall deal with many aspects of CR novels by considering their social content and significance, although the whole book is intended to lay stress on the novels' literary and stylistic 'form'.

Part I

Characterization of the Main Heroes

Introduction to Part I

Based on the then current literary policy and theory, the unprecedented promotion of heroic characters made this aspect the single most important literary factor in CR fiction, influencing other aspects such as plot, structure, style and aesthetic views. This part analyses the characterization of main heroes in the novels under investigation.

'Hero', as used in English literary analysis, can be ambiguous, used both for 'main character' and 'protagonist' as well as for a brave man. In Chinese literary analysis, the English term 'hero' may correspond to *zhurengong*, *yingxiong*, and *zhuyao yingxiong*. *Zhurengong* refers to the character who plays the main role in the stories, *yingxiong* to an important positive character who is admired for his/her goodness, bravery, great ability, etc., and *zhuyao yingxiong* to the most important positive character who is portrayed as the chief model personifying the current ideological and literary ideals. The 'main hero' under discussion (*zhuyao yingxiong*), corresponds to the 'main heroic character' in Yao Wenyuan's definition of the 'three prominences'. In addition, when used in a general sense, the 'main hero' refers to both males and females. In CR novels the main hero and the protagonist are always the same person. This is also true of most pre-CR novels, but there are some exceptions. For example, in the first volume of *Great Changes in a Mountain Village*, Liu Yusheng is the main hero, but Deng Xiumei is the protagonist [*zhurengong*].

This analysis is mainly qualitative, emphasizing the general characteristics of characterization of main heroes in the CR novels. For the sake of practicality, the analysis centres primarily on the following main heroes and works:

Main hero	Novel	Author
Gao Daquan	*The Golden Road*	Hao Ran
Jiang Chunwang	*Evergreen*	Chen Rong
Zhao Guang'en	*The Roaring Songhua River*	Lin Yu and Xie Shu
Lian Hua	*Qingshi Fort*	Zhu Jian
Wei Gengtian	*Mountains Green after Rain*	The 'Three-in-one' Group of Baise Prefecture
Shi Caihong	*The Long Rainbow*	Tian Dongzhao
Liu Wangchun	*The Mountains and Rivers Roar*	Gu Hua

These seven novels were originally selected as samples for linguistic analysis in Part II of this book. We have grounds to take them as samples for literary analysis because in addition to the points concerning linguistic aspects, the sampling has also taken literary elements such as time of writing, authorship, subject matter and time-setting into consideration. The detailed sampling principles and criteria are given in the Introduction to Part II. With regard to the multi-volume novels, the linguistic analysis covers only the first volume, but the literary analysis covers the novels in their entirety.

Apart from these seven focal heroes and works, some other main heroes and corresponding novels are also taken into account. They are Gao Jinfeng in Wang Dongman's *Spring Comes to Zhang River*, Wulan Tuoya in Wang Zhijun's *The Daughter of Slaves*, Gao Lisong in Sun Feng's *Mountains Emblazoned with Crimson*, Yue Yong in Feng Yunan's *Yinsha Beach*, Li Ke in Ke Fei's *Swift is the Spring Tide*, and Xiao Lin in Zhang Xue's *Mountain People*. More emphasis is placed on two women, Gao Jinfeng and Wulan Tuoya, because female main heroes constitute a minority.

However, in addition to qualitative analysis, in certain parts I generalize the features to a quantitative level in order to gain more substantive evidence on the basis of statistics. This being the case, I put the twenty-four main heroes of all the CR agricultural novels into a holistic perspective.

Another point concerning methodology is comparative analysis. Since some characteristics of the characterization of main heroes in the CR novels are inherited and developed from pre-CR literary theories and practice, I often compare the characteristics concerned with those of the pre-CR agricultural novels. This is not only helpful in revealing the CR novels' characteristics from a comparative angle but it is also conducive to analysing the characteristics in a historical perspective. The focal pre-CR novels concerned are Zhou Libo's *Great Changes in a Mountain Village*, Liu Qing's *The Builders*[1] and Hao Ran's *The Sun Shines Bright*. Once again, the samples are the same as those of the linguistic analysis except that entire works are taken into consideration in the present literary analysis.

Moreover, in view of the influence of Soviet literature on contemporary Chinese literature, I also sometimes bring Soviet novels such as Ostrovsky's *How the Steel Was Tempered*, and Sholokhov's *Virgin Soil Upturned* into comparison.

Chapter 1

Personal Background

The personal background under discussion covers the main heroes' age, sex, marital status, class origin, family background, education, and so on.

In Chinese terms, the period of youth continues up to the age of thirty, middle age occupies the years thirty to fifty, and old age is past fifty. Among the heroes of the twenty-four novels, two are set at old age (over fifty), seven at middle age (generally about thirty to forty), and the other fifteen at a young age (generally about twenty to thirty). Distinct preference is granted to youth; young main heroes make up 62.5 percent of the total. The reason for such age-setting is related to the content of the novels. As stated before, the basic motif of CR novels is the line struggle in which the main heroes and their followers fight against the wrong line pursued by people in power taking the capitalist road. This motif evidently corresponds with the ideological struggles which occurred during the Cultural Revolution, i.e. the Red Guards were encouraged to rebel against the capitalist-roaders. So it sounds reasonable to take the view that the overwhelming preference for young main heroes in CR novels suggests the novelists' inclination to match the age structure of the Red Guards in reality. It cannot be a coincidence that all the main heroes in the novels which are set in the Cultural Revolution are young, and they are exclusively the leaders of local organizations of Red Guards before they are promoted to the position of the paramount Party secretary.

As with age, the marital status of the main heroes is not random. Of all the twenty-four main heroes, seventeen are specified to be unmarried (all have never been married, i.e. none is divorced or widowed), accounting for 70.8

percent. Six are married, including two old heroes and four middle-aged ones. Of the other three middle-aged heroes, two are unmarried, and one is unclear. As for the young main heroes, no one is married although most of them have passed the legally marriageable age.

Love was proclaimed a 'forbidden zone' in literary writing during the Cultural Revolution. In the 'Forum Summary' the authorities severely criticized the theme or descriptions of love in pre-CR literary and art works: '. . . still others are concerned only with love and romance, pandering to philistine tastes and claiming that love and death are the eternal themes. All such bourgeois and revisionist trash must be resolutely opposed.'[1] So no main heroes in the CR novels are in love. However, no stipulation has been found for the avoidance of married heroes. The preponderance of single people suggests there was a tacit agreement to promote the unmarried state in the characterization of main heroes. Even in the novels, some characters express their surprise as to why the heroes are so indifferent to their own marriage prospects. For example, in Feng Yunan's *Yinsha Beach*, Dong Liang, the director of the production brigade, cannot understand why his old friend Yue Yong, the main hero, does not worry about his unmarried situation:

> He has been making revolution for over ten years, and he has experienced charging under heavy fire and crossing high mountains. But now he has neither got a house nor found a wife. He is thirty years old, but is still unmarried. It is really quite strange.[2]

One reason for the tendency towards bachelorhood of the main heroes is the more highly promoted ideology of collectivism and altruism, which will be taken into account later. As they are single, the heroes may wholeheartedly devote themselves to the interests of others rather than to their own families. In other words, the unmarried condition is conducive to showing the main heroes' spirit of dedication to the Party's cause and to public affairs.

Another plausible reason for the inclination to bachelorhood can be linked to the prevailing advocacy of 'marrying and raising children late' [*wan hun wan yu*]. Although the preference for late marriage existed in the 1950s, it was then mainly based on the dictate that marrying and raising children too early hindered one's own development in work and study. Moreover, it often represented the views of educated individuals. For example, in the pre-CR novel *Great Changes in a Mountain Village*, learning that Sheng Shujun and Chen Dachun have a tryst, Deng Xiumei, an educated cadre coming down to the countryside, talks to Sheng: 'You may now be in love, but it would be better to marry later. It's not good for a woman to produce and raise children too early.'[3] According to the narrator, Deng Xiumei's advice arises mainly out of her personal bias and concern for women's interests.

Because 'marrying and raising children late' was mainly an individual phenomenon rather than official advocacy before the Cultural Revolution, the authors of pre-CR agricultural novels seemed not to avoid married main heroes. For instance, Liang Shengbao in *The Builders* and Xiao Changchun in *The Sun Shines Bright* both had family-arranged child-brides, although the child-brides died early which made way for the main heroes to find new partners. Furthermore, in *Great Changes in a Mountain Village*, Liu Yusheng married twice.

However, the advocacy of marrying and raising children late became official during the Cultural Revolution. In the government's propaganda, the practice of this principle became a kind of obligatory collective awareness. Its promotion concerned not only the work and study of individuals but more importantly the more imperative pressure of population. In her research into the poetry of the Cultural Revolution, while talking about the disappearance of wives, husbands, and lovers from poetry, Bonnie S. McDougall points out: 'The reassertion of traditional puritanism, heightened by the need for population control, has made these themes unacceptable in poetry in the seventies.'[4] Under such circumstances, people who married late were often commended by local authorities as good examples for other people. Thus we have grounds to believe that in characterization of the main heroes, who were thought to be models to be emulated by readers, authors may have taken this point into consideration.

As for the gender of the main heroes, of the twenty-four main heroes, four are females, accounting for 16.7 percent of the total. The proportion of female main heroes is small; the overwhelming majority are males. Nevertheless, by comparison with pre-CR agricultural novels, in which I could find no female main heroes, this rate is noticeable. Furthermore, the four female main heroes all appear in the novels set in the Cultural Revolution. Thus, among the total of six agricultural novels set in the Cultural Revolution, there are four in which the main heroes are females, accounting for a dominant majority (66.7 percent). The four female main heroes are all young and unmarried.

Male supremacy [*nan zun nü bei*] was prominent throughout the ages of traditional Chinese civilization. After the May Fourth Movement (1919), in correspondence with Western feminism and communist ideology, the feminist trend of thought gradually became popular in China. In the pre-CR period, the propaganda of the Chinese government supported the equality of the sexes. It was claimed that women 'held up half the sky'. The promotion of the status of women through propaganda developed to an even higher level during the Cultural Revolution. Male supremacy was taken to be part of traditional customs and old culture, and became one target of the movement. *Shidai bu tong le, nan nü dou yi yang* [The times have changed, male and female are the same now] became a household phrase.[5] Therefore, the higher rate of female main heroes and some other factors in the CR novels might be viewed as a reflection of the current propaganda attacking male supremacy. The changes might remind people of the Western feminist literary trend. However, since the changes were based on the promoted communist ideology, we have no grounds to attribute them to the influence of Western feminism in literature, even though we may find certain similar elements between Chinese CR literature and Western feminist literature.

Class and family origin are another aspect of the main heroes' personal background. Under the People's Republic before the end of the Cultural Revolution, class origin was an important criterion in judging people's political stance and ideological consciousness. In brief, the proletarian class had superiority over the propertied class and the rich. This standard of evaluation in society was naturally reflected in the literature of that period. Thus, the main heroes in both the pre-CR and CR agricultural novels are all from poor families.

However, although the main heroes in the pre-CR and CR novels share the same general proletarian class status, their parentage in the CR novels has some new characteristics. In the pre-CR novels, the parents of the main heroes are described as ordinary poor farmers. They suffered from hard labour, hunger and illness, and they did nothing extraordinary in the old society. So, except for poverty (which could be taken as an identification of their proletarian class origin), we cannot find other typical relationships between the heroes' parentage and the heroes' character.

In CR novels the family background of old main heroes and some middle-aged main heroes is not emphasized. In most cases, their parents are not mentioned. The reason could be that the heroes' personal sufferings or revolutionary experiences overshadowed those of their parents in the old society.

However, as stated above, the majority of the main heroes in the CR novels are young. The parents of the young and some middle-aged heroes are given certain prominence in the CR novels. Most parents, especially the fathers of the heroes, are not ordinary poor peasants but revolutionaries or heroic persons. For instance, with respect to revolutionaries, in all the fifteen novels in which the main heroes are young, both parents of three heroes, and fathers of seven heroes are revolutionaries. The typical design is as follows: As an army commander, the father led troops to fight for the interests of the given locality, but he laid down his life in the fighting. The mother also died. The orphaned main hero was brought up by poor local peasants. After growing up in the People's Republic, he was promoted to the top leadership of the village in a certain politicized agricultural campaign.

Another type of parent of the young or middle-aged main hero, mainly referring to fathers, did not join the revolutionary ranks, but was distinguished from other common poor villagers by heroic qualities, such as being brave, generous, righteous, and especially unyielding in the face of brute force. Jiang Chunwang's father Da Lao Jiang [Senior Old Jiang] in *Evergreen* is an example. One day in 1940, Da Lao Jiang and some other young villagers were caught by the Japanese army and subjected to conscription. They were locked up in a temple. At midnight, Da Lao Jiang broke the rope on his body by biting through it. Then he helped others untie their ropes and escape. After five people succeeded in fleeing, a fifteen-year-old boy awakened the enemy because of his nervousness and clumsiness. The rest of the villagers, including the boy and Da Lao Jiang, were caught again. The next morning, the Japanese forced the people to stand in the courtyard and paraded the boy in front of them, threatening to kill him if they were unable to find the ringleader. 'Then and there, Da Lao Jiang stepped forward bravely and said: "Set free the child, I shall answer for everything!" With his voice like a bell and his posture like a pine, Da Lao Jiang stood straight in front of the Japanese soldiers, like an imposing mountain. The Japanese soldiers were frightened and fell back before they finally killed him in cold blood.'[6] The story and description show Da Lao Jiang's heroic spirit of self-sacrifice and awe-inspiring fortitude in facing an evil force.

The above analysis indicates that CR novelists elevated the main heroes' origins, i.e. poor parentage, which is typical in pre-CR novels, is elevated to revolutionary and heroic parentage of CR heroes. This may be analysed as follows:

Firstly, the new patterns of origin reflect the 'theory of descent' [*xuetong lun*]. During the Cultural Revolution, on the basis of further emphasis of class status, the traditional theory of heroic descent became prominent. The Red Guards openly shouted out such a slogan: *Laozi yingxiong er haohan, laozi fandong er hundan* [If the father is a hero, his son is a true man; if the father is a reactionary, his son is a wretch]. In terms of the 'theory of descent', it becomes inevitable that the main heroes in the CR novels are from a heroic parentage. They are therefore described as resembling their fathers in appearance and qualities. In *Qingshi Fort*, the villagers comment on Lian Hua: 'His features and figure look exactly like his father's!'[7] In *Yinsha Beach*, after Yue Yong was demobilized and returned to his native village, Xiang Liangao, the old Party secretary, proposed to transfer his position to Yue Yong because Xiang 'saw Yue's father's image in this young Party member'.[8] 'Image' [*yingzi*] here refers to both external and internal likeness. With reference to the above story of Da Lao Jiang in *Evergreen*, his son, Jiang Chunwang, the main hero of the novel, inherited his father's awe-inspiring bearing in the face of evil forces. In front of the enemies in the temple courtyard, Da Lao Jiang's simple words spoken in a resonant voice frightened the fully armed Japanese soldiers into falling back. Similarly, one night just after Land Reform, when Jiang Chunwang was on sentry duty as a militiaman, he saw three people each with a wheelbarrow on their way to resell grain at a profit, which was illegal. The hero shouted: 'Stop!' 'The voice resounded through the skies and the earth.'[9] The three backward middle peasants were so frightened that they could not control the wheelbarrows, which consequently turned over. 'From then on, it became a well-known saying in the village to indicate the hero's power that "one shout from Chunwang can turn over three wheelbarrows".'[10] A revolutionary and heroic origin is thus one of the factors leading to the superiority of the main heroes in CR novels.

Secondly, the new patterns of origin are related to the current promotion of 'the theory of continuous revolution under the dictatorship of the proletariat', which was claimed by the authorities to be the theoretical foundation of the Cultural Revolution.[11] In CR novels, the young main heroes are generally idealized as model successors to the cause of proletarian revolution. Thus, apart from inheriting the qualities of the revolutionaries of the older generation, the main heroes should have the revolutionary will to carry the revolutionary cause through to the end. In *Spring Comes to Zhang River*, the main hero, Gao Jinfeng, was born in an enemy prison. She was only two months old when her parents, both revolutionaries, died a martyr's death in the prison. She was then transferred to the village. Her father wrote a poem in blood on the lining of a jacket wrapped around the baby: 'I have been making revolution all my life, but now I shall die in Taihang Mountain; I have only one wish in my mind: that my daughter can carry on my revolutionary will.'[12] According to the narrator, 'Gao Jinfeng could already recite the poem when she was in primary school. She gained a better and better understanding of the poem as her age increased. When she was taking the oath on being admitted to the Party under the bright Party flag, she also recited the poem silently . . .'[13] In the main story, when the capitalist-roaders put pressure on her, it is the poem that encourages her to go ahead. She stares at the jacket, 'as though the images of her father and mother had emerged from the twenty characters in the poem, written in her father's blood. Although she was unable to imagine their real appearance and voice, she could perceive clearly the two red hearts loyal to the Party and the martyrs' forceful voices urging her to carry on the revolutionary cause.'[14]

Lastly, the new patterns of origin are in accordance with the fashionable literary and artistic principle of 'giving prominence to the main heroes'. The revolutionary and heroic parentage is designed to provide a foil to set off the main heroes. On the one hand, it adds honour to the main heroes, i.e. to achieve the effect of *shui zhang chuan gao* [when the water rises, the boat goes up]. On the other hand, it intensifies the love, esteem and support of other characters for the main heroes. For example, in *Qingshi Fort*, Lian Chunshan, the father of the main hero Lian Hua, had established prestige among the masses during his lifetime. People thus have not allowed anybody to attack his son since his death. Below is a passage showing people's feelings towards Lian Hua which are interwoven with their love and esteem for his father:

> The image of Secretary Lian Chunshan could never be erased in the mind of Qingshi Fort's villagers. People always cherished his memory. Whenever people talked about the evening when he died a martyr, their eyes brimmed with tears. Over the last eighteen years, people poured their love for Secretary Lian into Lian Hua. Who did not regard him as his own child? Who dared to speak one sentence against him or make one move to insult him? Who dared to separate the people of Qingshi Fort from him . . .[15]

A high rate of orphanhood is another characteristic which features in the heroes' personal background. Of the twenty-four heroes, seventeen are orphans, accounting for 71 percent. In the pre-CR novels, the main heroes also had a hard childhood. Some heroes' father or mother died early, and the heroes grew up in a single-parent or stepparent family. For example, in *The Builders*, Liang Shengbao's father died of hunger when Liang was four years old, and he was brought up by his mother and stepfather. In *The Sun Shines Bright*, Xiao Changchun's mother died early of illness, and he was looked after by his widowed father and some relatives. Such a background contributes to intensifying the poverty of the heroes' family and the hardship of their personal experience in the old society. In the CR novels, however, most main heroes' father and mother both died early. This is not simply intended to manifest the hardship of the heroes' background but has other effects. According to D. E. Pollard's investigation, the main heroes in short stories of the Cultural Revolution are also usually orphans. He attributes this to a desire to emphasize the main heroes' gratitude to the Party, i.e. the heroes claimed that the Party was their parents.[16] With respect to this phenomenon in CR novels, in addition to the point made by D. E. Pollard, there are some other reasons. First, the orphanhood of the main heroes is related to the promotion of their parentage as analysed above, that is, the fact that many parents died for revolution leads to the characterization of the main heroes as successors to the cause of proletarian revolution at the same time as it gives rise to orphanhood.

The second reason for orphanhood is in accordance with the above-analysed reason for the tendency towards bachelorhood of the main heroes, i.e. the heroes need not serve their family, including parents, so that they could be completely dedicated to the revolution and the interests of the collective.

Finally, orphanhood contributes to proletarian class love. According to the Communist doctrine, proletarian class friendship is more important than blood kinship, as illustrated in the model revolutionary theatrical work, *The Red Lantern*, 'How can you say that only kinship is weighty? Class love is weightier than Tai Mountain.'[17] So, in spite of their orphanhood, the main heroes enjoyed class care in their childhood. Some of them had foster parents, who had no kinship with the heroes but showed profound loving care for them. In *The Mountains and Rivers Roar*, the main hero Liu Wangchun tells Uncle En: 'My mother [foster mother] has treated me very well. Her loving care for me is 100% more than for her own children!'[18] In fact, Liu's foster mother went so far that when she had to make a choice in the war, she handed in her own son to the enemies who were searching for Liu. In many other cases, the main heroes in their orphaned childhood had no formal foster parents. They got class care and love from the poor people of the whole village, and they accordingly took the whole village as their family. In *The Long Rainbow*, the main heroine Shi Caihong was claimed by the old Party secretary to be the 'descendant' of all the poor and lower-middle peasants. She was surnamed 'Shi' not with reference to any specific family but from the name of the village 'Shi Zhuang' [Shi Village]. Furthermore, the class love under discussion means collective friendship instead of individualistic affection. So, on the basis of the heightened proletarian class friendship, the orphanhood of the main heroes in the CR novels has further symbolic significance. That is, the fact that the adolescent main heroes grew up amid love based on class relations rather than kinship is conducive to the formation of their class feelings and collective consciousness, which are among the most important factors dominating their future thought and action.

Another point about the main heroes' personal background is education. Generally, the educational levels of the heroes are related to their age. The young and middle-aged main heroes who grew up under the People's Republic are all graduates from middle schools. The old and middle-aged who grew up before socialist China had no chance of going to school during their childhoods because of poverty. But, some of them joined the army led by the Communist Party and learned to read in the army, and others in the countryside went to a local literacy class in the new society. Therefore, none of the main heroes in the twenty-four novels are illiterate.

In addition to showing the advantages of the Party's leadership under which poor people can receive education, more importantly, literacy is necessary for the main heroes' political life. In all the CR novels, studying political documents, especially Mao's works, and criticizing non-proletarian ideology occupy an important place in the development of the stories. The main heroes play the main role in organizing such activities and interpreting the documents. It stands to reason that the .ould not play their parts properly without the appropriate educational background.

Besides, with regard to the young and middle-aged main heroes who finished middle school, the narrators attached certain importance to the main heroes' will and determination to work as farmers in the countryside. In the Cultural Revolution, the Chinese government launched a massive campaign in which school-leavers were settled in the countryside to receive so-called 're-education' from the poor and lower-middle peasants. This propaganda raised attitudes towards working in the countryside to an ideological level. It was said that according to bourgeois ideology, working in the countryside was inferior to working in cities because of heavier labour, lower income and poorer living conditions, but on the basis of proletarian ideology, there was no difference between the two choices. As stated in the CR novel *The Long Rainbow*, ' . . . to join the army, to go to school, to work in factories, and to plant crops are all revolutionary work. What you will do should serve the needs of revolution and follow the arrangement of the Party. This is the right attitude taken by a revolutionary descendant.'[19] The authors of CR agricultural novels set a high value on the will and actions of the local school-leavers to settle down to farm work, and the authors put this value especially into the characterization of the main heroes. In *Spring Comes to Zhang River*, on the basis of her 'magnificent and beautiful aspiration' — 'to build the new socialist countryside', Gao Jinfeng has given up the chance of furthering her education and returned home on her own initiative to be a farmer. Later, Tian Guifa, a capitalist-roader, tries to tempt her with a promise to recommend her for urban employment. He says,

> . . . Some factories will soon recruit workers from our village. I promise to recommend you. A young person should strive for a brighter prospect: to go to large cities to be a worker or a cadre and to have white flour and rice. There, you may go to the theatre or the cinema for enjoyment. That is much better than staying in the remote mountains. Your qualifications are favourable: being literate, being capable of writing and calculating, having revolutionary martyr parentage and a poor family background, and being a young Party member. In a few years, you may probably become a senior official, then you may travel by sedan. Oh, if I were as young as you, I would have left long ago . . .[20]

Tian's statement is representative of the views of those backward or negative characters in all the novels on the difference between working in the countryside and in cities. Feeling insulted, Gao Jinfeng is in a great rage and refuses Tian Guifa's offer.

The last aspect concerning the main heroes' personal background is their military experience. Of the twenty-four main heroes, one-third have been professional soldiers in the past. Some (the old or middle-aged) joined the militia in the Sino-Japanese War (1937–45) and then enlisted in the PLA (the Chinese People's Liberation Army); some (the middle-aged) joined the PLA in the War of Liberation (1945–49) or joined the Chinese People's Volunteers in the Korean War (1950–53); and the others (the young) joined the PLA in the peaceful period under the People's Republic. About another one-third of the twenty-four main heroes did not enlist formally and had no professional military background, but they either joined aid-front contingents in the war years or joined the militia around the time of Land Reform, and experienced some military action. As for the remainder, about one-third of the main heroes, they grew up in the 1950s or 1960s and had no experience of war. Nevertheless, they had the experience of being local militiamen in the socialist society. Most of them were the head of the militia in the village before taking the post of village Party secretary and accordingly received some military training.

The significance of emphasizing the military experience of the main heroes in characterization could include the following factors. Firstly, a military background adds honour to the main heroes. On the one hand, the ex-servicemen have usually rendered meritorious service in the wars. In Ke Fei's *Swift is the Spring Tide*, Li Ke is celebrated as a combat hero and the pride of his hometown. He captured an American colonel alive and blew up an enemy blockhouse in the Korean War. For those main heroes who had only experience in local militia, some also did unusual deeds in fighting against local evildoers and evil deeds, which showed their bravery and power. At the beginning of *Evergreen*, as mentioned above, on his sentry duty in the village, Jiang Chunwang shouted at three grain smugglers, single-handedly frightening them out of their wits. On the other hand, during the Cultural Revolution, the prestige of the PLA was raised to an unprecedented level by the authorities. According to Mao, Daqing was the model in industry, Dazhai the model in agriculture, and the PLA the model for the whole nation (although the three collective models were established in 1964, the campaigns of learning from them did not reach their peak until the CR). Thus, to characterize the main heroes as demobilized soldiers has a symbolic meaning, i.e. the status of having been a member of the collective model of the whole nation adds to the heroes' worthiness of imitation. Moreover, in the propaganda, as the set model of the whole nation, the PLA was claimed to be a great school of Mao Zedong Thought. The 'graduates' from this school were thought to have a high level of political consciousness and to be reliable leaders of socialism.[21] This could be the reason that some main heroes, who did not have a chance to join the PLA, were also described as having gained political guidance from the members of a working team [gongzuo dui] of the PLA. In this experience, they were impressed by the discipline and collective awareness of the PLA men, which influenced their future thinking and action.

Secondly, the military background of the main heroes is related to the story-line of the novels. As stated before, the class and line struggles are the most important motif of the CR novels, which are generally likened to wars. So the dual status of soldiers — in both a political and military sense — is conducive to intensifying the fighting power of the main heroes. For instance, the villains, usually hidden class enemies, generally try to make a last desperate counter-attack when their real status and conspiracies are brought to light near the end of the stories. At the climax of the confrontation between the positive and negative sides, it is the main heroes who subdue the villains with their superior combat power and skills derived from their military background.

Lastly, just as how, in the above analysis, the will of school-leavers to settle down in the countryside is highly valued, so demobilized soldiers who return to their native place to settle down to do farm work are also highly regarded. Therefore, setting the main heroes as ex-servicemen also reflects the current policy of encouraging people to settle down to do farm work in the countryside. In *Mountain People*, the main hero Xiao Lin is often challenged about whether or not he will remain in the village forever to do farm work. His actions not only prove his will but also give an example for those backward people who look down upon working in the countryside.

Chapter 2

Physical Qualities

During the Cultural Revolution, the main value regarding the beauty of human beings was *xinling mei* [spiritual — literally 'heart' — beauty]. With relation to the restraints on sexual love, preference for physical or outward beauty was criticized as a sentiment of the bourgeoisie or petty bourgeoisie. This value was represented in CR literature.

In CR novels, the 'spiritual beauty' of the main heroes is to a great extent related to their ideological qualities such as correct political standing, ideological consciousness and altruistic spirit. However, in spite of the stress laid on descriptions of 'spiritual beauty', authors were by no means careless in portraying the physical characteristics of the main heroes. This analysis is intended to show how the authors describe the heroes' physical appearance, which is one aspect of the manifestation of the heroes' 'loftiness, greatness and perfection', and what characteristics their exterior shows, indicating current aesthetic views on the physical portrayal of heroes.

The description of the physical characteristics of the main heroes in CR novels is not simply for the sake of showing their physique and appearance. The authors intentionally tried to integrate the heroes' outward appearance with their inward character to create a 'unity'. Usually, authors adopted the method of description plus commentary, that is, the direct description of their constitution, features, expression, manner, style etc. was interspersed with the narrators' commentary on the symbolic significance of these elements and the impression they make on other people. Below are two examples, of which the former is a description of the hands of hero Liu Wangchun in *The Mountains and Rivers*

Roar, and the latter a portrayal of the face and eyes of heroine Wulan Tuoya in *The Daughter of Slaves*.

> (1)   Liu Wangchun clenched his hands. These were a pair of labouring hands, a pair of creative hands, a pair of sturdy and big hands, and a pair of strong and powerful hands. Looking at this pair of hands, Li Zhichuan almost shouted out his admiration. But looking at this pair of hands, Long Youtian [the villain] couldn't help being scared. Such hands could crush stones into pieces and push mountains down.[1]

> (2)   Her face glowed with a sun-tanned and rosy colour, and her forehead looked broad, which always gave a dynamic impression to people. Her eyes were not too big, but they were bright and piercing, and, with eyelashes moving, flashed with resourcefulness and bravery.[2]

In general, CR novelists' portrayals of main heroes' physical qualities follow some set characteristics and include a number of stereotyped words and expressions. I have enumerated below the five most prominent features.

STRONG CONSTITUTION AND VIGOROUS AIR

Expressions such as *kuan jian kuo bei* [broad shoulders and back], *da shou da jiao* [big hands and feet], *jiejieshishi* [sturdy], *zhuangzhuangshishi* [sturdy], *hei li tou hong* [skin glows with sun-tanned and rosy colour], *shengqi bobo/huhu* [full of vigour], *qiangjian youli* [strong and powerful], *shencai yiyi* [glowing with health and radiating vigour], *jingshen huanfa* [be fresh with energy], and *zhengzheng yinghan* [a man of iron] are commonly used. Below is a portrait of Wei Gengtian in *Mountains Green after Rain*, in which his strong constitution and vigorous air are conspicuous:

> On the mountain road, a man in his thirties with a load on his shoulder . . . was walking towards the village with vigorous strides. He was not too tall, but he was sturdy. A sweaty white shirt closely covered his broad and muscular chest. The muscles on his shoulders, glowing with sun-tanned and rosy colour, were like ripe litchis. A pair of dark blue trousers were rolled up to his knees, under which his shanks looked like two short stone posts. As his big feet trod on the stone road, his heavy footsteps sounded clearly. Wiping the sweat away from his face with a towel, he strode forward steadily. His face was glowing with ruddy health. Under his heavy eyebrows were big bright piercing eyes. The bridge of his nose was straight and his lips were slightly thick. The whole figure was likely to leave an impression of warm-heartedness and honesty. It was the Party secretary of Longrong Brigade.[3]

During the CR period, the expressions *jiankang mei* [healthy beauty], *laodong mei* [labour beauty], and *zhandou mei* [martial beauty] were the terms in vogue to indicate physical beauty. It stands to reason that the strong constitution and vigorous air of the main heroes in CR novels conform to this standard of outward beauty. With respect to vigour, in addition to strong physique, the heroes' powerful movements are emphasized with inflated language. The following paragraph from *The Golden Road* describes Gao Daquan's splitting wood with a broad axe. It is clear that the author has intentionally exaggerated the hero's movements to play up his vigour and power.

> The young people at the gate were struck dumb by Gao Daquan's movements . . . They saw that beads of sweat were dripping from his muscular chest when Gao Daquan straightened his back. They saw the broad axe in his hands lift up to the sky, drop down to the ground, and cut deeply into the tree root with a lightning flash and a rush of wind. They saw the tree root shiver and jump under his axe; it split like a mine blowing up, and wood chips flew around with the deafening sound . . .[4]

With the context of CR novels taken into consideration, such a strong constitution and vigorous air has a symbolic meaning, that is, it indicates that physically the idealized heroes have the power to withstand trials and tribulations and to win the struggles for ideology and production.

UNSOPHISTICATED FEATURES AND EXPRESSION

The common expressions include *lüe hou de zuichun* [slightly thick lips], *pushi de biaoqing* [simple and honest expression], *hanhou de weixiao* [honest smile], and *shuanglang de xiaosheng* [hearty laughter]. The above portrayal of Wei Gengtian in *Mountains Green after Rain* also shows the hero's 'unsophisticated features'. In *The Daughter of Slaves*, the heroine Wulan Tuoya has 'slightly thick lips beaming in an honest smile'.[5]

According to communist propaganda, simplicity, honesty and lack of sophistication were relative to the proletariat. Their opposites, cultivation, hypocrisy and sophistication, were relative to the bourgeoisie. During the CR period, many people, including officials, proudly claimed to be *dalaocu* [simple, uncouth or uneducated fellows]. It is only natural that the simple, honest and unsophisticated qualities are emphasized in the portrayal of CR novel heroes.

Furthermore, the above features are also designed to show the heroes' open-hearted and upright character, which was also affirmed in communist rhetoric. It is well known that during the Cultural Revolution inner Party struggles were the most fierce in the history of Chinese Communist Party. After Lin Biao fell in the middle of the CR decade, the level of propaganda promoting *jinhuai tanbai* or *guangming zhengda* [being open and aboveboard] and opposing *yinmou guiji* [intrigues and conspiracies] reached a climax.[6] It stands to reason that CR novelists were inclined to emphasize such characteristics in portraying the heroes' exteriors.

Moreover, apart from the ideological significance, the portrayal of heroes as honest and upright is also in accordance with the characterization according to the heroes' temperamental qualities which will be discussed in Chapter 4.

DIGNIFIED MANNER AND AWE-INSPIRING BEARING

Such expressions as *shense gangyi* [expression full of fortitude], *wenjian de jiaobu* [firm steps], *bu bei bu su* [neither humble nor vulgar], *luoluo dafang* [natural and graceful], *tanran ziruo* [calm and confident], *congcongrongrong* [confident and composed] and *weiyan* [awe-inspiring] are commonly used. The main heroes often show their poised manner and dignified style when speaking on public occasions. In *The Long Rainbow*, at the grandest mass rally since she had become the village Party secretary, 'Shi Caihong looked neither flurried due to excitement, nor short of passion due to calmness'.[7] The heroine's poised bearing and inspiring speech impresses the audience deeply.

In many cases, the main heroes' dignified manner is displayed in front of negative superiors who try to force the heroes to carry out the wrong line. This indicates their fortitude and heroic spirit in upholding the correct line. In *Evergreen*, for instance, the deputy county secretary Huang Guang is dissatisfied with the main hero Jiang Chunwang's disobedience in pursuing the policy of fixing output quotas on a household basis. When Jiang goes to visit him, he rudely gives Jiang the cold shoulder. But 'taking his tobacco bag out of his pocket, Jiang filled his pipe, lit it, and started smoking. He carried himself with dignity, looking confident and composed'.[8]

Usually, such a dignified manner is integrated with an awe-inspiring bearing, of which the descriptions are often inflated in tone. In *Evergreen*, after meeting Jiang Chunwang as described above, the capitalist-roader Huang Guang convenes a mass rally and forcefully announces in public the practice of the policy of fixing output quotas on a household basis. Jiang Chunwang decides to go to the platform to debate with Huang face to face. 'Then and there, Jiang Chunwang stood up. His movement aroused the attention of the masses. Many people stopped talking. Chunwang walked forward confidently and vigorously ... Wearing a white shirt, his strong arm raised high, he passed through the crowd and stepped forward steadily. He looked like a silver sailing boat bravely forging ahead in a blue rolling sea.'[9] His dignified bearing and imposing manner makes Huang Guang feel shocked and defeated.

Again, in precarious situations when other people are likely to be thrown into panic and confusion, the main heroes always remain calm and collected.

In *The Mountains and Rivers Roar*, at the critical stage in which the irrigation works were near completion, torrents of water rushed down the mountains, and some people were frightened. However, 'staring at the surging and roaring mountain torrents, Liu Wangchun's large eyes set under heavy eyebrows glistened with unyielding brightness; through the furious storm, his face showed amazing and solemn composure'.[10] The main heroes' awe-inspiring presence, combined with their strong constitution and vigorous air, becomes even more evident in the eyes of the class enemies, as detailed in the following two features.

BIG AND BRIGHT PIERCING EYES

In portraying the main heroes' features, special emphasis is placed on their eyebrows and eyes, which generally have the same shapes, i.e. *nong mei da yan* [heavy eyebrows and big eyes]. Furthermore, the expressions *mingliang de yanjing* [bright eyes], *jiongjiong you shen* [eyes bright and piercing] and *xili de yanjing* [piercing eyes], *fuyu biaoqing de yanjing* [expressive eyes] are, almost without exception, used in describing the heroes' eyes. Such portrayal of eyes is related to some of the points analysed above. For example, according to Chinese convention, 'heavy eyebrows' are associated with an awe-inspiring expression, and 'bright eyes' with a vigorous and healthy air.

However, in addition to suggesting the above associations, the stereotyped portrait of the main heroes' eyes has a special symbolic meaning concerning their ideological qualities. The authors tried to unify political insights with physical visions, i.e. 'big eyes' and 'bright eyes' are associated with ideological insight and foresight, and 'piercing eyes' signify political sensitivity and vigilance. By means of their keen sight and sensitivity, they are able to distinguish the wrong line or policy from the correct one, and identify the disguised class enemies. Therefore, the heroes' eyes have extraordinary awe-inspiring force before negative characters. For instance, in *The Mountains and Rivers Roar*, the main villain, Long Youtian, has a face-to-face confrontation with the main hero Liu Wangchun. 'When he raised his sly eyes and looked at Liu Wangchun, Long Youtian saw Liu staring at him closely. Liu's flashing and piercing big eyes were like two sharp swords, ready to prick through his internal vital organs. Long Yongtian suddenly felt cold to the bone. His whole body couldn't help shrinking down.'[11]

A SONOROUS AND FORCEFUL VOICE

The tone of voice of the main heroes is another point emphasized in descriptions of their physical qualities. Its characteristics are reflected in the following commonly used words and expressions: *hongliang* [sonorous], *kengqiang youli* [sonorous and forceful], *hongzhong ban de* [like the sound of a large bell, i.e. having a stentorian voice], *leiming ban de* [thunderous], *pili ban de* [as loud and powerful as thunderclaps], etc. Obviously, such characteristics add to the main heroes' vigorous air and awe-inspiring bearing from another angle. The hero's voice can often strike awe into negative characters. As stated earlier, in *Evergreen*, 'one shout from Jiang Chunwang can turn over three wheelbarrows'.[12] In *The Daughter of Slaves*, during the height of combat with the class enemy, the heroine Wulan Tuoya's voice, 'though peaceful at ordinary times, sounded like a series of thunderclaps'.[13] Not only her words but also the tone of her voice caused the villain Jia Wushiliu to become mouth agape and tongue-tied in fear and trepidation.

The above set features and stereotyped expressions cause the main heroes of CR novels to share a general resemblance. On the one hand, the ideological significance of the portrayals as mentioned above plays an important part in forming the characteristics. On the other hand, the patternized physical features could also be attributed to the influence of the model theatrical works.

The model theatrical works were primarily modern Peking operas. Peking opera is the most representative of Chinese traditional dramatic art forms, created and developed over a period of several centuries. It conventionally stresses the physical features of an actor. For example, actors playing main roles must have big, bright and expressive eyes. Below is a narrative describing the attempts of renowned modern Peking opera artist Mei Lanfang to cultivate 'a pair of bright and piercing eyes'.

> He had, for instance, a pair of lack-lustre eyes when he was a child. To remedy this, he exercised his eyes relentlessly. He would practise gazing at the movements of an incense flame in a dark room; fly kites and stare at them drifting in a blue sky; keep pigeons in order to look at them soaring higher and higher until they disappeared into the clouds . . . These were some of the ways in which he managed to give himself a pair of bright, keen, highly expressive eyes.[14]

Apart from actors' physical features, Peking opera places emphasis on the appearance of actors in make-up and costume. According to Wu Zuguang, a well-known Chinese playwright and dramatic critic, 'Like other types of traditional drama, Peking opera was originally a folk art. It has been suggested that its staging in the open air in the early years led to the use of excessively heavy make-up, using heavy paint in bright colours.'[15] Moreover, the representation of classification of social values is clear in the make-up. 'The audience is able to distinguish the loyal from the treacherous, the good from the wicked by studying the make-up and costumes . . . The hero or villain is usually recognized without difficulty by the way his face is painted or the costume he wears.'[16]

Between February and August of 1930, Mei Lanfang and his operatic troupe visited the United States and staged Peking opera in many American cities, becoming sensational for a time. Many American literary and art critics commented on the traditional form of Chinese theatre. A generally expressed view is that this Chinese theatre form has an idealistic flavour. The dramatic critic Stark Young explained such flavour by drawing a parallel between Peking opera and Chinese painting and sculpture. Following this parallel, Chinese critics borrowed a term from Chinese painting and sculpture to indicate the keynote of Peking opera, i.e. *xieyi*, of which no English equivalent has been found. According to Huang Zuolin, a noted Chinese stage and film director, the *xieyi* in Peking opera is reflected in the following four characteristics: the life represented is sublimated and refined; the human movements are eurhythmicized to a higher plane; the language is elevated to lyrical height; the decor is designed to achieve an artistic effect.[17]

The idealistic nature of Peking opera was also shared by the well-known German playwright Bertolt Brecht. In 1935, during Mei Lanfang's visit to the Soviet Union, Brecht had fled from Hitler's persecution to live as a political refugee in Moscow. After seeing Mei's performance, he wrote, 'This way of acting is healthier and (in our opinion) worthier of a rational being; it demands . . . an acute understanding of social values. Naturally, here too a creative process is at work; but its value is higher, because it has been transmuted to the plane of the conscious.'[18]

Guided by Jiang Qing, the model theatrical works of the Cultural Revolution greatly reformed traditional Peking opera. However, in spite of changes in many aspects, the model theatrical works retained and even developed certain conventionalized principles of the traditional form of theatre. The above idealistic nature regarding form was further developed under the slogan of 'revolutionary romanticism'. As regards the appearance of actors in make-up and costume, on the one hand, substantial changes were made in arranging the stage features of actors. On the other hand, the rearrangement still retained the conventional characteristics of heavy make-up and the spirit of contrast between hero and villain. Certainly the heroes' appearance in make-up and costume was designed to embody current social values such as 'healthy beauty', 'labour beauty' and 'martial beauty'.

Along with the campaign to promote and popularize the model theatrical works, the typical stage features of ideal heroes became established. These stereotypes contributed to certain set physical qualities of heroes in other forms such as literature, painting, film, and other theatrical forms, although no documents have been found with regard to literary imitation of the theatrical heroes' exteriors. Virtually all the above-mentioned five set features of the main heroes in CR novels can be found in the stage images of the main heroes of the model theatrical works.

During the Cultural Revolution, the concepts of pure physical beauty such as *haokan* [good-looking], *piaoliang* [handsome] and *meili* [beautiful] were ideologically denigrated. Although they are not mutually exclusive, the connotation of beauty as 'health, fitness for labour and fitness for fighting' is different from the generally recognized concept of physical beauty embodied by such terms as 'handsome' and 'beautiful'.

Nevertheless, in CR fiction, the concepts of pure physical beauty and ugliness are clearly taken into consideration in authors' characterizations, i.e. positive characters are good-looking and negative characters ugly. With regard to the main heroes of the CR novels, although the authors avoided using the most common and direct words '*piaoliang*' and '*meili*' in portraying the heroes' appearances, they clearly and unequivocally described the heroes/heroines as being handsome or beautiful persons. When the heroine Shi Caihong appears for the first time in *The Long Rainbow*, there is a passage describing her physically: 'She was about twenty-five years old. Two pigtails hung down to her shoulders. There was a pair of dimples on her rosy egg-shaped face. Under delicate heavy eyebrows, her big eyes were aglow with radiating vigour . . . From head to foot, she looked nimble, natural and graceful.'[19] At the end of the story, another passage reads: '. . . Those big eyes looked even brighter, and glowed with a radiant pride and confidence; that pair of pretty [*haokan*] dimples looked even clearer, radiant with a triumphant and happy smile.'[20] Actually, in the CR novels, it is because the main heroes' appearance is unusually impressive that strangers are able to distinguish them from others by their appearance. In *The Golden Road*, before she meets Gao Daquan, the female county cadre Xu Meng has only heard about some of Gao's uncommon deeds. When she comes down to the village Fangcaodi, Xu Meng immediately identifies Gao Daquan in a large crowd 'by his jet-black hair, his ruddy face, his bright eyes, and his steady and vigorous steps'.[21]

Moreover, in the portrayals of the main heroes' appearance in the CR novels, although the two words *piaoliang* [handsome/beautiful] and *meili* [beautiful] are seldom used, some synonyms such as *yingjun* [handsome], *junmei* [beautiful] and *junxiu* [beautiful] can be found. Semantically, these two groups of words have the same notional meaning — 'good-looking'. This is why in common Chinese-English dictionaries, the respective translations are the same, i.e. *piaoliang* and *yingjun* [handsome], *meili*, *junmei* and *junxiu* [beautiful]. Yet there is a slight difference in emphasis between the two groups of words. While *piaoliang* and *meili* only mean 'good-looking', *yingjun*, *junmei* and *junxiu* can suggest 'strength' and 'health' in addition to the same notional meaning 'good-looking'. Nevertheless, in spite of the fact that 'strength' and 'health' may be associated with some of the above-stated symbolic meanings, as synonyms of *piaoliang* and *meili*, the three words all clearly indicate physical beauty. In *The Golden Road*, when the head of the county Gu Xinmin meets the main hero Gao Daquan, he cannot help looking Gao up and down, because he is surprised at Gao's 'handsome appearance' [*waibiao yingjun*].[22]

In the conventions of traditional Chinese literature the description of a person's appearance is a means to show his/her character and temperament. Positive figures generally have better appearance than negative figures. People with advanced temperamental and behavioural qualities often have a handsome or beautiful appearance, but people with ferocious characters usually have hideous features.

A similar tendency can be found in Western literature, especially traditional romantic literature. For example, Walter Scott, a romantic British writer of the nineteenth century, is renowned for his talent in describing the appearance of people representative of different classes and origins. He pays obvious attention to the unity of people's inner and outer qualities. Below is a paragraph from *Ivanhoe* describing the heroine Rowena's appearance, in which the author combines her beauty and nobility.

> Formed in the best proportions of her sex, Rowena was tall in stature, yet not so much so as to attract observation on account of superior height. Her complexion was exquisitely fair, but the noble cast of her head and features prevented the insipidity which sometimes attaches to fair beauties. Her clear blue eye which sate enshrined beneath a graceful eyebrow of brown sufficiently marked to give expression to the forehead, seemed capable to kindle as well as melt, to command as well as to beseech. If mildness were the more natural expression of such a combination of features, it was plain, that in the present instance, the exercise of habitual superiority, and the reception of general homage, had given to the Saxon lady a loftier character, which mingled with and qualified that bestowed by nature. Her profuse hair, of a colour betwixt brown and flaxen, was arranged in a fanciful and graceful manner in numerous ringlets, to form which art had probably aided nature.[23]

The following quotation from the same novel is a description of Front-de-Bœuf's appearance, which shows vividly the ferocious character of 'the formidable baron'.

> Front-de-Bœuf, a tall and strong man, whose life had been spent in public war or in private feuds and broils, and who had hesitated at no means of extending his feudal power, had features corresponding to his character, and which strongly expressed the fiercer and more malignant passions of the mind. The scars with which his visage was seamed, would, on features of a different cast, have excited the sympathy and veneration due to the marks of honourable valour; but, in the peculiar case of Front-de-Bœuf, they only added to the ferocity of his countenance, and to the dread which his presence inspired.[24]

In Soviet novels based on Socialist Realism we can also find examples in which heroes have impressive appearance. In Sholokhov's *Virgin Soil Upturned* the main hero Semyon Davidov, whom the party sends to supervise and speed up the collectivization campaign in a Cossack village, impresses the local cadres deeply with his physical qualities at the beginning. After Davidov relays to the village activists the directive of the higher level about the collectivization, Andrei, chairman of the village Soviet, worries about possible opposition from the villagers, and doubts Davidov's ability to lead their campaign. However, it is Davidov's physical qualities that make Andrei confident in his leadership:

> He [Andrei] remembered Davidov's stocky, solidly built figure, his determined, tightly bunched face with its firm folds at the sides of the mouth, and the humorously wise expression of his eyes, he remembered the way he had leaned over to him behind Nagulnov's back at the meeting and the clean youthful tang of his breath as he had said during Lubishkin's speech . . . And as Andrei remembered this, he decided joyfully, 'No, that one won't let us down.'[25]

The main difference between CR novels and other types of novel in terms of description of physical qualities has two aspects. Firstly, the convention that heroes have a good appearance and villains have poor appearance is carried out in CR novels in terms of absolutes. In other types of novel there are exceptions to this convention. For instance, in Scott's *Ivanhoe* Maurice de Bracy, a villain, is described as being 'handsome', 'whose manners partook alike of the grace of a courtier, and the frankness of a soldier'.[26] In *Virgin Soil Upturned*, Sholokhov describes Timofei, a villain, as follows: 'Even in death he was handsome, this women's darling. A dark lock of hair had fallen on the clear white forehead that the sun had never touched, the full face had not yet lost its faint rosiness, the curling upper lip with its soft black moustache was raised a little, exposing moist teeth, and a faint shadow of a surprised smile lingered in the blooming lips . . .'[27]

Secondly, CR novels lay much more stress on the uniqueness and prominence of the main heroes. The heroes are not only morally the most prominent but also physically the most impressive. Since CR novels tend to patternize their main heroes' physical qualities and follow the model of Peking opera, some features become not merely set heroic attributes but are also possessed exclusively by the main heroes. Some expressions are thereby exclusively used to portray the main heroes. For instance, the idioms *jiongjiong you shen* and *shencai yiyi* cannot be found to describe any other characters in the twenty-four CR agricultural novels. Moreover, the main heroes of CR novels appear with advanced physical qualities which scarcely change according to the heroes' circumstances, which could be designed to embody the principle of perfection of heroes. According to the principle, therefore, the following description of Semyon Davidov's appearance in *Virgin Soil Upturned* would be shocking. As noted above, Davidov has impressive physical qualities at the beginning. However, he becomes lifeless and dispirited when he is obsessed with Lushka.

> Davidov had grown a bit slack. An unaccustomed irritability appeared in his character, and even outwardly he looked by no means so brisk and sturdy as

he had when he first came to Gremyachy Log . . . Glancing quizzically into Davidov's gaunt face, Razmyotnov said one day, 'Losing weight, Semyon? You look like an old ox after a bad winter; you'll soon be dropping in your tracks. And you're sort of peeling and scurvy: Are you moulting, or what? You'd better keep off our girls, specially wives who've just been divorced. It's awful bad for the health . . .'[28]

As regards pre-CR Chinese novels, the portrayals of the main heroes' appearance also form a stark contrast to those of CR novels in many aspects. For example, in *Great Changes in a Mountain Village*, the main hero Liu Yusheng is nicknamed 'Yu Xiazi' ('Yu' is the first character of his given name, and 'Xiazi' means a blind man) by the villagers because of his short-sightedness, which would be one of the most forbidden defects in the portrayals of a CR main hero. In *The Builders*, the main hero, Liang Shengbao, who is acclaimed by many Chinese critics as a successful heroic image in pre-CR fiction, is unremarkable in his looks. This contrast indicates the different views of the authors of pre-CR and CR novels on the relationship between the heroes' physical qualities and their ideological or temperamental characteristics. From another angle it also reflects the different degrees of idealization in the characterization of pre-CR and CR novels' main heroes.

Chapter 3

Ideological Qualities

The main ideological motifs of CR agricultural novels were summarized by Chinese commentators in the Cultural Revolution as the struggle between two classes (the proletariat and the capitalist class), two roads (the socialist road and the capitalist road), two lines (the line of Marxism–Leninism guided by Mao and the line of revisionism) and two ideologies (altruism/collectivism and egoism/individualism). In the novels, the main heroes are representatives of the proletariat, of the leaders [daitouren] of the socialist road, of the followers of Mao's line, and of the values of altruism and collectivism.[1] Therefore, the idealization of the main heroes' ideological qualities occupies a prominent position in the novelists' characterization of the heroes, emphasizing the heroes' 'loftiness' and 'greatness'. The following analysis concentrates on the method and extent of such idealization, and consists of two parts: the heroes' consciousness of class, road and line struggles, and the heroes' consciousness of altruism and collectivism.

CONSCIOUSNESS OF CLASS, ROAD AND LINE STRUGGLES

Of the class, road and line struggles, the road struggle is usually attached to class and line struggles. So the main heroes' ideological consciousness of class, road and line struggles is primarily concerned with class and line struggles. In pre-

CR agricultural novels, the ideological motif of class and line struggles is not as conspicuous as it is in CR novels. The only subject matter in pre-CR agricultural novels is the collectivization movement, which represents the policy of the Party's orthodox line. The main heroes actively pursue the Party's policy and lead villagers to take the road of collectivization. Thus, their loyalty to the Party and its line, their understanding of the Party's policy, and the leading role played by them in local collectivization, all reflect the heroes' ideological consciousness.

In *Great Changes in a Mountain Village*, Liu Yusheng understands that collectivization is part of the Party's cause and that he should play a vanguard role in the movement. Thus to uphold the Party's honour and discipline, he devotes himself to the movement regardless of his wife's opposition and other backward villagers' attacks. In *The Builders*, Liang Shengbao, who has been very much acclaimed in orthodox mainland Chinese literary circles as a lofty, heroic image of a socialist peasant, has a deep understanding of the significance and urgency of the collectivization movement. According to Liang, 'Private property was the source of all evil . . . He wanted to take this task of removing the ownership of private property as soon as possible, as his noble responsibility.'[2] He plays an even more active role in leading local collectivization than Liu Yusheng.

As pointed out by some commentators, the heroes' ideological consciousness in carrying out the collectivization in pre-CR novels was idealized.[3] Generally, the idealization is based on a single standard of evaluation, i.e. exclusive obedience to the calls and instructions of higher authorities who represent the Party or government. What the main heroes do in the collectivization movement is to carry out the intentions of the higher levels. Liu Qing, the author of *The Builders*, stated that he 'tried to describe Liang Shengbao as a loyal son of the Party', i.e. 'a young Party member of peasant origin who obediently did as the Party said'.[4] From another angle, the degree of idealization of the main heroes' ideological level is within such a range that their ideological consciousness and qualities are presented as being higher than those of their colleagues and subordinates, but lower than those of their leaders in higher positions of authority. Their understanding of the collectivization movement comes from the leaders' interpretations and guidance. In brief, the 'heroic' role they play in the stories is to learn the Party's policies from high-level superiors, to propagate these policies in the villages, to educate and organize villagers to carry out these policies, and to set examples for them. In view of the above characteristics, Joe C. Huang gave an unfavourable comment on the characterization of Liang Shengbao in *The Builders*: 'He is not a hero . . . He is merely faithfully executing official policy and is perfectly well aware that the Party is behind him . . . The difference between a hero and a socialist man is that between a man who makes a decision on his own judgement at his risk and a Party member who sees himself merely as the agent of Party policy.'[5] T. A. Hsia also pointed out that heroism in pre-CR novels is subject to command, discipline and other restrictions.[6]

As regards the CR novel heroes' ideological consciousness in class and line struggles, the situation is different. The present analysis centres on the hero Gao Daquan in *The Golden Road* and the heroine Shi Caihong in *The Long Rainbow* as examples. Gao's story is about the collectivization movement, and Shi's about the campaign of learning from Dazhai.

The Golden Road is set in a village in north China. Its main story begins in the winter of 1951 when Land Reform had just ended. The higher authorities put forward the slogan 'to build up family fortunes', which is intended to encourage peasants to develop production. Responding to the call of the authorities, the head of the village Zhang Jinfa starts to put the slogan into effect. But Gao Daquan, Zhang's colleague, doubts whether carrying out 'the new policy' is socialist work, and goes to consult the higher authorities. Later Wang Youqing, the secretary of the district Party committee, firmly tells him in person that 'this is socialist work', yet he still is not convinced for the following reason:

> The socialist work that he had expected should be more exciting, more forceful, . . . But now the pattern unfolding before him was so different from that beautiful blueprint in his mind that nothing anyone could do could make them compatible. . .[7]

Later, primarily on the basis of his own understanding of socialism, he organizes local peasants to resist the policy of building up family fortunes, and then sets up a mutual aid team in the village. He clings to his course, and the confrontation between him and the higher authorities lasts two years. Finally, the policy pursued by the top authorities of the Party affirms Gao Daquan's actions. Thus, unlike Liu Yusheng in *Great Changes in a Mountain Village* and Liang Shengbao in *The Builders* who are encouraged and guided by higher authorities to organize the local collectivization, Gao Daquan leads the movement in his home village on his own initiative. His thinking and actions indicate his unusual ideological insight and political foresight.

The story of *The Long Rainbow* is about learning from Dazhai in a mountain village during the Cultural Revolution. The heroine Shi Caihong, the newly appointed Party secretary of the village, is dissatisfied with the past work of learning from Dazhai undertaken under the leadership of the previous secretary, Shi Changqing. According to the heroine, 'the campaign of learning from Dazhai is concerned with the struggle of the two roads and the two lines', and the main reason for past failures is 'that some village leaders only took Dazhai as an example of production and paid all attention to production, but could not smell the scent of the gunpowder of class struggle or distinguish different lines'.[8]

Shi Caihong's plan and practice in leading the villagers to build a dam encounter not only sabotage by the class enemies, but also the opposition of her colleagues and superiors. The commune director Sun Qizhi, who stays in the village as a representative of the higher authorities to guide its work, backs the previous village secretary Shi Changqing, who is in charge of production and now the second most important leader in the village. They disagree with the heroine because the engineers' surveys and calculations disprove the practicability of the project plan. Then, hoodwinked by the hidden class enemy, they assert that the project will only waste manpower and material resources, and they put pressure on the heroine. Sun Qizhi warns her, 'If you still act in disregard of others' opinions, and cause unnecessary losses for the collective and the masses, you should know the consequence for your position and Party membership!'[9] However, Shi Caihong, confident in her own correctness, and sure that Sun Qizhi is carrying out a revisionist line, organizes the masses to criticize Sun irrespective of his higher position. Her actions at last gain the support of the higher authorities and the project is completed well ahead of schedule. At the end, even Sun Qizhi and Shi Changqing are convinced of the heroine's higher ideological qualities in pursuing Mao's line in learning from Dazhai.

It is evident that disobedience to certain higher authorities and their policies is a prominent aspect of the characterization of the heroes. This seems contrary to the situation criticized by Joe C. Huang and T. A. Hsia in pre-CR novels. However, the disobedience is not substantially based on the heroes' individuality. The correct line is dominated by Mao, the supreme authority. Although the stories of CR novels seem to centre on the heroes' actions against the wrong line, there exists a shadow central story-line in the novels, namely that the heroes are pursuing the correct line. Therefore, CR novelists held a dual criterion of evaluation when dealing with consciousness in the line struggles, i.e. loyalty to the correct line and opposition to the wrong line. In order to show the heroes' extraordinary ideological qualities, the authors put emphasis on the heroes' thoughts and actions which indicate that they are able to distinguish the correct line from the wrong line. In fact, both the correct and wrong lines are from higher authorities.

As the correct line is Mao's line, the unusual ideological insight and foresight of the heroes actually render their ideas as being in accordance with Mao's thought. Therefore, in the CR novels, the novelists played up the connection between the heroes and Mao. For instance, for those works set during the Cultural Revolution, some young main heroes went to Beijing and saw Mao at the beginning of the movement. Such an experience always inspired them and reminded them to carry out Mao's line. In *The Mountains and Rivers Roar*, the night after Liu Wangchun saw Mao at Tiananmen Square in 1966, he wrote his pledge in a notebook: '. . . I vow to be a red successor to the cause of revolution. My will became still stronger when I stood in front of Tiananmen, the will to resolutely combat and prevent revisionism.'[10] Six years later, when the struggle in the campaign of learning from Dazhai becomes more acute, he holds the notebook in both hands and speaks with excitement: 'Chairman Mao, Chairman Mao! As a soldier reviewed by you six years ago, when I now think of you, my confidence has increased hundredfold, and my courage thousandfold! . . .'[11] During the night, he sees Mao in a dream and becomes even more inspired.

For those stories set before the Cultural Revolution, it became a stock episode for the heroes to write to Mao or to plan to go to Beijing to ask Mao for instructions when the conflicts between them and the wrong line become intense. Consequently, the higher authorities' replies on Mao's behalf confirm the main heroes' correctness and help them win the struggles. Generally, however, to go to Beijing to ask Mao for instructions is merely a symbolic trope. In *The Golden Road*, Gao Daquan, disappointed at the explanation of socialism made by the district leaders, and receiving no reply from the county Party committee, decides to visit the county leaders in person. He is sleepless the previous night because of the fear that he will fail to convince the leaders concerned to change the policy of 'building up family fortunes'. Before dawn, 'he got up and lit a lamp. As he raised his head and saw the portrait of Mao, he was suddenly enlightened. He turned back and spoke to his wife, "If I don't return home tomorrow evening, that means I shall have left for Beijing."'[12] This description indicates that Mao is the supreme authority in the hero's heart, and moreover, that he is confident that Mao and he are in mutual understanding. However, he need not go to Beijing because on the way he meets higher-level leaders who approve his actions and guide him to study Mao's article 'Get Organized'.

Another way to link Mao's line and the main heroes' ideology is to emphasize the heroes' study of Mao's works. In The *Golden Road*, after the county Party secretary Liang Haishan gives Gao Daquan a copy of Mao's article 'Get Organized', he realizes that Mao's words are 'the golden road' of socialism in the countryside. Again and again he studies the article and takes the words 'get organized' as his motto. In *The Long Rainbow*, the heroine Shi Caihong often studies Mao's works late into the night. She claims that all the questions raised in her work have been answered in Mao's works.

The above analysis mainly concerns the heroes' consciousness of line struggle. Another important aspect of the main heroes' ideological qualities is their awareness of and sensitivity to class struggle. In The *Golden Road*, the hidden class enemy Fan Keming disguises himself so well that even leaders of the higher levels have not discovered his true colours. It is only Gao Daquan who begins to suspect Fan's real background. This quality is shared by all the main heroes in the CR novels. They are good at analysing information with respect to hidden class enemies which others cannot see through, and they are the first to keep a close watch on the disguised enemies. In *The Long Rainbow*, Shi Caihong's acute political sensitivity makes her the first to suspect the hidden class enemy Zhao Deming, vice-chairman of the village revolutionary committee. The heroine's superior, Sun Qizhi, and other cadres have been hoodwinked by the enemy for a long time. At the end of the story, Zhao Deming is arrested as a proven traitor in the War of Resistance against Japan. Sun Qizhi and other cadres are once again convinced of the heroine's ideological consciousness.

With respect to pre-CR fictional heroes' awareness of and sensitivity to class struggle, the situation is very different from CR novels. Generally, in pre-CR novels the class enemies are outside the Party; their identities are open and their activities are often under people's surveillance. What a hero does is to organize his/her followers to keep watch on the class enemies' movements and attack them at the proper time. During the Socialist Education Movement between 1964 and 1966, there appeared a few novels describing local inner-Party class struggles. Hao Ran's *The Sun Shines Bright* was representative, and was acclaimed by the authorities during the Cultural Revolution. However, even in this novel, the class enemies' activities are more overt and their disguises and intrigues are often observed not only by the main hero Xiao Changchun but also by other people such as Jiao Shuhong.

By comparison, although the heroes' consciousness and sensitivity to class struggles are important, their awareness and foresight in line struggles are given more prominence. However, the line and class struggles are usually interwoven, that is, the wrong line is pursued by negative higher authorities and supported by class enemies. It is mainly through distinguishing the wrong line, opposing the negative authorities, and attacking the class enemies, that the heroes' high ideological qualities are shown. The heroes' ideological qualities in the class and line struggles are not only higher than those of their subordinates but also higher than those of their superiors. They are so high that their thought is connected to Mao.

CONSCIOUSNESS OF ALTRUISM AND COLLECTIVISM

Unlike ideological consciousness of the class and line struggles, which is mainly shown in the main heroes' struggles against capitalist-roaders and class enemies, altruistic and collective consciousness is primarily manifested in the heroes' thinking and actions in service of the public or others' interests.

Throughout China between the 1950s and 1960s, altruism and collectivism were promoted by propaganda. The campaign of learning from Lei Feng in 1962 was an example of embodying this ideal. Nevertheless, the Cultural Revolution carried the promotion of altruism and collectivism to an unprecedentedly high level. Three of Mao's early articles [*lao san pian*] were acclaimed as the people's mottoes.[13] Zhang Side in 'Serve the People', Bai Qiu'en [Norman Bethune] in 'In Memory of Norman Bethune', and Yu Gong [the Foolish Old Man] in 'The Foolish Old Man Who Removed the Mountains' were intended as examples for the people. Mao's phrases from these articles such as *wei renmin fuwu* [serve the people][14] *hao bu li ji, zhuanmen li ren* [utter devotion to others without any thought of self][15] became people's pet phrases. Ideologically, the promotion of altruism and collectivism went so far that 'to fight selfishness' became parallel with one of the most prominent principles of the Cultural Revolution — 'to repudiate revisionism', which directly concerns the class and line struggles.

In pre-CR agricultural novels, as stated before, the ideological motif of the class and line struggles is not conspicuous, but the ideological conflicts between collectivism/altruism and individualism/egoism are emphasized. According to Joe C. Huang, 'The goal of the Communist Party in the transformation of individual farming into agricultural co-operation was not only a change from private to collective ownership but also a reshaping of the peasants' attitude.'[16] The 'reshaping of the peasants' attitude' should indicate the cultivation of altruism and collectivism. The main role played by the heroes as described in the movement of collectivization is to set examples for the masses in taking the road of collectivism and practising altruism. So for the pre-CR novels, we may take collective and altruistic consciousness to be the most important ideological aspect of the authors' idealization in characterization of the main heroes.

Individual interests in the novels primarily concern personal and family affairs, of which love and marriage are significant. Thus, it becomes a stock treatment in the pre-CR novels to have the heroes place collectivization work before their own love and marriage. In *The Builders*, Liang Shengbao, twenty five years old, puts the work of his mutual aid team first, although his family and the villagers feel very anxious about his marriage. He loves Gaixia deeply, but he tries hard to control his feelings because he fears that love and marriage would divert attention and energy from the collective work. As Gaixia musters her courage to express her love for him, he is moved. But, 'considering his responsibility for the cause and the Party's reputation, he could not allow his personal affairs to interfere with the public cause. He thought that he had no right to be self-indulgent'.[17] He refuses her affection on the spot, and eventually he loses her. In *Great Changes in a Mountain Village*, Liu Yusheng's devotion to public interests leads to his wife's dissatisfaction and becomes the reason for her leaving him. When alternative choices have to be made between collective work and his marriage, he chooses the break-up of his marriage so that he can continue to work wholeheartedly for the common good.

However, in these stories we also see another side to the heroes. In *The Builders*, Liang Shengbao is fascinated by Gaixia's physical beauty, and thereby falls in love with her. 'Shengbao had to confess that he liked her large expressive eyes; he liked her musical voice; he liked her charming way of walking, and he liked her graceful steps. He admitted that he liked such external beauty.'[18] Whether he is sleepless at the railway station in the county town, or lost in thought in the mountains, he cannot restrain himself from thinking about his mother, father, sister and Gaixia. Especially, when Liang Shengbao mistakenly thinks that Gaixia has changed her love for him, his grief further reveals his ordinary feelings:

Misery! Misery! The change in Gaixia's attitude made him miserable and upset . . . Every man's spirit is sustained by a few emotional pillars — the way he feels about his parents, about his faith, about his ideals, about his intimate friends, about love. If any of these pillars snap, no matter which, his heart is bound to ache. Until such time as Shengbao could form an interest in another girl, whenever he thought of this matter, he would be unhappy.[19]

Furthermore, in the conflict of choice between collective interests and love or marriage, pre-CR-novel heroes feel certain impulse, hesitation, sentimentality and even anguish, even though their ideology of collectivism and altruism finally gains the upper hand. The following description in *The Builders* shows Liang Shengbao's feeling and emotion before he declines Gaixia's affection, and shows how hard he restricts his impulse through reason.

Liang Shengbao's heart had already been reduced to liquid by the flames of love. He was burning all over, as if something within Gaixia were being transmitted to him through her loving words, her intelligent expression, her gentle hand. Shengbao was intoxicated. He felt vitally alive . . . He longed to wrap this girl who loved him in his strong arms and kiss her . . . A communist's reason controlled his feeling . . . He must control his basic instinct and feeling using his noble spirit . . .[20]

In *Great Changes in a Mountain Village*, Liu Yusheng finally agrees to his wife's request for divorce, but his heart is full of reluctance and he behaves weakly and sentimentally. He sheds tears again and again, imploring his wife not to leave him. As shown in the following passage, his sorrowfulness and frailty even move his wife temporarily.

When he was about to write the application for divorce, Liu Yusheng cried sadly. Standing outside the window, Chairman Li deliberately raised his voice as he talked with the people on the outside in order to prevent the sound of his crying from being heard by them. Seeing him crying so grievously, and the hand in which he held the pen shaking, Zhang Guizhen could not help feeling sorry.[21]

The descriptions of the heroes' sentimentality, hesitation and sorrowfulness have a dual significance. On the one hand, they show realism, although the heroes on the whole were products of idealization according to the then current ideological standard and artistic theories. In other words, the descriptions added truth [*zhenshi xing*] to the works by revealing the heroes' normal human feelings. On the other hand, the authors emphasized the heroes' sentimentality, reluctance and anguish in order to intensify the difficulty of their choice. The fact that the heroes overcome these feelings indicates their high level of altruism and collectivism.

As for the CR novels, although the altruistic and collective ideology is overshadowed by political ideology concerning the class and line struggles, the degree of idealization of altruism and collectivism in the characterization of the main heroes is further heightened in comparison with pre-CR novels. The descriptions are greatly simplified through exclusively accentuating the side of absolute altruism. Love is basically excluded from the main heroes' life. Human feelings relating to love, such as physical attraction, passion for physical contact with the opposite sex, sentimentality over absent or lost loves, are consequently not a part of the heroes' thoughts and actions.

With regard to family, many main heroes are orphans and unmarried, so the only emotional connection between them and others is a class relationship, and what they think and do is related to the public or others' interests. In other words, their origin and marital status themselves reflect an intensification of altruistic and collective ideology in the characterization of the main heroes.

For those main heroes who are married and have families, their altruistic and collective awareness is so heightened that there appears to be no clear line of demarcation between family and the collective. Below is a dialogue taken from *The Golden Road*, showing the fused relation between family and collective in Gao Daquan's heart. Not long after the main story begins, the hero leads some villagers to some temporary work at the Beijing Railway Station. Far from their homes, some are homesick. Early one morning Gao Daquan is flushed with excitement. Holding his fellow villager Deng Jiukuan's hands tightly, Gao is too excited to speak, with his lips trembling:

> Deng Jiukuan was rather surprised and asked him immediately, 'What happened? Are you okay?'
>
> After a long pause, Gao Daquan only said, 'Brother Jiukuan, I am homesick.'
>
> Deng Jiukuan felt relieved and smiled, 'Oh, that would be a bit weak. Are you thinking of your wife?'
>
> Gao Daquan shook his head.
>
> 'Are you thinking of your son?'
>
> 'No.'
>
> 'What on earth are you thinking of?'
>
> 'I'm thinking of our village Fangcaodi, and those people who shared joys and sorrows with us.'
>
> 'But exactly who is the dearest among them?'
>
> 'I'm thinking of all of them. They are all equally close to me.'
>
> 'Nonsense. I know you're in fact thinking of your wife and son. You needn't be ill at ease. You may ask for leave and go home for some time.'
>
> 'Brother Jiukuan, what I'm saying is true, do you know? I am not only Lü Ruifen's husband and Xiao Long's father, but, more importantly, as a Party member I belong to the Party and to all the poor villagers.'
>
> 'I can't understand what you mean.'
>
> 'You should understand . . .'[22]

In *The Golden Road*, Gao Daquan's younger brother Gao Erlin decides to split from the family. From Gao Daquan's reaction to the unforeseen break-up of his family, we can see that in his mind family is a mere trifle when compared to his work for collectivization. In the story, during the absence of Gao Daquan, and under the instigation of negative characters, Gao Erlin proposes to break up the family and live apart because he cannot stand that 'his brother and sister-in-law crazily help other people from morning till night, but do not pay any attention to the family and to his marriage'.[23] Seeing that the two brothers have shared weal and woe for so many years, villagers are shocked by the news and grieved at the failure to stop it. In such a gloomy atmosphere, Gao Daquan returns home at last. He is speechless as Liu Xiang, a poor peasant, tells him what has happened and tearfully comforts him. But he immediately raises his head and says,

> Uncle Liu Xiang, . . . I am not angry nor disconsolate . . . The root of all evil is private ownership. Before extinction of the ownership, such a thing can't be eliminated . . . I can stand it. To say nothing of breaking up the family and living apart, even if my family had been bombed flat with no trace left of the adults and child, I would still go ahead to make revolution as before. Please set your mind at ease.[24]

These words may lead the reader to feel that the hero's dedication to collectivization reaches such an extent that he is cruelly indifferent to his family. His words and actions surprise all the villagers on his side and they unanimously praise the loftiness of his altruism. In brief therefore, while facing the contradiction between family and public interests, the main heroes of CR novels privilege public interests without the sentimentality, hesitation or reluctance of the main heroes of the pre-CR novels.

There are some other characteristic points of CR novels indicating the main heroes' ideology of altruism and collectivism which are not emphasized in pre-CR novels. The first is their anti-departmentalism. In the heroes' mind, family interests are subordinate to the collective interests of their village, yet the public interests of the village are subordinate to the collective interests of higher administrative levels, of which the highest is the state. Evidently, the main heroes' anti-departmentalism overshadows other cadres who overemphasize the collective interests of their village. In *The Long Rainbow*, Shi Laifu is a member of the leadership of the village in charge of sideline production. In his opinion, 'A cadre should try to make a contribution to the collective interests. This is completely reasonable. Otherwise, what is his use to the public?'[25] The previous night, before selling a number of pigs of the village-owned piggery to the state purchasing station, he attempts to play a little trick. From his own experience, he knows that feeding pigs with salty food is helpful in maintaining their weight during transport. He reckons that using this method can at least earn more tens of *yuan* for the village collective. Thus, without hesitation, he takes all his family's salt to the piggery. But his 'unselfish' intention and act meet with the main hero Shi Caihong's severe criticism: 'Your intention is absolutely out-and-out capitalist ideology . . . The relationship between the state and the collective of the village is just like that between the village and a family. The state is a big collective, and our village Shizhuang is a small collective. . .'[26]

Secondly, the main heroes are willing to risk their lives to save others. Some cases are chance encounters along the heroes' way, but more scenes are set at a construction site. A typical picture is as follows: Due to sabotage by the class enemy, an accident takes place which puts a person or a crowd in imminent danger. At the moment when the common people are shocked and other supporting heroes have yet to decide how to act, the main hero rushes forth courageously. The expected consequence is that the hero's action averts the catastrophe although he might be slightly wounded.

In *The Mountains and Rivers Roar*, there are two such detailed descriptions of the main hero Liu Wangchun's deeds. The first is in the prologue, which first introduces Liu in the novel. When Liu and other passengers share a ferry boat across the Hulong River, a girl takes fright and falls off the boat. Liu immediately dives into the torrent to rescue her. Another scene is near the climax of the story. At the demolition site, because of the villain Long Youtian's sabotage, some explosive packages fail to explode as expected after the fuse burns and they must be quickly removed. Having refused to be dissuaded, Liu Wangchun personally leads two others to do the work. This is very dangerous because the explosive could blow up at any time. However, irrespective of the personal danger this poses, Liu remains unusually composed. He is prepared to die for the sake of others' safety. Suddenly, seeing one explosive package ready to explode, he covers one of his companions with his own body without the least hesitation.

Of the 24 CR agricultural novels, over two-thirds have one or two episodes in which the main heroes save others without regard to their personal safety. It is evident that such descriptions are intended to emphasize the main heroes' altruistic awareness and heroic spirit. We thus have reason to take scenes such as these as stock elements in the characterization of the main heroes.

It goes without saying that altruism based on ideology exists in not only Chinese novels but also in the novels of other countries. For instance, the altruism of the protagonist in Voynich's *The Gadfly* is also remarkable. In particular, the hero's letter written on the eve of his execution shows his altruistic stature, which by no means pales beside that of fictional communist heroes. Pavel Korchagin, the hero of Ostrovsky's *How the Steel Was Tempered*, comments, 'I still stand for what is most important in *The Gadfly*, for his courage, his supreme endurance, for the type of man who is capable of enduring suffering without exhibiting his pain to all and sundry. I stand for the type of revolutionary whose personal life is nothing as compared with the life of society as a whole.'[27]

Ostrovsky's *How the Steel Was Tempered* was claimed by some CR writers as a novel exerting an important influence on their lives. The hero Pavel's following words were popular among young Chinese during the 1960s and 1970s.

> Man's dearest possession is life. It is given to him but once, and he must live it so as to feel no torturing regrets for wasted years, never know the burning shame of a mean and petty past; so live that, dying, he might say: all my life, all my strength were given to the finest cause in all the world — the fight for the Liberation of Mankind.[28]

Like other Soviet novels, this novel includes descriptions of love. Pavel falls in love several times, but ideological value and the public interest always come first. Among all the girls he falls in love with Tonya occupies a special position, because this love is not only his first, but also the longest. Dissatisfied with Tonya's lack of proletarian ideological awareness, Pavel eventually breaks off his relationship with her in spite of his initial sadness when he makes this decision.

Later, Pavel is attracted by Rita. Like Liang Shengbao in *The Builders*, who severs his love with Gaixia for whole-hearted devotion to the work of collectivization, Pavel stops further progress of his feelings because he thinks love needs time which he is willing to spend only on revolution. The following description shows his self-restraint, similar to Liang Shengbao's.

> To Pavel, Rita was sacred. She was his friend and comrade, his political guide. Yet she was a woman as well. He had first become aware of this over there at the footbridge, and that was why her embrace stirred him so much now. He felt her deep even breathing; somewhere quite close to him were her lips. Proximity awoke in him a powerful desire to find those lips, and it was only with a great effort of will that he suppressed the impulse.[29]

Rita, also a revolutionary, cannot help blaming him: 'You ought not to be so harsh to yourself, Pavel. Our life is not all struggle, there is room in it for the happiness that real love brings.'[30]

In this classic of Soviet Socialist Realism we are made aware of the complexity of the hero's mind which is sometimes full of hesitation, sentiment, regret, and so on. Pavel and Rita meet again after three years of separation. Below is a section of the dialogue between them during their reunion, in which the hero's sentiment and regret are fully articulated.

> 'Let's sit here,' Rita said, indicating two seats in a corner at the back of the stalls.
>
> 'There is one question I must ask you,' said Rita when they were seated. 'It concerns bygone days, but I am sure you will not refuse to answer it. Why did you break off our studies and our friendship that time?'
>
> And though Pavel had been expecting this question ever since they had met, it disconcerted him. Their eyes met and Pavel saw that she knew.
>
> 'I think you know the answer yourself, Rita. That happened three years

ago, and now I can only condemn Pavel for what he did. As a matter of fact Korchagin has committed many a blunder, big and small, in his life. That was one of them.'

Rita smiled.

'An excellent preamble. Now for the answer!'

'It is not only I who was to blame,' Pavel began in a low voice. 'It was the Gadfly's fault too, the revolutionary romanticism of his. In those days I was very much influenced by books with vivid descriptions of staunch, courageous revolutionaries consecrated to our cause. Those men made a deep impression on me and I longed to be like them. I allowed *The Gadfly* to influence my feeling for you. It seems absurd to me now, and I regret it more than I can say.'

. . .

'It is a pity, Pavel, that you did not tell me this three years ago,' said Rita with a smile that showed her thoughts to be far away.

'A pity, you mean, because I have never been more to you than a comrade, Rita?'

'No, Pavel, you might have been more.'

'But surely that can be remedied.'

'No, Comrade Gadfly, it is too late for that . . .'

. . . She could tell by his eyes that he was deeply hurt by her confession . . .[31]

It is the complexity of the hero's mind that differentiates the altruistic hero of Soviet Socialist Realism from his CR novel counterpart.

We may also compare Sholokhov's heroes with CR novel heroes in terms of ideological qualities. Sholokhov has been the most popular contemporary writer in the Soviet Union since the 1930s. His *Quiet Flows the Don* was acclaimed by critics as a Cossack *War and Peace* or an epic reflecting the reality of Russia between 1912 and 1922. The novel *Virgin Soil Upturned* depicts the collectivization of agriculture among the Don Cossacks. It has been said that 'this novel of Sholokhov's does more to help one understand the realities of collectivization than all the official Soviet literature on the subject put together'.[32]

In *Quiet Flows the Don* Sholokhov's presentation is generally taken to be on the whole objective and balanced. He neither idealizes all his Reds as heroes nor portrays all Whites as unmitigated villains. His principal character, Grigory Melekhov, is shown changing sides and deserting the Reds, and in the third volume we even see him fighting on the side of the Whites. The fourth volume was written with the specific object of setting this straight and of showing Melekhov's final change of heart, but the ending is somewhat ambiguous, and Melekhov's adherence to the new order of things somehow incomplete. His following monologue near the end of the novel shows the protagonist's ideological confusion and complexity.

I've always envied men like the young Listnitsky or our Koshevoi . . . Everything was clear to them from the start, and to me even now nothing is clear. They've both got their own straight roads, their own goals, but ever since 1917 I've been swinging this way and that staggering along like a drunk: I left the Whites but didn't stick to the Reds, so here I am, floating about like dung in an ice hole . . . I should have been in the Red Army all the way through, then things might have worked out all right for me.[33]

Without clear ideological awareness he does not show unusual altruism.

Virgin Soil Upturned shows the contradictions in the dispossessed peasants, the conflict between their proprietary instincts and the doctrine of Communism, and the harsh process of the movement. The protagonist Davidov was meant by the author to serve as the embodiment of revolutionary heroism. It is evident that Davidov sets store on the party's interests. He claims that he is ready to die for the party and for the cause of the working class. His ideological qualities are particularly evident in his indomitable spirit of opposition to enemies. However, in spite of his heroic qualities based on ideological discipline, we also see aspects of Davidov's personal indulgence. For instance, he fornicates with the ex-wife of his colleague Nagulnov. The woman is known for her beauty and dissoluteness in the village. He is so madly infatuated with her that he walks hand-in-hand with her in the village regardless of his colleagues' criticism and villagers' gossip. Since the woman has secret contacts with villains, the hero's relationship with her leads to a series of losses in the campaign of collectivization.

Most of Sholokhov's works were translated into Chinese. The Chinese translation (by He Fei) of the first two volumes of *Quiet Flows the Don* was published in Shanghai in 1931. Lu Xun, who himself translated a short story by Sholokhov entitled 'Fuqin' ['The Father'] into Chinese, wrote a postscript for He Fei's translation. The great influence of Sholokhov's fiction on Chinese writers is undeniable. For instance, Zhou Libo, who was the Chinese translator of Sholokhov's *Virgin Soil Upturned*, wrote *Hurricane* [*Bao feng zhou yu*][34] and *Great Changes in a Mountain Village*. These two novels show the obvious influence of Sholokhov, and they correspond to *Quiet Flows the Don* and *Virgin Soil Upturned* in terms of storyline. However, Sholokhov became known as representative of revisionist writing in China during the Cultural Revolution. From the above discussion we may see the substantial differences between the characterization of CR novels and Sholokhov's, thereby also seeing the difference between the Combination of Revolutionary Realism and Revolutionary Romanticism of CR writers and the Socialist Realism represented by Sholokhov. Moreover, through this comparison, we can see more similarities between pre-CR Chinese novels and Soviet novels than between CR novels and Soviet novels.

Chapter 4

Temperamental and Behavioural Qualities

In CR novels ideology is evidently an important part of the foundation of the thinking and actions of the main heroes. This is especially true when the thinking and actions are concerned with class and line struggles. Nevertheless, apart from ideological consciousness and qualities, which cannot explain all their feelings, manners and behaviour, CR novel heroes have their temperamental and behavioural qualities. Like the ideological qualities, temperamental and behavioural qualities also contribute to the heroes' 'loftiness, greatness and perfection'.

CATEGORIES OF TEMPERAMENTAL AND BEHAVIOURAL QUALITIES

Generally, the following characteristics with regard to temperament and behaviour are prominent and are shared by all of the main heroes of CR novels.

Being Kind, Generous and Above-Board

First, in respect of kindness and generosity, the previously analysed spirit of being willing to sacrifice their own personal interests for others concurrently reflects such temperamental and behavioural qualities of the heroes.

Another noticeable manifestation of kindness and generosity in the heroes' thinking and actions is their good intentions and magnanimous attitude towards backward characters. As shown in *The Golden Road*, Gao Daquan's family affair does not shake his resolution to pursue collectivization, that is, on the point of ideology, Gao Daquan does not show any sentimentality about the separation of his brother Gao Erlin. On the other hand, personally, Gao Daquan's magnanimity towards Gao Erlin goes beyond the mere category of ideology. He does not accept the advice of his colleagues and other villagers who all regard Gao Erlin's behaviour as being devoid of gratitude: '. . . From now on, just think that he is dead and decomposed, make a clear break, and never think of him again.'[1] On the contrary, Gao Daquan goes so far as to feel sorry for Gao Erlin. In front of the villagers who come to comfort him, Gao Daquan says,

> I'm sorry that our family has held its wedding ceremonies in dilapidated houses for generations. I wish I could build a tile-roofed house and let them (Gao Erlin and his fiancée) get married in the new house. But I can't afford it now. Of the present two rooms, ours is larger. So I intend to decorate this larger room carefully . . . and then let them hold a ceremony in this room and stay here later on. My wife, son and I will move into the smaller room. . .[2]

It is evident that Gao Daquan's speech above does not include any resounding ideological words, but his thinking and manner show the moral qualities of consideration and generosity.

In *Evergreen*, because the main hero Jiang Chunwang refuses to carry out the policy of fixing farm output quotas for each household, the county secretary Huang Guang, a capitalist-roader, comes down to the village in person to supervise and speed up its implementation. On the one hand, Jiang Chunwang does not make any concession in the line struggle on an ideological level. But on the other hand, realizing that pursuing the new policy is not Huang Guang's personal error but a wrong Party line, Jiang Chunwang is considerate towards Huang on a human level. In spite of Huang's indifference and arrogance, Jiang Chunwang goes to visit Huang and attempts to dissuade him. He tells Huang that it is not only his own view but the will of all the poor and lower-middle peasants to take a collective road and to oppose the new policy of individual farming. With excitement and sincerity, and full of warm-heartedness towards Huang, he describes the future of the village.

> The Party and the poor and lower-middle peasants entrusted me to develop the land well, but I feel ashamed that I have not yet fulfilled the task. Secretary Huang, you will see our future. So long as we still rely on the collective economy, the village will change a lot. Two years hence, when you come to our village, we shall not treat you with only *jiaozi* and pancakes as now, but we shall present you with savoury rice. Oh, then on both sides of Yi River, we shall smell the fragrance of rice flowers.[3]

However, Jiang Chunwang's good intentions and sincere words do not change Huang Guang's course. After he makes the decision to discharge Jiang Chunwang from his position as head of the village and to prosecute him, Huang Guang proposes to convene a mass rally to announce the implementation of the new policy. Knowing that the villagers will struggle against Huang face to face at the meeting next day, Jiang Chunwang decides to make a last attempt to dissuade Huang. He thinks that at least he should try to persuade Huang to cancel the meeting in order to protect Huang from public humiliation. Once again, Huang Guang does not accept his advice but gives him a dressing-down with an even more imperious bearing. However, although Jiang Chunwang fails in his efforts, his action shows the utmost forbearance and consideration. This indicates that the narrator goes so far in playing up the hero's kindness and generosity as to put the hero in a temporary position of weakness, full of innocence and magnanimity, which arouses the reader's sympathy. So it is only natural that Deng Daniu, one of Jiang Chunwang's colleagues, cannot help sighing, 'The biggest shortcoming of Chunwang is that he is too kind and generous.'[4] In *The Long Rainbow*, Sun Qizhi, the backward superior of Shi Caihong, has opposed the heroine's thinking and actions from the beginning until he is relieved of his post for self-examination. At the end of the story, after he heightens his ideological awareness through political study, Sun Qizhi is reassigned to supervise the work of the village. However, the villagers, who are on Shi Caihong's side, have a strong aversion to Sun Qizhi and disagree with the arrangement. There and then, Shi Caihong dissuades the cadres and villagers from opposing him and warmheartedly welcomes his return. Her generous action moves the formerly backward superior so deeply that he cannot refrain from shedding tears in front of the welcoming crowd.

Next, in CR novels, being above-board is another conspicuous factor in the main heroes' personality. As analysed in Chapter 2, the heroes' nature to be above-board is so emphasized that it is integrated into the portrayals of the heroes' physical features. In *The Golden Road*, Gao Daquan asserts sternly that deception and scheming have nothing to do with his character. 'All the words and expressions from my mouth are candid, like straight steel rails in the broad daylight.'[5] Even Zhang Jinfa, who is Gao Daquan's direct opponent in the line struggle, confirms that this is a characteristic of Gao: 'When Gao Daquan finds something done by me out of keeping with his principles, he contradicts and argues with me to my face. I have never found that he played underhand tricks.'[6] In *Evergreen*, when the capitalist-roader Huang Guang keeps exerting pressure on Jiang Chunwang and his colleagues to force them to pursue the policy of fixing farm output quotas for each household, Jiang's colleague Deng Dianju, the director of the village, proposes that they carry out the new policy in the open but take the old way in secret. Deng Dianju is pleased to think that this is a measure satisfactory to both sides, neither disobeying Huang Guang's directive nor losing Jiang Chunwang's ideological principles. However, risking being discharged from his post by Huang Guang, Jiang Chunwang disagrees with such feigned compliance and seriously criticizes Deng. What Jiang thinks and does indicates not only his ideological staunchness but also his quality of being open and above-board.

Being Level-Headed, Polite and Modest

There is no exception to the rule that all the main heroes in CR novels are described as being level-headed and polite. As for level-headedness, in Chapter 2 we have analysed Jiang Chunwang's dignified style in the confrontation with the capitalist-roader Huang Guang, and Liu Wangchun's composed and awe-inspiring manner in front of mountain torrents. Those external expressions and manners also indicate the heroes' temperamental quality of level-headedness.

Another common manifestation of this quality is their reactions in emergencies. The heroes are described as emerging with perfect ease to deal with emergencies. For instance, as discussed in Chapter 3, rescuing other people from accidents is a stock element in CR novels. In such scenes the heroes' cool-headedness is accentuated. Seeing others in danger, the heroes dash to rescue them without any hesitation or nervousness. Such descriptions are evidently designed to show not only the heroes' spirit of self-sacrifice but also their character of bravery and level-headedness.

Next, the heroes' cool-headedness is shown in emotional situations such as being insulted by other characters. In *The Mountains and Rivers Roar*, the backward character Hou Laowu abuses the main hero Liu Wangchun in his absence for being ill-informed and inexperienced. He even attacks Liu for having been promoted solely because of his political involvement in the Cultural Revolution. His abuse arouses public indignation, and he comes under attack from the crowd headed by Tai Zai. Just as both sides are engaged in the heated argument, Liu Wangchun himself appears. Tai Zai is so indignant that his eyes brim with tears. He proposes to convene a public accusation meeting to criticize Hou Laowu. However, after hearing the facts, Liu Wangchun stops the indignant crowd from attacking Hou Laowu. He says calmly to Hou Laowu, 'Go home to think it over carefully. We shall have a good talk sometime later.'[7] Liu Wangchun's unusual cool-headedness calms peoples' emotions, and he goes on to advise them to get at the truth concerning Hou Laowu's backstage supporters.

Politeness is another aspect of the heroes' behavioural qualities. Although the main heroes are at first described as playing a main role in class and line struggles, they never lose their politeness and urbanity. We have investigated through statistics the distribution of vulgar expressions such as taboo words and/ or swearwords according to the type of speaker. The result indicates that among the rates of vulgar expressions spoken by all characters of the CR novels, that of the main heroes is the lowest. The rate is also lower than that of the main heroes of the pre-CR novels (see Chapter 6).

In many descriptions, we may see a sharp contrast between the main heroes' politeness and other characters' crudeness. For example, unlike the capitalist-roaders who are often arrogant and impertinent in front of the cadres at lower levels, the main heroes are never impolite or crude towards their subordinates. In struggles against capitalist-roaders and class enemies, other positive people are often rude in their attitude and their manner. In *Evergreen*, Guiying, an active female cadre, pays a visit to the capitalist-roader Huang Guang. Her impolite manner and blunt words criticizing Huang for pursuing the policy of fixing farm output quotas for each household make Huang irritated. He cannot help shouting, 'How dare you take such liberties!' But, regardless of Huang's reaction, Guiying continues her rebuke. At last, 'Guiying's dressing-down in a louder and louder voice threw Huang into a totally awkward predicament.'[8] Here Guiying's visit forms a contrast to the main hero Jiang Chunwang's two visits, in which Jiang always keeps his self-control and grace, although the ideological conflict is even more serious. Later, most cadres and the common villagers treat Huang Guang and other cadres of the county work team rudely. But Jiang Chunwang explains the difference between a courteous reception towards the cadres of the work team and the struggle against their ideology. Even after he is discharged from his post by the work team, he still exhorts the village cadres and the masses to be warm and sensible towards the work team.

In their struggles against class enemies, other positive characters' attitude and actions are even ruder than against the capitalist-roaders in the line struggles. They hastily convene public accusation meetings to criticize a class enemy, abuse the class enemy with vulgar expressions, point the finger of scorn at the class enemy, and occasionally even slap the class enemy on the face. However, there is not a single instance of the main heroes inflicting such personal humiliation on a class enemy. (Even in the model theatrical works, with a military setting, the heroes may shoot the enemy but they never try to beat him up.)

Modesty is another aspect of the main heroes' character. They are modest not only in front of positive superiors and elders but even with other characters as well. As is well known, intellectuals and technical specialists had a lower political status than workers, peasants and soldiers during the Cultural Revolution. In the countryside, they were instructed to learn from poor and lower-middle peasants to remould their ideology, which was called 'to receive re-education' [*jieshou zai-jiaoyu*]. But before these technical specialists, the main heroes are always modest and self-effacing. For example, in *The Long Rainbow*, the heroine Shi Caihong brings her plan to build a huge dam to the attention of the authorities in hydrology. Some engineers and other advanced specialists at the level of both county and province gather at the village to discuss the feasibility of the plan. At the meeting, the engineer Li Zhiyao is the only supporter of Shi Caihong's plan, but he is outnumbered by the opposers. He then asks Shi Caihong to explain the plan by herself at the meeting because he thinks that she is more eloquent than himself in debate. The villagers also place their hopes on her. But Shi Caihong politely declines. Finally, responding to Li Zhiyao's repeated requests, she speaks to him sincerely: 'If I were asked to talk to the villagers, I would be pleased to do so. But now all the people present are engineers or technicians. What they want to listen to is theoretical knowledge. So, it's better for you to talk. After your speech, I might make some additional remarks.'[9] Shi Caihong's courteous and modest behaviour impresses the audience on the spot. It is evident that the narration is intended to emphasize the heroine's modesty.

Being Rebellious

During the Cultural Revolution, rebelliousness was promoted in both rhetoric and behaviour. At the beginning of the decade, the Red Guards were encouraged to revolt against the capitalist-roaders. The saying *Shede yi shen gua, gan ba huangdi la xia ma* [He who is not afraid of death by being cut to pieces dares to unhorse the emperor], which Mao had quoted from *Hong lou meng* [*The Dream of the Red Chamber*], became a fashionable slogan.[10] Later, rebellious disposition was described as *tou shang zhang jiao, shen shang zhang ci* [having horns growing on their heads, and having thorns growing on their bodies].[11] A rebellious spirit was not only encouraged as one aspect of the Red Guards' disposition but was even regarded as one of the inherent qualities of all the proletariat. It was claimed by CR literary authorities that in pre-CR literature and art the poor peasants are portrayed as passively accepting oppression and humiliation by the landlord class, whereas in CR literature and art the poor peasants are described as rising up against the landlords. In her analysis of the revisions in the adaptation of *The White-haired Girl* from an opera to a dance-drama, Hua-yuan Li Mowry indirectly pointed out such a change. The opera had been considered a proletarian classic since it was written in Yan'an in the early 1940s. It was rearranged as a dance-drama in 1964, and became one of the eight model theatrical works in 1966. It was claimed that, in the original opera, Xi'er and her father Yang Bailao are passive sufferers of the oppression of the landlord Huang Shiren and his followers, but in the dance-drama, they both show strong rebellious spirit. For instance, in the latter, Yang Bailao does not commit suicide but is beaten to death as he fights against his oppressors. Similarly Xi'er in the ballet is consistently rebellious in the face of the landlord's oppression.[12]

However, since CR novels are generally set in socialist society, the manifestations of the heroes' rebellious spirit cannot only be limited to struggle against the landlord class. More commonly, the rebellious spirit of the heroes is shown in their behaviour towards the capitalist-roaders. In those stories set in the Cultural Revolution, the main heroes generally start off as *geming zaofan-pai* [revolutionary rebels], and maintain their rebellious spirit after being promoted to the Party leadership. Shi Caihong in *The Long Rainbow*, Wulan

Tuoya in *The Daughter of Slaves* and Liu Wangchun in *The Mountains and Rivers Roar* are all described as 'having horns growing on their heads, and having thorns growing on their bodies'. In *The Mountains and Rivers Roar*, a senior Party cadre warns Liu Wangchun, the main hero, that as a commune Party secretary as opposed to the head of a Red Guard group, he should not continue to be rebellious against leaders and colleagues. But Liu's answer is, 'I shall forever keep the revolutionary spirit of revolt against capitalism, revisionism and all other reactionary forces. No matter what banner they flaunt and what garb they wear, I shall rebel against them, without compromise or concession.'[13]

The main heroes in stories set in the pre-CR period also have a similar rebellious spirit. In *Evergreen*, the main hero is nicknamed *Jiang-bu-zhu* [cannot be controlled]. Even his exterior shows his rebellious temperament: 'His heavy eyebrows looked awe-inspiring, and his big eyes were brightly aggressive, which clearly indicated that he was not easily dealt with.'[14] He struggles against his superiors throughout the novel.

The rebellious spirit of heroes is also displayed in pre-1949 revolts against landlords. The drama *The White-haired Girl* is one such example. In *Swift is the Spring Tide*, Li Ke leads a revolt against the landlord. When the landlord makes use of a local superstition to collect grain from the villagers, Li Ke finally sets fire to the landlord's house and then leaves to join the communist army.

Next, the main heroes' unconventional social views could also to some extent be attributed to their rebellious spirit. One typical manifestation is that they give up chances of working in cities and insist on labouring in the countryside. Usually, as mentioned before, before the main heroes are demobilized from the army, their relatives and other villagers expect that they will be given an assignment to work in the city. The heroes challenge convention, coming back to their native places, usually backward mountain areas. Moreover, according to traditional convention, unmarried adults often think of their marriage prospects. But the heroes ignore other people's remarks about their single status and devote themselves to collective work and ideological struggles.

Lastly, the heroes' rebelliousness sometimes combines with adventurism. In those novels whose motif is learning from Dazhai, the main heroes all attempt miracles in construction projects and belittle difficulties produced by natural and human conditions which are thought by others to be insurmountable barriers. For instance, in *The Long Rainbow*, Shi Caihong insists on building a huge dam in a local river. In view of a previous failure, her superior, some of her colleagues and the villagers criticize the plan for ignoring natural laws. Some experts in water conservancy flatly deny its practicability on the basis of their geological surveys and calculations. But challenging all opposition, the heroine clings obstinately to her own course and works wonders. In *The Mountains and Rivers Roar*, Liu Wangchun's adventurous spirit is even more conspicuous. He decides to complete a large irrigation project ahead of schedule. According to the original plan, the project would take three years to accomplish, but Liu proposes to complete it within six months. He is criticized by his colleagues for ignoring practical considerations and striving for miracles, but Liu persists in his way.

The main heroes' rebelliousness is to a great extent shown in ideological struggles and politicized agricultural campaigns. The nature of rebelliousness will be discussed further with relation to submissiveness and loyalty below.

Being Submissive and Loyal

In the analysis concerning the main heroes' ideological consciousness, we noticed that the heroes' compliance with Mao's thought indicates the height of their ideological awareness. But many such descriptions show another aspect of their temperament, i.e. submissiveness and loyalty. In *The Mountains and Rivers Roar*, Liu Wangchun recalls the scene in which the Red Guards were reviewed by Mao in Tiananmen Square. The night before the review, he and his comrades-in-arms recited Mao's quotations until dawn. He recalls,

> Then and there, I swore an oath in my mind: I must become a good soldier of Chairman Mao! I should bring credit to Chairman Mao, and win honour for Chairman Mao! I should fight for Chairman Mao's revolutionary line! I should become a reliable successor to the cause of proletarian revolution.[15]

Even in his dreams, Liu Wangchun repeats his oath. Both his previous fanaticism in Tiananmen Square and his later piousness in recalling the scene indicate not only his ideological loyalty but his temperamental submissiveness.

Usually, in order to persist in Mao's line, the heroes take Mao's quotations as mottoes. According to our investigation into the frequency and distribution of Mao's quotations in CR novels, about 60 percent of the quotations are made by the main heroes (see Chapter 7).

The heroes also claim to be loyal to the Party and the Party's causes such as socialism and communism. In *Evergreen*, Jiang Chunwang says, 'To struggle for the Party and its causes is the whole happiness of my life, and is also the only need of my life.'[16] In *The Golden Road*, when he takes the oath on being admitted to the Party, Gao Daquan makes a pledge 'to hand over more than one hundred *jin* (referring to his life) to the Party' [*ba zhe yi bai duo jin jiao gei dang*], which later becomes his standard phrase.[17]

If the above piousness towards Mao and the Party is too abstract to show submissiveness and loyalty in their character, their attitude and manner in front of those superiors who represent the correct line of higher levels indicate such personal traits more concretely. For example, in *The Golden Road*, the first superior whom Gao Daquan admires is Luo Xuguang, who led the Land Reform at the village, recommended Gao for Party membership, and then left before the main story of collectivization begins. Luo gave Gao Daquan a notebook as a souvenir before he left, in which he wrote a few lines of encouragement and predicted the coming socialism. From then on, Gao Daquan often takes out the notebook to review these words and to remind himself to adhere to Luo's guidance. The second superior whom Gao Daquan admires is the county secretary Liang Haishan, who is the authoritative representative of collectivization in the county. When Gao Daquan is introduced to Liang for the first time, sweat keeps oozing from his face because of excessive reverence. He tries to remember everything that Liang says and decides to follow Liang's guidance all his life. In short, Gao Daquan's implicit obedience to and faith in superiors such as Luo Xuguang and Liang Haishan form one important aspect of his character.

The heroes' submissiveness and loyalty are not only shown in their reverence for their ideological superiors, but also in their filial piety towards their parents, including foster parents. This filial piety is often intentionally emphasized in CR novels by authors, and is in sharp contrast to class enemies' disobedience and impiety to their parents.

It seems paradoxical that the character of submissiveness and loyalty and the above spirit of rebelliousness are integrated into the temperamental and behavioural qualities of the main heroes of CR novels. However, of the two qualities, submissiveness and loyalty take a leading position. In other words, although rebelliousness is an emphasized factor of the heroes' character, it is subordinate to their submissiveness and loyalty, i.e. their rebellious behaviour is based on their loyalty to Mao and the Party. It is in pursuing Mao's line that the heroes rebel against the wrong line, so that when facing negative elements such as capitalist-roaders and class enemies, they manifest a rebellious spirit. Before the superiors who represent the correct line, they behave obediently and submissively.

Being Optimistic and Indomitable

According to the method of Combination of Revolutionary Realism and Revolutionary Romanticism, optimism is an important aspect of heroism.[18] In the characterization of the main heroes of CR novels, an optimistic character and an indomitable spirit are combined. In pursuing the line set by the Party and Mao, the heroes experience a series of difficulties. They endure many trials especially in their struggles against capitalist-roaders, but they remain filled with confidence. In *Evergreen*, in spite of the pressure put on him by the capitalist-roader Huang Guang, Jiang Chunwang refuses to carry out the policy of fixing farm output quotas for each household. Finally, Huang Guang removes Jiang from his position as Party secretary of the village. The villagers feel upset and disheartened, but Jiang is still optimistic about the victory of their struggle. 'No expression of grievance, complaint, agony or discontentment could be found in his face'; '. . . he was all smiles'.[19] The following paragraph shows his thoughts on the night after he is removed from his post and is warned of further disciplinary action.

> Oh, the black clouds have melted, the moon comes out now, the quiet field is so clear, and the sound of flowing water seems like light laughter. Tomorrow will be a fine day, the golden sun will be shining over the ground as before, the water of the Yi River will be flowing as before, and the poor and lower-middle peasants of Wannianqing Village will go forward under the banner of the people's commune as before. Huang Guang cannot withstand the historical trend. It doesn't matter for me to lose the position of secretary. I am still a Party member and I shall persist in struggling. If they expel me from the Party, I shall still be a commune member, and I shall still struggle to the end. Even if they put me into jail or put me to death, I shall not be scared and shall not yield. Without me, Wannianqing Village still has other Party members and a large number of poor and lower-middle peasants. The socialist cause will still develop triumphantly.[20]

Many other main heroes in CR novels have similar adverse experiences and share similar optimistic reactions.

Other setbacks encountered by the main heroes include natural adversities and accidents in the workplace. In *The Long Rainbow*, when the dam project is nearly finished and the villagers are in high spirits looking forward to its completion, a section of the dam collapses, representing a great waste of manpower and material resources. For the heroine Shi Caihong, the main leader of the project, this setback has particular significance: the accident reveals the impracticability of her project plan, as pointed out by her colleagues and superiors at the beginning. The collapse thus gives them further reason to abandon the project. At night, the villagers gather in a temple courtyard, gloomy and disheartened. After a while, Shi Caihong appears. 'She looked calm. No-one could see any sign of pessimism from her. On the contrary, her face was scarlet, as if she were excited.'[21] Seeing her supporters shed tears, the heroine criticizes them for not smiling, and gives three reasons why they need not be pessimistic. Firstly, the accident is negligible by comparison with the accidents experienced at Dazhai. Next, they may draw lessons from the accident which are helpful to their later work. Lastly, the future is bright and the project will be completed as long as they go ahead. Shi Caihong's optimistic spirit infects her colleagues and subordinates, who then continue with the construction.

Being 'Artistic'

Apart from the above qualities which mainly concern behaviour and morality, the main heroes of CR novels are described as having an 'artistic' temperament.

According to the Combination of Revolutionary Realism and Revolutionary Romanticism, proletarian heroes are revolutionary idealists and are inclined to look forward to the future.[22] In CR novels, the main heroes are not only inclined to look to the future but have the sensibility to form a picture of the idealized future. The 'artistic' temperament here mainly concerns the heroes' inclination and ability to connect reality and the future with poetry, paintings and music. In *The Golden Road*, after he has come back from Beijing Railway Station, where he witnessed the organized collective in action, Gao Daquan looks forward to the future of the collectivized Fangcaodi Village. He imagines 'the happy scene full of vitality', 'the great upsurge in production' and 'the marvellous fruits of victory'. 'Then and there, the gold-like grain and the silver-like cotton would fill all vehicles, big and small. Forming a long line and raising red flags, the villagers would move vigorously towards the state storehouse . . .'[23] Gao's 'poetic' imagination is intensified by the poetic style of narration.

In *Mountains Green after Rain*, while the hero Wei Gengtian is looking at a map of the county, a picture forms in his mind: It is as if the mountains of his village appeared on the map, covered with crops and trees, as beautiful as brocade. He thinks, '. . .We should paint the newest and the most beautiful pictures. We paint pictures in our minds with lofty sentiments and aspirations. We also paint the pictures on the vast land of our country with our strong hands, using perspiration as paint and using iron hammers, hoes and shoulder poles as brushes. . .'[24] In *Evergreen*, seeing people transporting manure into the field, Jiang Chunwang forms a picture in his mind: 'Heaps of manure were put in order in the vast field. It was as if waves were moving forward in a peaceful sea. The diligent commune members had painted so many beautiful pictures in the vast land with their miraculous hands.'[25]

In many other cases, 'poetry' and 'painting' or 'poetry' and 'music' are interwoven. The hero Liu Wangchun in *The Mountains and Rivers Roar* says, 'Our magnificent poetry is written on the mountains and rivers with iron arms, silver hoes, hammer drills and blasting powder. What we write are the newest and the most beautiful writings, and what we paint are the newest and the most beautiful paintings.'[26] In *Evergreen*, in Jiang Chunwang's mind, the productive activities engaged in by the poor and lower-middle peasants are beautiful pictures, and their ideological struggles are heroic poetry.[27] Later, after he is removed from leadership, Jiang Chunwang encourages himself excitedly:

> Oh, life, how beautiful you are! But your road is tortuous. The past is gone forever, and the present will never come back. The more beautiful poetry and the greater music need more dauntless struggles to compose. Compose, and compose! . . . dipping into every drop of blood which comes from services to the people, and dipping into every drop of sweat which comes from dedication to the great socialist cause, to compose more magnificent poems.[28]

Here, the political struggles are transformed into images of 'music' and 'poetry'.

In some CR novels, the main heroes are directly identified as 'poets' and shown as being able to express themselves in poetic language. In *The Long Rainbow*, the heroine Shi Caihong explains her project plan and delineates a future to Li Zhiyao, a professional hydrologist, with clear water, verdant trees, diving fish, red flowers, green rice seedlings, and so on. Li Zhiyao responds, 'You are really like a poet, a romantic poet. You have described your prospect so well . . .'[29]

Readers might regard these so-called artistic characteristics as a linguistic phenomenon, i.e. the heroes are fond of using figures of speech. However, taking the following facts into account, we have grounds to believe that they are not merely a linguistic tendency. From a linguistic point of view, in matters of form, figures of speech are usually on the level of words and phrases, whereas the above 'artistic' expressions are usually on the level of sentences and paragraphs. Semantically, figures of speech cover varieties of associative meaning, whereas the 'artistic' expressions only cover poetry, paintings and music. The contexts generally indicate that the 'artistic' expressions are designed to accentuate the heroes' 'poetic' imaginative quality rather than a linguistic tendency to use figures of speech. In fact, according to our investigation into the lexical style of CR novels, figures of speech do not form a conspicuous characteristic of the heroes' language.

Apart from the literary requirements of the Combination of Revolutionary Realism and Revolutionary Romanticism, some social factors also contributed to the characterization emphasizing the heroes' 'artistic' qualities. It is known that in the Great Leap Forward of 1958, along with the politicized production movement, a nationwide campaign was launched to write new folk songs which were also called poems. This campaign was echoed during the Cultural Revolution, when workers, peasants and soldiers were encouraged to write poems, which were regarded as ammunition for occupying the positions of the socialist cultural front and promoting the prosperity of socialist literature and art. The recitation of improvised and self-written poems were commonplace in factories, farms, barracks and schools.

This fashion of writing and reciting poems was intensified by the promotion of Mao's poetry. It is known that Mao had followed with interest the development of Chinese literature and art since Yan'an period. But his personal practice in literature was confined to poetry. As commentators have pointed out, Mao was a highly proficient craftsman of traditional classical forms of Chinese poetry.[30] In the immediate aftermath of the Cultural Revolution, Mao's poetry was almost the only poetry in official circulation. During the campaign of learning Mao's works, his poetry, which was also graced by his calligraphy, became widely known. Although Mao's poems were in classical style, and not as easily intelligible as the modern new poems, the powerful propaganda by which they were clarified, taught, broadcast and reproduced promoted their popularity. Therefore, the prominence given to poetry in society made poetic ability lofty, and this thereby became a part of the heroes' characteristics.

Another social factor was the campaign to popularize the model Peking operas. As noted in the analysis of the CR novel heroes' physical qualities, although it is the operatic heroes' ideological qualities that were emphasized in the CR literary policy, other stage characteristics shown by the stage heroic images also became part of the current aesthetic values on the characterization of heroes. CR novelists might deliberately endow the novel heroes with some of the stage images' artistic qualities. The stage heroes' recitation of actors' lines, which were often poetic, bore similarity to the novel heroes' improvization of poems. Music and painting require more professional training, and were accordingly less emphasized in the novel heroes' 'artistic' quality. In fact, the association with paintings and music in the heroes' 'artistic' expressions was complementary to their poetic imagination, and their 'identification' was also usually noted by the narrators or other characters as 'poet' rather than 'painter' or 'musician'.

In the above examples, the CR novel heroes' poetic quality is mainly displayed through their imaginative association, with the heroes themselves seemingly unaware of their poetic quality. Below is another example, in which the hero demonstrates his poetic talent by improvising and commenting on poetry. In this case he is perfectly conscious of his own poetic quality.

In *The Mountains and Rivers Roar*, Mai Qing, an educated young woman working in the countryside, is fond of poetry and writes poetry herself. According to her, 'In composing a poem, one must have regard for artistic conception, rhythms, syllables and rhymes . . .'[31] She later becomes well-known as an amateur poet in the commune. One day, Mai tells Liu Wangchun, the main hero, that her classmates ridicule her (thinking her *chi* [crazy] and *sha* [foolish]) because she is willing to settle down in the countryside. Liu Wangchun replies,

(To show the poetic characteristics of the language, the original is quoted.)

Rang zichanjieji qu xiaohua women 'chi' he 'sha' ba! Women chi zai nongcun xiu diqiu, sha wei geming ba gen zha! Tamen da de shi jing bu qi fengyu de geren anlewo, women jianzao de shi shi gongshe shanhe yi xin de xingfu diba!

[Let the bourgeoisie ridicule us for being 'crazy' and 'foolish'. We are proud of being 'crazy' because we are embroidering the earth in the countryside; we are proud of being 'foolish' because we settle in the villages for the revolution. What they are striving for is only constructing their own cosy but flimsy nests, but what we are building is a dam of good fortune, which will bring an entirely new look to the commune.][32]

Liu's response is full of inflated language, symbolic imagery, and verse-like rhythms and rhymes, in accordance with current poetic styles. Filled with admiration, Mai Qing praises Liu Wangchun for his poetic feelings and inspiration, and Liu replies with confidence that he will write poems later when he has time. He then improvises another poetic description, and concludes with a long speech about composing poems:

In order to rearrange the mountains and rivers of the commune, we struggle against the heavens, the earth and evil people. We should have a passion for composing poems . . . Poets in the past played with the pen and indulged in narcissism behind doors. They could only intone empty chants because they stood outside the thick of realistic struggles and their minds were empty. The poems and songs of the proletariat ought to be the drumbeats of time and the clarion call for marching forward. 'I think that the problem of fundamental importance is whether the author is a revolutionary . . . What comes out of fountains is water, and what comes out of blood vessels is blood.'[33]

Mai Qing by now is absolutely convinced by Liu Wangchun's speech and full of admiration for his poetic ability.

Lu Xun's well-known saying about the source of literary talent, quoted here by Liu Wangchun, gives Liu's speech theoretical weight. The combination of such theoretical knowledge about poetic inspiration and his own spontaneous talent indicates the depth of his 'poetic' temperament.

The 'artistic' quality of the main heroes in the CR novels is unusual with regard to their status of agricultural cadres. For instance, Liu Wangchun's casual verse-like remarks, and his theorized speech about poetry seem awkward in the context. This implies that the authors are determined to play up the heroes' 'artistic' temperament, regardless of plausibility.

SOCIAL AND CULTURAL FOUNDATIONS OF TEMPERAMENTAL AND BEHAVIOURAL QUALITIES

In the preceding section, I have generalized a number of characteristic temperamental and behavioural qualities of the main heroes in CR novels. Except for 'artistic' qualities, of which the social background has been taken into account, the other qualities are primarily concerned with personal cultivation and moral principles. This raises a question: What are the internal relations of the other qualities? In other words, what are the social and cultural foundations of the values and standards shown in the characterization of the heroes with regard to their personality and behaviour?

The characterization of CR novel heroes concerning their personal and moral qualities may readily remind readers of traditional Chinese novels such as *The Romance of the Three Kingdoms* [*Sanguo yanyi*] and *Outlaws of the Marsh* [*Shui hu zhuan*]. Some heroes (not only main heroes) in these novels are morally and behaviourally impressive. In them we can also see the qualities of kindness, generosity, 'above-boardness', bravery, level-headedness, politeness, dignity, loyalty, etc., although, unlike the CR novel heroes, such qualities may not be comprehensively shown in each of them. For example, Zhang Fei is an important hero in *The Romance of the Three Kingdoms*. He is generous, above-board, brave and loyal, but he is often not level-headed or polite. In *Outlaws of the Marsh*, whereas Song Jiang is well known for his generosity, his bravery is not as prominent as many other heroes. Lu Junyi impresses readers through his well-cultivated personal qualities, but he lacks rebellious spirit against villains in power before he is driven to join the rebels on the Liang Mountain.

CR Chinese novels also bear a certain resemblance to some Western romantic novels in terms of heroes' moral and behavioural qualities. Walter Scott's historical romances are good examples. Some critics label Scott's characterization of the hero as seeking 'perfect heroism', 'who may be of heroic stature'.[34] Scott's typical hero is known as a passive hero and a symbolic figure of noble principles and values. P. F. Fisher has a statement concerning Scott's hero: 'The most favored of Providence are men of character; character is based on principle, and principle is derived from the moral law . . . It is evident . . . that any principle, however rigorously, and perhaps, mistakenly interpreted, is better than no principle, and any ideal is better than no ideal.'[35] Marian H. Cusac points out, 'The hero of the Waverley Novels . . . represents, however, a social ideal, and acts or refrains from acting according to the accepted morality of his public . . . Instead of a commander, this hero is an ideal member of society.'[36]

In *Ivanhoe* the protagonist is representative of the best in Norman chivalry. Although, as a 'passive hero', Ivanhoe does not appear in the stories frequently and actively, Scott intends to describe the hero as being humane, tolerant, informed, faithful, generous, confident, and brave. His rebelliousness is shown in his forsaking his origin, which leads to the break-up between him and his father. His loyalty is manifested in his devotion to the Norman King Richard. Since he is brave he takes up the challenge to rescue Rebecca without the least hesitation, in spite of his incompletely recovered health. He is so level-headed and grave that he warns Richard against his 'wild spirit of chivalry' which impels the King to seek dangers needlessly.

Apart from his hero and heroine, Scott's other characters may also be described as representing ideal moral principles. Rebecca is an example. Joseph E. Duncan points out, 'Critics have found many anachronisms in *Ivanhoe*, but they have tended to neglect the one which Scott intended to present — the adherence to ideals that have outlived their usefulness . . . It is ominous that Rebecca, who seems to represent the ideals of the past that are really worth preserving, leaves England because the nation is not prepared to nurture these ideals.'[37] Rebecca is always ready to help others who find themselves in an unfavourable situation, and many times she saves others' lives with her masterly medical skill without considering reward. After she hears that her father has received the eighty zecchines as reward given by Ivanhoe's retainer on his master's behalf, Rebecca gives one hundred to the retainer; twenty is awarded to the retainer, and eighty is returned to his master. So even the main hero Ivanhoe cannot help admiring her generosity after the retainer tells him the story. Later, in Front-de-Bœuf's castle, surprised at her extraordinary beauty,

Ivanhoe almost forgets his Rowena, and impulsive affection springs up in his mind. Rebecca deliberately mentions her background to indicate that their opposing religions do not allow sexual affection between them. Thus she tries to heal the hero's wound at the risk of her life not for money or for love. She is neither haughty nor humble in front of supercilious or ferocious aristocrats. She adheres to her Jewish religion and refuses to convert to Christianity whether she is threatened by Templar Bois-Guilbert, or persuaded by Ivanhoe's bride Rowena. All her actions reveal her virtues and nobility.

It goes without saying that the description of the above ideal characters in traditional Chinese and Western novels reflects related social and cultural values. In the Chinese novels, the heroes' qualities show traditional Chinese morality and principles. As regards Scott's novels, the cultural foundation of the heroes' personality and behaviour is medieval chivalry and religious principles, which are fully shown in Ivanhoe's following speech.

> Thou wouldst quench the pure light of chivalry, which alone distinguishes the noble from the base, the gentle knight from the churl and the savage; which rates our life far, far beneath the pitch of our honour; raises us victorious over pain, toil, and suffering, and teaches us to fear no evil but disgrace. Thou art no Christian; and to thee are unknown those high feelings which swell the bosom of a noble maiden when her lover hath done some deed of emprise which sanctions his flame. Chivalry!—why, maiden, she is the nurse of pure and high affection—the stay of the oppressed, the redresser of grievances, the curb of the power of the tyrant—Nobility were but an empty name without her, and liberty finds the best protection in her lance and her sword.[38]

With respect to CR Chinese novels, the social and cultural foundation of the main heroes' temperamental and behavioural qualities seem to be complex. One of the most fashionable slogans during the Cultural Revolution was *po jiu li xin* [to eradicate the old and to establish the new]. However, there is no evidence to indicate that a complete set of new norms concerning people's behaviour, temperament and morality was created and established during the Cultural Revolution. What the propaganda authorities mainly did was to select a number of Mao's quotations and promote them as people's mottoes, some of which concern not merely purely ideological principles, but behavioural and temperamental standards as well. It might be taken that this selection and promotion, with the relevant quotations, reflected current values and standards of ideal human character. For instance, as previously noted, at the outset of the Cultural Revolution, the authorities declared that Mao's 'three early articles', namely 'Serve the People', 'In Memory of Norman Bethune' and 'The Foolish Old Man Who Removed the Mountains', were to be nationwide required reading. At the end of 'In Memory of Norman Bethune', in addition to emphasizing the spirit of absolute selflessness, Mao proposed *wu zhong ren* [five types of human] as ideal humans: 'a man being noble-minded, a man being pure, a man of moral integrity, a man above vulgar interests, and a man of value to the people'.[39] The five attributes 'noble-minded', 'pure', 'being of moral integrity', 'being above vulgar interests' and 'being of value to the people' were then evidently concerned not only with ideological principles but also with behavioural and temperamental standards.

However, sporadic sayings such as these, which generally appeared in Mao's works written before the foundation of the People's Republic, did not form a complete set of norms and standards concerning personal cultivation. In many cases these sayings were simply general principles requiring other sub-standards in order to ascertain their meaning. For example, the standards of the above 'five types of human' could be taken as a group of behavioural norms promoted in the Cultural Revolution. But the standards are too abstract for us to ascertain their specific contents because no official definition and demarcation of the five attributes can be found. With regard to literature, it stands to reason that as promoted standards of ideal human behaviour and style, the five attributes could influence current novelists' characterizations of the idealized heroes. But novelists also needed more concrete standards to embody these general principles. In short, other behavioural and temperamental standards and values exist behind Mao's quotations and other ideological documents concerning human behaviour, in accordance with which people could complement or interpret those current principles.

My investigation suggests that traditional norms concerning personal cultivation occupy a significant position in latent popular values and standards. Historically, China had a set of established conventions and standards concerning human morality, behaviour, and temperament. They were mainly based on the doctrines of Confucius and Mencius, and they formed part of traditional Chinese culture. According to Chinese scholars' research, this set of traditional principles mainly includes *ren* [benevolence, kind-heartedness], *yi* [righteousness], *zhong* [loyalty, specifically, being loyal to emperors], *shu* [forbearance, which was also explained by Confucius as 'not doing to others what you do not want done to yourself'], *xiao* [filial piety], *ti* [fraternal duty], *zhi* [wisdom, intelligence], *yong* [bravery], *gong* [respect, politeness], *li* [etiquette, courtesy], *kuan* [generosity, magnanimity], *xin* [honesty], *zhi* [will, personal integrity, self-respect], *hui* [favour, which means doing favours for others] and *gong* [selflessness].[40] Throughout history, representative figures of Confucianism have given a series of accounts or explanations of these basic principles or norms. For example, with respect to *ren* [benevolence, kind-heartedness] and *li* [etiquette, courtesy], according to Confucius, 'To exercise self-restraint and to act on etiquette/courtesy are one aspect of benevolence . . . No watching except things according with etiquette/courtesy, no listening except to things according with etiquette/courtesy, no speaking except things according with etiquette/courtesy, and no acting except on things according with etiquette/courtesy [*Ke ji fu li wei ren . . . Fei li wu shi, fei li wu ting, fei li wu yan, fei li wu dong*].'[41] With relation to *zhi* [will, integrity, self-respect], Mencius defined the standards of *dazhangfu* [a true man]: 'Neither riches nor honours can corrupt him, neither poverty nor lowly condition can make him swerve from principle, neither threats nor force can bend him. These are the qualities of a true man [*Fugui bu neng yin, pinjian bu neng yi, weiwu bu neng qu, ci zhi wei dazhangfu*].'[42]

During the Cultural Revolution, as the name of the movement suggests, old Chinese culture bore the brunt of the struggle. As part of traditional Chinese culture, the above principles or norms concerning behavioural and temperamental conventions were attacked through propaganda. The criticism was that these traditional norms failed to emphasize the class nature of humankind. During the CR decade, one noticeable ideological trend was the promotion of the theory of the class character of human nature [*ren de jieji-xing; jieji de renxing*]. According to this theory, traditional principles concerning human behaviour and temperament were taken to represent 'supra-class feelings and temperaments' [*chao-jieji de renxing*], which were thought to be non-existent. The argument is that people of the propertied class could not practise such norms as 'benevolence', 'generosity', 'honesty' towards the proletariat, and vice versa. So the proletariat should practise 'benevolence', 'generosity', 'honesty' etc. only within the proletarian class.[43] However, on ideological grounds, this criticism concerns only the applicable range of norms rather than the norms themselves. In other words, the criticism does not refute the general tenets of those traditional norms. For example, critics labelled traditional principles such as 'benevolence' [*ren*], 'righteousness' [*yi*], 'generosity' [*kuan*], 'honesty' [*xin*] and 'politeness' [*gong*] as feudal or bourgeois norms, but they could not affirm their opposites 'malevolence', 'non-righteousness', 'ungenerosity', 'dishonesty' and 'rudeness' as general qualities of the proletariat. As analysed in the previous section, the actions of the main heroes of the CR novels hardly leave the reader with the impression that they are malevolent, non-righteous, ungenerous, dishonest or rude towards negative characters.

In his account of the Anti-Confucian campaign launched in the fall of 1973, Merle Goldman observed, 'At one level, the attack on Confucianism was what it appeared to be, a continuation of the effort to eradicate traditional habits and attitudes that had persisted despite the Cultural Revolution . . . At another level, however, the campaign became a vehicle through which the Shanghai group and the party bureaucratic leaders, by means of historical analogy and symbolism, carried on their personal and ideological power struggle.'[44] These words include two points relative to the present discussion. One is the persistence of traditional values, and another the campaign's nature of using historical analogy and symbolism to carry out ideological power struggle. The first point implies the existence of certain traditional values during the Cultural Revolution, and the second point indicates that Confucianism is not the real target of the campaign.

We may compare some of Mao's fashionable quotations in the Cultural Revolution with some of the popular traditional norms of Confucianism.

According to Mao, 'Our attitude towards ourselves should be "to be insatiable in learning" and towards others "to be tireless in teaching".'[45] Here 'to be insatiable in learning' [*xue er bu yan*] and 'to be tireless in teaching' [*hui ren bu juan*] were quoted directly from Confucius. Confucius promoted *xue* [learning or studying] and *hui* [teaching] to the level of temperamental qualities, which are related to *zhi* [knowledge, intelligence], one of his fundamental principles about personal cultivation.[46] Then, according to Mao, 'A communist should be honest and faithful . . .'[47] As stated above, 'honesty' and 'faithfulness' are two of the basic principles of Confucianism. Below, as a further comparison, I list several of Mao's and Confucius's most popular quotations.

Mao	*Confucius*
It is not hard for one to do a bit of good for others. What is hard is to do good all one's life. [*Yi ge ren zuo dian haoshi bing bu nan, nan de shi yibeizi zuo haoshi.*][48]	A gentleman is always ready to perfect the good of others. [*Junzi cheng ren zhi mei.*][49] Be never tired of doing good for others. [*Le shan bu juan.*][50]
selflessness; self-denial and whole-hearted devotion to the public [*da gong wu si; ke ji feng gong*][51]	self-denial and seemliness [*ke ji fu li*][52] People are all devoted to the public interest. [*Tianxia wei gong.*][53]
We should be modest and prudent and guard against arrogance and impetuosity. [*Women yinggai qianxu, jinshen, jie jiao, jie zao.*][54]	A gentleman is self-respected, well-behaved, modest and courteous. [*Junzi jing er wu shi, yu ren gong er you li.*][55] If a man has gifts as admirable as those of Duke Chou, yet be vain and mean, his other gifts are unworthy of notice. [*Ru you Zhou Gong zhi cai zhi mei, shi jiao qie lin, qi yu bu zhu guan ye yi.*][56]
Knowledge is a matter of science, and no dishonesty or conceit whatsoever is permissible. [*Zhishi de wenti shi yi ge kexue de wenti, lai bu de ban dian xuwei he jiao'ao.*][57]	To know something is to know it, not knowing is not knowing — that is knowledge. [*zhi zhi wei zhi zhi, bu zhi wei bu zhi, shi zhi ye.*][58]

It is clear that in terms of personal cultivation, Mao's and Confucius's norms quoted above share a common spirit. This fact further confirms that some of Mao's sayings, selected by the authorities to represent the then promoted behavioural values and standards, are in accordance with, or are rooted in those orthodox traditional principles. In other words, some of the idealized standards of evaluation, as dictated in traditional behavioural and temperamental norms, existed, and were even promoted during the Cultural Revolution.

However, traditional norms, rooted in a long standing civilization and culture, formed a set of consistent and systematic standards for the traditional orthodox personality. During the Cultural Revolution, however, in principle the current behavioural and temperamental standards mainly played a complementary part in ideology. They also did not form a consistent system in Mao's holistic doctrine. Although we can find Mao's sayings rooted in traditional norms, in different contexts there are other examples in direct opposition to those traditional principles. For example, in contrast to his promotion of qualities such as 'modesty', 'prudence', 'non-arrogance', 'non-impetuosity', 'respectfulness', 'politeness' and 'generosity' — all in accordance with Confucianism — on another occasion Mao opposed Confucius's *wen zhi binbin* [being gentle] and *wen liang gong jian rang* [being temperate, kind, courteous, restrained and magnanimous].[59] Nevertheless, with regard to the main heroes of the CR novels, qualities which are in accordance with the traditional standards are consistently embodied in their characters.

It is not my intention in this presentation to specifically analyse the traditional elements of moral and behavioural principles during the years of the Cultural Revolution, or to discuss in detail the relation between the views of Mao and Confucius on human temperamental and behavioural qualities. What I intend is to set the CR fiction's idealized hero's character and personality against a more realistic background and to understand them within a unified perspective including both the promoted standards and those within traditional norms. The reason is that an analysis based solely on ideology is not enough to reasonably explain the holistic character of the CR novel heroes, i.e. the qualities and characteristics concerning the heroes' behaviour and temperament cannot be entirely attributed to ideological standards.

We shall see in Chapter 7 that the heroes of CR novels often quote from Mao. But the quotations are generally related to ideological activities rather than to personal cultivation and temperamental qualities. In other words, therefore, the heroes' thoughts and actions concerning class, line, road or ideological struggles are clearly shown to be based on their conscious following of ideological principles. Generally, however, few references are made to ideological documents which deal with the heroes' feelings, manner and behaviour with respect to their temperament and personal cultivation. This fact also confirms that it is insufficient to put the heroes' temperamental and behavioural qualities into a single perspective of ideology.

When we put the heroes' temperamental and behavioural qualities within a unified perspective which includes traditional norms, the references may generally be to the satisfaction of one and all. CR novels consistently emphasize the heroes' qualities and characteristics such as kindness, righteousness, generosity, gentleness, honesty, intelligence, reasonableness, and politeness. All these qualities and characteristics have references within the traditional norms we have discussed. However, it seems that rebelliousness has no foundation in those traditional principles. Yet as analysed in the preceding section, the rebellious spirit is subordinate to loyalty (to Mao). 'Loyalty' is one of the basic principles of traditional norms. In some cases, references to certain traditional norms may be subtle, but they exist. For example, the heroes always avoid the use of vulgar words and expressions. We may also find grounds for this in Confucian doctrine. Confucius pointed out, 'As for language, a man of noble character pays attention to words and expressions' [*Junzi yu qi yan, wu suo gou er yi yi*], and 'A man of noble character is careful about his language' [*Junzi . . . shen yu yan*]. He even advocated the use of a spoken standard language [*yayan*].[60] Moreover, if we see the CR novels' heroes in a comprehensive perspective, we find that their experiences generally include poverty, temptation by class enemies, and threats by capitalist-roaders, yet they nevertheless stand firm. Their integrity is consistent with the above-quoted spirit of Mencius's 'a true man': 'Neither riches nor honours can corrupt him, neither poverty nor lowly condition can make him swerve from principle, neither threats nor force can bend him.'

Given that traditional culture was under attack in the propaganda of the Cultural Revolution, it is only natural that support for traditional norms and standards was usually indirect or non-indicated. In some cases, reasons for the heroes' character and behaviour may be directly attributed to ideological principles, including literary policies, nonetheless we can also find references to traditional norms. For instance, the heroes' behaviour generally has nothing to do with love and sex. It is evident that this characteristic is related to the literary policies of the time, according to which love and sex belong to revisionism. Yet it is indirectly supported by traditional norms. For example, 'Sexual desire comes first on the list of evil deeds' [*Shou e wu ru se yu*], 'Man and woman should not be close to each other when giving and receiving' [*Nan nü shou shou bu qin*].[61]

With regard to the heroes' ideological qualities, it stands to reason that we have attributed their collective and altruistic spirit to their ideological awareness. On the one hand, the authors played it up intentionally at the level of ideology, i.e. communist qualities and style. On the other hand, the heroes practise it consciously as an ideological principle, that is, the way of taking the socialist road. But it still has reference to traditional norms. Apart from those Confucian norms enumerated above concerning selflessness and devotion to the public and others' interest, there existed numerous similar sayings in the writings of other representative Confucian figures. Thus, according to modern scholars such as Guo Moruo and Chao Yue, Confucian 'benevolence' is 'a kind of altruism, which encourages people to get rid of all selfish motives and to cultivate the spirit of devotion to the public'.[62] Joseph S. M. Lau and Howard Goldblatt observed, 'Confucianism, insofar as it was identified as China's state religion', is 'coterminous with the concepts of altruism, compassion, and benevolence'.[63] In the pre-CR novel *Great Changes in a Mountain Village*, Li Huaiqin, an old retired teacher from the old-style private school of the village, says in public, 'Mencius said, "to treat others' aged parents or grandparents like my own [*Lao wu lao, yi ji ren zhi lao*]." So even our ancestors had intended to make socialism . . .'[64] These quotations show the subtle connection between modern collectivism and traditional norms. Moreover, in Chapter 3, we have attributed the heroes' unusual ideological foresight and insight to their ideological consciousness. But, if we exclude the ideological factor and take 'foresight' and 'insight' as a kind of personal quality, they are both supported by Confucian 'intelligence' [*zhi*].

Now, therefore, we return to the question proposed at the beginning of this section: What are the social and cultural foundations of the values and standards shown in the temperamental and behavioural qualities of the main heroes in the CR novels? According to the foregoing analysis, we can tentatively conclude that these foundations are a combination of the then current ideological principles and orthodox traditional moral, behavioural and temperamental norms, that is, traditional norms which offered concrete content to abstract ideological principles.

Chapter 5

Prominence Given to the Main Heroes

It is evident that the physical, ideological and behavioural qualities analysed in the preceding chapters showed the main heroes' prominence in the CR novels. However, such prominence, as discussed in this section, refers in particular to those aspects intended by the authors to set the characters off through following the 'three prominences' and other established ways.

PRACTICE OF THE 'THREE PROMINENCES'

As noted in the Introduction, according to the 'three prominences' (and also 'three foilings'), all other characters are destined to serve as foils to the main heroes. The basic methods for using other characters as foils include *fanchen* [setting off a character through stressing others' demerits], that is, setting off the heroes by emphasizing other characters' inferiority to the heroes, and *hongtuo* or *pudian* [setting off a character through stressing others' merits], i.e. setting off the heroes by heightening other characters' qualities such that the better the supporting characters, the better the heroes. This is also done by playing up other characters' feelings such as appreciation, praise and love towards the heroes. Both *fanchen* and *hongtuo/pudian* may be called *peichen* [setting off].

The four-level hierarchical classification of the 'three prominences' is initially based on the conventional bifurcation, i.e. classifying all characters into positive characters and negative characters. The other two types of character defined in the 'three prominences' — heroic characters and main heroic characters — are sub-classifications of the positive characters. Therefore, in view of the initial bifurcation and for the sake of practicality, the present analysis is designed to be along two dimensions: the positive characters' *peichen* and the negative characters' *fanchen*.

Setting off the Main Heroes by Providing Positive Characters as Foils

Before we go into any depth in this topic, it is necessary to explain the make-up of the positive characters according to the relationship between the main hero of a novel and other positive characters. Initially, there is a core of positive characters in a novel. A typical positive core in the agricultural novel consists of four people: the main hero, an old male, a middle-aged male and a young male or female. The constitution of the core is roughly in accordance with the structure of the basic-level leadership of the countryside during the pre-CR and CR periods. With the exception of Gu Hua's *The Mountains and Rivers Roar*, which is set at the level of the people's commune, the remaining twenty-three CR agricultural novels are set in the basic administrative unit, 'production brigade' or village. In a production brigade, the standing political/administrative bodies included the brigade itself as an administrative unit, the Party branch, the Youth League branch, the militia company, the shock youth brigade, the poor peasant association, the public security group, the women's association, and the sideline production group. The leadership of a production brigade was formed by the heads of each of these organizations. Among the leadership, the Party secretary was certainly paramount. Not long after the Cultural Revolution began, a new political/administrative body, the revolutionary committee, was set up in each brigade, but the practical administration still operated under the original pattern. In fact, the posts of the revolutionary committee were concurrently held by former leading members, for example, the Party secretary was often concurrently the chairman of the revolutionary committee.

The relationship between the core of positive characters in a CR agricultural novel and the membership of the leadership in a production brigade is as follows: The main hero is generally the secretary of the Party branch, the old man is the head or retired chairman of the poor peasant association, the middle-aged man is the director of the brigade [*daduizhang*] (the head of the brigade as an administrative unit), and the young male or female is usually the head of the militia or shock youth brigade, or sometimes the secretary of the Youth League branch. Thus the four members of the positive core represent the central political, administrative and military organizations in the village.

The director of the production brigade might only be regarded as a quasi-member of the positive core. He is usually the predecessor of the main hero's official position, and his current position and power take second place in the leadership of the set village. He is in charge of village production and labour, and he cares more about crop yields and the masses' income than he does about politics. In politicized agricultural campaigns, he remains cautious, playing a conservative role. In conflicts between the positive core and capitalist-roaders, he vacillates and plays the role of an intermediary. The negative characters can often take advantage of his ideological unawareness. Yet his disagreements with the main hero and other core members are not motivated by evil, but rather by his inferior ideological consciousness and political sensitivity. And he also has qualities in common with other core members, such as selflessness, devotion to the collective, and loyalty to the Party. Moreover, his disagreements are temporary, and he later allies himself with other core members against the common opponents. With regard to the classification of characters according to the 'three prominences', the old man and the young person are Heroic Characters ('secondary heroes' or 'supporting heroes'), and the middle-aged person may be categorized as a Positive Character. Therefore, among the positive core, the main hero, the old male, and the young male or female form a hero group.

In their study of the model theatrical works Lowell Dittmer and Chen Ruoxi use a metaphor to indicate the relationship among important positive characters, i.e. 'an extended family'.[1] In the extended family, there are usually three characters who represent three generations and play important roles: a grandfather or grandmother, a hero, and a young male or female. The structure of the three generations represents the currently promoted organizational structure of the three-in-one combination of the old, the middle-aged and the young. Their symbolic meaning is evident, i.e. the hero is representative of the Party, and he/she is a revolutionary in his/her prime; the 'grandfather or grandmother' represents revolutionaries of the older generation; and the young person represents the future successors to the revolutionary cause. The hero group of CR novels is analogous to the 'extended family', although the group's constitution in terms of age may not be parallel to the three generations because CR novels tend to employ youthful heroes. The symbolic significance of the group is similar to that of the 'family'. The main heroes always appear ideologically mature in comparison with the young supporting heroes.

In addition to the positive core, there are three other important categories of positive character. The first is that of members of the main hero's family. They usually support the hero in a particular way, i.e. managing all the housework so that the hero can devote himself/herself fully to the collective without family consideration. The second category is that of positive superiors. Although they are on the main hero's side, when the hero is in confrontation with negative superiors, they are generally absent from their duties because of illness or other assignments. Yet they are offered chances to express their support directly or indirectly for the hero and his followers, most especially at the end, when they appear to affirm the correctness of the hero and to help him/her win the confrontation with their opponents. The last category is the masses, i.e. positive characters as common people. Some are very active. In its broadest sense, 'the masses' sometimes refers to all positive people except the main hero. The masses are the social basis of the prescribed correct line of the Party.

Generally, with respect to the three core members, *hongtuo* is the main way to provide the old poor peasant as foil. For the young male or female, both *hongtuo* and *fanchen* are adopted. For the head in charge of production, *fanchen* is more important.

As stated in Chapter 1, the old supporting heroes in the CR novels, such as Jiang Yutian in *Evergreen*, Zhou Zhong in *The Golden Road*, or Zhao Yiliang in *Mountains Green after Rain*, used to be the main heroes' teachers of farming skills and models of morality. In the main stories, these characters play the role of advisor to the heroes' political activities.

In *Evergreen* Jiang Yutian is described as the most prestigious figure in the village before the foundation of the People's Republic. Jiang Chunwang, the main hero of the novel, was often with Jiang Yutian in his orphan childhood. He learned a variety of farming skills from the old man. More importantly, however, the old man's morality, behaviour, and feelings influenced Jiang Chunwang's personal cultivation. In the present story, the old man raises livestock in the village. He devotes himself heart and soul to the work of the collective. In order to give livestock more space, he and his wife move out of their three main rooms and convert them into a livestock shack. The old man often uses his own grain rations to feed the livestock. These activities indicate his high level of consciousness of collectivism. Moreover, as advisor to the main hero Jiang Chunwang, the old man also displays unusual political insight and sensitivity. At the beginning, after hearing of the new policy of fixing farm output quotas for each household, he judges it an evil trend which may have powerful support and urges the hero to be careful.

In order to demonstrate the close relationship that has developed between Jiang Yutian and the main hero, the narrator intentionally plays up the similar qualities between them, both internal and external. 'How alike the two were. Their labourers' weather-beaten skin colour, unyielding spirit, and even style of dress — including the simple home-made clothes and the broad cloth waistbands — were alike. The age difference was insignificant. The hearts of both were beating for the future of the people's commune.'[2]

In the pre-CR novels, we also find representative poor peasants who place collective interests before their personal affairs. For example, in *The Sun Shines Bright*, the old poor peasant Ma Laosi, who also raises livestock, has a story similar to that of Jiang Yutian in *Evergreen*. He too lets livestock share his rooms and feeds sick livestock with his grain ration. However, in contrast to Jiang Yutian in *Evergreen*, and though not inferior with respect to collective consciousness, Ma Laosi does not reach the same loftiness as Jiang in terms of other qualities.

For instance, he is sometimes rude, especially when he uses abusive language and resorts to beating his son. But more importantly, he does not have the same ideological foresight or insight as Jiang, and he is unable to play the role of advisor to the hero Xiao Changchun's political activities. The following dialogue between him and Xiao indicates that the old man's part in the village is labour rather than ideology. He says to Xiao, 'The loads on your shoulder are heavy. It's a pity that I cannot help you.'[3] Xiao answers, 'That you work hard [raising livestock] every day is a help to me.'[4]

There is another piece of evidence which highlights the significance of the ideological level of the representative old poor peasants in the CR novels. It is the linguo-stylistic analysis in Chapter 7 which indicates that the distribution of ideological words and expressions used by old poor peasants in CR novels is much greater than that in pre-CR novels.

In brief, as the main hero's teacher, examplar and advisor, the old poor peasant's temperamental qualities, ideological consciousness, political sensitivity and life experience are highly idealized in a CR novel. The primary reason for this idealization is to *hongtuo* the main hero, i.e. to achieve the effect of *shui zhang chuan gao*.[5]

The young supporting hero, such as Zhu Tiehan in *The Golden Road*, Zhao Tie in *Mountains Green after Rain* or Jing Chunhong in *Qingshi Fort*, is described as the main hero's important assistant. As a member of the leading group of a village, he/she is always on the main hero's side. His/her character is also intentionally idealized so as to *hongtuo* the main hero. In *Mountains Green after Rain*, the head of the militia of the village, Zhao Tie, demonstrates his heroic spirit by struggling against the landlord Da Jinya and accompanying the main hero Wei Gengtian down a mountain cave to kill a large poisonous snake. Moreover, after Wei Gengtian has been called by the capitalist-roader Nong Liji to commune headquarters, it is Zhao Tie who leads the villagers in their continuing struggle against the class enemies and negative superiors. In *Qingshi Fort*, the supporting heroine Jing Chunhong heads the village shock youth brigade. She foregoes the opportunity to live and work in a large city and settles down in the countryside to do farm work. As the strongest supporter of the main hero Lian Hua in the village, she experiences a great deal of face-to-face conflict with negative characters, especially with the negative female A Gui, in which she demonstrates her political sensitivity, bravery and resourcefulness in the class and line struggles.

We can also find corresponding characters in the pre-CR novels who demonstrate heroic qualities. But some other descriptions of their thinking and behaviour indicate the lower level of idealization in their characterization. An example is Chen Dachun in *Great Changes in a Mountain Village*. As the secretary of the Youth League of the village, he stands firmly with the main hero Liu Yusheng on collectivization. When the backward character Fu Jiangeng proposes the abandonment of collectivization and criticizes the main hero, Chen Dachun refutes him immediately and indignantly. When tracking down the stolen ox, Chen disregards his girlfriend's warning that the thief has professional combat skills and he rushes to the spot immediately. He dashes to the ox without the least hesitation when it gets angry and fiercely rushes towards the crowd. However, he sometimes lacks self-restraint in other aspects. For instance, he refuses to recruit Sheng Shujun as a Youth League member because he is swayed by personal feelings. His rude manner sometimes causes him to swear at people in public. He falls in love and has a tryst with his lover. It is evident that characteristics such as these cannot be found among the young supporting heroes in CR novels.

In spite of their highly idealized characterization in CR novels, these young supporting heroes sometimes show immaturity and impetuosity in class and line struggles, which are used as foils to *fanchen* the main heroes' maturity and reasonableness. In *The Golden Road*, Zhu Tiehan is the main hero Gao Daquan's important assistant in carrying out collectivization. He is highly regarded in the village for his high level of ideological awareness, righteousness, honesty, bravery, and so on. Yet he is not as circumspect and far-sighted as Gao Daquan. In Gao's absence, and under the instigation of the negative characters, Gao's brother Gao Erlin proposes to break up the family and live apart. After Gao Erlin refuses to be dissuaded, Zhu Tiehan decides indiscreetly to call the village militia to intervene with force because he is unable to see clearly the complex inside story and to find a proper way to deal with the incident. Fortunately, his abrupt action is interrupted by Zhou Zhong, the old supporting hero. Later, Zhu Tiehan is convinced by the reasonableness of the main hero Gao Daquan's solution. With respect to collectivization, Zhu Tiehan is so excited to learn that the Party and Mao are calling for the campaign that he immediately draws up a plan. But his plan ignores people's actual collective awareness and does not comply with Party policy. Gao Daquan criticizes him personally for his impetuosity, and his plan for its impracticality. Thus, Zhu Tiehan's naivety, indiscretion and impetuosity are accentuated to provide a contrast with Gao Daquan's political maturity and temperamental level-headedness.

Unlike the old and the young core members, the other member of the positive core, such as Li Bao'an in *Mountains Green after Rain*, Deng Dianju in *Evergreen*, or Shi Changqin in *The Long Rainbow*, almost always act as foils to the main hero through *fanchen*. The contrast between this core member and the main hero is most visible in their different ideological consciousness of the class and line struggles. In *Mountains Green after Rain*, Li Bao'an fails to see through Wei Junping, a class enemy in disguise. Even after the main hero Wei Gengtian calls his attention to Wei Junping, he continues to think highly of the enemy's 'collective spirit' until his full self-exposure towards the end. By contrast, Wei Gengtian is suspicious of the enemy even at the beginning of the story. In the campaign of learning from Dazhai, as his name implies, Li Bao'an is conservative and content with the status quo.[6] He is dissatisfied with Wei

Gengtian's plan to launch a large-scale water conservancy project, but favours going all out for production and output. So within the village leadership, there exists an internal contradiction between himself and Wei Gengtian concerning the campaign of learning from Dazhai. Later, he only passively resists the interference of capitalist-roader Nong Liji, even though he agrees with Wei's plan. After the uncompleted project fails to prevent the flood from inundating the village's corn fields, he becomes more hesitant. When Nong Liji flies into a rage and criticizes both him and Wei Gengtian severely, Li Bao'an, in contrast to Wei Gengtian's composure, is at a loss and is so nervous that he is sweating. The author plays up his political insensitivity and temperamental conservatism and hesitation so as to set off Wei Gengtian's political insight, venturous spirit, awe-inspiring dignity and dauntless heroism.

Apart from the positive core, the positive characters can further be classified into another three groups, i.e. the main heroes' family members, the positive superiors and the masses. There is different emphasis between the three groups and the positive core in providing them as foils to the main heroes, because the core members have more opportunities to work closely together with the main heroes. Generally, the positive core members' *peichen* to the main heroes is primarily shown in their interaction with the heroes. But for the characters of the other three groups, their feelings towards the main heroes are accentuated in their *peichen* to the heroes. Nevertheless, 'interaction' and 'feelings' are not unconnected. For instance, the core members' activities or interaction with the main heroes always contain their feelings towards them. Furthermore, there are also some direct descriptions of feelings of the core members such as admiration and concern.

With regard to members of the main heroes' families, *hongtuo* is the main way to set off the heroes. That is, family members are idealized to achieve the effect of *shui zhang chuan gao*. This characterization is especially revealed in the family members' understanding and support of the heroes' devotion to public interests and their involvement in political struggles. With the exception of Gao Erlin in *The Golden Road*, in an episode in which he complains about his elder brother Gao Daquan's altruism, no other member of the main heroes' families in the twenty-four CR agricultural novels exhibits a negative attitude towards the heroes' work. Moreover, even in the case of the only exception Gao Erlin, his negative attitude towards his brother's actions does not all originate with him, but rather derives from the negative characters' deceptions.

In *The Golden Road*, Gao Daquan's wife Lü Ruifen 'firmly believed in the importance and nobility of her husband's actions, and thought what he did was for the sake of poor people's happiness. . . She was determined to work in concert with him, not letting family affairs vex him in the slightest, so that he could do his important things with all his energy'.[7] After failing to dissuade her brother-in-law Gao Erlin from living separately, she reprimands him indignantly and expresses her love and loyalty to Gao Daquan:

. . . Right, you don't like the Communist Party member Gao Daquan, but I like him! You want to leave Gao Daquan, who takes the socialist road, but I shall accompany him as long as I live. Even if he goes to climb a mountain of swords, or plunges into a sea of flames or a cauldron of boiling oil, I shall accompany him![8]

This resolute pledge indicates not only her personal feelings towards her husband but also her faith in her husband's socialist cause. More importantly, however, her unswerving support and loyalty to Gao Daquan add to the 'greatness' and 'loftiness' of the hero's image.

In *Mountains Green after Rain*, Wei Gengtian's mother is also supportive of her son's devotion to the collective. She says to her son, 'The things you are doing are revolutionary work for the public interests. You must do them hard and well. You just go ahead with all your might; don't worry about family affairs.'[9] The story of Wei Gengtian's wife Huang Xiuzhen, who supports Wei's work, is even more impressive. 'In the recent campaign of learning from Dazhai, Wei Gengtian rarely came home. She did not have any complaints at all. What she expected of her husband was that he wholeheartedly led the villagers forward. Three months earlier, the Jinfeng Mountain Project had started. She could have avoided the heavy labour because she was pregnant. But thinking that as the wife of a cadre she should set an example for the masses, she offered, on her own initiative, to go to work on the construction site. Staying and working there she did not return home until the cadres and the masses repeatedly urged her to leave since she was close to delivery'.[10]

Later, in the scene depicting Wei Gengtian's departure for the commune government office, Huang Xiuzhen's action in supporting her husband seems even to overshadow his own heroic behaviour. As the conflict between Wei and his superior Nong Liji approaches a climax, under the instigation of the class enemies Nong gets angry and orders Wei to the commune office to justify his actions. The villagers, including Wei's wife, are afraid that Nong will put greater pressure on Wei. Before leaving Wei comes home to say goodbye to his wife. At first he finds his wife looking a little flurried, but he does not pay much attention to it. Then he enters the kitchen to have a meal, and she goes into their bedroom. After the meal, he goes to collect a change of clothes in the bedroom, but she comes out in a hurry and lightly closes the door behind her. While handing him a small parcel with his clothes inside, she urges him to leave right away. Now Wei begins to suspect his wife's behaviour, guessing that something unusual has happened in the bedroom. Then a cry from their three-year-old child comes out from the bedroom. She dissuades him from entering to see the child with the excuse that he is late and must leave. He becomes even more suspicious of the situation. Catching her unawares, he pushes open the door. He is surprised to see that their son's face is scarlet because he is running a high fever. The truth is that the child has been ill since the previous day, but she has tried to cover this up in order not to vex him.

Among the main heroes' family members, even little children naively tend to support their parents to help others. In *The Golden Road*, when Gao Daquan knows that the poor peasant Liu Xiang's family is going hungry, he returns with a heavy heart. His family's food is also limited; nevertheless, he decides to send a bag of corn to Liu. When his brother Gao Erlin, the exception mentioned above who does not fully understand the main heroes' actions, offers to weigh it for later return, Gao Daquan is irritated because he has no thought of having it returned later. He says nothing but stands there as if in a trance. His wife Lü Ruifen understands that her husband is insulted and comforts him by suggesting that they also give Liu some cabbages. But he is still despondent and remains silent until his three-year-old son Xiaolong heartens him.

> Xiaolong was quicker than his father. He was holding a Chinese cabbage in his arms and walking out of an inside room with faltering steps. He shouted repeatedly, 'I want to go, I want to go. No, let me hold it. I can do it!'
>
> A smile, like sunlight coming through the clouds, appeared on Gao Daquan's stern face. He held his son's round chin tenderly with his strong fingers and said, 'You are really my good son!' After speaking this sentence, he felt that comfort prevailed over the earlier gloom like a gentle breeze.[11]

Then all three go together to take the things to Liu Xiang's house. So the family is in harmony in their practice of collective altruism.

If we compare pre-CR novels, we see different descriptions of the main heroes' family members, indicating different ways of setting off the heroes. Usually, in pre-CR novels, some members of the main heroes' families, such as parents or spouses, are in a backward state of collective ideology. In *The Builders*, Liang Shengbao's stepfather Liang San is very disappointed at Liang Shengbao's devotion to the public interest. In addition to repeatedly complaining of Shengbao's 'foolishness', he sometimes causes trouble in the family in order to show his annoyance. In *Great Changes in a Mountain Village*, Zhang Guizhen cannot understand her husband Liu Yusheng's thoughts and actions on the village collectivization. Her complaints often cause Liu Yusheng to be downhearted. She finally goes so far as to insist on divorce despite Liu's reluctance to leave her. Therefore, in pre-CR novels, authors emphasized the egoistic thinking and behaviour of some members of the main heroes' families to use them as foils and set the heroes off by *fanchen*. By contrast, in the CR novels the authors heightened or idealized the altruistic spirit and collective consciousness of the members of main heroes' families to create the effect of 'setting off the higher with the high'.

The description of the heroes' family members in pre-CR novels bears similarity to Sholokhov's *Virgin Soil Upturned*. In this novel the main hero Davidov is single, and he is assigned to the village to guide the village's collectivization alone. So there is no evidence of either support or opposition from his relatives. However, Nagulnov, the village Party secretary, and Andrei, the village Soviet chairman, who form a positive core with Davidov, and are also described as heroic characters (supporting heroes), have miserable family situations. Before the main story commences, Andrei's wife committed suicide after she was violated by the enemy. In the main story Nagulnov's wife Lushka feels bored with her husband's 'world revolution' and divorces him, although he feels regret at parting from her. Andrei falls in love with Marina, the widow of a cavalry sergeant in the tsarist army who has been killed in a battle. They are not married, but they live together as a family for years. However, Marina opposes collectivization. Below is a description of Marina's reaction after she is told of the campaign by Andrei.

> After the meeting Andrei went straight to Marina's . . .
> 'What happened at the meeting?'
> 'Tomorrow we start gutting the kulaks.'
> 'You don't mean it?'
> 'The whole meeting, every poor man in the village, joined the collective farm this evening.' Without taking off his jacket Andrei lay down on the bed and picked up the kid in his arms, a warm woolly bundle. 'Take in your application tomorrow.'
> 'What application?' Marina exclaimed.
> 'To join the collective farm.'
> Marina flushed . . .
> 'Are you off your head? Why should I?'
> 'Let's not argue about that, Marina. You've got to be in the collective. Look at him, they'll say about me, makes people join the collective farm, but keeps his Marina out of it. I'll have a bad conscience.'
> 'I won't join. No matter what you say!' . . .
> 'Well, look out then, it'll be good-bye.'
> 'What a threat!'
> 'I'm not threatening, but I can't do otherwise.'
> 'Well, go then!'. . .
> 'You need a good spanking, but somehow I don't feel like it.' Andrei tipped the kid on to the floor, reached for his hat and whipped his soft scarf round his neck like a noose . . .[12]

Marina later marries somebody else. Their parting on bad terms increases the pressures on Andrei in his work. However, through his solving of problems from various sources, Andrei displays his ideological consciousness and heroic qualities.

As for the positive superiors in CR novels, their appreciation and admiration are important in setting off the main heroes. In *Mountains Green after Rain*, the deputy commune Party secretary often admits to Wei Gengtian's face that his ideological awareness is not as high as Wei's and he claims to be learning from Wei's example. In *The Golden Road*, one of the most impressive descriptions of a positive superior's praise is in a private talk between the secretary of the county

Party committee Liang Haishan and his wife. Late at night, his face glowing with excitement, Liang Haishan comes home after a conference and speaks highly of Gao Daquan to his wife. Unusually, the author did not emphasize Liang's language but highlighted Liang's wife's thinking and reaction.

> As a senior cadre, Liang Haishan did not casually belittle or praise a cadre on the basis of a brief impression. Although he was inclined to encourage his subordinates by affirming their work instead of criticising them too much, his affirmation was always within proper limits. So, if Gao Daquan was not much above average, Liang certainly would not speak as highly of him as he did today with such excitement . . . She was fascinated by her husband's account. She stopped sewing and stared closely at his face, anxious not to miss a single word . . . Finally, she could not help agreeing, 'Well, he really is a hero!'[13]

This description shows Liang Haishan's deep appreciation and admiration of the hero, thereby allowing Liang, the top positive superior in the novel's character setting, to contribute in setting off the hero.

Next, for the last group of positive characters, i.e. the masses or common positive characters, the people's feelings towards the main heroes are initially shown in their eagerness to learn from the heroes' examples. In struggles against negative characters, even if the main heroes are absent, the common positive characters often think of the heroes' deeds and follow their examples by actively participating in the struggles. In one important episode in the second volume of *The Golden Road* there is a conflict between several positive young people and the bosses of a temporary shoe plant in Tianmen Town. After they discover that the bosses are doing shoddy work and using inferior materials on government contracts, the young workers from the main hero Gao Daquan's village launch a campaign against the bosses. They encourage one another by invoking Gao's spirit of struggling against evildoers and evil deeds. Inspired by what Gao Daquan did before for the collectivization of the village, Zhou Liping, the leader of the young group, decides to employ a tactic similar to the hero's. At last they win the struggle. This description emphasizes the main hero's lofty status in the positive characters' minds and indirectly indicates the hero's leading role in winning the struggle, all of which relates to giving prominence to the hero.

The numerous favourable comments made by the masses about the main heroes constitute another aspect of their feelings towards the heroes. Usually, such comments are full of inflated words and expressions. In *The Long Rainbow*, for instance, before the heroine Shi Caihong appears, Shi Fengyang, the well-known storyteller in the village, praises her in public by comparing her to a famous legendary heroine Mu Guiying: 'Hi, it is well said that Mu Guiying who broke up the enemy's *tianmen* battle formation was a great heroine. In my opinion, however, if she were alive, Mu Guiying would be far behind Caihong. She would not even be qualified to lead Caihong's horse!'[14]

In addition, in many cases the supporting heroes are also inclined to express their praise directly to the main heroes. In *The Golden Road*, while Gao Daquan cuts a stump with a broad axe, Zhu Tiehan, the young member of the positive core, praises Gao's might, '. . . Brother Daquan, you are even harder and sharper than the broad axe. You can't be turned nor ever broken. Anything negative, no matter what it is, or how hard it is, or how strong it is, or how stubborn it is, will be cut into pieces and become dust in cooking stoves as the stump will do, whenever it touches you!'[15]

Another aspect of the masses' feelings which is accentuated to set off the main heroes is their concern for the heroes' health and safety, indicating the central position the heroes occupy in their minds. In *The Golden Road*, Deng Jiukuan has no ox to help him plough. Yet he and his wife Zheng Suzhi do not have the heart to turn to the hero Gao Daquan for help because they think Gao is too busy managing the work of the whole village and they worry about his health. Then, unexpectedly, Gao Daquan comes to their house in person to discuss their difficulties because he knew something of it from his own observations. Learning their problem, Gao promises to try his best to resolve it. Later, there is a dialogue between the couple.

> After Gao Daquan left, Zheng Suzhi sighed, 'We intended not to tell him our troubles. Whoever had a loose tongue and told him about that?'
>
> Deng Jiukuan said, 'You didn't want him to know, but you couldn't lock our land up in a cabinet.'
>
> Zheng Suzhi said, 'We must care for him. On no account must we add to his worries. Have you seen how thin he has become now? A man's energy is limited. Although he is vigorous, how can he stand so many problems?'[16]

In *Mountains Green after Rain*, after he learns that Wei Gengtian has been notified by the negative superior Nong Liji that he must go to the commune office to justify his actions, Huang Runsheng, an old poor peasant, is worried. The next morning before daybreak, the old man comes to the hero's house to give him a bottle of tiger-bone liquor, which was bought for him from the county city by Tang Qun, a positive superior, and which the old man has cherished for a long time. Seeing that Wei Gentian has not yet got up, the old man squats down outside the door and sighs to himself, 'You have worked for all of us day and night. Some people put pressure on you from above, and some play tricks in the village . . . You are too tired. I hope you can sleep well and long.'[17] In order not to awaken the hero, the old man keeps quiet in the bitter cold of the early winter morning, and even tries not to cough.

With respect to personal security, the masses and cadres often put the main heroes before themselves. In *The Long Rainbow*, after they find a clue indicating that the villain Zhao Deming attempts to murder the heroine Shi Caihong, the masses and cadres are worried. Although the heroine herself thinks that people have exaggerated the potential danger, the people insist on taking measures to protect her. The one in charge of the task, Shi Huying, makes a solemn vow on behalf of the militia in a meeting: 'We are ready to die in defence of Sister Caihong. So, even if the class enemy bombs all the militia to death, we mustn't let him injure her in the slightest!'[18] In *Mountains Green after Rain*, before descending into the mountain cave to kill the large poisonous snake, a 'debate' takes place between the hero Wei Gengtian and the old poor peasant Zhao Yiliang. According to Wei, as the head of the village he has an obligation to forge ahead in the face of danger. Zhao refutes Wei, 'There must be a chief-commander in a powerful army, and a main pillar in a high building. You are the chief-commander or main pillar in our Longrong. Who can be in charge of the village if anything should happen to you?'[19] In such ways, the sincere concern of these positive characters adds to the prominence of the hero in the characters' minds.

Moreover, the masses and cadres spontaneously vindicate the main heroes' reputation at all times. In *The Mountains and Rivers Roar*, Hou Laowu, a backward middle peasant, makes some unfavourable comments about Liu Wangchun. According to Hou, Liu's rise to commune secretary is not because of his competence but is largely the result of his taking advantage of the revolts of the Cultural Revolution. Hou Laowu's remark immediately arouses public indignation. Some people are so angry that they attempt to beat him, while others propose to convene a public accusation meeting. Later, after an accident has occurred on the construction site, Hou Laowu and other backward people seize the opportunity to bring Liu personally to account. As the news spreads over the construction site, another great disturbance occurs:

> Now, crowds of people streamed towards the headquarters . . . On the way, running down to the foot of the mountain, the cadres and poor and lower-middle peasants shouted curses one after another:
> . . . 'Whoever dare lay a finger on our young militant [*xiaojiang*], we shall surely break his leg!'
> Tai Zai and Xiong Xiaomang from Hongsonggu brigade took the lead running down like two young tigers. They encouraged each other by shouting: 'Quick! Quick! We can't allow the bastards to attack our young militant even if we die.'
> Old Zhao, the secretary of Sanwanquan brigade, and a woman from Chunlingjiang brigade, who were not able to keep pace with the two young men, simply shouted behind, 'You must protect Secretary Liu!'
> The streams of people, like tides from different directions, were surging towards the headquarters and their *xiaojiang* secretary.[20]

The masses' intense emotion and feeling are intentionally emphasized by the narrator to enhance the hero's image.

This scene may remind people of the sensational 'women's riot' in *Virgin Soil Upturned*, which presents a striking contrast. Sholokhov describes the crowd's unscrupulous humiliation of the main hero and other heroes. The disorderly villagers crowd before the barns of the collective farm and clamour for the barns to be opened to distribute the seed inside. The village Soviet chairman Andrei attempts to control the crowd, but he fails and is put under public arrest. His boots are removed, and the people even threaten to take off his trousers. Davidov, the main hero, also fails to calm the crowd, and he comes under a joint attack from the women, although he displays a lot of calm, controlled composure in this scene.

> . . . several blows landed on his face and neck, and his arms were seized. He jerked his shoulders and shook off the women who were clinging to him, but they pounced on him again shouting, tore his shirt collar . . .
>
> A majestic old dame — Mishka Ignatyonok's mother — jostled her way grunting towards Davidov, swore at him filthily and spat in his face.
> 'That's for you, Satan, you godless creature!'
>
> Davidov turned pale and mustered all this strength to break loose, but failed . . .
>
> 'Citizenesses! My little love-birds! Don't hit me with sticks,' he pleaded, pinching the women nearest him and lowering his head with a forced smile.
>
> They battered mercilessly on his broad resounding back . . .
>
> 'Don't use sticks!' Davidov said grimly . . .
>
> His ear was bleeding, his lips and nose were cut . . . Ignatyonok's old woman, the one with the wart on her nose, gave him a terrible time. Her blows were painful and she tried to deal them on his temples or between the eyes . . .
>
> He had been beaten up more than once in his lifetime, but this was his first beating by women and it was an uncanny feeling. 'I'd better not fall down, or they'll go mad and might put an end to me.'. . .[21]

Finally, in CR novels there is a strong faith in the heroes' correctness and competence on the part of the masses. In *The Golden Road*, Liu Wan, a middle peasant, at the instigation of negative characters, refuses to join Gao Daquan's mutual aid team. In the busy farming season his wife has a baby. Seeing that her husband cannot manage the work in the fields alone, the wife is unwilling to rest in the house after giving birth and tries to work outside. She finally breaks down from overwork. Her illness is too serious to be cured. On her death bed she asks to see the hero Gao Daquan. Liu Wan agrees to invite the main hero to come to her in person. Many villagers crowd around her with anxiety. As the patient regains consciousness, she looks at Gao Daquan weakly and says in an imploring voice, 'Secretary, please let my two children and their father join you. Promise. . .'[22] After the hero promises, 'a trace of a smile of satisfaction appeared on the patient's face, then she closed her eyes slowly . . .'[23]

Moreover, the common people not only have confidence in following the heroes to take part in political activities but also display their trust in them by asking them for help in dealing with personal affairs. In *The Long Rainbow*, Wang Xiaomei, a twenty-two-year-old girl who is the barefoot doctor of the village, meets 'a hard nut to crack'. Two years ago, she was engaged to Guo Quanshan in the neighbouring village. In spite of their engagement, the couple rarely have a chance to talk to each other in private. Now Wang Xiaomei intends to postpone their wedding day. She has received a letter from Guo Quanshan in which he asks to visit her to talk. The letter places her in a predicament because she is so shy that she feels embarrassed reading his letter, let alone talking face to face with the young man. 'In short, in the shy barefoot doctor's mind, nothing in the world is more difficult than being in love.'[24] She needs somebody to give her advice on how to be in love. She decides to ask the heroine Shi Caihong for advice. In her opinion, 'Caihong has a high level of ideological consciousness and working ability. She is surely capable of dealing with this affair'.[25] Actually, even though Shi Caihong is three years older than Wang Xiaomei, she has never been in love. Yet the heroine nevertheless answers all her questions, including the most naive one: 'In front of him, I feel so shy that I blush with nervousness and my heart beats much faster. I am too nervous to speak. What should I do?'[26] The girl at last finds the courage to meet her fiancé. Thus the emphasis on the deep personal trust other positive characters have for the heroes shows the special position the latter have in their hearts.

Setting off the Main Heroes by Providing Negative Characters as Foils

Of all the negative characters in a CR novel, three types play active roles in the plots. The first is negative superiors, i.e. capitalist-roaders. Among them, one tends to be the most important, such as Huang Guang in *Evergreen*, Nong Liji in *Mountains Green after Rain* and Gu Xinmin in *The Golden Road*. Sometimes the capitalist-roaders are villains which here refer to class enemies, such as Jia Weimin in *The Roaring Songhua River*, and Long Youtian in *The Mountains and Rivers Roar*. But in most cases, the capitalist-roaders differ from villains. The former pursue the wrong line not out of their evil motivation towards the government and the Party, but because of a lower level of ideological awareness. Yet the latter support the wrong line because of an ulterior motive — to sabotage the Party and its causes. The negative superiors also differ from the 'quasi-member' of the positive core. Whereas the latter changes his course half-way in support of the wrong line, the former usually persist in pursuing the wrong line through to the end.

The second category of negative characters is villains, i.e. class enemies. Typically, the main villain in a CR novel has a dual identity, namely, as a member of the leadership of the village and as a hidden enemy. As a member of the leadership, he is usually in charge of sideline production, and as an enemy, he could be a landlord who escaped being classified as such, a historical traitor, or even a hidden enemy agent. Overt class enemies are relatively unimportant. The reason is that their activities are limited because they are under public surveillance. It is evident that the CR novels' authors generally try to connect overt class enemies with the main villain and the negative superiors, and sometimes they even cause the chief overt class enemy to manipulate the villain from behind the scenes, although the connection is merely superficial and symbolic.

The last category is the backward middle peasants. They are designed to be the primary social basis of the wrong line. They claim to represent 'the masses' in supporting the negative superiors in pursuit of the wrong line. However, their activities are usually manipulated by the main villain.

Fanchen is the exclusive method for setting off the main heroes in providing the three categories of negative character as foils. For the capitalist-roaders, normally, they pursue the wrong line because their ideological qualities are not sufficiently sharp as to enable them to distinguish the right line from the wrong. This is in contrast to the main heroes who have extraordinary political foresight and ideological insight allowing them to see through the nature of the wrong line. The narrators emphasize this difference between the capitalist-roaders and the main heroes so as to give more prominence to the heroes.

As analysed in Chapter 3, from the beginning of the main story when he is not the village Party secretary, the hero Gao Daquan in *The Golden Road* has pursued collectivization, which represents the correct line. But his superiors, from village to county level, Zhang Jinfa, Wang Youqing and Gu Xinmin, attempt to carry out the policy of 'building up family fortunes', which represents the wrong line. The confrontation between Gao Daquan and the higher authorities continues for two years before instructions from the highest authorities confirm the correctness of the hero's position. This causes the senior leader Gu Xinmin, who has been advocating the slogan of 'building up family fortune', to become confused, and to feel inferior. According to Gu, the slogan which was propagated in newspapers and magazines originally came from his higher authorities. How could he on his own be discerning enough to discover the error of the slogan? In all events, it is difficult for him to understand how Gao Daquan could sense, even from the beginning, that it was a wrong slogan. He is so ashamed that he is unwilling to identify himself to the hero. The following quotation indicates both his perplexity and his envy.

> How could a common Party member in a village become aware of its error, but he, an old revolutionary and a county-grade cadre with theoretical expertise, fail to discern its error . . . Whatever Gao Daquan did was correct. How could he make such miracles happen? . . . Did he do it blindly and by chance, or did he really have such a high level of political awareness?[27]

It is evident that the emphasis on Gu Xinmin's inferiority contributes to setting off the main hero in comparison.

In addition to emphasizing their ideological inferiority, another point is to accentuate the capitalist-roaders' inner weakness during the confrontation between them and the main heroes. On the one hand, the capitalist-roaders are the main heroes' superiors and they have the power to discipline the heroes. So they may act with outward blustering in front of the heroes. On the other hand, they represent the wrong line and as such they are foils to heroes, thereby destined to be in a weaker position. In the analysis of Jiang Chunwang's awe-inspiring air in Chapter 2, we have seen the capitalist-roader Huang Guang's inner feebleness.

In *Mountains Green after Rain*, after the flood, the commune Party secretary Nong Liji comes down to criticize the hero Wei Gengtian for the impracticality of his irrigation project. Although several times during a face to face confrontation, he threatens to give Wei Gengtian disciplinary punishment, Nong Liji is still in the weaker position. The hero criticizes the superior's finding fault with the campaign of learning from Dazhai by stressing the temporary difficulties of his project. 'After hearing this series of questions raised by Wei Gengtian, like a deflated rubber ball, Nong Liji sat and gasped for breath . . . He found himself devoid of all argument . . . "You . . . you . . . needn't preach to me like this. If . . . if you cling to your course, you will . . . have to be held responsible for the consequences." Owing to inner feebleness, he could not help stammering.'[28] On his hurried return, he bumps into Li Bao'an, the head in charge of production. He is so upset that he forgets to untie the halter of his horse from a tree before he mounts and whips it, so that he nearly falls off the horse. Obviously, in a comparative sense, the capitalist-roader's embarrassment and inner weakness contribute to setting off the hero's righteousness and heroic spirit.

The inferiority of class enemies, the second category of negative characters, is different from the capitalist-roaders described above. For the latter, inferiority concerns ideological foresight and insight. But for the former, inferiority is shown in the descriptions in which their attempted sabotage is thwarted by the main heroes. As noted above, the active class enemies or the main villains in the CR novels are often hidden enemies with dual identity. Usually, with respect to the class struggle motif, they are the main heroes' most important opponents and as such they plot and sabotage. However, in spite of the complex and mysterious nature of their plots, the main heroes are always able to see through their schemes and intrigues. Actually, in many cases the main heroes have seen through the class enemies and their plots for a long time, but deliberately adopt a temporary *laissez-faire* attitude in order to allow the enemies to fully expose themselves and thereby teach others a lesson.

In *The Long Rainbow* the hidden enemy Zhao Deming has played tricks for a long time and has gained the confidence of the villagers. As deputy director of the village revolutionary committee, he takes advantage of his position and conducts a series of plots and intrigues in the campaign of learning from Dazhai. He fails to deceive the heroine Shi Caihong however, who begins to notice him not long after the campaign starts. In mid-story, Zhao Deming murders Wang

Huaishan to prevent him from divulging his secrets. He creates an elaborate, false suicide scene and then pretends to be active in the investigation of the case. He congratulates himself on his scheme and on the fact that people trust him. But he does not recognize Shi Caihong's suspicion. In the following dialogue, the heroine intentionally encourages the enemy to do his best, designing ultimately to cause him to fully expose himself.

> Caihong said with a smile, ' . . . Old Zhao, you are wise and full of stratagems. Go ahead by all means.'
>
> Waving his head, Zhao Deming looked modest and said, 'I am not a capable person. But under your leadership, I feel more confident and I shall do my best.'
>
> 'I believe that you will do your best.' Caihong's words were full of overtones. She continued without betraying her feelings, 'As you know, at present, an engagement of life-and-death has begun; how can you not do your best?'[29]

The fact is that the heroine has the enemy's motives at her fingertips, although the enemy is kept in the dark. In sum, on the one hand, the hidden enemies' craftiness is accentuated in CR novels to indicate the complexity of class struggles. On the other hand, their craftiness and their schemes are described as self-exposing acts under the complete control of the main heroes. In the end, the enemies are destined to suffer a crushing defeat. Thus their craftiness and tricks pale into insignificance next to the heroes' keen insight and extraordinary manoeuvres. In other words, their craftiness, their tricks and their inevitable failure are designed as foils to set off the main heroes' resourcefulness and ultimate triumph.

Another important aspect concerning the class enemies' characterization as foils is that which accentuates their weakness in front of the main heroes. In The *Mountains and Rivers Roar*, Long Youtian is both a class enemy and a capitalist-roader. Before the main hero Liu Wangchun, 'he feels as if he were stripped naked in sunlight'.[30] As noted in Chapter 2, Long Youtian is especially frightened by the hero's flashing eyes. 'As if Liu Wangchun's eyes were like two sharp swords, which were about to prick through his internal vital organs.'[31] The following passage contains Long Youtian's feelings and response as Liu Wangchun points out his mistakes.

> As for Long Youtian, the *xiaojiang* [young militant] secretary's words were like thunder and lightning, which made him feel dizzy, break out into a cold sweat and become totally dispirited. Under the great power contained in Liu Wangchun's language, Long Youtian could not but nod, 'yes, yes', looking completely convinced.[32]

This exaggerated description of Long Youtian's undignified weakness is clearly intended to set off the hero's awe-inspiring power.

The weakness of the backward middle peasants, the third category of negative character, is also played up to *fanchen* the power of the main heroes. Unlike the class enemies who mainly conduct sabotage covertly, the backward middle peasants take liberties in support of the wrong line of developing capitalism because they can rely on their advantage of not being classified as class enemies. However, although the backward middle peasants are usually swollen with arrogance in front of other cadres and villagers, they are diffident before the main heroes. Among the backward middle peasants of the CR novels, Li Fugui in *The Roaring Songhua River* is one of the most overbearing. He even thinks nothing of Chen Qingshan, who is nicknamed *tie hanzi* [iron man] because of his powerful physique and strict discipline, concurrently deputy Party secretary and general commander of the project of transforming wasteland. But the middle peasant stands in awe of the main hero Zhao Guang'en, so much so that he is alarmed and nervous even at the mention of the hero's name. Once, while inciting Liang Mantun, the deputy head in charge of production, to oppose Chen Qingshan's arrangement to transform the wasteland, Mantun's wife enters and says, 'Mantun, Uncle Guang'en is coming.' "'My God! Why is he coming?!'" Li Fugui slid down from the *kang* [a kind of heatable brick platform used for sleeping and sitting] hurriedly, as if bounced out by a spring . . . "Don't let him see me. I am going . . ." He slunk off.'[33]

In *Evergreen*, as mentioned before, there is an episode highlighting the main hero Jiang Chunwang's awe-inspiring power, i.e. 'one shout from Chunwang can turn over three wheelbarrows'. It is clear that the three backward middle peasants' weakness is provided as a foil to set off the hero. Later in the main story, Jiang Hongyun, the ringleader of the three middle peasants, actively supports the capitalist-roader Huang Guang in carrying out the policy of fixing farm output quotas for each household. Near the end of the story, Jiang Yulin, the local agent of the capitalist-roader Huang Guang, secretly promises to let Jiang Hongyun lease ten *mu*. That day when the poor and lower-middle peasants are sowing in the field, Jiang Hongyun rushes onto the scene and declares with bluster that he has leased the ten *mu*. As he stands in front of the Youth League secretary Jin Zhu who is ploughing, the story continues as follows:

> Jin Zhu was so angry that he clenched his teeth and urged the horse to go on straight towards Jiang Hongyun.
>
> Jiang Hongyun was ready to die. With hands grasping the harness on the horse, he stood on tiptoe and caught hold of the harness of the horse desperately. He did not move at all.
>
> 'Get out of the way!' Suddenly, Jiang Chunwang shouted.
>
> The voice was even more powerful than that 'which had turned over three wheelbarrows'. Jiang Hongyun at once trembled with fear. . . .[34]

Then, both Jiang Hongyun and Huang Guang's agent Jiang Yulin shrank back helplessly.

Setting Off the Main Heroes by Means of Pathetic Fallacy and Natural Description

In CR novels, there are many descriptions of natural scenery which are related to the portrayal of the main heroes. That is, the scenic surroundings are intended to serve as foils to set off the heroes. The above-analysed forms of giving prominence to the main heroes are based on the relationship between the heroes and other characters. The scenic descriptions under discussion, however, concern the relationship between the heroes' image and nature. Although the natural description is not within the definition of the formula 'three prominences', it reflects the spirit of giving prominence to the heroes. Two kinds of such scenic description are important. One is where the author intentionally plays up the beauty and prosperity of the scenic surroundings at certain places where the hero appears. The author selects a series of scenic objects which have symbolic meanings, such as bright sunlight, blue sky, green trees, green grass, fresh air, peaceful water and beautiful flowers. In *The Golden Road*, one early morning, after saying goodbye to the positive superiors who have given him instructions about the collectivization in Xiongji Village, Gao Daquan starts to walk towards his home village. On the way the surroundings present a beautiful and lively scene:

> In the bright sunlight, walking through the emerald green grasses, and breathing the fresh air which seemed infused with sweet honey and mellow wine, he was striding south.
> The towering mountains, the dense fruit trees, the lively springs, the soaring goshawks, the slopes with varieties of flowers, the fields with green crop seedlings, the vast Jidong Plain . . . All these attracted him, inspired him, and encouraged him.[35]

The scenery is full of life, which impressively sets off the hero's happiness and rosy prospects.

In many cases the beautiful flowers/blossoms are emphasized, giving rise to an impression of 'presenting fresh flowers to heroes'. For instance, in *Mountains Green after Rain*, while on the way to the commune office, Wei Gengtian seems to walk in a world of blossoms.

> . . . There was a chill in the air in spring, but the cold could not keep off the flourishing prosperity of nature . . . At front and back of the small wooden dwellings, and on both sides of the mountain roads, the white plum blossoms and pink peach blossoms seemed to be smiling in the breeze. The tung trees also came into bloom with a shining white colour. And the kapok trees all over the mountains were in blossom. The petals on the strong branches were red as fire. Look! Emblazoned with crimson, the mountain village became even more buoyant . . . Looking at the flourishing kapok blossoms, Wei Gengtian was in high spirits. . . .[36]

This type of scenic description highlights the main heroes' high spirits and bright future by emphasizing the beauty and prosperity of the scenery. Another kind of scenic description highlights the heroes' powerful and unyielding qualities by playing up the harshness and relentlessness of the natural surroundings. In this case, the symbolic objects include high mountains, strong winds, heavy rain, surging waters, hardy pines, lightning, thunder, etc. In *Mountains Emblazoned with Crimson*, there is a paragraph describing the scene of Huayang Mountain in which the main hero Gao Lisong is walking in vigorous strides. The scenery on the way is evidently provided as a foil to set off the hero's power.

> . . . The thousands of mountains were like surging billows. Huayang Mountain stood there with its head held up, and on it the wind in the pines was soughing. The young communist Gao Lisong walked the mountain road with head and chest held high. His mind was in a tumult. His every strong step was like thunder booming . . .[37]

Usually, the second type of natural description appears in scenes depicting struggle against natural calamities. The following quotation from *The Mountains and Rivers Roar* is typical.

> . . . In Hulong Valley, the dense clouds covered the ground, the wind blew hard and the rain came down in sheets. The towering cliff stood firm despite the attack of the violent storm. The tall pines powerfully waved their branches and crowns, as if making fun of the rain and thunder. The mountains and rivers were roaring violently . . . Liu Wangchun stood under a hardy old pine . . . Staring at the surging and roaring mountain torrents, his big eyes, set under heavy eyebrows, glistened with unyielding brightness; through the furious storm, his face showed an amazing and solemn kind of composure. Watching the mountain torrents, he seemed a general staring at a battle map and held spellbound on the eve of a fierce battle . . . Suddenly, a great boom and a powerful flash of light appeared on the top of the pine under which he stood. The shining light illuminated the unyielding iron man under the tree, who looked like a straight stone statue.[38]

It is evident that the narrator mixes the image of the hero and the scenic objects together. The harsh natural surroundings represented by those characteristic objects set off the hero's unyielding will and power by showing nature's might. Most especially, the towering cliff and hardy pine symbolize the hero's image and add to the effect of serving as foils.

OTHER STOCK POINTS CONCERNING PROMINENCE OF THE MAIN HEROES

According to the literary doctrine current during the Cultural Revolution, a novel's story-line must centre on main heroes, that is, the heroes become involved in all main contradictions. Moreover, 'the heroes play the dominant roles in the development of contradictions, and they are the decisive factors in their resolution'.[39] Based on these principles, there are other noticeable stock elements in CR novels which are designed to give prominence to the main heroes. Below are four examples.

More Appearances Made by the Main Heroes

Since the plots of CR novels are designed to centre on the main heroes, the heroes are more likely to appear often in the novels. According to our quantitative investigation, in CR novels the chapters where the main heroes appear in person on average account for over 80 percent of the total. This is about twice as often as in pre-CR novels. For example, *Mountains Green after Rain* has thirty-two chapters in total, of which the hero Wei Gengtian appears directly in twenty-nine. The rate reaches 90.6 percent. In *Qingshi Fort*, the total number of chapters is twenty-eight. The hero Lian Hua appears in twenty-five chapters. The rate is 89.3 percent. However, the pre-CR novel *The Builders* (Vol. 1) includes thirty chapters, in thirteen of which the hero Liang Shengbao appears in person. The rate here is 43.3 percent. In *Great Changes in a Mountain Village* (Vol. 1), the main hero Liu Yusheng appears in nine chapters, accounting for only 34.6 percent of the total of twenty-six. Moreover, in Part II of this book, our statistics show that the number of words spoken by the main hero in a CR novel is much higher than in a pre-CR novel. That is, the average rate of words spoken by the main heroes per 1,000 Chinese characters is 42.59 versus 19.45. So, in comparing the above-enumerated four novels, the numbers of words spoken by Liu Yusheng and Liang Shengbao in the two pre-CR novels are 2,023 and 5,948 respectively, accounting for 9.41 and 16.57 per 1,000 Chinese characters. But in the two CR novels, the figures for Wei Gengtian and Lian Hua are, respectively, 17,602 and 20,720, making up 49.86 and 60.06 per 1,000 characters (see Table 20). From the analysis of language this fact indicates that the main heroes in CR fiction are more involved or play a more active part in the stories.

The Exclusive Longitudinal Structure of the Novels

The principle that stories are mainly centered around the main heroes is also shown in the structure of CR novels. In pre-CR fiction, there are different structures. For example, the pre-CR novel *Great Changes in a Mountain Village* takes parallel structure, in which each chapter roughly centres on one different character, although the main hero and other important characters play leading roles in the main story of the agricultural collectivization. This type of structure is common in traditional Chinese fiction, such as *Outlaws of the Marsh* for example. The structure of another pre-CR novel, *The Sun Shines Bright*, is longitudinal, but with regard to the main hero, the stories basically cover a section of his life within the time setting. However, the situation in the CR novels is different. The novels exclusively take a 'longitudinal' [*zongxiang*] structure. More importantly, although the main plots are set within certain periods of time, the stories about the main heroes generally cover their life from childhood to the end of the main stories. Therefore in many cases CR novels have a prologue [*xiezi*] and an epilogue [*weisheng*]. Generally, the prologues centre on the childhood of the heroes, and the epilogues précis their prospects such as new promotions and new assignments, indicating that they are continuing their struggles. In short, the exclusive longitudinal structure contributes to a centring on the main heroes, and gives CR novels a biographical fictional style.

The Heroes' Presence at a Critical Point

In the stories, there are a number of scenes in which controversies or accidents are checked by the main heroes. The heroes' presence is specially arranged so as to give prominence to the heroes. That is, the heroes have not appeared in the scene until the controversies or accidents reach a critical point, i.e. an unfavourable decision is being made or a great danger is impending. For instance, in *The Long Rainbow*, in discussing the practicability of the plan of an irrigation project proposed by the heroine Shi Caihong, the engineers and technicians of hydrology are arguing heatedly in a special meeting. Obviously, Li Zhiyao, who supports the plan, is overpowered by those who oppose him, and the situation is leading towards the negation of the plan. At the critical moment, Shi Caihong arrives at the meeting-place. After a heated dispute, the heroine and her followers win. In *The Daughter of Slaves*, also at the critical point when Dong Lingyun's life is threatened by a ferocious wolf, the heroine Wulan Tuoya gallops on horseback to the spot in time. She kills the wolf and Dong Lingyun is rescued from a desperate situation. It is evident that such descriptions are intended to give readers the impression that the main heroes are the decisive factors in solving problems.

The Heroes' Absence in Troubled Time

Unlike the above situations, a number of incidents or accidents fail to be checked by the heroes. These incidents or accidents are often caused by the class enemies' sabotage. When these incidents or accidents brew or occur, the heroes are absent. In *The Golden Road* the sensational incident in which Gao Erlin breaks up the family and sets up a separate home has been manipulated by villainous characters. But it happens during the time when the hero Gao Daquan has gone to Xiongjizhai to meet with superiors. In *The Long Rainbow*, the most serious accident is the collapse of the dam under construction. The direct cause of the accident is the villain Zhao Deming's sabotage, conducted during the heroine Shi Caihong's absence because of illness. Although the heroine arrives at the spot in time and directs people to deal with the immediate emergency as the accident occurs, she is powerless to prevent it in the first instance because of her earlier absence. It stands to reason that this kind of absence is not coincidental but intentionally arranged. That is, the absence is intended to exclude a contradiction, i.e. the main heroes, who are described as having a keen insight into class enemies, if present could not fail to see through them and prevent their sabotage. In other words, the heroes' absence is engineered by authors to give them prominence by avoiding miscalculation and fault.

Part II

Lexical Style

Introduction to Part II

Here Ferdinand de Saussure's distinction between *langue* and *parole* is adopted, *langue* being the system of rules common to speakers of a language, and *parole* being the particular uses of this system.[1] The *langue* during the CR period was still the Modern Standard Chinese [*putonghua*] system, and there is no indication of any change in official policy in regard to its phonological, lexical or grammatical norms. Nevertheless, although the Cultural Revolution did not change the existing Chinese *langue*, it substantially affected the style of Chinese speech and writing, which pertains to *parole*.

The definition of style in the present investigation is based on the following points summarized by Geoffrey N. Leech and Michael H. Short:[2]

i)   Style is a way in which language is used.
ii) Style consists of choices made from the repertoire of the language.
iii) A style is defined in terms of a domain of language use.

Style is also applied to the linguistic habits of a particular writer ('the style of Lu Xun, of Mao Dun', etc.); at other times it refers to the characteristics by which language elements are selected in a particular period, genre, school of writing, or some combinations of these ('the style of "the thirties of this century"', 'the poetic style', 'the style of "the lotus-lake school"', 'the style of novels from 1949 to 1965', etc.). The present study focuses on the lexical style of CR Chinese novels, with a view to revealing the trends in vocabulary usage of the whole CR literary language.

Concentration on the investigation of the lexical style — rather than syntactic, phonological, contextual, or other styles — was determined by the following factors. Theoretically, vocabulary is the most active and sensitive factor of a language to reflect social change. Of the many facets of style, lexis is believed by many linguists to be the most basic and most profitable area of study.[3] What readers are intuitively most aware of in the language of novels is vocabulary.[4]

How to assess style has been controversial. The statistical approach to style has been criticized by some linguists as claiming too much. Nevertheless, many linguists agree that it remains the most important and practical way because unlike purely impressionistic statements, it has the support of objective and concrete evidence.[5] Quantitative analysis is the basic method used in the present research.

SELECTION OF THE SAMPLE

Style is a relative concept, and the study of style is essentially comparative and contrastive.[6] Seven novels published during the Cultural Revolution and three before the period are selected as samples. The sampling of the seven CR novels is supposed to take the following aspects into account in order to avoid unnecessary preference or negligence produced by some variants.

i) Writing time. The novels must originate from the time of the Cultural Revolution in order to avoid probable inconsistency in lexical style. For instance, *Swift is the Spring Tide*,[7] was not chosen because its draft was produced between 1956 and 1959, although the final version was completed in 1974.

ii) Authorship. Considering that diverse authorship can lead to inconsistent language use, the sample includes works by authors from different categories.

iii) Subject matter and time setting. The sampling covers four of the five categories of sub-types of subject matter of agriculture, which are concerned with four periods and four politicized agricultural campaigns (see the Introduction). Particular fashionable words and expressions appeared in each of the periods and campaigns; they consequently exist in the corresponding novels. However, works set during a later period can embrace time-specific words and expressions of earlier periods, but novels set in earlier periods cannot comprise those items appearing and in vogue during later periods. It is thus necessary for the sampling to cover different sub-types of subject matter and time setting. The quantity of sample novels with a certain sub-type of subject matter and time setting is in direct proportion to the total ratio of novels under the corresponding category.

iv) Geographical setting. The Chinese language is well known for the great diversity of its dialects.[8] Modern Standard Chinese is based on the Northern Dialect which consists of a good few sub-dialects. The geographical setting may relate to the distribution of dialectal words and expressions. For this reason, the sample avoids settings with an unusually high frequency of dialect lexical items. For example, *The Peacock Flies High* is set among the Dai ethnic minority, and is known for being 'rich in local colour';[9] its language includes evidently more local elements than many novels set in Chinese nationality. The novel is thus excluded. Moreover, the majority of CR novels are set in North China, whose dialect is the nearest one to Modern Standard Chinese. So proper care ought to be taken to pick some works set in other dialect regions.

v) The sample must include only novels written in Chinese in their original form. *At the Foot of Kezile Mountain*, which is translated from the Uighur, is not on the list.

The seven sample CR novels, *The Golden Road* (Vol. 1), *The Roaring Songhua River* (Vol. 1), *Evergreen*, *Qingshi Fort*, *Mountains Green after Rain*, *The Long Rainbow*, and *The Mountains and Rivers Roar*, have also been adopted as focal works for literary analysis in Part I.

As the agricultural novels published between 1956 and 1966 focus only on the agricultural cooperative movement, and authorship is usually a single one, the sampling of pre-CR novels is less complicated. The three samples, *Great Changes in a Mountain Village* (Vol. 1), *The Builders* and *The Sun Shines Bright* (Vol. 1), are acknowledged to be the most influential agricultural novels of the pre-CR period. *Great Changes in a Mountain Village* is set in South China, *The Builders* in West China and *The Sun Shines Bright* in North China.

All the ten sample novels and relevant information are tabulated in Table 1.

UNITS AND LEVELS OF ANALYSIS

Since the present investigation takes account of stylistic rather than grammatical (morphologic and syntactic) aspects of the novels' vocabulary, the analytical unit may exist in units on various grammatical levels, that is, a stylistic item may be in the form of a word, a phrase, a clause, or a sentence, which all depend on different categories of stylistic item. Nevertheless, the range of items mainly covers words and set expressions.[10]

Words can be classified according to different criteria: e.g. by origin, by notion, by usage, etc. Here the classification is by level of usage, according to which the words are categorized as common, bookish or literary, colloquial, dialectal, slang, technical, and so on.[11] Since 'common words' are stylistically neutral, and hence not related to a particular period, genre, school of writing, etc.,[12] they are not included here.

The most common kinds of set expression in Chinese are idioms, proverbs and *xiehouyu*. Structurally, most Chinese idioms are four syllable phrase, but proverbs and *xiehouyu* take the form of concise sentences.

The detailed criteria and rules by which the items are determined and counted are given in the following section and under corresponding categories in the specific sections.

The next operative procedure presents another problem, i.e. the unit in the text against which the stylistic items are set in proportion so that the percentages can be achieved. The ideal unit is no doubt the word. A difficulty, however, rises from the fact that the word is not a unit in the Chinese writing system. Neither orthography nor lexicography is sufficient to establish word divisions in the absence of any well-defined phonologic criteria for distinguishing words from morphemes or phrases.[13]

In order to avoid unnecessary complication, I have therefore decided to take the written character as the unit under all circumstances except some analyses with regard to some item distributions according to representative people in the novels. For the latter analyses, it sounds more reasonable and illustrative to put the stylistic items in proportion to the amount of word units (see Chapters 7 and 8). With regard to the word as a unit under such circumstances, I take *A Modern Chinese Dictionary* [*Xiandai Hanyu cidian*] as the main reference.[14] For exceptions beyond the reference book due to the indistinctness of Chinese word boundaries as noted above, I have to decide intuitively, a method affirmed by some scholars.[15]

Here some detailed explanations are given of our rules and procedures for counting Chinese characters in the investigation. Among the ten novels, there are six in which the character numbers were noted by publishers, but the other four were not. Conventionally, the calculation formula is that the total character number of one novel is the product of the number of characters per line multiplied by the number of lines per page and then multiplied by the total number of pages. However, there exist some inconsistencies in the publishers' counting and calculation of the number of characters of the novels. Firstly, the publishers adopt different conventions for rounding up/down. For instance, in *Great Changes in a Mountain Village* and *The Sun Shines Bright*, the error rate is ±500, but in *Evergreen*, *The Roaring Songhua River*, *Mountains Green after Rain*, and *The Long Rainbow*, it is ±5,000. Secondly, the publishers adopt different criteria in counting punctuation marks (according to Chinese convention, punctuation marks are taken into account in counting Chinese characters). For example, in composition, a comma usually occupies half a space of a character while a full stop occupies a full space. We can discern by investigation that in counting *The Sun Shines Bright*, *Evergreen*, *The Roaring Songhua River* and *The Long Rainbow* the publishers took two commas for one unit, but for *Great Changes in a Mountain Village*, the publisher counted one comma as a unit. Thirdly, among the six novels with characters numbered by publishers, there are five whose noted numbers are the same as those that I counted in accordance with the above formula. But the calculation of the other one, *Mountains Green after Rain*, cannot be reasonably understood in this manner. If the calculation is done in the way adopted in *Great Changes in a Mountain Village*, the total number should be approximately 7,000 more than that noted; if it is done in the way adopted in the other four novels, the number should be approximately 7,000 fewer than that noted.

In view of the above, therefore, the following rules are set in our counting and calculation in order to reduce discrepancies and produce more appropriate results:

i)   The approximate rounding is to one thousand, i.e. the accuracy rate is ±500.
ii) The representative lines must be lines containing either all characters or characters and full stops, i.e. two commas are taken for one unit, which is the counting method adopted in *The Sun Shines Bright*, *Evergreen*, *The Roaring Songhua River*, and *The Long Rainbow*.
iii) All characters outside the main body, such as in tables of contents, prefaces, and postscripts are excluded from the counting.

CATEGORIES OF STYLISTIC ITEMS VERSUS REFERENCES

The categories of stylistic item are listed as follows, and are defined under the corresponding categories in the following sections: vulgar expressions, ideological words and expressions, idioms, proverbs, *xiehouyu*, classical verse, dialectal words, 'bookish', 'colloquial', military expressions, meteorological terms in metaphorical use, and inflated expressions. Of the twelve stylistic categories, the first ten are statistically analysed. But for the last two categories, the analysis is mainly qualitative. Thus the present description with respect to statistics is only concerned with the first ten categories.

In order to decide under which of the ten categories the individual items should be classified, I have chosen the following dictionaries and books as basic references: *A Modern Chinese Dictionary*, *Hanyu chengyu xiao cidian* [*A Small Dictionary of Chinese Idioms*],[16] *Xiehouyu cidian* [*A Xiehouyu Dictionary*],[17] *Hanyu yanyu cidian* [*A Dictionary of Chinese Proverbs*],[18] *Changyong kouyu yuhui* [*Colloquial Vocabulary in Common Use*],[19] *Hanyu fangyan cihui* [*A Word List of Chinese Dialects*],[20] *A Dictionary of Military Terms: Chinese-English and English-Chinese*,[21] and *Glossary of Chinese Political Phrases*.[22]

In spite of their authoritativeness, however, these references are insufficient to cover all the items (no reference books in fact so far published can possibly do that) because of the peculiarity of the extensive originating sources and the peculiarity of Chinese word-formation. Therefore, my intuition is occasionally used to decide the classification after failing to get sufficient recorded information.

EXHAUSTIVE OR SAMPLE MEASUREMENT

The ideal methodology would be to make a thorough analysis of all the stylistic categories in the ten novels. But for practical reasons, seven of the ten categories, i.e. vulgar expressions, ideological expressions, idioms, proverbs, *xiehouyu*, classical verses, and military expressions, are treated exhaustively. The other three categories, dialectal expressions, 'bookish', and 'colloquial', are measured by random sample. The length of sampling generally accounts for 10 to 15 percent of the complete work.

The ten stylistic categories are generally mutually exclusive, but there exists some overlapping. For example, a large number of idioms come from writings in classical Chinese; they are bookish as well as idiomatic. Some vulgar expressions have a dual identity, both vulgar and dialectal. In order to avoid missing any possible stylistic items, overlapping items are entered in both categories.

THE STATISTICAL PROCESS

As for counting, no current software package in Chinese is available that can cope with the complexity of the semantic and stylistic analysis. The only way to reach the goal is the crude and laborious way of counting by hand. The next stage is to calculate the figures as required with the aid of a computer. The whole statistical process consists of the following steps:

i) Underlining the items in the novels.
ii) Copying the items under corresponding categories. Each item is identified by the following points: (1) Spoken by character or narrated by narrator. (2) If by character, the character's name; in monologue[23] or dialogue. (3) For an abusive expression, the target's name added. (4) Page.
iii) Making a series of tables according to respective analysis requirements and purposes of the stylistic categories; counting the items and points concerned, then calculating the percentages; filling the tables with the figures.
vi) Calculating the means of the two groups; tabulating the results.

The final presentation of the statistical analyses covers two aspects, i.e. under one heading, there are two tables: x - 1 and x - 2. Table x - 1 presents the ten individual novels so that any one of them can be compared with any of the others. Table x - 2 is designed for presentation of the mean value of the two groups so that comparisons can be made between the three pre-CR novels and the seven CR novels.

Chapter 6

Vulgar Expressions

VULGAR EXPRESSIONS DEFINED

Here the concept 'vulgar expression' roughly corresponds to 'swearing' plus a small part of 'slang' described by Lars-Gunnar Andersson and Peter Trudgill in their *Bad Language*.[1] English and Chinese contain some specific sorts of vulgar expression which exist only in one of the two languages. For instance, according to Andersson and Trudgill, 'a typical form of swearing in English and most other European languages involves *blasphemic* utterances',[2] but in Chinese few words can be found to refer to religion in a derogatory way. According to the specificity of Chinese vocabulary, the vulgar expressions under discussion cover the following sorts of items:

i) Set swearing expressions, which are labelled as 'swearword' in *A Modern Chinese Dictionary*.
    Examples: *hundan* [bastard] (G, p. 95 — for reference codes of the novels, see Table 1, the same below), *si biaozi* [a damned whore] (G, p. 347), *ta ma de* [Damn it] (F, p. 61).

ii) Taboo words relating to sex, bodily organs or functions.
    Examples: *diao-mao* [pubes] (C, p. 150), *jiba* [penis] (B, p. 320), *fangpi* [to fart] (G, p.181).

iii) Offensive metaphors used to call human beings things, animals or ghosts.
    Examples: *xialiu huo* [a dirty thing] (C, p. 401), *xiao tu-zaizi* [a young rabbit — a brat] (D, p. 611), *gou niang yang de* [son of a bitch] (G, 347), *gui zisun* [descendants of tortoise (bastards)] (B, p. 41).

This category excludes two varieties: (1) idiomatic phrases with morphemes referring to animals or ghosts even though some are derogatory. The reason is that the literary flavour of them overshadows their vulgar colouring. For example, *hai qun zhi ma* [an evil member of a horse herd — one who brings disgrace on his group] (D, p. 612), *niu gui she shen* [monsters and demons — forces of evil] (H, p. 526). (2) nicknames relating to abominable animals. For example, *Qingzhushe* [a kind of snake] (H, p. 40), *Chuanshanlang* [a kind of wolf] (G, p. 199). Although their metaphoric meaning is rather offensive and vulgar, they have nevertheless gained the nature of proper names.

iv) Slang self-referent words/phrases referring to elder generations.
Examples: *laozi* [father] (H, p. 82), *laoniang* [old mother] (G, p. 347), *ni nainai* [your grandmother] (G, p. 398).

Usually, using such self-referent words/phrases in speech is regarded as being self-aggrandizing and rude. It is sometimes especially offensive because people being addressed think that they are put in the position of juniors of the speakers of such items.

v) Phrases or sentences used to lay a curse on somebody.
Examples: *ni zhege ai qian dao de* [you who will be cut by a thousand knives] (G, p. 351), *lao bu dao hao si de* [you who will die a tragic death] (A, p. 178).

THE DENSITY OF VULGAR EXPRESSIONS

It seems to be generally acknowledged that vulgar expressions were very prevalent during the Cultural Revolution. In his famous *Language versus Social Life* [*Yuyan yu shehui shenghuo*], Chen Yuan, one of the most authoritative Chinese socio-linguists writes: 'During the Cultural Revolution, Chinese language was heavily polluted; people's writings and speech were full of empty, big, stereotyped and vulgar expressions . . .' 'In the decade, too many vulgar expressions existed in the social life . . . it was as if the more you used vulgar expressions, the more revolutionary you were.'[3]

Such an observation concerning vulgar expressions fits the writing style of *dazibao* [big-character poster] or leaflets by Red Guards or other rebels [*zaofan pai*] during the early and most intense period of the Cultural Revolution. However, the language in formal official documents or literature during the CR period does not contain more vulgar expressions than previously. Furthermore, written spoken language in formal publications does not show an increase in vulgar expressions.

Contrarily, the present statistics of the ten novels reveal that CR novels include fewer vulgar expressions than pre-CR novels. The number of vulgar expressions per 100,000 characters in the three pre-CR novels is nearly twice as many as those in the seven CR novels (33.75 vs. 16.98, see Table 3 – 2). Individually, the rates in *The Golden Road, Evergreen, The Long Rainbow,* and *The Mountains and Rivers Roar* respectively account for only a quarter or so of the mean of the pre-CR novels.

The Golden Road versus *The Sun Shines Bright,* both by Hao Ran, provides good evidence of the tendency. The rate in the latter is about four times as much as that in the former (see Table 3 – 1).

According to Table 3 – 1, the tendency towards fewer vulgar expressions in the seven CR novels is regular except for *Qingshi Fort,* which ranks the second highest among the ten novels. My investigation shows that this novel is exceptional in having a high rate of vulgar expressions not only among the seven samples, but also among all other CR agricultural novels. There is insufficient material to explain the phenomenon fully. For example, we lack information about the author Zhu Jian and his personal style because there is no sign of any other publication from any period by him. However, the character setting in the novel could from one angle give reasons for the novel's exceptional status. In the CR novels, the relation and contacts between negative characters are generally indirect or covert. They usually act in isolation and speak cautiously. In *Qingshi Fort,* however, the negative characters group together, acting rather boldly and overtly. Their language is full of vulgar expressions, especially when they talk to one another. For instance, the percentage of vulgar expressions by 'other negative characters' in the novel is over twice as much as the mean of Group II, and nearly five times more than that of Group I (see Table 6). Therefore, irrespective of other factors, the special character setting in the novel is conducive to the high rate of vulgar expressions.

DISTRIBUTION ACCORDING TO FUNCTIONAL VARIETIES

Five Functional Types

I have categorized the vulgar expressions into the following five functional types.[4]

Abusive

Directed towards others; includes name-calling and curses.

Examples:
(1) *Che le ni de zhi la, wangba-dan!*
[You have been discharged from your post, you bastard! — 'wangba' is a popular name for the tortoise; in an abusive way, it means someone whose wife has sex with other men.] (G, p. 272)

(2)   *Wenshou*!
      [You beast!] (H, p. 553)

(3)   *Ni xiashuo, ni fangpi*!
      [You are talking rubbish. Shit! — literally, 'fangpi' means to fart; abusively, it means to talk nonsense.] (G, p. 354)

(4)   *Da si ni ge gou ri de*!
      [I hit you beast to death! — 'gou ri de', which is a nominal phrase ('de' phrase), literally means somebody who was fucked by dog.] (C, p. 401)

(5)   . . . *zhe zao qiang beng de* . . .
      [. . . he who will be shot by gun . . .] (E, p. 503)

Expletive

Used to express emotions; not directed towards others, but derogatory; as an independent grammatical unit, with a pause.

Examples:

(6)   *Pi! Laozi jiu shi bu pa*!
      [Shit! I am just fearless!] (H, p. 182)

(7)   *Niao! Ting de jiao ren naozi teng*!
      [Hell! What he said made me get a headache! — 'niao' literally means bird, but is also euphemism for 'diao' which means penis.] (B, p. 319)

(8)   *Ta ma de, wo suan renshi nimen le*!
      [Damn it, I have really seen through you at last! — 'ta ma de' literally means his mother's.] (C, p. 254)

(9)   *Mama de*!
      [God damn it! — it literally means mother's.] (G, p. 387)

(10) *Nainai, ni rang laozi shang daoshan, laozi ye rang ni xia you guo*!
      [Damn it, you want to force me to climb a mountain of swords; I shall compel you to plunge into a cauldron of boiling oil! — literally, 'nainai' means grandmother.] (G, p. 314).

All these references to mother/grandmother in examples (8), (9) and (10) have connotations of 'fuck your mother/grandmother'.

Generally uncouth

Not directly offensive; most are taboo words, literal or metaphorical; some are special slang referring to elder generations.

Examples:

(11) *Bu ji guonian qian neng e chulai ma*?
      [If we don't take measures right away, our only hope will be to shit the money for the New Year Festival. — 'e' literally means to discharge

excrement or urine. This sentence means no way to get money for the New Year Festival.] (H, p. 4)

(12) *Liu xia name piguyan yidianr* . . .

[Just left us a place as small as an arsehole . . .] (C, p. 91)

(13) *Ta nüren-jia dong — dong ge pi!*

[She, a woman, can understand nothing! — '*pi*' literally means fart, here it means nothing.] (H, p. 111)

(14) *Pa you shi duo guan le ji zhong mao niao* . . .

[I'm afraid he's pissed again . . . — '*mao niao*' literally means urine of cats, but it here means alcoholic drink.] (F, p. 420)

(15) *Laozi bu gan le!*

[I give up the post! — no English equivalent, '*laozi*' literally means father, but as a self-aggrandizing slang self-referent, it means I or me.] (G, p. 181)

(16) *Yemen lai-tian fang ba huo* . . .

[We shall sometime later set fire to . . . — '*yemen*' is similar to '*laozi*' above, but it is a plural.] (J, p. 148)

Auxiliary

Swearing, as a way of speaking; has no clear syntactic or semantic relation with other elements in a sentence; usually unstressed; without pause.

Examples:

(17) *Wo ta ma dao cun kou lan zhu xing Huang de, xian gao ta yi zhuang.*

[I'll bloody well go to the entrance of the village to meet Huang, making a complaint against him (referring to the hero). — '*tama*' literally means his mother.] (E, p. 190)

(18) *Nimen ta ma de kan dao nali qu le* . . .

[What a bloody mistake you made . . . — ref. (8) above.] (C, p. 597)

(19) *Zhe jiao ta niang de shenme shir ya?*

[What is this bloody thing called? — '*ta niang de*' is synonymous with '*ta ma de*' above.] (D, p. 90)

Humorous

Directed towards others or self but not really derogatory; playful rather than offensive.

Examples:

(20) *Ai dao de, zongshi mei da mei xiao.*

[You, a regular mischief, always ignore the difference between the elder and the younger. — the '*de*' phrase '*ai dao de*' literally means somebody who will be stabbed with a knife, but here it is of comedial colour, addressed by Jiao Erju towards her nephew Xiao Changchun, the hero of the novel, who is making fun of her.] (C, p. 53)

(21) *Ni yao si le, ni zhege gui-zaizi?*
     [Are you going to die, you naughty boy? — '*gui-zaizi*' literally means son of ghost.] (A, p. 273)

(22) *Feng pozi! Ni ba . . .*
     [Naughty girl! Your father . . . — '*feng pozi*' literally means mad woman] (J, p. 185)

(23) *Ni zhe lao dongxi, yibeizi mei xin guo gui . . .*
     [You old thing, you've never believed in ghosts . . . — this sentence is uttered by Uncle En to himself, in which calling himself 'old thing' is rather playful.] (J, p. 66)

'Humorous' often takes the form of abusive swearing but has the opposite function, decided not by the literal meaning of the expressions, but by the relationship between speakers and listeners, and/or by the intention of speakers. Usually, it appears in the dialogue of positive characters who intend to joke, such as examples (20), (21), or to express love for or appreciation of children, such as (22). Sometimes it refers to mockery directed towards the speaker himself, such as (23). Another kind of humorous abuse comes from the contrivances of speakers. They pretend to abuse each other for others' attention; the abusive expressions could be called performance swearing. Their humorous and playful nature could be supposed to relate to both plot setting and language use, but here the latter is emphasized. For example, in *Great Changes in a Mountain Village*, a backward couple, Wang Jusheng and his wife, play a farce of threatening the cadres with divorce if they are compelled to join the agricultural producers' cooperative. The pretence of the wife's abusing her husband is conducive to the episode's comical effect.[5]

Although the five functional categories are conceptually clearcut, under some circumstances, the same expression can be sorted into different categories, determined by actual context. For instance, the same phrase *ta ma de* in examples (8) and (18) is respectively put under Expletive and Auxiliary. The same word *pi* in (3), (6) and (13) also belongs to different corresponding categories.

As the amount of Abusive plus Generally Uncouth in each group surpasses eighty percent of its total vulgar expressions (see Table 4), we may take them as major types, and the others as secondary types. The statistics show two features about the distribution of the functional varieties of Group II in comparison with Group I: Firstly, it has a rather higher rate of Generally Uncouth, even without individual exceptions. Secondly, it has lower rates of the other four categories, among which Humorous is the most evident.

Classification of Vulgarity

From the above definition and description, we may see that the degrees of offensiveness and vulgarity of the five categories are different. They can be roughly classified into five corresponding 'vulgar levels'. The rankings are as follows:

Categories of expressions	Vulgar levels
Abusive	Strongest
Expletive	Strong
Generally uncouth	Middle
Auxiliary	Weak
Humorous	Weakest

In addition to the above classification of vulgarity by comparison of the five functional categories, there are two obvious inner distinctions with regard to vulgar extent within the categories. (1) Within any category, the expressions which relate to sexual organs are supposed to be with stronger taboo meaning, and intuitively more vulgar. (2) Within Abusive, those expressions targeting the elder generation are taken to be more offensive.

Some interesting findings can be gained from the distribution of the functional varieties accounted above. Firstly, for the two major types Abusive and Generally Uncouth, because Group II has a lower rate of Abusive, it may be taken for granted that vulgar expressions in CR novels decrease not only in quantity, but also in semantic extent. In other words, since Abusive is at the top vulgar level as noted above, the decrease of Abusive but increase of Generally Uncouth (middle level) demonstrates that the vulgar expressions in CR novels are stylistically milder and more restrained. This phenomenon can also be confirmed by my extended examination into the internal vulgar distinctions of the categories, i.e. expressions relating to sexual organs and Abusive expressions concerning the elder generation in Group II are much less frequent than those of Group I. For these reasons, we cannot find from Group II such highly vulgar expressions as the following examples which appear in Group I.

(24) *Wo <u>cao ni de mama</u>.*
      [I'll fuck your mother.] (A, p. 83)
(25) *<u>Cao ni ge baijun qin mama</u>!*
      [Fuck your White army's mother! — 'qin' or 'lao' is sometimes put before 'mama' or 'niang' for stronger offensiveness.] (B, p. 453)
(26) *Wo <u>ri ta zuzong</u> le!*
      [I'll fuck his ancestors.] (C, p. 617)

(27) *Jiba mao* dang toufa!
[(He's) got pubes for hair.] (B, p. 140)

(28) *Ma de bi*, ni shenqi shenme, zhang nage de shi-zi . . .
[Your mother's cunt, what makes you so cocky, and whose power do you rely on . . .] (A, p. 57)

Secondly, as the rate of Humorous in Group I is about three times as much as in Group II, it would be reasonable to judge that the use of vulgar expressions in CR novels is with less comical flavour and less free scope. As a matter of fact, from Group II, we have found neither performance swearing as in *Great Changes in a Mountain Village*, nor playful but abusive jokes cracked by protagonists and other positive characters such as examples (20) and (21) above.

Lastly, for the other two secondary types Expletive and Auxiliary, the rates in Group II are lower than those in Group I. Unfortunately, there seems no general regularity to suit all the individual novels because of exceptions. For example, *Evergreen* has no Expletive, but has the highest rate of Auxiliary; while *The Golden Road* has a lower rate of Auxiliary compared to *The Sun Shines Bright*, it has over twice the number of Expletive. Moreover, within Group I, the rates of the two categories for each novel are also without regular pattern. The inconsistency could probably be attributed to other factors such as personal style and local style rather than period style.

DISTRIBUTION BY SEX

My next investigation into the style in using vulgar expressions is to analyse the distributions according to characters. The first I deal with is the distribution of the expressions in the monologues and dialogues by different sexes, with Narrators forming a separate category. Here I categorize the vulgar expressions under three types of speaker: Male, Female, and Non-specific (see Table 5). 'Non-specific' in discussion refers to those characters whose sex is not specified in the text. Usually, their expressions are collective abuse or vulgar interruptions of somebody from a crowd. For example,

(29) You *yi gu gu xiang chaoshui shide renliu*, xiang zhihui-bu yong lai . . . jiao ma bu jue: '*Gou ri de* di fu fantian, xian za ta ge xibalan!'
[Crowds of people streamed towards the headquarters . . . successively shouting curses: 'Now that the bastard landlords and rich peasants are attempting to wreak vengeance, we will smash them to pieces first!] (J, pp. 371–2)

(30) Xiang li de *renmen you ma Fu-laizi de*, ye *you guai Sheng Shujun de*: . . .
'Sheng jia li de na ge meizi ye *bu shi hao huo* . . .'

[Among the people in the village, some were cursing Fu-laizi, and some others were blaming Sheng Shujun: 'The girl of the Sheng family is no good (not a good thing) either . . .'] (A, p. 84)

For Male and Female, I expected before the analysis that the rate for males in Group II would be lower than that of Group I, but the rate for females in Group II would be higher than that of Group I. The expectation was based on the following reasoning: As mentioned above, the level of emphasis by propaganda on the equality of sexes reached a new stage in the Cultural Revolution. Although no reliable research was conducted into actual change of speech patterns in the sexes, it seemed reasonable to suppose that the female speaking style was influenced by the Cultural Revolution and that the stylistic differences between the different sexes were lessened. Consequently, the change would be reflected directly or indirectly in the speaking of the characters of CR novels.

The statistical result (see Table 5) shows that the rate of Male in Group II is really lower than that of Group I (63.8% vs. 69.4%), but the difference is not so noticeable as to need further attention, and the individual patterns are not regular enough to prove the existence of a trend. As for Female, more unexpectedly, the rate in Group II, instead of increasing, drops compared to that in Group I, despite the slightness of the scale (27.0% vs. 27.8%). Therefore, on the basis of the statistics, I have to conclude that by comparison with pre-CR novels, no substantial change may be detected as regards the distribution of vulgar expressions between the proportion of Male to Female in CR novels, no matter what happened in reality.

After the above analysis, I further investigated some distributions within the category of Female. Firstly, I examined Female distribution according to age: young, middle, and old. The result, disappointingly, shows no obvious change. The basic pattern of both groups is as follows: The rate for the middle is the highest, the old the second, and the young the last. The slight difference in actual rates between the two groups can be reasonably ignored because no regular pattern can be generalized from the individual novels.

Secondly, I examined the distribution by class status within the Female category. There is also no statistically regular change found by comparison of the two groups.

Thirdly, by combining the above two aspects, I examined the distribution of functional varieties within Female; two interesting points emerge.

i) Very few old female poor peasants in Group II use vulgar expressions except for Humorous. In Group I, however, almost all old female speakers of vulgar expressions are poor peasants. So we cannot find a single old female poor peasant in the CR novels who like Aunt Five [Wu shen] in *The Sun Shines Bright* abuses a backward element (Ma Lianfu) roundly,[6] or who like Chen Dachun's mother in *Great Changes in a Mountain Village* abuses her children constantly.[7]

ii) Although a reduction in the level of vulgarity is a general tendency in CR novels, there was an actual increase in the level of vulgar expressions by young girls in CR novels. The readers of pre-CR novels thus could not possibly encounter such highly vulgar abusive expressions spoken by young girls as in CR novels:

(31) *Zhe ji tian, Wang Huaishan he Bai Erxian zhe <u>yi dui gui-sunzi,</u> ti ti zhao zhao you shen chu lai le· . . .*
[These days, Wang Huaishan and Bai Erxian, the couple of sons of bitches, have been getting ready to start something again . . . — 'gui-sunzi' literally means grandson of a tortoise, for which the popular name is 'wangba'; this item is a very vulgar expression of abuse. ref. example (1) above.] (I, p. 78)

(32) *Zhe liang ge <u>gou dongxi</u> lai suanji wo le. Hao ba! Ni <u>gunainai</u> bu gao ni ge bi ta zui wai, jiu bu pei zuo Qingshibao de xin dang-jia . . .*
[The two bastards have schemed against me. Well! If I can't have your faces bashed in, I shall not be qualified to be a new leader in Qingshi Fort . . . — the two items, the former used to call others animals, and the latter used to refer to the speaker herself as great-aunt of the listeners, are so offensive and vulgar that according to general literary conventions, they would be more suitable if spoken by a negative shrew rather than by a young educated heroine.] (G, p. 332)

Another feature concerning the change is the manner of speaking. Most vulgar expressions by young girls in pre-CR novels are spoken in monologue or behind people's backs, but those in CR novels are generally spoken in public or to people's faces. We may compare the following two examples:

(33) 'Mei lian!' <u>Gaixia zai xin li ma,</u> 'Ni jian tian dao Huangbao wenhua zhan qu tigao, zhao bu xia duixiang, gan zhaoji!' <u>Dan ta zui li yi sheng bu keng</u> . . .
['What a nerve! (or Shameless!) You go to the culture station of Huangbao for improvement every day, but you still can't find a girlfriend, and you have to be anxious to no avail.' Gaixia was abusing him in her mind, but outwardly she did not utter a sound.] (B, p. 220)

(34) <u>Chunhong da he yi sheng:</u> 'Zhu kou! <u>Ni zhe tiao lanpigou</u>!'[8]
[Chunhong shouted loudly, 'Stop! You loathsome creature!' — 'laipigou' literally means mangy dog.] (G, p. 336)

While analysing the above changes concerning the use of vulgar expressions by female characters, we cannot separate them from changes in characterization. A reasonable explanation for the fact that old female poor peasants are not allowed to use abusive expressions is that the authors deliberately try to present the sensible and rational side of their disposition. Moreover, to let young women use more abusive expressions in a more open and bolder manner is one aspect of the measures taken by the authors to reflect the characters' anti-traditional and rebellious temperament.

Lastly, I examined Female distribution concerning the targets towards whom the abusive expressions are directed. The result shows that the proportions relating to both family and non-family members in both groups are similar. However, within the distribution of family members, there is a noticeable change, i.e. almost all abusive expressions concerning family members by female characters in Group I are directed towards children, whereas most of such expressions in Group II are directed towards husbands. This characteristic will be discussed further in a later section.

Next, the category of Non-specific is small in both groups. Either the small numbers of actual expressions or the slight differences between the percentages of the two groups can be reasonably ignored in the present investigation.

Then, for the category of Narrator, the distinctly contrastive distributions in the two groups are worth taking into further consideration. Functionally, vulgar expressions by narrators generally belong to Abusive only, with a few exceptions which can be classified into Generally Uncouth. Most of the vulgar expressions by narrators are offensive metaphors used to call human beings animals or other things, and the others are taboo words relating to bodily organs or functions. For example,

(35) *Zhe ge gua zhe Gongchandangyuan zhaopai de <u>chailang</u>, ren mian shou xin de <u>chusheng</u>* . . .
[He, a wolf under the signboard of a member of the Communist Party, and a beast in human shape . . .] (G, p. 209)

(36) *Yong Ma-Liezhuyi, Mao Zedong Sixiang zhe mian zhaoyaojing qu zhao, jiu neng zhao de <u>wugui-wangba</u> xian yuanxing!*
[When we try to spot them with the monster-revealing mirror of Marxism-Leninism and Mao Zedong Thought, we can make the bastards show their true colours. ref. example (1) above.] (H, p. 347)

(37) *Yi ge <u>shuo qu fangpi</u> de meipo ye lai quan ta* . . .
[A woman matchmaker, who always talked a pile of maggoty shit, also came to persuade her . . . ref. example (3) above.] (G, p. 209)

From the examples, we can see that the vulgar expressions are used to express the narrators' highly partial attitude towards the characters, in this context to denigrate negative characters. The targets of the vulgar expressions by narrators are exclusively negative characters, and under most conditions are main villains.

The statistical analysis (Table 5.2) shows that the rate of vulgar expressions by narrators in Group II is about five times higher than that of Group I (6.5% vs. 1.4%). The situation could, from one angle, show that the narration and description by narrators in CR novels are more partial relative to pre-CR novels.

DISTRIBUTION ACCORDING TO TYPE OF SPEAKER

The characters of the novels are here classified into five types according to ideology: Main Hero, Other Positive Characters, Backward Elements, Other Negative Characters, and Main Villain. This classification is based on the conventional bifurcation (positive and negative) and the CR novel character set-up noted in Chapter 5.

From Table 6.2, we may see the following two characteristics by comparing the two groups:

i)   The distribution ranking of the five types of speaker is the same. From the highest to the lowest, they are Other Positive Characters, Backward Elements, Other Negative Characters, Main Villain, and Main Hero.

ii) The distribution rate under each type of speaker in Group II is different, i.e. the rates under Main Hero, Other Positive Characters, and Backward Elements decreased, but the rates under Main Villain and Other Negative Characters increased.

As for the highest and lowest ranking of distribution, firstly, it is expected that Main Hero ranks last, because, as a way of characterization, vulgar expressions generally reflect speakers' irrationality or crudeness, which are naturally at odds with the heroes' cool-headed and rational temperament. Secondly, why Other Positive Characters rank first seems hard to understand. It is in fact attributed to two main factors. One is that the total amount of speaking by Other Positive Characters accounts for an overwhelming majority of the dialogue and monologue in the novels, which may proportionally comprise most vulgar expressions. Another is that nearly all Humorous vulgar expressions come from this type.

The consistency of the distribution ranking in both groups is noticeable, which indicates that before and during the Cultural Revolution, the authors kept the same general pattern.

The different pattern of the rates of vulgar expressions under the five types of character in Group II (a reduction in the rates of vulgar expressions spoken by positive characters, but an increase in the rates by negative characters) is noticeable. The phenomenon shows that as a measure of characterization the use of vulgar expressions in these novels is more closely related to characters' ideological identities.

How far is it true to say that the distributions of vulgar expressions in CR novels are more closely related to the ideological identities of characters? From Table 6.1, we found out that the rates in individual CR works fluctuate within a wide range. For example, under Main Hero, the rates range from zero to 7.9; under Main Villain, from zero to 20.8; under Other Negative Characters, from zero to 30.3. The irregular rates reflect that ideological identities are not the only criterion by which the authors distribute vulgar expressions. In other words, the authors of the CR novels did not ignore other aspects of characterization in using vulgar expressions, while they in general put more stress on the ideological identities of characters. The rates under Main Villain can be taken to illustrate the situation.

For Main Villain, *The Roaring Songhua River* and *The Mountains and Rivers Roar* are contrary to the whole tendency of increasing the rates of vulgar expressions spoken by negative characters. In the two novels, the main villains have double ideological identities. Their public status is Party cadre, but actually they are villains. The authors' distribution of vulgar expressions seems to relate to several factors over and above villain classification. The rate of vulgar expressions spoken by Long Youtian in *The Mountains and Rivers Roar* is very low. Long had been educated in the traditional Confucian way in his youth (see J, pp. 161–2), and later becomes the vice-director of the revolutionary committee of the commune and the deputy commander-in-chief in charge of the irrigation project in construction. That he seldom uses vulgar expressions is more in keeping with standard literary conventions about his educational background and official status. Jia Weimin in *The Roaring Songhua River* is the deputy Party secretary of the county. As a well-educated intellectual, he is interested in classical Chinese literature and Western classical music. He does not use vulgar expressions in conversation. Thus no vulgar expressions spoken by him are found in the novel.

DISTRIBUTION ACCORDING TO TARGETS OF ABUSE

The vulgar expressions in discussion in this section mainly refer to Abusive. The investigation concerns the differences of distribution of targets of abuse between the two groups.

Types of Character as Targets of Abuse

Related to the classification of the types of character made in the previous section, 'Others' here refers to those whose ideological identities cannot reasonably be determined. They are mainly young children behaving neither well nor badly, disregarding what types their elders belong to. For example, Meng Qishan in *The Golden Road*, a pre-school boy, who is much abused by some middle characters, is under Others, although his father is a negative character (a big landlord).

In Table 7.1 – 2, obvious differences between the two groups can be seen. With the exception of Backward Elements, under which the rates of both groups rank highest, the rates under all the other four types rank differently between the two groups. For example, the second highest rate in Group I is under Other Positive Characters, but in Group II is under Other Negative Characters. The lowest rate in Group II is under Main Hero, but in Group I is under Main Villain.

Generally speaking, with each group considered (see Table 7.1 – 2), within Group I, positive characters (Main hero and Other positive characters as indicated in the table) as targets of abuse rank higher than negative characters (Main villain and Other negative characters as indicated in the table) as targets of abuse, i.e. 38.3 (10.8 + 27.5) vs. 13.6 (4.9 + 8.8) — numbers in this paragraph are percentages of abusive expressions targeted towards characters. Within Group II, however, a contrary pattern appears: positive characters account for 18.8 (3.3 + 15.5), but negative characters 43.7 (13.1 + 29.6). In comparing the two groups, the rate for positive characters in Group I is nearly twice that in Group II (38.3 vs. 18.8), but the rate for negative characters in Group I is only less than one third of that of Group II (13.6 vs. 43.7).

On the basis of the above comparison, horizontal and vertical, we may reasonably assume that ideological criteria were not adopted or emphasized in pre-CR novels when the target of abuse was taken into consideration. However, the rate pattern in CR novels indicates that the authors deliberately followed a principle based on ideological partiality: causing abusive expressions to be mainly directed towards negative and middle characters. The practice of the principle can be evidenced further by the distribution of the individual novels, in which the rates are rather regular in accordance with the whole mode (see Table 7.1 – 1).

The changes in the extent of offensiveness according to types of character also prove the prominence of the ideological criteria in the novels of Group II. In Group I, we have not perceived obvious differences between the offensive extents relating to positive and negative characters as targets of abuse. We can thus find some highly offensive expressions of abuse directed towards Main Heroes. For example,

(38) *Liang-laosan de xiao duzi* . . .
[Liang-laosan's bastardy son . . . — 'xiao duzi' literally means small son of ox.] (B, p. 275)
(39) *Gou ri de, hao hui shi shouwan ya* . . .
[How skilfully that bastard plays tricks . . .] (C, p. 181)

However, in Group II, similarly offensive expressions of abuse can only be found being directed towards middle and negative characters, being spoken by both opposite-side and same-side characters, but can hardly be found used towards Other Positive Characters, and are never found towards Main Heroes.

The subtle change in which even Main Villain and Other Negative Characters do not abuse positive characters severely is worthy of notice. It indicates that, with the two opposite sides taken into consideration, in the pre-

CR novels, the highly offensive expressions of abuse are mutual between positive and negative characters, but in CR novels, they are only directed from positive characters towards negative characters.

In the end, therefore, with regard to vulgar expressions versus the types of character, if we do not have enough confirmation that the authors of CR novels paid strict attention to ideological criteria in the distribution of speakers, we may reasonably conclude that they consciously arranged the distribution of targets of abuse according to ideological principles.

Family Members as Targets

From Table 7.2 – 1.2, we may see the similarity between the two groups as regards the distribution rates of family members and non-family members as targets of abuse: for Family Members, 26.5% in Group I vs. 25.4% in Group II, and for Non-family Members, 73.5% vs. 74.2%. For both groups, over seventy percent of targets of abuse are non-family members. That would reveal that the confrontation which is reflected by using abusive expressions dominantly exists among non-family members. Because the internal differences concerning non-family members between the two groups are mainly reflected in the distribution over the ideological types of character as discussed in the previous section, the present analysis concentrates on family members.

Firstly, comparing the families of the two groups in which some members are abused by others, I have found that such families in Group I can be classified into three types according to constituents of ideological identities (small children beyond ideological classification are not included): (1) Family with only positive characters, such as Chen Xianjin's family in *Great Changes in a Mountain Village*, Liang Shengbao's family in *The Builders*, and Xiao Changchun's family in *The Sun Shines Bright*. (2) Family with positive and backward characters, such as Wang Shuanshuan's family in *The Builders* and Ma Laosi's family in *The Sun Shines Bright*. (3) Family with backward and/or negative characters, such as Ma Zhiyue's family and Ma Liben's family in *The Sun Shines Bright*. In the first type of family, only children are the targets of abuse, but in the second and third types of family, the targets may be husbands, wives, or children. In Group II, however, the families with targets abused by family members absolutely exclude type (1). They are normally types (2) and (3). The targets of abuse may be also husbands, wives, or children.

The next is within the families, i.e. the differences between the two groups as regards the internal distribution over family members as targets of abuse. According to Table 7.2 – 2.2, the sharpest contrast is the rates under Husbands: 7.4% in Group I and 50.9% in Group II. Actually, in Group II, husbands as targets of abuse rank first among the three types of family member, but in Group I, husbands rank last. With wives taken into account, the number of abusing expressions towards them in Group I is over three times more than the number towards husbands, but in Group II, is only under one third of the number towards husbands. The rate under Wives in fact ranks last in Group II.

The Group II phenomenon of husbands as predominant targets of abuse, with wives rarely targeted, is a significant stylistic characteristic in the use of vulgar expressions. It is typical that in the dialogues between husbands and wives in Group II, while the wives frequently abuse their husbands face to face, the husbands seldom make counterattacks with abusive expressions. The situation is consistent no matter what the ideological identities of the abusing wives or the abused husbands are. For instance, in *Qingshi Fort*, the backward element Geng Jiaquan and the main villain Shi Jigen habitually use abusive expressions towards non-family members in dialogue and monologue. However, Shi, being frequently abused by his wife Qingyun, a positive character, rarely abuses her; Geng never abuses his wife Agui, a negative character, who abuses her husband severely and constantly. In *Mountains Green after Rain*, the positive character Li Yinlan uses a lot of abusive and vulgar expressions towards her husband Wei Chaoben, a middle character, usually in public, but the latter also does nothing but swallow them, refraining from using abusive expressions in retort.

On the level of ideological identities, as targets of abuse by a spouse, both husbands and wives in the two groups belong to middle or negative characters; as abusers towards spouse, husbands in both groups and wives in Group I are also middle or negative characters, but wives in Group II may be positive, middle or negative characters, among which the positive accounts for most.

The above features concerning husbands and wives as abusers or targets of abuse can be summarized as follows: (1) By comparison of the two groups, husbands in Group II are much more passive than husbands in Group I in being abused by wives, but wives in Group II are much more active than wives in Group I in abusing husbands. Moreover, wives as abusers in Group II have more diverse ideological identities. (2) In the comparison between husbands and wives within Group II, wives are more active in using abusive expressions towards husbands. On the other hand, husbands are more passive as targets of abuse by wives.

Lastly, according to the ranking pattern in Group I, it seems plausible to suppose that pre-CR novels are more tinged with patriarchal tradition in the arrangement of targets of abuse. In the light of the tradition, wives are subordinate to husbands, and children are subordinate to parents. Among family members, children are naturally the most common targets of abuse because they may be abused by both father and mother. For this reason, although Chen Xianjin's wife in *Great Changes in a Mountain Village* abuses her son and daughter constantly, she never uses a single abusive expression towards her husband.

As noted above, in the Cultural Revolution, the heightened rhetorical support for the equality of the sexes influenced young women's psychology and behaviour. The relationships between family members, as depicted in fiction, inevitably reflected the change. Another fact emerging from my examination is thus also conducive to revealing the differences between the older and younger generations. In Group II, there are a few abusive expressions towards wives, but all the expressions are used by old men, such as Yu Laonian in *The Roaring Songhua River*, and Yu Si in *Qingshi Fort*. No abusive expressions directed towards wives appear in the dialogues of middle-aged or young couples, but all abuses against husbands exist in such couples. In other words, for old couples, it is husbands that abuse wives; but for middle-aged or young couples, it is wives that abuse husbands.

Chapter 7

Ideological Expressions

IDEOLOGICAL EXPRESSIONS DEFINED

Compared to the other categories of stylistic items, ideological expressions are very difficult to count because of the following two factors:

Firstly, on a semantic level, some political and ideological expressions are well-established, but some are not. There are three semantic categories of these expressions:

Specific

This covers words and expressions whose political and ideological meaning are literally determined and distinct, including the following categories:
1. Ideological terminology.
   Examples: *zhengzhi* [politics], *geming* [revolution], *yishixingtai* [ideology], *shehuizhuyi* [socialism], *wuchanjieji* [the proletariat], *Mao Zedong Sixiang* [Mao Zedong Thought].
2. Names of political organizations and political figures plus their associated epithets.
   Examples: *gongqingtuan* [the Youth League], *gongchandang* [the Communist Party], *Hongweibing* [the Red Guards], *Mao Zedong Sixiang xuanchuandui* [Mao Zedong Thought propaganda team], *weida lingxiu Mao Zhuxi* [Great Leader Chairman Mao].

3. Names of political campaigns.

Examples: *Tugai* [the Land Reform], *hezuohua* [cooperative transformation], *Fanyou* [the Anti-Rightist Struggle], *Siqing* [the 'Four Clean-ups' Movement], *Shehuizhuyi Jiaoyu Yundong* [the Socialist Education Movement], *nongye xue Dazhai* [In agriculture, learn from Dazhai], *Wuchanjieji Wenhua Da Geming* [the Great Proletarian Cultural Revolution].

4. Terms denoting class status.

Examples: *pinnong* [poor peasant], *pin-xiazhongnong* [poor and lower-middle peasants], *zhongnong* [middle peasant], *funong* [rich peasant], *dizhu* [landlord].

5. Political slogans.

Examples: *Zaofan you li!* [It is right to rebel!] (H, p. 532)

Jianjue ba Wuchanjieji Wenhua Da Geming jinxing daodi! [Resolutely carry the Cultural Revolution through to the end!] (H, p. 587)

6. Quotations from Marx, Lenin, Stalin and Mao.

Examples: *qiong ze si bian* [poverty gives rise to a desire for change] (H, p. 95)

Qianwan bu yao wangji jiejidouzheng. [We must never forget class struggle.] (J, p. 428)

7. Titles of political documents.

Examples: «*Shiliu tiao*» [The Sixteen Articles] (H, p. 485), «*Qian shi tiao*» [The Previous Ten Articles] (G, p. 383), «*Ba Jie Shi Zhong Quanhui gongbao*» [Communique of the Tenth Plenary Session of the Eighth Central Committee] (G, p. 330)

Quasi-specific

The literal sense of some words and idiomatic phrases does not concern politics and ideology, but they have an established metaphoric meaning or colouring relating to politics and ideology.

Examples: *daolu* [road], *sixiang* [thought], *xuexi* [study], *juewu* [awareness], *pipan* [criticize], *douzheng* [struggle], *guojia* [country], *zi li geng sheng* [self-reliance], *jianku fendou* [work hard].[1]

Non-specific

Some word groups or sentences contain no specific or quasi-specific political terminology but they have political and ideological meaning in the specific context.

Examples: *Tamen ren hai zai, xin bu si.* [They are still alive, and have not lost ambition. — 'Tamen' in the context refers to class enemies. The sentence means that class enemies are ready to wreak vengeance.] (H, p. 219)

Yi dao jinguang zhao si fang. [A golden ray shines upon all quarters. — In the context, this is a figure of speech indicating the publication of Mao's article 'About Cooperative Transformation of Agriculture'.] (E, p. 18)

Secondly, on the morphological and syntactic level, the structures of political and ideological expressions are manifold.

Words and Fixed Word Groups

Examples: *jieji* [class], *jiejidouzheng* [class struggle], *gongchandang* [communist party], *gongchanzhuyi* [communism], *Makesizhuyi* [Marxism], *Wuchanjieji Wenhua Da Geming* [the Great Proletarian Cultural Revolution], *zi li geng sheng* [self-reliance].

Non-fixed word Groups and Sentences

Examples: *shehuizhuyi geming he shehuizhuyi jianshe* [socialist revolution and socialist construction] (H, p. 65)

Wuchanjieji Wenhua Da Geming shengli wansui! [Long live the victory of the Great Proletarian Cultural Revolution!] (J, p. 527)

For the first category, i.e. words and fixed word groups, no controversy exists in collecting and counting items because their forms are established. For the second category, i.e. non-fixed words and word groups, however, there are problems related to collecting and counting criteria:

i) A word group or a sentence can include some words which in isolation are irrelevant to politics and ideology, but which are indispensable constituents in forming the word group or sentence.

Example: *Hezuohua yundong shi yi chang yanzhong, fuza he weimiao de douzheng* [The movement to organize co-operatives is a serious, complex and subtle struggle] (A, p. 36)

ii) A word group or a sentence can consist of various grouping levels and there are no established criteria for determining demarcation of levels. In other words, because the word group or sentence is as a whole an expression having meaning concerning politics and ideology, we lack grounds as to determining which level is to be selected. For example,

pipan xiuzhengzhuyi luxian [to criticize the revisionist line] (J, p. 27) — on the first level;

pipan | xiuzhengzhuyi luxian — on the second level;

pipan | xiuzhengzhuyi || luxian — on the third level.

On the first level, the whole group is an ideological expression which could be regarded as one stylistic item; on the second level, the two immediate constituents are two separate ideological expressions, so that two items could be counted; on the third level, the three constituents are three ideological words which could be taken as three stylistic items.

In view of the complication stated above, two specific criteria have been set as follows in order to avoid possible ambiguity and imprecision in collecting and counting the ideological items:

i) Semantically, of the three categories above, only the first two (Specific and Quasi-specific) are collected and counted.

ii) Structurally, of the above two categories, only the first one (Words and Fixed Word Groups) is used as a basis for counting units.

According to these criteria, therefore, the stylistic items from the following expressions, which were given above, can be determined as indicated:

Jianjue ba <u>Wuchanjieji Wenhua Da Geming</u> jinxing daodi! (see above) — One item.

<u>Hezuohua</u> <u>yundong</u> shi yi chang yanzhong, fuza he weimiao de <u>douzheng</u> (see above) — Three items.

Here are some comparative pairs or groups:

1a) . . . *Zhao Guangming xi guo lian, dai shang saozi zuor wanshang wei ziji fengbu hao de <u>maozi</u>, . . .* [. . . after washing his face, Zhao Guangming put on the cap which was mended by his sister-in-law last night, . . .] (F, p. 42) — Here 'maozi' is not an ideological item.

1b) . . . *gei ta ba <u>maozi</u> dai shang guanzhi qilai.* [. . . declare him officially a landlord and put him under surveillance.] (E, p. 345) — As a kind of political label of class status, here 'maozi' is an ideological item.

2a) *<u>huzhuzu</u> shi shehuizhuyi de mengya* [mutual-aid-team is the seed of socialism] (B, p. 424) — 'Huzhuzu' is an elementary form of organization in China's agricultural cooperation. Setting up the organization was a campaign launched by the government during the early years of the 1950s. When the word is used as a general term, it is an ideological item, such as this example.

2b) *Liang Shengbao <u>Huzhuzu</u>* [Liang Shengbao Mutual-aid-team] (B, p. 33) — Here 'huzhuzu' is a specific term referring in particular to the team organized by Liang Shengbao, and the whole word group is like a proper noun. The word is thus not counted as an ideological item.

3a) *ba gongchanzhuyi <u>jingshen</u> da da fayang* [carry on the communist spirit energetically] (H, p. 230) — Here 'jingshen' is an ideological item (quasi-specific).

3b) *You zai gao jiuji jiu hefa, zhe shi Zhongyang de <u>jingshen</u>, shangtou xie zhe de.* [It is lawful to help the people tide over a natural disaster; this is the instruction of the Party Central Committee, which was set out in black and white] (G, p. 115) — Here '*jingshen*' is an ideological item (quasi-specific).

3c) *Lao Wei, ni <u>jingshen</u> bu shuang, wo huiqu la, ni hao hao xiuxi!* [Old Wei, you are low-spirited, so I am going home now; you then have a good rest!] (H, p. 354) — Here '*jingshen*' is not an ideological item.

DENSITY OF IDEOLOGICAL EXPRESSIONS

On the whole, the statistical results matched my expectation that the CR novels include more ideological expressions than the pre-CR novels. In the pre-CR group, there are 4.27 ideological items per 1,000 Chinese characters, while in the CR group, the figure is 7.23 (see Table 8).

When we consider the rates and their differences, we should be aware of the fact that the rates of ideological expressions presented are based on restrictively established counting criteria. Unlike other stylistic categories, which are not very relevant to context, ideological items are usually directly related to context. Compare the following examples (in the first, non-ideological stylistic items are underlined for counting; in the second, ideological items are counted):

(1) *Wei Gengtian qingmie de xiao le xiao: 'Kan, zhe hui shi <u>yi tiao xian shang bang de liang zhi mazha, shui ye pao bu diao</u>!'*

    Li Bao'an shuo: 'Kanlai shi <u>gou ji tiao qiang</u> la!'

    'Dui, <u>gou ji tiao qiang</u>!' Gengtian <u>dang ji li duan</u>, 'Liji fentou ba Feiba jia baowei qilai, ba ta qinna daoshou!'

[Wei Gengtian laughed scornfully, 'Look, this time, (they) are like two locusts bound with the same string — no one can flee away!'

[Li Bao'an said: 'It looks as if he wants to risk danger in desperation now.'

['Right, he wants to risk danger in desperation.' Gengtian made a prompt decision: 'Split up and encircle Feiba's house right away, and catch him!'] (H, p. 570)

(2) *Ta fanshen zuo qilai, silu yue lai yue kaikuo: Shi a, <u>weida lingxiu Mao Zhuxi</u>, nin weile women nianqing yi dai de zhuozhuang chengzhang, bu zhi hua le duoshao xinxue; nin qinzi fadong, lingdao de <u>Wuchanjieji Wenhua Da Geming</u>, ba <u>fanxiu fangxiu</u> de wan li changcheng, zhu zai women yi dai ren de xin li . . . Liu Wangchun a, Liu Wangchun! Cong lao yi bei <u>wuchanjieji gemingjia</u> shen shang, yao jicheng xia de shi <u>jieji</u> de guang he re, yao jie guo de shi <u>douzheng</u> de jian he qi! Tamen kaipi le women guojia <u>shehuizhuyi</u> de <u>hongse</u> tiandi. Women zhe yi dai, jiu shi yao zai zhe <u>hongse</u> tiandi jian, ba <u>wuchanjieji zhuanzheng</u> xia de <u>jixu geming</u> jinxing daodi!*

[He turned over and sat up, thinking farther and farther: Right, the great leader Chairman Mao, you have made all painstaking efforts for the healthy growing of our young generation; you personally launched the Great Proletarian Cultural Revolution which constructed a Great Wall to prevent revisionism in the heart of our generation . . . Hey, Liu Wangchun, Liu Wangchun! What you must inherit from the proletarian revolutionaries of the old generation are the honour and energy [literally, light and heat] of the class, what you must take over from them is the sword and flag of struggle! They set up the socialist red world of our country. In the red world, our generation must carry through to the end the continuing revolution under the dictatorship of the proletariat.] (J. p. 378)

For (1), '*yi tiao xian shang bang de liang zhi mazha, shui ye pao bu diao*' is a *xiehouyu*, in which '*mazha*' is a dialectal word; '*gou ji tiao qiang*' and '*dang ji li duan*' are idioms. The content or semantic context of the whole quotation has no clear connection with the stylistic meaning of the items. In other words, as stylistic units, the items are relatively independent from the neighbouring words and expressions. For (2), however, the whole paragraph forms a whole ideological context, which is not made up by only the twelve underlined ideological items but by the combination of the items and the other eighty-six words (excluding the first sentence which leads to the protagonist's monologue). So although they are irrelevant to politics and ideology in isolation, the other eighty-six words are indispensable to constitute the wholly stylistic meaning of an ideological context. Actually, according to my sampling statistics, the total words and expressions which form the ideological contexts including the ideologically stylistic items are over seven times more than the number of the items alone.[2] It is therefore conceivable that the quantity of ideological component elements of the novels would become much more striking if all the contextual expressions were taken into account. But the present analysis can only be based on the ideological items under discussion because of the complexity of the statistics as stated in the previous section.

With the individual works taken into consideration, below are my findings concerning the density of ideological expressions:

Firstly, the statistical result (see Table 8 – 1) shows that Liu Qing's *The Builders* and Chen Rong's *Evergreen* rank first within their respective groups. In China these two novels are claimed by critics to be relatively less politicized compared to others. The former has been taken by many pre- and post-CR Chinese scholars as the most important post-1949 agricultural novel.[3] The latter is also regarded by some post-CR critics as one of the better novels of the CR period. Such positive comments are attributable to literary, stylistic and other aspects, regardless of high rates of ideological items. In fact, no literary comments about or linguistic analysis of the two novels relates to their high density of ideological items. It stands to reason that the comprehensive ideological colour of a novel is not equivalent to the ideological style of a work's language. The latter is mainly represented by the quantity and distribution of ideological items, but in the former case, in addition to the density and distribution of ideological expressions, other factors such as stories, characterization, and other stylistic items, are all taken into account. However, in spite of this phenomenon, the fact that the above novels are taken to be less politicized than many other current novels, but are statistically shown to have higher rates of ideological expressions than others, is nevertheless worth consideration by literary critics.

Secondly, it was expected that there would exist a certain relationship between subject matter and density of ideological expressions, but the statistics show that the relationship is only relatively established. For instance, the three novels, *Mountains Green after Rain*, *The Long Rainbow*, and *The Mountains and Rivers Roar*, in all of which the subject matter is 'learning from Dazhai', have similar rates of ideological expressions. On the other hand, there is a wide gap between *Evergreen* and *The Roaring Songhua River* (9.10‰ vs. 5.96‰), although they have the same subject matter of 'opposition to fixing output quotas on household basis'. Moreover, *The Roaring Songhua River* has a different subject matter from *Qingshi Fort* ('socialist education'), but they have a similar density of ideological items (5.96‰ vs. 6.82‰).

Thirdly, it was expected that time-setting would be a clue to the density of ideological expressions, and that the density would increase as time goes on. According to convention, contemporary political events in the different time periods, which contribute to the production of ideological items, are often described as having some relation to the previous political campaigns. So the ideological expressions in vogue during earlier periods could appear later, but the items coming into being during the later period could not have appeared in the earlier time. For example, *Zongluxian* [the General Line], *Dayuejin* [the Great Leap Forward], and *renmin gongshe* [people's commune], which all emerged and were prevalent during the late 1950s, appeared in *Evergreen*, *The Roaring Songhua River*, *Qingshi Fort*, *Mountains Green after Rain*, *The Long Rainbow*, and *The Mountains and Rivers Roar*, in which the time-setting is post-1961, but they could not appear in *The Golden Road* which is set in the early 1950s. Generally, the CR novels closely followed the expected pattern. But for the pre-CR novels, we cannot find an obvious relationship between time-setting and ideological expressions. For instance, the time-setting of *The Builders* is earlier than that of *Great Changes in a Mountain Village* and *The Sun Shines Bright*, but its rate of ideological items is about twice that of *Great Changes in a Mountain Village*, and also much higher than that of *The Sun Shines Bright*. Besides, although the time settings of *Great Changes in a Mountain Village* (1955, winter) and *The Sun Shines Bright* (1957, summer) are quite close, there is also a rather wide gap in the density of ideological expressions between them.

Lastly, among the seven CR novels, the two with the lowest rates of ideological expressions are Hao Ran's *The Golden Road* and Lin Yu's *The Roaring*

Songhua River. This fact could be to some extent attributed to authorship or authors' personal style. Hao Ran and Lin Yu are well-known professional novelists in China. Among the authors of the sample CR novels, they are the only ones who had published novels before the Cultural Revolution. Hao Ran was the best-known novelist during the Cultural Revolution, and his pre-CR novel *The Sun Shines Bright* and CR novel *The Golden Road* were the best-known novels in the period. Both novels were criticized by some scholars after the Cultural Revolution for being excessively marked by ideological flavour.[4] However, the present investigation shows that from the linguo-stylistic point of view, the two novels have low rates of ideological expressions compared to other works. Among the seven CR novels, *The Golden Road* has the lowest density of ideological items. The rates of ideological items in some sample CR novels, such as *Evergreen*, *Mountains Green after Rain* and *The Mountains and Rivers Roar*, are about twice that in *The Golden Road*. The density in *The Golden Road* is even lower than the pre-CR novel *The Builders*.

DISTRIBUTION OF IDEOLOGICAL ITEMS BY CHARACTER

In the present investigation, I have selected four characters from each novel in order to compare the distribution of ideological expressions among them: an Old Poor Peasant, a Young Woman, the Main Hero, and the Main Villain (see Table 9). As for the procedure and criteria of selection, the Main Hero and the Main Villain are clear-cut in the novels (see Chapter 5 for the identification of the Main Villain). But for the other two, the following principles are set to maintain comparability among the corresponding characters of the ten novels:

i) Both the Old Poor Peasant and the Young Woman are generally supposed to be the most active among the characters of similar ages, for example, in talking and thinking more than the others. With the principles ii) and iii) below taken into consideration simultaneously, the Old Poor Peasant and the Young Woman are not necessarily from the positive core group elaborated on in Chapter 5, although some do belong to the core.

ii) For the Old Poor Peasant, preference is given to those who are uneducated, and without political status, because literacy and political position would enhance the speakers' ideological vocabulary. For this reason, from *The Mountains and Rivers Roar*, I select Du-er Lao Xiong rather than Lu Linhan because the latter is a village Party secretary, although he has more monologue than the former. In *The Long Rainbow*, of Shi Longfu and Shi Fengyang, two close friends who are both active old poor peasants, the latter is selected because the former is a Party member and was once the chairman of the peasant association of the village during the Land Reform.

iii) For the Young Woman, emphasis was placed on progressive women, who are supposed to represent the new generation with a new spirit, new views, and new behaviour. They are usually open-minded and outspoken, conducting support activities for the main heroes. For this reason, from *The Roaring Songhua River*, Liu Yingzi was selected instead of Li Xiaojun because as a Party member and the head of the shock youth brigade, she has the same typical characteristics in her social activities as the selected young women in the other novels, whereas the latter mainly conducts activities against her backward parents, although she talks more than Liu Yingzi.

Before further considering the distribution under discussion, the following incidental fact observed from the statistics needs to be pointed out, although it relates more to characterization than to stylistics: There is no wide gap between the total quantities of words uttered by the Old Poor Peasant and the Young Woman between a CR novel and a pre-CR novel (see Table 9 – 1.2).[5] However, big differences in the total numbers of words by the Main Hero and the Main Villain exist between CR novels and pre-CR novels, i.e. the numbers of words spoken by these two character types in a CR novel are greater than in a pre-CR novel.[6] This phenomenon is in keeping with the characterization characteristics of CR novels in which special prominence is given to main heroes, intensifying the contradiction between main heroes and main villains, and allocating more speech to the main characters (ref. Chapter 5).

As for the distribution of ideological items by the representative characters, according to the statistical results (see Table 9), the rates under the Main Hero in both groups rank first. This fact reveals that the authors of both pre-CR novels and CR novels paid attention to the ideological style of the main heroes' language. The situation, however, is even more conspicuous in CR novels. As shown in Table 9 – 2.1, the rate in Group II is nearly twice as much as that of Group I (4.30% vs. 2.39%). Meanwhile, no exception can be found from the distribution of the individual works, i.e. the lowest rate in Group II (2.93%, *The Golden Road*) is higher than the highest one in Group I (2.81%, *The Builders*).

A striking difference concerning the ideological style of the main heroes' language between the two groups is the way of speaking, i.e. the main heroes in CR novels often make long speeches with a high density of ideological expressions, especially in meetings which are a kind of popular form of class struggle or other political campaign. For example, in *The Mountains and Rivers Roar*, the main hero Liu Wangchun makes a long speech, which covers about seven pages, amounting to 2,026 words.[7] The number is more than the total number of words (2,023) spoken by Liu Yusheng, the main hero in *Great Changes in a Mountain Village*, and is over one-third of the total number of words (5,948) spoken by the main hero Liang Shengbao in *The Builders*. In the long speech by Liu Wangchun, there are 139 ideological items, 2.4 times as many as the total ideological items spoken by Liu Yusheng, and eighty-three percent of all ideological items attributed to Liang Shengbao.

Under the Main Villain, the rates of ideological items of both groups are similar (Group I, 1.57%; Group II, 1.74%). However, among the four categories of selected characters, the rate of Group I under the Main Villain ranks second, but the rate of Group II ranks last. Why do the main villains in CR novels use far fewer ideological expressions than the other three types of characters? The reason could be that the authors took the use of ideological expressions as a way of characterization, i.e. a positive aspect shown by characters, and paid attention to the ideological identities of characters in the distribution of the items.

The above analysis could be confirmed by the following two facts: (1) Within Group II, the main villains Jia Weimin in *The Roaring Songhua River*, Zhao Deming in *The Long Rainbow*, and Long Youtian in *The Mountains and Rivers Roar* use comparatively more ideological expressions. The authors certainly considered the three characters' open political identity, that of Party cadres. They thus need to use ideological expressions when they speak in public. (2) Distinct differences exist in the semantic range of the ideological items used by main villains and by positive characters. For example, the villains often use non-time specific expressions, seldom use positive political campaign slogans, and never mention or quote Mao.

Under both Old Poor Peasant and Young Woman, the rates of ideological items of Group II are around three times as much as those of Group I (see Table 9 – 2.2). As for the individual novels, even the highest rates under the two categories in Group I are lower than the lowest in Group II.

It is appropriate that the young women's speeches are full of ideological items in the CR novels because of their higher educational standard and political positions (usually, secretary of the Youth League, or head of the shock youth brigade etc.). It might be thought awkward, however, for an old poor peasant, often illiterate and without political status, to use a large quantity of ideological expressions, even including a large number of rather specialized political terms. For example, the following passage spoken by Du-er Lao Xiong in *The Mountains and Rivers Roar* sounds more like a speech by an educated Party cadre than an illiterate poor peasant.

(3) *Da gan da bian <u>xue Dazhai</u>, women jiujing xue shenme? . . . Dazhai de jiben jingyan shi san tiao: <u>zhengzhi guashuai</u>, <u>sixiang lingxian</u> de <u>yuanze</u>; <u>jianku fendou</u>, <u>zi li geng sheng</u> de <u>jingshen</u>; ai <u>guojia</u>, ai <u>jiti</u> de <u>gongchanzhuyi</u> fengge. Dazhai de tongzhi shuo de hao: Du bu zhu <u>zibenzhuyi</u> de lu, jiu mai bu kai <u>shehuizhuyi</u> de bu . . . Jintian women gongdi shang, shi an <u>Mao Zhuxi</u> de <u>jiaodao</u>, an <u>dang</u> de <u>jiben luxian</u> lai zhi shan zhishui da fanshen zhang? Haishi jixu gao <u>xiuzhengzhuyi</u> <u>hei xian</u> na yi tao? Zhihuibu li dang toutou de, ke bu yao ba women sheyuan yin dao <u>zibenzhuyi</u> de xielu shang qu ya, yao dailing dajia ben <u>shehuizhuyi</u> de da mubiao!*

[We get going and go all out to learn from Dazhai, but what on earth should we learn? . . . The basic experience of Dazhai consists of three aspects: the principle of putting politics in command and thought in the lead, the spirit of working hard and relying on one's own efforts, and the communist style of loving the country and loving the collective. The comrades of Dazhai said rightly: If you don't block the way to capitalism, you can't move a step along the socialist road . . . Today, on our construction site, should we follow Chairman Mao's teachings and the Party's basic line to transform mountains and tame rivers, or should we go on carrying out the same old black line of revisionism? The heads of the project headquarters must not lead our commune members to the evil ways of capitalism, but lead us in the direction of the great goal of socialism.] (J, pp. 266–7)

Such being the case, it is evident that the authors emphasized class identity more than other necessary conditions or potential such as educational background with regard to the frequent use of ideological expressions.

DISTRIBUTION OF HIGH-FREQUENCY IDEOLOGICAL ITEMS

I have investigated eighty-two high-frequency ideological items in order to reveal some distributive differences in semantic characteristics between CR novels and pre-CR novels (see Table 10). Quantitatively, an item listed in the table must appear at least ten times in one or more novels. Four semantic features are labelled: Time Specific, Non-time Specific, Meaning Specific, and Quasi-meaning Specific, which are defined as follows:

i)   Time Specific indicates that an item came into being and was prevalent at a specific time (usually in a specific political campaign).
      Examples: *Tugai* [the Land Reform], *dangan* [individual farming], *Dayuejin* [the Great Leap Forward], *Hongweibing* [the Red Guards], *zouzipai* [capitalist-roader].

ii) Non-time Specific indicates that an item's emergence and usage were not related to a specific time or campaign.
      Examples: *jieji* [class], *luxian* [line], *douzheng* [struggle], *geming* [revolution], *shehuizhuyi* [socialism].

iii) Meaning Specific indicates that an item's literal meaning concerns politics and ideology.
      Examples: *gongchandang* [the Communist Party], *Mao Zhuxi* [Chairman Mao], *gongchanzhuyi* [communism], *Wenhua Da Geming* [the Cultural Revolution].

iv) Quasi-meaning Specific indicates that an item has a metaphoric meaning or colouring concerning politics and ideology, although it does not have a literal political or ideological meaning.

Examples: *daolu* [road], *fangxiang* [orientation], *xuexi* [study], *lichang* [stand].

Time Specific is related to Meaning Specific, and Quasi-meaning Specific is related to Non-time Specific. However, not every Meaning Specific item is Time Specific although all Time Specific items are Meaning Specific. Similarly, all Quasi-meaning Specific items are Non-time Specific, but quite a few Non-time Specific items are Meaning Specific.

The statistics show that the rates of Group II under Time Specific and Meaning Specific are lower than those of Group I, but higher under Non-time Specific and Quasi-meaning Specific. The gap concerning 'meaning' is wider than that concerning 'time' (see Table 10.2). According to the results, and by comparison of the two groups, we can draw the following two general semantic characteristics about the ideological expressions:

Firstly, the ideological expressions in CR novels are on the more specialized semantic level. Time Specific generally covers those items relating to current political campaigns and slogans, and Non-time Specific mainly covers items of ideological terminology and the items with ideologically metaphoric meaning or colouring (Quasi-meaning Specific). The latter, the items of ideological terminology and the Quasi-meaning Specific items evidently have more theoretically political flavour than the former, the names of current campaigns and slogans. Therefore, the ideological expressions in the CR novels, which have higher rates under Non-time Specific and Quasi-meaning Specific, have consequently more specialized or theorized ideological colour. The following example is from a family dialogue in *The Roaring Songhua River*:

> (4) (To save space, the original is omitted here).
> [Zhao Yun held Chairman Mao's book, with her bright eyes glistening, and said: 'Chairman Mao says: "In the ideological field, the class struggle between proletariat and bourgeoisie is still protracted, complicated, and sometimes even acute." This means that even if the landlords and rich peasants all died, the class struggle in the ideological sphere would still exist.'
>
> 'Right!' Zhao Guang'en gave a pleased look at his niece, and nodded his head: 'Even if the old landlords and rich peasants all died, a new class enemy would appear. As to the class struggle in the ideological sphere, it would be still more complicated . . .'
>
> 'Auntie, you may wonder why Li Fugui is always thinking of making a mercenary marriage for his daughter, and trying to marry her off in the city?'
>
> 'It's because of his notorious bourgeois ideas.'
>
> 'Right, you may also wonder why Sister Yingzi, Zhinong, and

Guoyou, who studied at school, and deserve to be called intellectuals, are willing to work in the countryside for all their life? . . .'

'Oh, that is clear! It's because of the good ideas taught by Chairman Mao and the Party, which are our proletarian good ideas.'

'Right, the struggle between the two ideas is precisely the struggle in the sphere of ideology.'

'Hey, that means that after all the landlords die, the bad ideas will still struggle with those of our poor peasants and farm labourers for several generations . . . Just now, Suozhu said that Yu Bapi had tried to imbue his grandson with landlord class ideas. That is class struggle in the ideological sphere, isn't it?'

'Mum's right.' The eighteen-year-old Suozhu interrupted his mother. 'That means that struggle is necessary because the landlord class wants to remould the world according to their ideology, but we want to remould the world according to proletarian ideology. The struggle . . .'

Zhao Guang'en said: 'It's early days yet! In my opinion, we must struggle until the abolition of classes and the realization of communism.']
(F, pp. 336–7).

The topic of this dialogue is the so-called 'protracted and complex nature of class struggle'. It does not include any Time Specific items but is full of items of ideological terminology and Quasi-meaning Specific words and expressions. The ideological style permeating this dialogue is obviously different from that reflected in those family conversations in the pre-CR novels, which usually focus on the current campaigns and include repeated Time Specific items, such as *huzhuzu* [mutual aid team], *nongyeshe* [agricultural producers' cooperative], *rushe* [join the agricultural producers' cooperative].

Secondly, the ideological expressions in CR novels cover a more extensive semantic range. Under Meaning Specific, further observation shows that although the rates concerning frequency (the frequency under Meaning Specific to the total frequency of the eighty-two items) in the CR novels are lower, the rates of the items (the items under Meaning Specific to the eighty-two items) are much higher than those in pre-CR novels. The reason is that some items which came into being during the Cultural Revolution could not possibly appear in the pre-CR novels, but the items which emerged before the Cultural Revolution might appear in the CR novels. Thus, the semantic range covered by the ideological expressions in the CR novels is larger. For example, the following speech could not be found in a pre-CR novel:

(5) (To save space, the original is omitted).
[The Great Proletarian Cultural Revolution is a great revolutionary practice combating and preventing revisionism . . . Whenever a mighty mass movement had achieved a great victory, some people would come

out on the counterattack to settle old scores. There always appeared a struggle about whether to negate or to affirm the revolutionary movement, which was actually a struggle between progress and retrogression, or between restoration of the old order and opposition of the restoration. It almost became a law. Can you all remember the following things: The Great Leap Forward in 1958 was a great mass movement. But less than one year later, the capitalist-roader within the Party, Peng Dehuai, came out into the open, coordinating the class enemies in society, and stirred up an evil trend of Right opportunism, preaching that 'people's communes were set up too early', 'the Great Leap Forward left things in a mess', and supporting a return to individual farming. At the Tenth Plenary Session of the Eighth Central Committee, Chairman Mao issued a great call 'Be sure not to forget class struggle', and dealt head-on blows to Liu Shaoqi and Peng Dehuai's Right opportunist line. The evil trend was then stopped, and the achievements of the Great Leap Forward were consolidated. Today, the Great Proletarian Cultural Revolution is going forward both inside and outside the Party. There appear various revisionist phenomena of retrogression, and an evil trend of negating the Cultural Revolution . . .] (J, pp. 427–8)

This paragraph includes a lot of Time Specific items concerning past political events but few items of ideological terminology, which seems to accord with the feature of the pre-CR novels. But the items in it cover much more extensive political content, because they relate to a series of campaigns which concerned different periods or phases, and could not be included in pre-CR novels. The ideological style formed by these expressions and their extensive semantic range is thus very different from that of pre-CR novels.

Next, further investigation into the distribution of some specific high-frequency items shows some specific findings concerning semantic range:[8]

i)   The total frequency of the items including the morpheme -zhuyi [-ism] in one CR novel is 3.9 times on average as much as in a pre-CR novel (175.3 vs. 45.3 for one novel). The items include *shehuizhuyi* [socialism] (excluding *shehuizhuyi*- in *Shehuizhuyi Jiaoyu Yundong* [the Socialist Education Movement]), *zibenzhuyi* [capitalism], *gongchanzhuyi* [communism], *Makesi-Lieningzhuyi* [Marxism-Leninism], and *xiuzhengzhuyi* [revisionism]. This fact conforms with the characteristic stated above that CR novels have higher rates of specialized ideological terms.

ii) The frequency of items referring to Mao and Mao's thought in a CR novel is on average 6.2 times that of a pre-CR novel (116.9 vs. 19). The items are *Mao Zhuxi* [Chairman Mao], *Mao Zedong*, *Mao Zedong Sixiang* [Mao Zedong Thought], and *(weida) lingxiu* [(great) leader]. This fact is attributed to the idolatry of Mao, which reached a new level during the Cultural

Revolution.[9] In novels, it is not only shown in characters' psychology and action, but also reflected in characters' speeches and narrators' narration. In rhetoric, firstly, various epithets are added to Mao, such as *weida lingxiu* [great leader], *ta laorenjia* [literally, he the old man], *nin laorenjia* [literally, you the old man], *jing'ai de* [beloved]. Secondly, a large number of phrasal expressions containing *Mao Zhuxi* [Chairman Mao] / *Mao Zedong* as a constituent appear in CR novels. For example, we may find the following nominal phrases with *Mao Zhuxi* [Chairman Mao] as an attributive adjunct from *Mountains Green after Rain*:

> *Mao Zhuxi de zhishi* [Chairman Mao's instructions] (p. 12), *Mao Zhuxi de shu* [Chairman Mao's books] (p. 14), *Mao Zhuxi de haozhao* [Chairman Mao's calls] (p. 94), *Mao Zhuxi de hua* [Chairman Mao's words] (p. 97), *Mao Zhuxi de jiaodao* [Chairman Mao's teaching] (p. 95), *Mao Zhuxi de luxian* [Chairman Mao's line] (p. 507), *Mao Zhuxi yulu* [quotations from Chairman Mao] (p. 448), *Mao Zhuxi de zhuzuo* [Chairman Mao's works] (p. 457).

Use of the items concerning Mao is related to the characters' ideological identities. In other words, idolatry of Mao is the privilege of positive characters. For instance, the item *Mao Zhuxi* [Chairman Mao] occurs over 700 times in the seven CR novels, but issues not once from the mouth of a negative character. Even those negative characters who take open political status and administrative positions never use expressions concerning Mao. The idolatry of Mao relating to the ideological style of CR novels' language is also reflected in the fact that Mao's words are frequently quoted (see the following section).

iii) The frequency of items indicating general concepts about class struggle in one CR novel is on average 5.5 times as much as that in a pre-CR novel (284.6 vs. 51.7). The items include *jieji* [class], *wuchanjieji* [the proletariat] (excluding *wuchanjieji-* in *Wuchanjieji Wenhua Da Geming* [the Great Proletarian Cultural Revolution]), *zichanjieji* [the bourgeoisie], *jieji douzheng* [class struggle], *jieji diren* [class enemy], *dou* [struggle], *douzheng* [struggle]. During the Cultural Revolution, class struggle was stressed to an unprecedented degree,[10] and was also the general motif of CR literature. This is the reason for the high distribution of the above items in CR novels, which imbues more 'fighting flavour' into the ideological style of CR novels' language. The other three words which also relate somewhat to class struggle are *geming* [revolution], *qunzhong* [the masses], and *yundong* [movement]. Their total frequency in one CR novel is on average 3.2 times as much as in a pre-CR novel (346.6 vs. 109).

iv) The frequency of items referring to the Party, the Youth League, and membership of them in a CR novel is on average 0.83 times that of a pre-CR novel. The items include *gongchandang* [the Communist Party], *dang* [the

Party], *gongchandangyuan* [member of the Communist Party], *dangyuan* [Party member], *gongqingtuan* [the Communist Youth League], *qingniantuan* [the Youth League], *tuan* [the League], *gongqingtuanyuan* [member of the Communist Youth League], *qingniantuanyuan* [member of the Youth League], and *tuanyuan* [League member]. It is surprising that such items appear less frequently in the CR novels than in the pre-CR novels. The reason for this could be explained as follows: Firstly, the extreme adulation of Mao overshadowed the authority of the Party. Secondly, other organizations such as the Red Guards and the shock youth brigades make the Youth League appear less important.

v) The frequency of items indicating class status in a CR novel is on average 0.63 times that of a pre-CR novel. The items include *pinnong* [poor peasant], *pingunong* [poor peasants and farm labourers], *pin-xiazhongnong* [poor and lower-middle peasants][11], *zhongnong* [middle peasant], *shangzhongnong* [upper-middle peasant], *fuyuzhongnong* [rich-middle peasant], *funong* [rich peasant], and *dizhu* [landlord]. The lower rate in CR novels seems to contradict the fact that the motif of class struggle is much more emphasized in CR novels than in pre-CR novels as stated above. An explanation could be the different forms of class struggle in the novels of the two groups. The class conflict and relations reflected in pre-CR novels exist between the various classes which were classified in the Land Reform. In CR novels, however, class struggle is interwoven with line struggle, which was then taken to be the new form of class struggle under the dictatorship of proletariat.[12] Although there still exist some old conflicts and relations between various classes as in pre-CR novels, a new more important 'class confrontation' runs through the stories of CR novels, i.e. the contradiction between poor peasants and the Party leaders taking the capitalist road. This could be the reason why, in CR novels, the items referring to class status set in the Land Reform have lower frequency.

QUOTATIONS FROM MAO

Frequent quotation from Mao in CR novels is another relevant aspect of the ideological style of the novels' language. In the previous sections, for convenience of counting, only the defined ideological items included in the quotations from Mao were taken into account together with other ideological items. In fact, holistically, quotations from Mao may be regarded as ideological stylistic components, because, according to CR fashion, Mao's speeches were quoted as the most authoritative ideological norm to highlight speeches and conversation.

Below is a special investigation into the quantity of the whole quotations and Chinese characters included in them. For precision in counting, only the contents with formal marks are taken into consideration, which include two situations:

i)   Direct quotations with quotation marks. In CR novels, the quotations are all printed in boldface type in addition to quotation marks. These include words, sentences, or paragraphs from Mao's speeches or articles (see H, p. 579, and E, p. 135), and also lines from his poetry, which only appear in the CR novels (see F, p. 378).

ii) The titles of Mao's articles with double angle brackets (not in boldface type). For example, «*Zai Yan'an Wenyi Zuotanhui shang de jianghua*» [Talks at the Yan'an Forum on Literature and Art] (D, p. 198), and «*Maodun lun*» [On Contradiction] (G, p. 371). Some book titles which were not given by Mao in person are not counted. For example, «*Mao Zedong xuanji*» [*Selected Works of Mao Zedong*] (E, p. 546), «*Mao Zedong zhuzuo xuandu (yi zhong ben)*» [*Selected Readings of Mao Zedong (second version)*] (H, p. 13).

As shown in Table 11 – 2, the number of quotations from Mao in each of the seven CR novels is on average over eleven times as much as in a pre-CR novel (19.1 vs. 1.7), and the average quantity of characters of the quotations in the CR novels is more than seven times as much as in the pre-CR novels (650.9 vs. 90.7).

As for the individual works (see Table 11 – 1), among the pre-CR novels, Zhou Libo's *Great Changes in a Mountain Village* ranks first in number of quotations, and Liu Qing's *The Builders* ranks first in number of Chinese characters of the quotations. Surprisingly, Hao Ran's *The Sun Shines Bright* has no quotations from Mao. The CR novels generally include a large number of quotations from Mao although the numbers vary greatly. Hao Ran's *The Golden Road* ranks last, but even it includes many more than any of the pre-CR novels. As to the length of texts, the longest quotation comprises 355 Chinese characters (see J, pp. 385–6), and the shortest consists of 4 (see D, p. 648).

Among all agricultural novels produced during the Cultural Revolution, *Battle Chronicles of Hongnan*, which was the first novel published during the decade, ranks first.[13] It includes 177 quotations in total (97 text quotations and 80 title quotations), totalling 6,953 Chinese characters. In fact, the density of the quotations is so great that there is one quotation per 2,200 Chinese characters in the novel. This novel is claimed by post-CR critics to be 'purely politicised' and to have 'a preaching style'.[14]

Indirect quotations (i.e. without quotation marks) of Mao in the CR novels are by no means fewer than direct quotations in number, but they are too indefinite to ascertain precisely, especially concerning the number of Chinese characters, although their ideological style is established. For example,

(6) *Shijie shang, renhe shiwu, renhe difang dou shi chongman zhe maodun de,*

youqi shi jieji maodun, geng shi cunzai yu zhengge shehui zhi zhong. Zhe zhong maodun, houjin danwei you, xianjin danwei you, guoqu you, xianzai you, jianglai hai hui you! Mao Zhuxi shuo le, maodun shi pubian de, douzheng shi juedui de.
[In the world, everything and everywhere are full of contradictions, especially class contradiction. Such contradiction exists in both backward and advanced units, and in the past, the present and even the future. Chairman Mao said that contradictions existed ubiquitously, and struggles absolutely.] (G, p. 371)

In form, it seems that only the last sentence is an indirect quotation because it uses the introductory words 'Mao Zhuxi shuo le'. In fact, the whole paragraph might be regarded as an indirect quotation, because the whole paragraph, full of Mao's original words, is wholly an interpretation of Mao's idea, made by a character in analysing the class struggle in his village. The ideological meaning of both the last sentence and the whole paragraph is definite.

Moreover, in addition to Mao, Lenin is also quoted in CR novels (but never in the pre-CR novels). The direct quotations are also in boldface type (see examples in H, p. 265, and J, p. 490 and pp. 372–3).

In short, the great increase in quotations from Mao and other political figures in the CR novels intensifies the ideological colour of the novels' language.

Lastly, investigation shows that various quotations from Mao are exclusively made by narrators and positive characters in both pre-CR and CR novels (especially the main heroes in CR novels). As for negative characters, we can find some quotations from Liu Shaoqi, who was referred to during the Cultural Revolution as the 'number one capitalist roader' (see example in F, pp. 353–4). However, in pre-CR novels, quotations from Liu are only made by positive characters (see example in A, p. 117), because he was then the president of the country. The distribution pattern of quotations according to a character's ideological identity reveals from another angle the ideological nature of the quotations from Mao and other political figures in the novels, of which CR novels go even farther in degree and in kind.

Chapter 8

Idioms, Proverbs, *Xiehouyu*, and Classical Verses

THE FOUR CATEGORIES OF ITEM DEFINED

In the present investigation, the definitions and range of idioms, proverbs, *xiehouyu*, and classical verses are based on the corresponding reference books indicated in the beginning of Part II. Below are complementary counting criteria concerning each category:

i)   The forms of Chinese idioms are sometimes allowed to be modified for the sake of literary rhetoric although they are generally established.[1] Some modified forms have gradually become established variant forms, such as *ru ku han xin* reversed from *han xin ru ku* [endure all kinds of hardships], and *ba xian guo hai, ge xian qi neng* modified from *ba xian guo hai, ge xian shen tong* [like the Eight Immortals crossing the sea, each one showing his or her special prowess], which are also listed in the reference books. But some other modified forms which are not contained in reference books are individual creations, or are in the transitional stage towards being accepted variant forms. Considering that the modified forms generally have a similar linguistic style to the original idioms if the modification is within some restrictions, the rule here is that the modified idioms not in the reference books which comply with the following restrictions are also counted:

   Firstly, the modification must keep the same morphological structure as the original form. For example, '*ci qiong li qu*' [having nothing left with which to justify oneself] (E, p. 393) and '*gao fei yuan zou*' [go away to a distant place] (B, p. 215), which are reversed from the established forms *li qu ci qiong* and *yuan zou gao fei*, but keep the original coordinate structure, are taken as two items. But '*zan kou bu jue*' [be full of praise] (H, p. 307) and '*si ye bu ming mu*' [die without closing eyes, i.e. with regret] (H, p. 31), which come from *zan bu jue kou* and *si bu ming mu*, retain the original meaning but not the original structure, and are not counted.

Secondly, only one character (representing a morpheme) may be replaced within an idiom, and the substitute is usually synonymous with that being replaced. For example, '*zhan ding qie tie*' [decisively or categorically] (A, p. 39) and '*gu bu ke cui*' [indestructible] (H, p. 296), which come respectively from *zhan ding jie tie* and *jian bu ke cui*, are regarded as two items. The substitute morpheme and the whole modified form are required to have similar stylistic characteristics to the original ones, such as the above examples, otherwise they are not included in the discussion, no matter whether the phenomenon comes from coincidence or deliberate modification. For instance, '*gu qian gu hou*' [look ahead and behind — overcautious and indecisive] (C, p. 156) which might be from *zhan qian gu hou*, is not included because the former clearly has a less bookish colour than the latter. Occasionally, the substitute morpheme is not synonymous with the one replaced, but we also take the modified form under discussion if the linguistic style of the modified and original forms are alike. For example, '*chu jing shang qing*' [see something which arouses one's deep feelings] (B, p. 285) is the modification of *chu jing sheng qing* [the sight strikes a chord in one's heart], of which '*shang*' [sick at heart] and '*sheng*' [touch off] are not synonymous morphemes, but we take the modification into account.

ii) Proverbs generally consist of two forms: single-part and two-part. For the two-part forms, sometimes only one part appears, but normally their proverbial meaning and style are still determined. We take all the forms into account, i.e. each form is an item irrespective of length. Here are three examples which represent respectively the forms above:

Ruixue zhao fengnian. [A timely snow promises a good harvest.] (G, p. 514)

Ge ren zi sao men qian xue, bu guan ta ren wa shang shuang. [Each one sweeps the snow from his own doorstep and doesn't bother about the frost on his neighbour's roof.] (D, p. 352)

Youli zou bian tianxia [With justice on your side, you can go anywhere] (H, p. 513) — The second part '*wuli cun bu nan xing*' [without justice, you can't take a step], which is antithetical to the first part, is omitted.

iii) Every *xiehouyu* includes two parts, of which the first is descriptive, and the second carries the message. Usually, both parts are stated in writing, but occasionally, the second part is unstated. We take either form as a counting unit. For example,

Da niao zhengce — zheng zhi yan, bi zhi yan. [The policy of aiming at birds — with one eye opened, with another closed (it means turning a blind eye to something)] (H, p. 38)

Nuo fan cuo baba [Making cakes by kneading steamed glutinous rice] (H, p. 412) — The second part '*jiao cheng yi tuan*' [being stuck together (it means being in great confusion or disorder)] is omitted.

iv) Classical verses are quoted from three literary forms: *shi*, *ci*, and *qu*. Different counting criteria are adopted according to the sources and literary styles. For *shi*, we take the line as unit; for *ci* and *qu*, which are usually not separated into lines, we take a segment with a rhyme as a unit irrespective of length. For example,

Yue yi hua ying dong, yi shi yu ren lai. [While the moon moves, the shadow of flowers shifts; I suspect in illusion that it is the beautiful girl who is coming.] (C, p. 47) — These two lines of *shi* are taken as two units.

Mo dengxian, bai le shaonian tou, kong beiqie. [Don't fritter away your time, otherwise when you have gained hoary head, you will be sorrowful in vain.] (F, p. 194) — This segment of *ci* is taken as one unit.

Hulala, si dasha qing, han linlin, hunshen fa jin. [With a whistling sound, it is as if the mansion were collapsing; perspiring all over, she is stricken with shivering.] (G, p. 207) — These *qu* segments are taken as two units.

THE FOUR CATEGORIES ANALYSED

Idioms

Among all Chinese set phrases, idioms are the most frequently used and the most important category.[2] Readers of CR novels might expect that CR novels would include fewer idioms than pre-CR novels, because one aspect of the Cultural Revolution was its opposition to traditional literature, which is related to characteristics of Chinese idioms. In form, Chinese idioms often reflect the syntactic structures of traditional literary Chinese. They have their established syllabic and rhythmic structures, i.e. they generally consist of four syllables, and their rhythm pattern is two plus two irrespective of different grammatical and semantic structures.[3] The regular syllables and clear rhythms are one of the most prominent stylistic features of Chinese idioms. In source and meaning, a great number of idioms come from traditional literature.[4] So compared to some other vernacular set expressions such as folk proverbs and *xiehouyu*, idioms have more antique and literary colour in their literal meaning.

However, a careful reading of CR novels shows the opposite situation. This perception can be quantitatively evidenced by our statistical search. Table 12 – 2 shows that Group II has 83.52 idioms more than Group I per 100,000 characters (223.67 vs. 140.15). As for the individual works, six of the seven CR novels have higher rates than the three pre-CR novels. Only in *The Long Rainbow* which ranks last in Group II is the rate of idioms marginally lower than in *The Sun Shines Bright* (158.77 vs. 161.65). For some others, we see striking differences between them. The highest rate in Group II (*The Mountains and Rivers Roar*) is over twice that of the highest in Group I (*The Sun Shines Bright*) — 334.95 vs. 161.65, and more than three times the lowest in Group I (*The Builders*) — 334.95 vs. 110.03. We may also compare *The Golden Road* and *The Sun Shines Bright*, which were written by the same author Hao Ran. The rate of idiom-use in the former is substantially higher than that of the latter (217.58 vs. 161.65). For example, in *The Sun Shines Bright*, I have not found a sentence by the narrator with less than thirty Chinese characters which includes three idioms, but sentences such as the following are not rare in *The Golden Road*.

(1) *Ta jue zhe zhe feng xin yu wu lun ci, tong pian dou shi hu shuo ba dao, dou shi guyi daoluan, zhen shi qi you ci li.*
[He felt that the letter was incoherent, totally nonsensical and trouble-making; really, it was outrageous.] (D, p. 482)

(2) *Na xiang dao chushi bu li, yu shang le zheyang de ji feng baoyu, ba ta da le ge luohua liushui, langbei bukan.*
[He had not expected that he would unfortunately encounter such a heavy storm, which left him badly battered, and in a sorry plight.] (D, p. 610)

In addition to a high density of idioms, CR novels include more four-syllable phrases of other kinds than pre-CR novels, of which some are makeshift, but others are relatively established or semi-idiomatic. They are not as bookish as the established idioms because, unlike idioms, their sources are usually not directly related to classical literature. However, since they have the same syllabic and rhythmic structures as idioms, in form they also have the style of regularity or evenness in arrangement of phrase-forming elements. See the following example (the dot-underlined indicates the relatively established four-syllable phrases):

(3) *Tang Qun mian xiang qunzhong, ba zhe ge xiaoxi yi xuanbu, shunxi jian, huichang shang hongqi zhaozhan, luogu zhen tian, gesheng zhenzhen, bianpao qi ming. Qia shi chunlei gungun, songtao huxiao, jiao ren xinxian jidang, zhenfen buyi.*
[As soon as Tang Qun, who was facing the masses, declared the news, at the meeting place, red flags were fluttering, the sound of gongs and drums was deafening, the singing was resounding, and firecrackers were banging. It was as if the spring thunder were pealing, and the pines were soughing, which made people greatly excited and stirred.] (H, p. 585)

Why are idioms and other four-syllable phrases more prevalent in CR novels? Firstly, the vocabulary style of CR novels cannot transcend the general language fashion during the Cultural Revolution. According to post-CR scholars, '*kong*' [empty] and '*tao*' [stereotyped] are among the most prominent characteristics of the CR's general stylistic fashion.[5] The narration and description in CR novels perceivably lack minuteness and concreteness in comparison with pre-CR novels. Such style is considerably in accord with the expressive effect of idioms and formal idiom-like phrases, i.e. 'conciseness' in meaning and 'evenness' in form, which are attributed to the restriction of a fixed syllabic structure. So just as stated by some linguists, too frequent or excessive use of four-syllable phrases must reduce the minuteness and liveliness of description.[6] We may compare the following examples (unfortunately, it is difficult to differentiate the language styles properly through the translations):

(4) *Yuan shan, jin cun, conglin, tuqiu, quan dou* mengmenglonglong, *xiang shi zhao shang le tou sha . . . Yuanyuan de yuer gua zai you gao you kuo de tianshang, ba jinzi yiban de guanghui pao-sa zai shuimian shang, he shui wudong qilai, yong li ba zhe jinzi dou sui; sa shang le, dou sui, you sa shang le, you dou sui, kan qu shifen dongren.*

[The remote mountains, close villages, jungles, and hills, show a hazy view; it is as though they were covered with a gauze kerchief. The round moon is in the boundless sky, spreading golden light over the face of water; the river water is waving, breaking the gold vigorously; another sheet of gold is spread, and is again broken by the ripples; once more a new sheet of gold is spread, and is broken as before. It looks really beautiful.] (C, p. 357)

(5) *Jin ye ya, Hulongdang shang,* chunfeng qing fu, wei bo pai an, *man jiang li bu jian le ban ren gao de baitou lang, zhen ge shi* xi lang qian chong, liushui juanjuan, *xiang zai qingsu, xiang zai yinchang . . . Tianshang* fan xing zhayan, *yueliang pu sa xia* wan li qinghui, *yingzhao zhe* yi jiang chunshui, dou jun yan bi *. . .*

[Tonight, on Hulongdang, there are breezes stroking faces and ripples touching the shores. The tall terrifying waves have vanished. It is really a scene of thousands of ripples, and of soft flowing water, as though they were telling and singing lightly . . . In the sky, stars are glittering; the moon spreads a vast light covering the spring water of the river and the precipitous cliff.] (J, p. 532)

Both paragraphs are descriptions of night views of countryside. (4) has few four-syllable phrases, and presents a minute portrayal, but (5) is full of four-syllable phrases, and the 'empty' (sweeping or general) flavour is evident compared to (4). The last sentence of each passage (the original), which describes the bright moonlight over the river water, presents the reader with a sharp contrast in language style.

Secondly, in CR novels, conflicts between people are emphasized; people's speeches and dialogues include many criticisms of others. The criticisms are often full of overstated remarks with short and parallel structures, which sound forceful and overbearing. Idioms rhetorically possess the characteristics. A speech such as the one which follows, with so many idioms and four-syllable phrases, and so bookish a colour, directed towards a subordinate by a countryside cadre (commune secretary) in *Mountains Green after Rain*, cannot be found in pre-CR novels.

(6) *Ni de suo zuo suo wei, qishi zao jiu zai qunzhong dangzhong jiyuan hen shen, yijian fenfen le! Gan gongzuo hao da xi gong, bu gu keguan guilü, duduan zhuan xing. Rujin nao qi zheng di jiufen, qunzhong sixiang bodong, jiu shi ni zi xing qi shi de eguo! Dui ganbu paichi daji, dui qunzhong mo bu guanxin, piantan si ji . . . Zhexie, jiushi Longrong qunzhong gei ni de pinglun! Yi ge ren lü fan cuowu, que bu si huigai, fan'er qiao yan ling se, jili xishua, shenzhi dao da yi pa, zhe shi shenme taidu? Zai wo mianqian shangqie ruci, geng ke xiang zai Longrong shi hedeng feiyang bahu le!*
[The masses have had a lot of complaints about what you did for a long time! Disregarding objective laws, you have a fondness for the grandiose, and like to make arbitrary decisions and take peremptory actions. Now the quarrel about land boundaries, which upsets the masses, is precisely the evil consequence of your arbitrary action! Discriminating against other cadres, you are indifferent to the masses and partial to your personal friends . . . All these are comments on you by the Longrong masses! You have made mistakes again and again, but you have no intention of mending your ways; on the contrary, you have a glib tongue, try to gloss over your faults, and even make unfounded countercharges. What is this sort of attitude? Even to my face, you are so rude, I can thus imagine how arrogant and domineering you are in Longrong!] (H, p. 488)

The reason for criticism could also explain the fact that in CR novels the proportion of emotionally coloured idioms, in particular the rate of derogatory idioms, is greater by a big margin than in pre-CR novels.

Thirdly, as noted in Chapter 4, during the Cultural Revolution, improvised or self-written poems and slogans were prevalent. Scenes of reciting improvised poems, singing improvised songs, staging self-written plays, and shouting or showing slogans are popular in CR novels. Such forms also emphasize the evenness of syllabic and rhythmic structures. Idioms and relatively established phrases are good materials for the requirements of the forms. For example,

(7) *Feng bo lang li zhan shuang chi! Huohai daoshan wo gan chuang!*
[Fly through the wind and waves! I dare to climb a mountain of swords or plunge into a sea of flames!] (G, p. 219 — from an improvised poem)

(8) *Daoshan huohai* ye gan chuang. *Zhaoqi pengbo* gan geming . . .
[Dare to climb a mountain of swords or plunge into a sea of flames.
Make revolution vigorously . . .] (H, p. 33 — from an improvised song)

(9) *Liu Shuji, lin wei bu ju, fen bu gu shen jiu taren!*
[Facing danger fearlessly, and disregarding his own safety, Secretary Liu
rescued others!] (H, p. 454 — from a self-written play)

(10) *Zi li geng sheng, fenfa tuqiang, da gu ganjin, zhansheng chun huang* . . .
[Rely on our own efforts, work hard for the prosperity of our country,
go all out, and overcome spring famine . . .] (F, p. 26 — slogans)

Bearing some relation to the fashion in poetry and slogans, CR novels
definitely include more even sentences. In particular, the rhetorical formula
dui'ou [antithesis] is prevalent in narration, description, and even dialogue.[7]
Idioms and relatively established four-syllable phrases are also suitable elements
for antithetical forms due to their evenness of syllables and rhythms.[8] Most
examples above also illustrate the evenness and parallelism of the sentence
patterns. Below is another example which includes three antithetical
constructions (the capitalized expressions are idioms or four syllable phrases):

(11) *Zhexie changqing guo mu, jing dong bu diao:* MANTIAN FENG XUE, *da bu
diao ta de* TONGTONG YU GUAN; YANSHUANG LINLIE, *ta yuefa xian de*
CANGCUI YU DI. *Suoyi, rujin si shi ba jie, lai zi ge tiao zhanxian de* NANNÜ
GANBU, *lai zi bu tong gangwei de* LAO JIANG XIN BING, *zou jin xianwei jiguan
dayuan, dou shi man yan you lü, gandao* CHUNYI ANGRAN, SHENGJI BOBO.
[These evergreen fruit trees have not withered through the winter. The
strong wind and whirling snow cannot destroy their luxuriant crowns;
in the piercingly cold frost, they are still fresher and greener. So, now
all the year, the male and female cadres from various fronts, and the
veterans and the recruits from different posts, can see the green sight
full of spring air and vitality, when they enter the compound of the
county committee.] (J, p. 417)

In Chapter 4 we attributed the emphasis of main heroes' temperamental
quality of poetic association partly to the promotion of Mao's poetry and the
popularization of the model Peking operas. From a linguistic point of view, the
lines of Mao's poetry are in the classical style, and the language of the model
Peking operas, including monologue, dialogue and libretto, is full of poetic/lyric
style. We have grounds to conclude that the trend towards literary and poetic
language in CR novels, which is represented by more idioms and other literary
and poetic elements, is partly attributable to the promotion of Mao's poetry and
the popularization of the model Peking operas.

Lastly, in addition to having a different distribution of idioms, CR novels
also have a different density and distribution of some other stylistic categories

compared with pre-CR novels, as presented in other sections. For example, they have a lower density of vulgar expressions, folk proverbs, colloquial items, dialectal words, etc. More idioms in CR novels could to some extent complement the shorter distribution of other items.

Proverbs

According to Table 12 – 2, there is only a slight difference in the density of proverbs between the two groups (25.24 per 100,000 characters in Group I vs. 24.14 per 100,000 characters in Group II). While considering the individual distributions, we can see the following two rather significant points.

Firstly, *The Builders* and *Mountains Green after Rain* have an unusual density of proverbs in comparison with other novels within their respective groups. The rate in *The Builders* is so low that it is even lower than the lowest in Group II; the rate in *Mountains Green after Rain* is so high that it is even higher than the highest in Group I. The same situation also exists in the category of *xiehouyu*, which will be taken into account in the following section.

It is difficult to give a substantial argument to explain the two exceptions. The most plausible explanation is that the phenomenon relates to authors' personal language styles and the local vocabulary system of the place-setting. My investigation into Liu Qing's other works shows that they also have a low density of proverbs and *xiehouyu*.[9] *Mountains Green after Rain* was written by a 'three-in-one' group of a local government in southwest China, which is also the place-setting of the novel. According to the conventions of 'three-in-one' authorship, the writers should consult the masses widely.[10] That means that more established expressions of the locality such as folk proverbs and *xiehouyu* could possibly be put into the manuscript by some collective 'authors' (the masses). Nevertheless, I can neither obtain materials nor reach the locality to investigate the local language habits and vocabulary system which may have influenced the language of this novel.

Secondly, if we exclude the two exceptions *The Builders* and *Mountains Green after Rain*, we can see a very clear and regular pattern: all other pre-CR novels have a higher density of proverbs than all other CR novels. The previous average ratio of Group I to Group II of 25.24 vs. 24.14 becomes 32.61 vs. 18.43, and the original difference of 1.1 (25.24 minus 24.14) becomes 14.18 (32.61 minus 18.43), an increase of 12.89 times. Therefore, although Table 12 – 2 shows that the CR novels have an only slightly lower density of proverbs compared to the pre-CR novels, the actual extent of their difference is greatly blurred by the two exceptions. We may compare *The Sun Shines Bright* and *The Golden Road*, which were both written by Hao Ran who, as a well-known author before and during the Cultural Revolution, might be thought to have established his own language style in writing. The rate of the former is evidently higher than that of the latter (25 vs. 19.56).

Combining the two points above, in spite of the importance of the authors' personal styles and the probable local language characteristics of the place-setting, which could provide an explanation for the two exceptional samples, we could reasonably affirm that the period style still plays the main role in the holistic differences concerning the density and distribution of proverbs between pre-CR novels and CR novels. In short, proverbs in CR novels are less popular than in pre-CR novels.

Furthermore, Chinese proverbs can be divided into three categories according to their meaning: farming, meteorology, and social life, among which 'social life' can be divided further into three categories: admonition, local custom, and general knowledge.[11] My further investigation into the ten novels shows that no sharp contrast exists between the two groups with regard to the distribution of the different categories of proverb.

Moreover, according to various sources, proverbs may be divided into literary and folk categories. Literary proverbs are quotations from classical writings, and folk proverbs are from the sayings of working people, especially in the countryside. Owing to the difference in source, they have different stylistic characteristics. Unlike folk proverbs, which are basically formed from colloquial morphemes or words, and often have local colour, literary proverbs include quite a few literary morphemes, and have a bookish and elegant flavour. Besides the items directly quoted from classical poetry, other literary proverbs have characteristics of traditional poetic language. They have not only regular poetic grammatical and rhythmical structures (which some folk proverbs also have), but follow regular poetic tone patterns and rhyme rules, which obviously intensify the literary colour of the proverbs. Below are some examples of literary proverbs:

> *Yan guo liu sheng, ren guo liu ming* [Wild geese leave a sound after passing, man leaves fame after going] (D, p. 640). This is a sentence in *wenyan* prose (classical Chinese).
>
> *Renping fenglang qi, wen zuo diaoyu chuan* [Never mind the rising wind and waves, just sit tight in the fishing boat] (F, p. 444). This is a couplet featuring the prosodic structure of *wuyanshi* (a verse-form based on five characters per line).
>
> *Niannian you ru lin zhen ri, xinxin chang si guo qiao shi* [Always be vigilant as if being on the eve of a battle, constantly be on the alert as if walking on a dangerous bridge] (D, p. 412). This is a couplet featuring the prosodic structure of *qiyanshi* (a verse-form based on seven characters per line).

Investigation shows that with the proportion of literary proverbs among the proverbs as a whole taken into account, CR novels have a bigger proportion than pre-CR novels. That means it is the folk proverbs instead of literary proverbs that lead to the higher rates of proverbs in pre-CR novels than in CR novels.

Xiehouyu

In Table 12 – 2, we can see that the rate of *xiehouyu* in Group II is nearly twice of that in Group I (6.49 vs. 3.44). However, while considering the rates of individual works, we have no reason to conclude that the density difference is primarily attributed to the different period style because of the irregularity of individual distributions (see Table 12 – 1).

As stated above, *The Builders* and *Mountains Green after Rain* are not only exceptions in the range of proverbs used, but also in the scope of *xiehouyu*. For the CR novels, the high rate of the whole group to a great extent results from the exception *Mountains Green after Rain*, which contributes 43.98 percent of the total *xiehouyu* of the seven CR novels. Its rate is about ten times higher than that in *The Long Rainbow* (20.68 vs. 2.23) and *The Mountains and Rivers Roar* (20.68 vs. 2.30). For the pre-CR novels, the low rate of the whole group is mainly attributed to the exception *The Builders*, which has only one *xiehouyu*, accounting for 2.78 percent of the total number of the three pre-CR novels. Actually, except in *The Builders*, the rates of the other two pre-CR novels are not lower but higher than some of the CR novels. For example, as works by the same author, *The Sun Shines Bright* has a higher rate than *The Golden Road*, though the difference is not prominent (5.30 vs. 4.18). However, unlike proverbs, which, discounting the two exceptions, show a regular contrast between the two groups, the density and distribution of *xiehouyu* in the individual novels have no clear regularity after excluding the two exceptional samples.

Judging by the above irregularity within and outside the respective groups, it could be reasonably concluded that the density and distribution of *xiehouyu* in both pre-CR and CR novels depend mainly on the authors' personal language styles in writing and the local vocabulary characteristics of the place-setting.

With regard to the exceptional sample *Mountains Green after Rain*, the high density of *xiehouyu* could leave the impression that the authors introduced an excessive number of *xiehouyu* into characters' speeches, resulting in an unnatural effect.[12] For example,

> (12) *Na Wei Chaoben ting de you ren jiao ta, da zhuan tou, bian zheng da le yanjing:* 'Heyo, Zhao Tie huilai le! Wo hai yiwei ni shi <u>duan xian zhiyuan — yuan zou gao fei</u> le ne'
> Zhao Tie gu bu zhao gen ta fenbian, jingzhi wen dao: 'Ni gangcai yilu hengheng xie namen mingtang?'
> 'O, ni shi <u>banye chi huanggua, bu zhi touwei</u> ba? Cai huilai, ye nanguai! Ting wo gen ni bai.' . . .
> [Hearing someone calling him, Wei Chaoben turned round, opening wide his eyes: 'Oh, you have come back now! I thought you would be a kite with a broken string — having flown far and high.'

Zhao Tie, who had no intention of arguing with him, asked directly: 'What were you muttering just now?'

'Oh, are you like eating cucumber at midnight — unable to distinguish one end from the other? It's not surprising since you've just returned home. Let me tell you in detail.'] (H, p. 164)

Classical Verses

As in the case of idioms, my expectations before I conducted this investigation were that CR novels would include fewer classical verse quotations. However, statistical results prove the opposite. From Table 12 – 2, we can see that the rate in Group II is nearly twice as high as in Group I (1.21 vs. 0.67). Moreover, the individual rates also show a rather regular pattern by which pre-CR novels quote less classical verse than CR novels (see Table 12 – 1). For example, the rate in Hao Ran's *The Golden Road* is more than twice as much as that in his *The Sun Shines Bright* (1.10 vs. 0.42).

The classical verse quotations in CR novels come from more extensive sources and cover more formal styles (*lüshi, jueju, ci, qu,* etc.). Most of them come from famous poets such as Wang Zhihuan (H, p. 84), Li Bai (H, p. 196), Li Shen (D, p. 503), Luo Yin (G, p. 315), Wang Wei (D, p. 169), Bai Juyi (H, p. 200), Liu Zongyuan (F, p. 1), Li Shangyin (D, p. 228), Li He (H, p. 542), all from the Tang Dynasty; Yue Fei (H, p. 194), Zhu Xi (J, p. 530), both from the Song Dynasty; Guan Hanqing (E, p. 552), Wang Shifu (F, p. 370), both from the Yuan Dynasty; Feng Menglong (F, p. 429; I, p. 118), from the Ming Dynasty; and Cao Xueqin (E, p. 173; G, p. 207), from the Qing Dynasty. However, except for one line from a *lüshi* by the relatively obscure poet Zhu Qingyu (B, p. 216), from the Tang Dynasty, and two lines from a *qu* by Wang Shifu (C, p. 47), from the Yuan Dynasty, the other verse quotations in the pre-CR novels are either from anonymous folk songs (B, p. 274), or from educational poems for children (A, p. 147).

Therefore, stylistically, compared to the items in pre-CR novels, the classical verse quotations in CR novels are not only greater in quantity, but also in quality. The difference in quality can be indicated by their comparative frequency in Lü Ziyang's *Lidai shici ming ju cidian [A Dictionary of Well-known Lines of Classical Poetry through the Dynasties]* (1986):[13] Of the seven classical verse quotations in the pre-CR novels, only one (i.e. 14.29%) is included, whereas of the thirty-one classical verse quotations in the CR novels, twenty-five (i.e. 80.65%) are included.

This phenomenon can be attributed to the following three facts. Firstly, it corresponds with other characteristics of vocabulary style in CR novels, such as containing more idioms, and being more bookish, more regular, and less dialectal (see the relevant sections). It goes without saying that the holistic or comprehensive vocabulary style of CR novels is based on the complementarity and agreement of various stylistic features.

Secondly, the phenomenon is related to the character set-up of CR novels. As stated in Chapter 5, the capitalist-roader is an important type of character in CR novels. It seems to be a convention that the capitalist-roaders are described as well-educated cadres of exploitative class origins, who usually began their political life as students or teachers: they are presented as being endowed with so-called bourgeois sentiment but lacking proletarian feelings. These people are inclined to quote classical verse for inspiration or to express their mood or sentiments, as in the following examples,

> (13) *Nong Liji you da duan le Li Bao'an de hua dao: 'Jinjin jiu shi zhexie ma? Wo kan nimen shi xiang guren xie de yi ju shi: "You bao pipa ban zhe mian"! . . .'*
> [Nong Liji cut Li Bao'an short and said: 'Is that all? In my opinion, you are just as described in a classical poem : "Still holding the *pipa* (a plucked string instrument with a fretted fingerboard) covering half her face"! . . .'] (H, p. 200).
>
> (14) *Zhe shi, 'hao feng pingjie li, song wo shang qingyun', Xue Baochai de zhe liang ju shi, zai ta naozi li shan guo. Ta hen xihuan zhe liang ju shi, juede you yi zhong piaopiao yu xian de yijing, feichang de he kouwei.*
> [At this time, Xue Baochai's couplet 'the favourable wind relies on outside force, it helps me have a meteoric rise' flashed through his mind. He liked the couplet very much, feeling as if he were on wings, and thinking that the couplet perfectly suited his taste.] (E, p. 173)
>
> (15) *Jia Weimin zeze you sheng de zanshang zhe, 'A, zhe yi fu bu shi "Chang ting song bie" ma? "Bi yun tian, huanghua di, xifeng jin, bei yan nan fei, . . ."' Jia Weimin zai xinli yinyong zhe «Xi xiang ji» li de quzi, yi zhong moluo jieji de shanggan qingxu youran er sheng.*
> [Jia Weimin said in praise, clicking his tongue, 'Ah, this is a painting of "Farewell in the Long Pavilion", isn't it? "A clear blue sky, a chrysanthemum-covered land, the westerly wind is blowing hard, and the northern wild geese are flying south, . . ."' As Jia Weimin chanted the lines from *The Romance of the Western Chamber* [*Xi xiang ji*], a kind of sentimental regret for a class in decline welled up in his mind.] (F, p. 370)

It is known that Mao himself composed poems in traditional classical form, but he encouraged young people to write free verse in the vernacular. Although the main heroes' 'artistic quality' as regards poetry is emphasized in CR novels as analysed in Chapter 4, the quality mainly refers to poetic association and to the ability to write or recite improvised vernacular poems instead of classical poems. Moreover, although the educated villains of CR novels are described as being inclined to recite classical verses, they have never been presented as having the 'artistic quality' of writing poems by themselves, either in classical or in vernacular form.

Lastly, the situation is related to other current writings during the period, which at times include classical verse quotations. For example, verses from *The Dream of the Red Chamber* were often quoted in political articles, especially the critical writings which were then very important and popular.[14] Correspondingly, of the thirty-one items in the CR novels, five are from *The Dream of the Red Chamber*. These five items were frequently quoted in current writing in newspapers and political magazines. Two lines from Tang poems, '*shan yu yu lai feng man lou*' [the wind sweeping through the tower heralds a rising storm in the mountains], and '*xin you ling xi yi dian tong*' [hearts which have a common beat are linked] were also frequently quoted in political articles, both with some change to their original meaning or colour. The former was used to symbolize the imminence of serious political struggle, while the latter was applied to mutual understanding between discredited people. Thus we cannot exclude the influence of such popularity of the two lines while considering their quotation in the CR novels (H, p. 542; D, p. 228).

The Distribution of Idioms in Narration/Description and Dialogue/Monologue

As stated above, idioms are the most important category of established phrases in Chinese. Through the above investigation concerning the density of the three categories of established phrases (idioms, proverbs and *xiehouyu*), we have seen that the most regular and contrastive differences between pre-CR and CR novels exist in idioms.

The language of fiction can be divided into narration/description and dialogue/monologue, of which the former may be called narrators' language, and the latter characters' language. On the basis of the above analysis of the trend that CR novels have a higher density of idioms than pre-CR novels, I have studied the distribution of idioms between narrators' and characters' language (see Table 13).

The statistics show that there is a gap between the increase of idioms in narrators' language and the increase of idioms in characters' language in the CR novels. On the basis of Table 13 – 2, we may make two comparisons. Firstly, the total numbers of idioms in Group II vs. Group I are 5,717 vs. 1,466, i.e. the average increase is 3.9 times. But, the numbers of idioms by narrators in Group II vs. Group I are 3,560 vs. 1,062 (3.35 times, less than the average increase), whereas the numbers of idioms by characters in Group II vs. Group I are 2,157 vs. 404 (5.34 times, higher than the average increase). Secondly, in the narrators' language, the proportion of idioms to the total is lower in Group II than in Group

I (62.27% vs. 72.44%); for the proportion of idioms in characters' language to the total, Group II has a higher rate than Group I (37.73% vs. 27.56%). The differences are also confirmed by the individual distributions although there are some marginal exceptions which can be reasonably ignored.

In brief, the above analysis reveals that in the tendency towards a higher density of idioms in CR novels, characters' language goes still farther than narrators' language. The situation concerning the distribution of idioms in characters' language will be discussed further in the next section.

The Distribution of Idioms by Character

In Chapter 7 we analysed the distribution of ideological expressions by four types of representative character. In this section we investigate the distribution of idioms by the same four categories of character: Main Hero, Main Villain, Old Poor Peasant, and Young Woman.

Firstly, we refer to Tables 14 – 2.1 and 14 – 2.2, and compare the rates horizontally, i.e. the distribution over the characters within respective groups. We can see that the rankings of distribution rates between the two groups are the same, that is, from the highest to the lowest: Main Villain, Main Hero, Old Poor Peasant and Young Woman. Interestingly, unlike the rankings of ideological items, by which the rates under Main Hero rank first in both groups, the rates of idioms by Main Villain rank first in both groups, but for the distribution of ideological expressions by Main Villain, the rate in Group I ranks second, and the rate in Group II ranks last.

A possible reason why the rates of idioms by Main Villain rank first is educational background. As noted before, most Chinese idioms relate to literary documentation, especially to traditional literature. Normally, the main villains are from the exploiting class, which allows them to be better educated than the positive characters, who are generally from poor peasant families.

Among the other three types of character, Main Hero ranks first, Old Poor Peasant second, and Young Woman last. It is readily understandable that the rate of the Main Hero is higher than that of the Old Poor Peasant, because Old Poor Peasant is generally illiterate, while Main Hero, old or young, is literate. However, it seems difficult to understand why Young Woman ranks last, because this character always has a primary or middle school education. One explanation could be that some authors intentionally try to portray a new image in young women, stressing their challenge to traditional thought and culture. In other words, using fewer established or outmoded expressions is a way of highlighting an aspect of Young Woman's character. This corresponds with the previous findings on Young Woman's language, such as her use of a greater number of vulgar expressions than Main Hero and Old Poor Peasant, and of a greater number of ideological items than Old Poor Peasant. However, individual distribution is not completely consistent or regular, i.e. in some novels, Young Woman's speeches have a higher rate of idioms than Old Poor Peasant's (see samples C, D and I in Table 14 – 1.2), and even Main Hero's (see sample D in Tables 14 – 1.1 and 1.2).

Next is the vertical comparison of distribution rates between the pre-CR and CR novels (see Tables 14 – 2.1 and 2.2). Under all the four character types, the rates in Group II are higher than those in Group I by a large margin. The pattern is also proved by the basically regular individual distributions. Generally, therefore, by comparison with pre-CR novels, the language of characters in CR novels has a more literary or bookish flavour.

Chapter 9

'Bookish' and 'Colloquial'

'BOOKISH' AND 'COLLOQUIAL' EXPLAINED

In most if not all Chinese books concerning Chinese lexicology, rhetoric, and stylistics, there appear two terms: *shumianyu* [written language] and *kouyu* [spoken language]. Some vocabulary items are said to have *shumianyu secai* [the colour (flavour) of written language], being called *shumianyu ci* [bookish words], and some others to have *kouyu secai* [the colour (flavour) of spoken language], being called *kouyu ci* [colloquial words].[1] The vocabulary of Modern Standard Chinese is also often divided into three categories according to source: *guyu ci* or *wenyan ci* [old words or classical words], *fangyan ci* [dialectal words], and *wailai ci* [foreign words].[2] Here, old or classical words are differentiated from bookish words although all classical words fit into the category of bookish items. In brief, 'bookish' refers to stylistic classification, but 'classical' refers to etymological classification.

The practical classification of bookish and colloquial words is much more complex than can be explained by general theoretical description and definition. This could be the reason why no special comprehensive dictionaries of bookish or colloquial vocabulary in Modern Standard Chinese can be found.[3]

The compilers of *A Modern Chinese Dictionary* made a tentative effort to classify bookish and colloquial items. They labelled items as *shu* [bookish] or *kou* [colloquial] in the dictionary to distinguish them from neutral items.[4] However, in spite of their great effort, it is by no means the case that the classification is well established. We see inconsistency and confusion in the classification among linguists by comparing examples.

i) In Huang Borong and Liao Xudong's *Modern Chinese* (Vol. 1, p. 240), the following pairs of synonyms are listed as examples to illustrate stylistic classification. In each pair, the former is colloquial, and the latter is bookish:

gei	*jiyu*	[give]
xiahu	*konghe*	[frighten]
naodai	*toubu*	[head]
lian	*lianpang*	[face]
xin	*xinling*	[heart]
gebo	*bi*	[arm]

But in *A Modern Chinese Dictionary*, except for 'xiahu', 'naodai', and 'gebo' which are labelled colloquial, all the others are taken to be neutral (without label).

ii) In Zhang Zhigong's *Modern Chinese* (Vol. 3, pp. 36–8), the following items are classified as bookish:

> *yaoyue* [invite]; *zhanyang* [look at with reverence]; *yirong* [remains of the deceased]; *qinjing* [admire and respect]; *zhiyuan* [do something of one's own free will]; *rounen* [tender]; *rouhe* [soft]; *yingrao* [linger]; *dangyang* [ripple]; *mianyan* [stretch]; *xuanlan* [splendid]; *jiaojian* [vigorous]; *wucai binfen* [multicoloured]; *ru niao shou san* [flee helter-skelter]; *qiongqiong jie li, xingying xiang diao* [standing all alone, body and shadow comforting each other]

But in *A Modern Chinese Dictionary*, none of them is labelled bookish. The last three items are idioms, and it seems to be a rule that no idioms are labelled in the dictionary.

iii) In Yang Shuzhong's *Duoyici tongyici fanyici* [*Polyseme, Synonym and Antonym*] (pp. 40–1)[5], the first group of the following items is labelled bookish, and the second group labelled colloquial:

> Group 1: *furen* [wife], *cuoshi* [measure], *dajia* [everybody], *sanbu* [take a walk], *buxing* [go on foot], *han* [letter], *jijing* [quiet], *jincan* [have a meal]
> Group 2: *qizi* [wife], *laopo* [wife], *banfa* [measure], *dahuor* [all], *liuda* [stroll], *zhuanyou* [stroll], *zou* [go on foot], *xin* [letter], *jing* [quiet], *chifan* [have a meal]

But in *A Modern Chinese Dictionary*, except 'laopo', 'dahuor', 'liuda', 'zhuanyou' which are labelled colloquial, all the others are neutral.

iv) Zhang Jihua's *Colloquial Vocabulary in Common Use* includes the following items:

> *suihe* [amiable], *baoyuan* [complain], *qingjing* [quiet], *zhaoying* [take care of], *liushen* [be careful], *chuanshengtong* [somebody's mouthpiece], *ganbaba*

[dull], *lengbufang* [unawares], *liang mian san dao* [double-dealing], *zhijie liaodang* [straightforward], *xiang' an wu shi* [live in peace with each other], *qian pa lang hou pa hu* [fear wolves ahead and tigers behind — be full of fears]

But in *A Modern Chinese Dictionary*, none of them is labelled colloquial.

The above comparison shows the confusion in the classification of vocabulary on a stylistic level. In other words, 'bookish', 'neutral', and 'colloquial' are relative stylistic concepts, and no established criteria exist for their practical classification. In general, compared to other reference books, the stylistic classification in *A Modern Chinese Dictionary* covers a much narrower range. In order to avoid unnecessary confusion, the following principles are established.

i)   The classification is based on stylistic characteristics rather than the lexical source. It admits that linguistic intuition is necessary to determine bookish, neutral, and colloquial categories because of the relativity of the stylistic differences.

ii) The classification emphasizes the stylistic colour of an item, irrespective of its length. For instance, the following items include different syllable patterns and vocabulary units, which break with the convention in some reference books that set phrases (such as idioms) are not put under stylistic classification:

One syllable: *lü* [thread (bookish)] (C, p. 263); *sa* [three (colloquial)] (C, p. 263)
Two syllables: *qianxun* [modest (bookish)] (A, p. 143); *namen* [feel puzzled (colloquial)] (E, p. 560)
Three syllables: *lingyun zhi* [high aspirations (bookish)] (H, 392); *dajiahuor* [you/we all; everybody (colloquial)] (F, p. 3)
Four syllables: *jing er yuan zhi* [keep a respectful distance from somebody (bookish)] (J, p. 207); *lalatata* [slovenly (colloquial)] (C, p. 210)
More than four syllables: *yu jia zhi zui, he huan wu ci* [if you are out to condemn somebody, you can always trump up a charge (bookish)] (H, p. 497); *yi wen san bu zhi* [be entirely ignorant (colloquial)] (C, p. 66)

iii) The classification emphasizes relative differences between the different categories, which is in accordance with certain principles given in the four Chinese linguistic works cited above. For instance, we regard the former of each pair of the following synonyms as a bookish item, and the latter as either a neutral or a colloquial one:

po [very] (H, p. 203)	*hen* (H, p. 25)
qieyi [be pleased] (J, p. 483)	*gaoxing* (H, p. 416)
huangkong [terrified] (G, p. 195)	*haipa* (H, p. 537)

However, our classification is not as broad as in the four works. For example, in these books, the first group of the following items is classified into bookish words, and the second classified into colloquial words, but we regard them all as neutral items:

Group 1: *buxing* [go on foot]; *dajia* [everybody]; *sanbu* [take a walk]; *toubu* [head]
Group 2: *zou* [have a stroll], *qizi* [wife], *xin* [heart], *gei* [give], *lian* [face]

iv) The classification emphasizes the nature of each individual item regardless of the characteristics of a type of item as a whole. For instance, idioms as a whole are thought to have more formal and bookish colour than other vocabulary units, but the stylistic differences among the following three groups are quite clear.

Group 1 (bookish): *bolan zhuangkuo* [on a magnificent scale] (J, p. 123); *gengu wei you* [unprecedented since ancient times] (C, p. 528); *ting er zou xian* [risk danger when in desperation] (G, p. 271); *zhu Zhou wei nüe* [aid King Zhou in his tyrannical rule; help evil] (G, p. 254); *kun shou you dou* [cornered beasts will still fight] (J, p. 434)
Group 2 (neutral): *da chi yi jing* [be startled] (E, p. 256); *zi yan zi yu* [talk to oneself] (F, p. 312); *xin zhong you shu* [know fairly well] (G, p. 157); *ai sheng tan qi* [heave great sighs] (F, p. 218); *mo bu zuo sheng* [keep one's mouth shut] (A, p. 266); *yu zhong bu tong* [different from the others] (J, p. 149)
Group 3 (colloquial): *san yan liang yu* [a few words spoken] (J, p. 246); *qi shou ba jiao* [great hurry and bustle] (A, p. 117); *shi you ba jiu* [most likely]; *yi qing er chu* [completely clear] (C, p. 275); *luan qi ba zao* [in a mess] (C, p. 328)

In short, consequently, according to our classification, the range of bookish items is considerably broader than that in *A Modern Chinese Dictionary*, and the range of colloquial items is slightly broader, but the range of both types of item is substantially narrower than in the above-mentioned Chinese linguistic works.

As for colloquial items, we do not include the retroflex final suffix '*er*' as a mark of colloquial status.[6]

'BOOKISH' AND 'COLLOQUIAL' ANALYSED

Unlike the other categories analysed above, for which exhaustive statistics have been compiled, bookish and colloquial words are only counted in sample passages for practical reasons. We have taken two pages (the second and third) from each chapter as the sample in all the novels with these exceptions: *The Golden Road*, *Evergreen*, and *The Roaring Songhua River*. *The Golden Road* and *Evergreen* both have an exceptionally large number of chapters (their chapters are thus shorter). In *The Golden Road*, we have sampled 1.5 pages in every chapter (the second in each chapter, and the third in odd chapters), and in *Evergreen*, one page in each chapter. This is not only in order to reduce the labour involved but more importantly to keep a balance in sampling, i.e. the proportion of number of Chinese characters in sampled pages to total number of Chinese characters in each novel is set around 10–15%. In *The Roaring Songhua River*, which has relatively few chapters (its chapters are generally longer), we have sampled three pages in each chapter (second to fourth). All the detailed sampling processes are presented in Table 15.

The statistical results concerning the density of the two categories are shown in Table 16. According to Table 16 – 2, in comparison with pre-CR novels, CR novels include a higher density of bookish words (5.01 vs. 3.94 per 1,000 characters), and a lower density of colloquial words (0.73 vs. 0.88). But from Table 16 – 1, we find in both groups some individual exceptions to the general pattern. The most noticeable exception is *Evergreen*, which has the lowest rate of bookish words and the highest rate of colloquial words among all the ten novels. This novel is substantially out of line with respect to the two stylistic categories. Another exception is *Great Changes in a Mountain Village*, where the density of bookish words is above the average of the CR novels.

We may analyse the above facts from two aspects. On the one hand, we can affirm the general tendency towards an increase in bookish words and a decrease in colloquial words in the CR novels by comparison with the pre-CR novels, since with only two exceptions, the novels in both groups comply with the pattern. For instance, the contrast between *The Golden Road* and *The Sun Shines Bright* is consistent with the general pattern although the works have the same author. Moreover, this general tendency in CR novels is in accordance with other characteristics stated before, such as including fewer vulgar expressions, more idioms, more literary proverbs and more classical verse segments.

On the other hand, in view of the existence of the two exceptions, *Evergreen* and *Great Changes in a Mountain Village*, we cannot deny the role played by the authors' personal vocabulary style in the distribution of the two stylistic categories. It goes without saying that personal vocabulary style of authors always exists although it may change to some extent under the influence of period style. In the CR novels, the personal vocabulary style of the authors becomes more manifest when those non-politicized lexical items such as idioms, proverbs, *xiehouyu*, bookish words, colloquial words and dialectal words are used.

Chapter 10

Dialectal Expressions

DIALECTAL EXPRESSIONS DEFINED

Dialectal expressions under discussion consist of two categories: one refers to the words and expressions which may still not be counted into the vocabulary of Modern Standard Chinese,[1] but are in rather common use in writings in the standard language. Such items are labelled *'fang'* [dialectal] in *A Modern Chinese Dictionary*. For example, *'sha'* [what] (E, p. 222), *'jinr'* [today] (E, p. 386), *'ganqing'* [indeed] (G, p. 61), *'gouqiang'* [terrible] (D, p. 231), *'duozan'* [when] (F, p. 245). Another category covers items which do not appear in *A Modern Chinese Dictionary*. They can be classified into two sub-categories: (1) items totally unrelated to the elements of Modern Standard Chinese, since the characters only play a role of phonetic transcription. In many cases, they are only intelligible to the speakers of the specific dialects to which the items belong. They are sometimes given footnotes by the authors of the novels under examination. For example, *'huizi'* [slogan] (A, p. 91), *'manman'* [term of endearment for uncle] (A, p. 93), *'dinggang'* [offset] (F, p. 418), *'zhagu'* [cure] (F, p. 344), *'gaoxinhe'* [go about something in a haphazard way] (A, p. 109). (2) items having some relation to the elements of Modern Standard Chinese, such as sharing the same word forms, including the same morphemes, but having the following dialectal characteristics by which they can be distinguished from the lexical items of Modern Standard Chinese.

Dialectal Affixation

A root and an affix may be elements of Modern Standard Chinese, but the derived form (by prefixation or suffixation) is not within the vocabulary of Modern Standard Chinese.

Examples: *lao-di* [younger brother] (A, p. 160), *lao-mei* [younger sister] (A, p. 127), *guniang-jia* [woman] (I, p. 322), *jianbang-zi* [shoulder] (C, p. 328), Qingming-*zi* ['Qingming' is here a person's given name] (A, p. 31).

Dialectal Reduplication

Some morphemes and words are elements of Modern Standard Chinese, but the reduplicated forms cannot be found in the vocabulary of the standard language.

Examples: *didi* [the truth or root of a matter] (I, p. 37), *chaoshishi* [moist] (C, p. 26), *lachelache* [chat] (B, p. 168), *toutounaonao* [head or tail of something] (D, p. 313), *fanbaifanbaiyan* [show the whites of one's eyes] (D, p. 170).

Dialectal Meaning

Some items have the same form as words of Modern Standard Chinese but have a different meaning.

Examples: *yeye* [D: father; S: grandfather — here in translation, D stands for dialect, and S Modern Standard Chinese] (A, p. 96), *popo* [D: wife; S: grandmother] (A, p. 96), *sihai* [D: unaffected and casual; S: the whole world] (A, p. 31).

Dialectal Grammatical Function

Some items have the same meaning as words of Modern Standard Chinese, but have a different grammatical function in usage.

Examples: . . . *Zhuang Yao guniang, . . . nayang ye bu cha nanzihan.* [. . . the girls of the Zhuang and Yao nationalities, . . . do not fall short of men at all. (D: a transitive verb; S: an intransitive verb)] (H, p. 393); . . . *naxie laotouzi zhen gou yangxiang de* . . . [. . . those old men are really making an exhibition of themselves . . . (D: an adjective; S: a noun)] (C, p. 195).

Dialectal Morpheme Order

Some items have the same meaning and grammatical function as the words of Modern Standard Chinese, but have a different morpheme order.

Examples: *baijie* [(S: *jiebai*) spotlessly white] (A, p. 14), *tuxi* [(S: *xitu*) harbour the intention of] (F, p. 392), *shiqi* [(S: *qishi*) as a matter of fact] (A, p. 237), *tanxu* [(S: *xutan*) chat] (B, 168).

Dialectal Collocation

Some words of Modern Standard Chinese are used in dialectal collocation.

Examples: *yi pian laosao* [(S: *yi tong/zhen laosao*) some grievances] (A, p. 265), *gan le yi jia* [(S: *da le yi jia*) have a fight] (G, p. 272), *lao lan bu weijin* [(S: *jiu lan bu weijin*) old blue scarf], *chi de qi* [(S: *shou de qi*) be able to suffer wrong] (A, p.143).

Dialectal Idiomatic Phrases

In these idiomatic phrases, there may be some constituents which can be found in Modern Standard Chinese, but the phrases as a whole cannot be found in the vocabulary of the standard language.

Examples: *liao xian pian* [chat] (D, p. 132), *chuifeng zhuangdan* [boost somebody's courage] (H, p. 228), *jiji feng yin* [very quiet] (A, p. 116), *le tou bao yan* [foam with rage] (G, p. 104), *ri biao ye zhang* [grow/develop quickly] (H, p. 452).

Dialectal Figure of Speech

Some words or phrases, which can be found in the elements of Modern Standard Chinese, have dialectal figurative usage.

Examples: *huang gou-zi* [yellow dog, indicating policemen under the National Republic] (E, p. 97), *maomaoyu* [drizzle, indicating suggestion or criticism in advance] (H, p. 373), *che qi chang mianxian* [pull long cotton thread, indicating to chat long and casually] (A, p. 98), *da dianhua* [make a phone call, indicating to send a secret message to one's partner when playing cards] (A, p. 31).

DIALECTAL EXPRESSIONS ANALYSED

As shown in Table 17 – 2, the gap in the density of dialectal expressions between the two groups of novels is so wide that the density rate (number per 1,000 characters) in Group I is over twice as high as that in Group II (7.76 vs. 3.28).

The general tendency in which the density of dialectal expressions in the

CR novels is lower by a big margin is also shown in Table 17 – 1, according to which no sampled CR novel reaches the average of the pre-CR novels. Hao Ran's *The Golden Road* registers a decrease of around thirty percent compared to his *The Sun Shines Bright*. The density rate in *Great Changes in a Mountain Village* is over ten times as high as that in *The Mountains and Rivers Roar*, though both novels are set in the mountains of Hunan and belong to the Xiang dialect area.

The campaign to popularize Modern Standard Chinese began in the 1950s under the People's Republic and has been the fundamental language policy of the government ever since; that is, even the sample pre-CR novels were produced after the initiation of this campaign.[2] It is generally thought by post-CR scholars that the popularization of Modern Standard Chinese was impeded during the Cultural Revolution.[3] We have not so far found special official CR documents in favour of the popularization of Modern Standard Chinese, but neither have we found official statements against the campaign. However, our statistics show a trend of decreasing dialectal items in CR novels. In other words, if the popularization of Modern Standard Chinese is reflected in the frequency of dialectal expressions in CR novels, the campaign was not 'impeded' but promoted. The reasons for the reduction of dialectal expressions in the CR novels could be analysed as follows:

i) The ideology of seeking unity in all things or making all things uniform during the Cultural Revolution had some influence on the writers' language use. As stated by some scholars, the basic spirit of the Cultural Revolution was to unify people's ideology and behaviour, and to oppose individualism (including localism).[4] Seemingly, ideological unification is unrelated to the popularization of Modern Standard Chinese. But the campaign to popularize the standardized language also embodied a kind of spirit of unification. Thus it is plausible that the authors of the CR novels were inclined to use fewer dialectal items, consciously or unconsciously.[5]

ii) Another factor leading to the decrease in dialectal expressions is the complementary distribution of other stylistic items. For instance, higher density of ideological items may result in reducing dialectal words because ideological items cannot be dialectal. Again, a higher frequency of idioms, literary proverbs, and bookish words may also give rise to a lower density of dialectal items because they cannot be dialectal.

However, in spite of the general tendency, comparing individual distributions within the respective groups, we find noticeable irregularities. For example, in Group I, the highest rate (*Great Changes in a Mountain Village*) is over three times as much as the second (*The Builders*), and over five times in comparison with the lowest (*The Sun Shines Bright*). Within Group II, the lowest rate (*Qingshi Fort*) and the second lowest rate (*The Mountains and Rivers Roar*) only account for 16.24 percent and 25.5 percent of the highest (*The Roaring Songhua River*) respectively.

The inner irregularities within the two groups cannot be explained by time-setting and place-setting, which are often important factors in influencing the distribution of dialectal elements. For time-setting, some novels are set before the initiation of the popularization of Modern Standard Chinese, and some others after or under the campaign, although all of them were written after the start of the campaign. It could be expected that those novels with a time-setting before the initiation of the language campaign might have a higher density of dialectal items, but no consistency can be established. For example, within Group I, *The Builders* is set before the campaign, but it has a much lower rate of dialectal items than *Great Changes in a Mountain Village*. Within Group II, *The Golden Road* is the only CR novel set prior to the popularization of the standard language, but its rate of dialectal items is not the highest among the seven CR novels. Moreover, *Mountains Green after Rain*, *The Long Rainbow*, and *The Mountains and Rivers Roar* are all set in the Cultural Revolution, but there is no consistency among them. The rate in *Evergreen* accounts for only 63.49 percent of that in *The Roaring Songhua River* although both are set in 1962.

Place-setting could be expected to be related to the density of dialectal items because the settings are related to different specific dialects. We have actually found a number of dissimilarities concerning form and meaning of the items due to different place-settings. For example, the words meaning wife in Modern Standard Chinese are commonly 'qizi', 'airen' and 'laopo', but there is a series of different words for wife in dialects. In the sampled novels, we can find such items as 'poniang' (B, p. 133), 'poyi' (I, p. 110), 'popo' (A, p. 96), 'tangke' (A, p. 74),'xifu' (C, p. 299), 'niangmen' (D, p. 212), and 'shaohuopo' (H, p. 183), which reflect the differences produced by different place-settings. Nevertheless, we cannot find a clear relation between place-setting and the density of the items in the novels.

Our explanation for the irregularities within each group is that, under the prerequisite of period style by which the CR novels tend to have fewer dialectal expressions, the authors' personal styles play an important role in the density of dialectal items. For example, Zhou Libo, the author of *Great Changes in a Mountain Village*, is well known for his frequent use of dialectal items. It was his practice to learn local dialects for use in his writing when he went down to 'immerse himself in life' [*shenru shenghuo*] at the places which were claimed to be the original settings in his novels.[6] His well-known novel of 1952, *Hurricane*, which is set in the Northeast, also has a high density of dialectal expressions. So the two novels *Hurricane* and *Great Changes in a Mountain Village*, which not only have different time-settings and place-settings but cover different writing periods (the former written before the Modern Standard Chinese popularization campaign, the latter written after the start of the campaign) have in common a frequent use of dialectal items. However, Hao Ran is known to be familiar with the countryside and his observation of real life could not be inferior to Zhou's, but his works have a lower density of dialectal items in contrast with not only Zhou's but also those of the other sampled professional authors. Nevertheless, on the other hand, his personal style in using dialectal expressions is observably consistent in his two sampled novels, i.e. the rates of both are on a low level within the respective groups although the decrease in *The Golden Road* reflects the general trend of reduction of dialectal items in CR novels.

There is another characteristic concerning the irregularities which also relates more to the CR authors' individual style than to the CR period style, i.e. the young and new authors use fewer dialectal items than the older professional ones. A plausible explanation for this phenomenon is that the young and new writers had their school education during the 1950s and the early 1960s, when Modern Standard Chinese was being popularized. The government's campaign may have had more influence on their negative attitude towards dialectal elements.

The irregularities, which indicate the relative prominence of authors' personal styles in using dialectal items, confirm the former statement that the authors' individual language styles play a more important role in using non-politicized stylistic items.

Chapter 11

Military Words and Expressions

MILITARY WORDS AND EXPRESSIONS DEFINED

In practical contexts, military words and expressions can be classified into two categories according to their usage: One covers military words and expressions in literal use, i.e. they are used to refer to organizations, people, materials, and acts in a real military sense; the other category includes military words and expressions in metaphorical use, i.e. they are used to indicate organizations, people, materials, and acts which are not related to real military affairs. Compare the following examples:

(1) *Ta hai xiang dao Qi Zhixiong cong chuangdong sai gei ta de mianxie, Tianmen Zhen shang de qiangsheng, Ji-Yunhe bian de paohuo. Ta xiang dao zai feiji saoshe xia de yun liang che dui, zai xiaoyan zhong chongsha de qian jun wan ma.*
[He also thought of the cotton-padded shoes given him by Qi Zhixiong through the window, the shots in Tianmen Town, and the artillery fire at the Ji Canal. He thought of the grain transport corps under the strafing from the aircraft, and the thousands of soldiers charging forward in the smoke of gunpowder.] (D, p. 648)

(2) '*Hao, wo zhe yi qu, women jiushi zai liang tiao zhanhao, yi ge zhendi shang dazhang; shou de zhu hai bu suan, hai yao chong de shang cai suan hao zhanshi!*'
[Right, after I go there, we shall be fighting in two trenches which

belong to one battlefield. It is not enough to hold the position; only by charging forward can we be counted as good soldiers.] (H, p. 462)

The military items (underlined) in paragraph 1 are used in a literal sense, but those in paragraph 2 are metaphorical. In isolation, the literal meaning of paragraph 2 clearly concerns fighting, but in context the whole paragraph is related to political action rather than military affairs. Before he leaves for self-examination at the commune government office, the speaker, as the main hero, encourages other village cadres to continue opposing the secretary of the Party committee of the commune. Full of military words and expressions, this politicized speech has a distinctive military flavour. For the purposes of stylistic analysis, it is only military items in metaphorical use that are taken into account.[1]

As stated before, we lack an ideal reference book for identifying the military items, although Joseph D. Lowe's *A Dictionary of Military Terms: Chinese-English and English-Chinese* is helpful in determining the military connotations. However, linguistic intuition can take more effect here because as a class of specialized terms, military words and expressions have a relatively established meaning range.

According to our investigation, the military words and expressions under discussion included in pre-CR and CR novels roughly belong to the following semantic groups.

Military Organizations or Units

Examples: *tujidui* [shock brigade] (G, p. 26), *niangzijun* [detachment of women] (G, p. 499), *houqinbing* [rear-service units] (J, p. 123), *meng-hu pai* [fierce-tiger platoon] (J, p. 300), *canmoubu* [department of staff officers], *zhenggui budui* [regular troops] (J, p. 466).

Military People

Examples: *zhanshi* [soldiers] (H, p. 167), *jiangjun* [general] (J, p. 502), *zhanyou* [battle companion] (D, p. 507), *lao jiang xin bing* [veterans and new recruits] (J, p. 417), *nan bing nü jiang* [male and female soldiers] (J, p. 44), *xiaojiang* [young general or militant] (J, p. 17), *siling* [commander] (J, p. 123), *qian jun wan ma* [thousands of troops] (D, p. 648).

Military Materials

Examples: *zhanchang* [battlefield] (H, p. 315), *cidao* [bayonet] (G, p. 455), *wuqi* [weapon] (I, p. 80), *dapao* [artillery] (H, p. 418), *baolei* [fortress] (E, p. 106), *zhangu* [battle drum] (J, p. 299), *xiaoyan* [smoke of gunpowder] (I, p. 81), *paosheng* [boom of guns] (H, p. 392).

Military Acts

Examples: *tiaozhan* [challenge to battle] (A, p. 305), *xuanzhan* [proclaim war] (J, p. 216), *guashuai* [take command] (H, p. 72), *zhandou* [fight] (F, p. 378), *jingong* [take an offensive] (H, p. 357), *fanji* [counterattack] (I, p. 92), *paohong* [bombard] (H, p. 400), *chongfeng chu zhen* [charge forward] (H, p. 511), *xiu bing ba zhan* [truce] (I, p. 30).

In counting, the following two types of military items are excluded from the investigation, although they share some characteristics of military words in metaphorical use. (1) A military item used as a person's nickname. For example, in *The Builders*, Guo Zhenshan's nickname is 'Hongzhaji' [bomber, indicating his domineering character]; in *The Sun Shines Bright*, Ma Lianli's nickname is 'Dapao' [large gun, indicating his boldly outspoken character]; in *The Mountains and Rivers Roar*, the main hero Liu Wangchun is affectionately called 'Xiaojiang' (this term on the one hand is another name for the Red Guards ['Hongweibing'], and on the other hand means young general or militant. People call Liu 'Xiaojiang' because he used to be a Red Guard, and now he is the commander of the water conservancy works). (2) A military item used as a morpheme of a word which represents a non-military concept. For instance, 'Hongweibing' [the Red Guards] is an ideological item although the morpheme 'weibing' [guard] in it could be taken for a military word in isolation.

MILITARY WORDS AND EXPRESSIONS ANALYSED

It was expected that CR novels would include more military items in metaphorical use than pre-CR novels. According to present statistics, the density difference between the two groups is really striking. As shown in Table 18 – 2, the rate (the number of military words and expressions per 100,000 characters) in Group II is more than nine times higher than that in Group I. Meanwhile, the individual rates confirm the general pattern so well that the rates in the seven CR novels are exclusively higher than those in the three pre-CR novels and their average. There are six novels in Group II whose quantity of military items each surpasses the sum of the whole of Group I.

The prevalence of military items in CR novels might be shown by the following example. In *The Mountains and Rivers Roar*, the following expressions often appear, of which each includes '*zhandou*' [battle or fighting] as a modifier.

zhandou xili [the baptism through battle] (J, p. 11), *zhandou* de huhuan [the call for battle] (J, p. 89), *zhandou* haoling [the verbal command for battle] (J, p. 158), *zhandou* haoqing [the lofty sentiments of battle] (ib.), *zhandou* gangwei [battle station] (J, p. 375), *zhandou* xiwen [the denunciations of the enemy in battle] (J, p. 380), *zhandou* xiaozu [fighting teams] (J, p. 387), *zhandou* qixi [the flavour of battle] (J, p. 397), *zhandou* baolei [fighting fortress] (J, p. 421), *zhandou* kouhao [the battle slogans] (J, p. 482), *zhandou* tuhua [the picture of battle] (J, p. 486), *zhandou* de yongshi [the warrior in battle] (J, p. 508), *zhandou* jiti [the fighting collective] (J, p. 519).

T. A. Hsia has noted that military words and expressions were in vogue during the late 1950s and early 1960s.[2] His investigation seemed to be mainly focused on the contemporary language in newspapers rather than language in fiction. The present investigation shows that the language in the pre-CR novels does not have an impressive 'military flavour' because of the low density of military items. The plausible inference is that either the military words and expressions in metaphorical use in the pre-CR period were not popular enough to enter the novels in large numbers, or novelists consciously avoided using many military items.

In order to identify the reason for the much denser distribution of military expressions in metaphorical use in CR novels than in pre-CR novels, we focus the present analysis on the contexts in the CR novels where the military items appear. According to our investigation, the military items in the CR novels are mainly distributed in the following categories of context.

Class Struggle

Under the People's Republic before the post-CR period, the peasants in the countryside were classified into two large camps on the basis of their class status established during the Land Reform. The poor and lower-middle peasants were in one camp; the landlords and rich peasants in the other; the upper-middle peasants in either of the two. As H. C. Chuang pointed out, external enemies '*di xiu fan*' [imperialism, revisionism, and reactionaries] such as the United States (imperialism), the Soviet Union (revisionism), and the Kuomintang (reactionaries), only formed an atmospheric or imaginary threat.[3] The real and visible enemy in the countryside was the landlords and rich peasants (including those who escaped being classified or concealed their true status) who served as a practical reminder to positive people in their awareness of the need for struggle. Class struggle — the confrontation between the two camps — is likened to war, and military words and expressions are used. For example,

> (3) *Sheyuan men, bu neng wangji le jieji douzheng de cunzai, wang le* zhandou *a! Yao shike jizhu,* diren *bing meiyou sixin, erqie bi guoqu geng jiaohua le,*

women yao <u>lianxu jingong</u>, <u>jixu chongfeng</u>, <u>jixu dazhang</u>! Cai neng yongyuan zuo yi ge geming-zhe!

[Commune members, don't forget the existence of class struggle, nor forget fighting! You must remember at all times that the enemies have not given up their hope, and they have become even more crafty. We must fight continuously, charge continuously, and make war continuously! Only by doing so can we become eternal revolutionaries.] (G, p. 522)

The above passage is spoken by a character from the camp of poor and lower-middle peasants to boost morale against the class enemy. On the other hand, the class enemy also use military items in confrontation and counterattack. The following passage is from the thoughts of a class enemy.

(4) *Zenme ban ne? Liu Hai zao zhunbei hao le zai hui shang <u>da touzhen</u>, Kousanxian ye zai er dui zheteng le bantian, san dui, si dui dou you ren zhunbei <u>xiangying</u>. Zhengshi <u>liang jun duilei</u>, yijing dao le yi chu ji fa de shihou, pianpian lai zheme ge canguan, xingshi turan bian le, yan kan dui ziji buli. <u>Che</u> ba, laibuji le, ye bu ganxin; <u>shang</u> ba, fenming <u>di qiang wo ruo</u>, ye bu hui you haochu.*

[What should I do? Originally, Liu Hai was ready to fight in the van, Kousanxian had also spent several hours going about persuading people in the second production team, and some people from the third and the fourth teams were willing to respond. But just when the two armies were pitted against each other, and the battle might occur at any moment, we were called to visit this place. The situation suddenly changed and became unfavourable to me. Now I intend to withdraw, but it is too late, and meanwhile I won't submit willingly. But if we charge forward, it can't do us good because we are outnumbered by the enemy.] (E, p. 116)

Line Struggle

In line struggle, the opposing sides are the positive characters led by the main heroes versus the capitalist-roaders and their followers. By comparison, the line struggle 'war' is on a larger scale than the class struggle 'war'. The capitalist-roaders seem to arouse greater public indignation than landlords and rich peasants, although the former are Party cadres and the latter the branded enemy. The military items used in the context of line struggle greatly surpass those used in the context of class struggle, whether in quantity or in semantic degree of seriousness. The following examples are from the context of line struggle.

(5) *Gengtian Ge lin zou qian shuo de hao, zhe haobi <u>dazhang</u>, <u>shou de zhu</u> bu suan, hai yao <u>chong de shang</u>. Xianzai, wo xiang, jiu xiang <u>dazhang</u> nayang,*

qianmian de <u>zhanyou</u> *yijing* <u>chong shangqu</u>, *yao* <u>zha diao</u> <u>diren</u> *de* <u>diaobao</u>, *na,*
women jiu dei gankuai yong <u>huoli</u> *gei* <u>chong shangqu</u> *de* <u>zhanyou</u> <u>yanhu</u> . . .
[Brother Gengtian said before leaving, that just like fighting in a war,
it was not enough for us to hold the position, but we had to charge
forward. Now, I think, just like in battle, our comrade-in-arms has gone
in the van to blast away the enemy's blockhouse, we must screen his
advance with firepower . . .] (H, p. 511)

(6) *Zhao Yiliang ting ba, daxiao qilai dao: "Name shuo* <u>zhe yi zhang</u> <u>da de zhen</u>
<u>gou piaoliang</u>! *Women zai* <u>zhengmian jingong</u>, *Lao Tang nimen zai* <u>beihou</u>
<u>lanji</u>. *Zhe hui, hai bu ba Nong Liji* <u>da de luo hua liu shui</u>?!"
[After hearing that, Zhao Yiliang laughed and said, 'That means we have
fought a fine battle. We were making a frontal attack, and Lao Tang
and you were intercepting from the rear. This time of course Nong Liji
has been utterly routed.'] (H, p. 548)

Unlike the class struggle 'war', the 'war' of line struggle could be thought to be
unilaterally declared by the positive characters, or only the positive characters
promote the struggle to the level of war. This is justified by the fact that the
positive characters use military words and expressions to attack the capitalist-
roaders, but the opposing side rarely counterattacks with military items.

Struggle Against Nature

To struggle against nature [*tong daziran zuo douzheng*] and to conquer nature
[*zhengfu daziran*] were two pet phrases in China between the late 1950s and the
late 1970s. Among the battles against nature in the CR novels, the construction
of dams and other water-control projects is the most important. Compared to
the above two types of 'wars', the 'war' against nature provides a closer
representation of real military affairs, especially with the militarization of
organizations taken into consideration. In other words, following the example
of the regular army, the 'troops' are highly organized and manoeuvred.
Meanwhile, as the peasants are likened to soldiers, their labour tools are
correspondingly likened to army weapons. The following example sounds more
like a description of a real battlefield than a narration about a water project
site.

(7) *Chu shui suidao de* <u>si lu jingbing</u>: *Sanwanquan Dadui* <u>Menghu Pai</u>, *Shijiaopen*
Dadui <u>Zhengqi Lian</u>, *Hongsonggu Dadui* <u>Tie-guniang Dachui Ban</u>,
Chunlingjiang Dadui <u>Hongse Niangzijun Lian</u>, *kai guo* <u>shishi hui</u> *hou, jiu*
<u>fen lu jin bing</u>, <u>hui chui shangzhen</u>, *jin luo mi gu de gan shang le.*
[There were four groups of picked troops in the tunnel for leading water:
the Fierce-Tiger Platoon of Sanwanquan Brigade, the Bringing-Credit
Company of Shijiaopen Brigade, the Iron-Girl Sledge-Hammer Squad

of Hongsonggu Brigade, and the Red Women-Soldier Company of Chunlingjiang Brigade. After the oath-taking rally, they matched separately, brandishing hammers and going into battle in a blaze of martial glory.] (J, p. 300)

Furthermore, the 'war' against nature covers a very extensive range. From the following military expressions, we see other 'battles' and relevant 'enemies' in the 'war' against nature: *'xiang yandong xuanzhan'* [declare war against the severe winter] (J, p. 216), *'gen laotianye jue yi sizhan'* [fight the weather to the finish] (G, p. 24), *'zhan tian dou zai'* [fight natural disasters] (G, p. 25), *'xiang yi qiong er bai liang zuo shan jingong'* [attack the two mountains of poverty and blankness] (J, p. 203), *'ge cao zhandou'* [the battle of cutting grass] (F, p. 388), *'xiang qiong shan e shui xuanzhan'* [declare war against the barren mountains and unruly rivers] (H, p. 267), *'da liangshi chedi fanshen zhang'* [battle hard to bring about a great upswing in the grain production] (H, p. 287). Obviously, the 'war' against nature is only declared by the positive characters, and the 'enemy' cannot make counterattacks.

Militarized Activities Among Positive Characters

In addition to direct frontal engagement with the 'enemy' in the above 'wars', there are some other militarized activities within the camp of the positive characters, forming another type of military context. Unlike the above three types of context, which reflect the relation between the positive characters and the 'enemy' declared in the 'wars', the new one concerns the relationship between positive groups or individuals. Among these activities, mobilization and emulation are the most important. The former concerns the relationship between superiors and subordinates, and the latter the relationship between parallel groups. The common specific military items include *'dongyuan'* [mobilize] (F, p. 348), *'shishi'* [take a mass pledge before going to war] (J, p. 518), *'qingzhan'* [request a battle assignment] (J, p. 480), *'bushu'* [deploy] (H, p. 462), *'diaodong'* [manoeuvre] (H, p. 263) *'tiaozhan'* [challenge] (J, p. 273), *'yingzhan'* [accept a challenge] (J, p. 205), *'jinjun ling'* [the order to match] (I, p. 76), *'canzhan'* [enter into war] (H, p. 389), etc.

However, in many cases, the above four military contexts are not isolated but interrelated. For example,

(8) *Jiu zai zhe shihou, Jinfengshan shang, chuan lai le yi zhenzhen longlong de zha shi paosheng. Zhe, jinjin shi <u>xiang daziran xuanzhan</u> de <u>paosheng</u> ma? Bu, zhe ye shi zuzhi qianqianwanwan qunzhong, <u>diaodong haohaodangdang geming dajun</u>, xiang Zhongguo de Heluxiaofu fan-geming xiuzhengzhuyi luxian, xiang <u>na qiang he bu na qiang de jieji diren</u>, lei xiang le <u>da jinjun de zhentian zhangu</u>!*

[Just at this time, from Jinfeng Mountain came a series of booms from the rock-blasting. Was this merely the 'roar of guns' of declaring war against nature? No, this was also the sound made by thousands of the masses — the mighty revolutionary contingents who were pounding the resounding-through-the-skies drums of war to march massively against the anti-revolutionary revisionist line in China and class enemies with or without guns.] (H, p. 576)

The above four types of context represent the most common places where military items appear although they cannot cover all possible contextual ranges. Sometimes, a concrete context might not have direct connection with the four primary categories, but there is still some indirect relationship between them. For example, the following passage is intended to describe a scene where two oxen are driven by their breeder to go ploughing, and the two animals are likened to veterans going into battle.

(9) *Liang tou lao niu ye gei qian le chulai. Tamen zheng zhe tong ling ban de da yan, yi bu yi bu wenwendangdang de zou zhe, ting xiang liang yuan jiu jing zhengzhan de lao jiang, xiong you cheng zhu de zai shang zhanchang. Yutian daye musong ziji peiyang de "yongshi", xiongjiujiu de ta shang zhengtu, ye xingzhi bobo de gen qu le.*
[Two old oxen were led out of the door. With big eyes opened fully, they stepped forward steadily just like two old veterans of many campaigns going to a battleground self-assuredly once again. Seeing the warriors embarking valiantly on the road of expedition, Uncle Yutian then followed them in high spirits.] (E, p. 528)

Seemingly, the specific context has nothing to do with the above four main contextual categories, but it is in fact in a larger ideological context. The poor and lower-middle peasants are organized by the positive core of the village to sow in the collective field. Their action is the start of the climax of their struggle against the capitalist-roaders and class enemy. The oxen are led to join the 'battle' — to plough.

In short, among the four contextual categories, there is a general link: ideological conflict. Evidently, the first two types of context, class struggle and line struggle, are directly related to ideology. In the third type of 'war' (against nature), whether or how 'to fight or conquer nature' also embodies different ideological lines. The fourth category — militarized activities inside the positive camp — is subordinate to the other three categories and concerned with ideology.

The above analysis of military words and expressions shows the extent of the military lexical style of CR novel language. By comparison with pre-CR novels, the distribution of military words and expressions in CR novels is substantially increased.

The increase in military words and expressions could to a certain extent reflect the increase in militarization in real life during the Cultural Revolution, which serves the current politics. In CR novels the intensified military lexical style is related to the novels' politicized content, because the main contexts where the military items appear are concerned with ideological motifs. Moreover, the military lexical style is also related to other characteristics of language in CR novels. Since the ideological style in the language of CR novels is greatly intensified, the heightened military flavour adds to the intensification of ideological style in the language of CR fiction.

Chapter 12

Meteorological Vocabulary and Inflated Expressions

The above ten stylistic categories of vocabulary have been analysed quantitatively and qualitatively. The other two categories of stylistic items in this study are meteorological vocabulary and inflated expressions. Owing to the lack of thorough statistics, the following analyses concerning the two categories are mainly qualitative.

METEOROLOGICAL VOCABULARY

Like military words and expressions, meteorological items are also used in a literal or metaphorical sense. When used in a literal sense, they refer to weather and relative natural phenomena; when used in a metaphorical sense, they indicate political and social phenomena. Compare the following examples:

(1) *Zaochen qilai, <u>tianqi</u> haishi <u>qinglang</u> de, bang shangwu de shihou, turan jian <u>nong yun mi bu</u>, <u>kuangfeng da zuo</u>; jin jiezhe, <u>dian shan lei ming</u>, xiang yong da piao meng po meng dao de <u>yu shui</u>, longzhao le kuangye . . .*
[In the early morning, it was fine. But close to noon, suddenly, thick clouds were gathering and a fierce wind was blowing hard. After a while, with the lighting accompanied by peals of thunder, the rain was pelting down, covering the vast land . . .] (D, pp. 605–6)

(2) *<u>Pili</u> yi sheng kai xin yu, wan li <u>dongfeng</u> sao <u>can yun</u>.*

[A thunderclap opens a new world, the boundless east wind sweeps the remaining clouds away.] (H, p. 394)

Passage 1 is a factual description, in which the meteorological terms are in literal use. Passage 2 is a political slogan, in which the meteorological items are in metaphorical use. '*Pili*' refers to the Cultural Revolution, '*dongfeng*' to the revolutionary force, and '*canyun*' to the remaining forces or vestiges of feudalism and capitalism. For the purpose of stylistic analysis, it is only the meteorological items in metaphorical use that are taken into the present account.

In the pre-CR novels, very few meteorological items in metaphorical use can be found. For example, in *Great Changes in a Mountain Village*, only two typical items have been found: (1) '*xiaonong jingji jing bu qi feng chui yu da*' [small-scale farming by individual owners cannot stand the wind and rain] (p. 77), (2) '*geming fengbao*' [revolutionary storm] (p. 161). For the CR novels, however, especially for those novels set in the Cultural Revolution, readers cannot but be impressed by the frequency of meteorological items in metaphorical use. For instance, with only '*feng*' [wind] taken into consideration, we can find the following items in *The Mountains and Rivers Roar*: '*Lengfeng*' [cold wind — a way to stop revolutionary activities] (p. 52), '*jifeng*' [violent wind — mass movement] (p. 53), '*dongfeng*' [east wind — revolutionary force or inspiration] (p. 53), '*yaofeng*' [evil wind — evil tendency] (p. 58), '*qifeng*' [wailing wind — hard revolutionary experience] (p. 196), '*bu zheng zhi feng*' [unhealthy wind — politically unhealthy tendency] (p. 258), '*waifeng*' [evil wind — politically unhealthy views] (p. 264), '*chunfeng*' [spring wind — revolutionary spirit or inspiration] (p. 374), '*e xuanfeng*' [evil whirlwind — counter-revolutionary force] (p. 388), '*fengbao*' [windstorm — the movement of revolution] (p. 498).

In addition to typical meteorological terms such as *feng* [wind], *yu* [rain], *xue* [snow], *bing* [ice], *shuang* [frost], *yun* [cloud], *wu* [fog], *lei* [thunder], *shandian* [lightning], and so on, there are other elements (words or morphemes) with meanings related to meteorology in the language of the novels. Among those in metaphorical use, *lang* [wave] is commonly seen, used either in isolation, e.g. '*shengshi haoda de qunzhong yundong, taotao da lang*' [the momentous mass movement, the surging waves] (H, p. 405), or used together with *feng* [wind]. In the latter circumstance, they either form the compound '*fenglang*' [stormy waves — struggle] (F, p. 169), or are separately put in some parallel expressions such as '*da feng da lang*' [big wind and waves — serious struggle] (J, p. 551), '*fengfenglanglang*' [wind and waves — struggles] (J, p. 421), '*ba jin chuan duo ying feng qu, bu pa si mian lang lai dian*' [sailing the boat stably in the wind, and braving the waves from all around — dare to fight the politically evil forces] (H, p. 394). In addition, *lang* is sometimes used together with its synonym *tao*, such as '*jing tao hai lang*' [terrifying waves — acute struggles or severe tests] (E, p. 559).

Except for the two compounds *dongfeng* [east wind] and *chunfeng* [spring wind] which have established commendatory metaphorical meaning,[1] in isolation the meteorological elements are usually derogatory or occasionally neutral. For example,

(3) *Women gongdi de xinsheng-shiwu ye you zhe ge texing, zhe gu juejing, buguan feng chui ta, yu lin ta, shuang da ta, xue dong ta, ta que yue zhang yue wangsheng . . .*

[The newly emerging things at our construction site also have such unbending characteristics: although exposed to wind, rain, snow and frost, they become more and more exuberant . . .] (J, p. 421)

(4) *Zhe gongdi shang shi yao guafeng, qi yun le.*

[There will be wind and cloud in the construction site.] (J, p. 157)

(5) *jiu jing shenghuo fenglang*

[have long experienced the wind and waves of life] (J, p. 86)

In (3), the meteorological items '*feng*' [wind], '*yu*' [rain], '*shuang*' [frost] and '*xue*' [snow] are all likened to conservative and counterrevolutionary forces; in (4), '*guafeng*' [to blow] and '*qi yun*' [to cloud over] indicate the activities of the class enemy; and in (5), '*fenglang*' [wind and waves] refers to hard or unusual life experience.

However, meteorological elements are often modified by other morphemes or words. In such cases, the meteorological items have either commendatory or more obviously derogatory meaning, as shown in the following two groups:

Group 1: *geming fengbao* [revolutionary storm] (H, p. 477), *qunzhong yundong de ji feng zhou yu* [the tempest of mass movement] (J, p. 53)

Group 2: *zhen le yao-feng, ding le e lang* [have pressed the evil wind, and have set back the wicked waves] (H, p. 226), *Jiangnan chui lai na gu-zi xie feng* [the evil wind from the south of the Songhua River] (F, p. 231)

Because their metaphorical meaning in the CR novels usually concerns class and line struggles, meteorological items are often used together with ideological items. For example,

guo-neiwai jieji douzheng de bao-fengyu [the storm of class struggle at home and abroad] (F, p. 41), *geming lu shang conglai duo feng duo yu* [it is always windy and rainy on the revolutionary road] (J, p. 157), *Shehuizhuyi Jiaoyu Yundong de chunfeng* [the spring breeze of the Socialist Education Movement] (G, p. 23)

Moreover, because the political struggle is often likened to war, meteorological items are also used together with military items. For example,

(6) *Lao Wei, zhandou zai qian, zheng shi women jing fengyu, jian shimian de*

shihou. Wo shen shang ye hui zhan shang chentu, ye zheng gai dao <u>fengyu</u> li qu chongshuachongshua. Wo zheng pan zhe zaori chuyuan, qu xiang nimen xuexi, yu nimen gongtong <u>zhandou</u>!

[Old Wei, the battle lies ahead of us, we have reached the time to brave the storm and face the world. My body has also been besmirched with dust, and I intend to let the storm wash it away. I wish to leave the hospital soon in order to learn from you and fight together with you.] (H, p. 405)

Actually, under many circumstances meteorological items are used together with both ideological and military items due to the interrelated metaphorical meanings. The combined use of the three categories of stylistic items enhances the seriousness of the political struggles described in the novels. For example,

(7) *<u>Jieji douzheng</u> de <u>da feng da lang</u>, <u>dang-nei</u> liang tiao <u>luxian dou zheng</u> de <u>jing tao hai lang</u>, zengjin le Wannianqing de <u>gongchandangyuan</u>, <u>pin-xiazhongnong</u> he guangda sheyuan zhijian de <u>zhandou</u> tuanjie.*
[The great storms of class struggle and the terrifying waves of inner-Party struggle promoted the militant solidarity of the Communist members, the poor and lower middle peasants, and the masses of the commune members in Wannianqing.] (E, p. 559)

Finally, in keeping with the descriptions that political struggles and evil forces are likened to meteorological phenomena, the heroes who experience the struggles and oppose the evil forces are often likened to those plants and animals which are resistant to harsh weather. For example,

(8) *Ta xiang Longrong'ao kou de <u>changqing rong</u>, you si Jinfengshan shang de <u>ao xue song</u>.*
[He was like an evergreen banyan at the Longrong Col, and also like a braving-snow pine on Jinfeng Mountain.] (H, p. 578)
(9) *Baba xiang <u>shanying</u>, <u>chuanyue mi wu nong yun, ku yu qi feng</u>, xiang zhe geming, xiang zhe guangming, qianjin!*
[Like a mountain eagle, passing through the dense fog, thick cloud, weeping rain and wailing wind, Dad forged ahead towards revolution and brightness!] (J, p. 196)

INFLATED EXPRESSIONS

Inflated expressions here refer to those items produced by rhetorical exaggeration. As stylistic units in this study, they are limited to the scope of vocabulary use. Below are some examples:

(10) *lianxu san nian de ziran zaihai, yanjun de kaoyan le <u>Taishan ya ding bu</u>*
<u>*wan yao*</u> *de renmin gongshe sheyuan!*
[The natural calamities in the last successive three years severely tested
the members of people's communes who did not bend their heads even
if Mountain Tai toppled on them.] (F, p. 29)

(11) *Qunzhong shi zhenzheng de yingxiong, zhe liliang, <u>he shan shan rang lu</u>, <u>ji</u>*
<u>*shui shui zhi liu*</u> . . .
[The masses are real heroes, and their power is so great that when they
shout at mountains the mountains get out of the way, and when they
attack waters the waters stop flowing . . .] (G, p. 487)

Inflated items commonly appear in pre-CR poetic language, especially in
the new folk songs of the Great Leap Forward, but they are scarce in pre-CR
fiction language. However, inflated words and expressions are commonly used
in CR novels, forming another stylistic feature of the novels' language.

As noted above, CR novels include a number of improvised poems and
songs. Similar to the style of folk songs of the Great Leap Forward, they include
many inflated expressions. Below are two examples, of which (12) is a part of
an extemporaneous folk song, and (13) is a rhyme by the crowd cheering for
the main hero Liu Wangchun in *The Mountains and Rivers Roar* as he is
hammering stones.

(12) *Qie kan qingnian tuji-dui,*
    dao shan huo hai ye gan chuang.
    Zhaoqi pengbo gan geming,
    gan jiao Longrong huan xin zhuang.
    [We may look at the shock youth brigade; its members dare to climb a
    mountain of swords or plunge into a sea of flames. Making revolution
    vigorously; they dare order Longrong to change its appearance.] (H,
    p. 33)

(13) *Liu Dachui, you shen wei! Da de zhun, chui de mei! Meng shijin, bantian*
    lei! Shuijinggong, yao zhen sui! Longwang Ye, mang xiagui . . .
    [Big Hammer Liu has the power of the Gods! He is hammering precisely
    and beautifully! He does it hard, and his hammering is as powerful as
    thunderbolts! The Crystal Palace is about to be shaken to pieces! The
    Dragon King hastens to kneel . . .] (J, p. 28)

Apart from such improvised poems and songs, the prose language of CR
novels, with which we are more concerned in the present investigation, also
includes a large number of inflated expressions. Contextually, the inflated items
are often related to struggles with nature, such as in the above examples.
Nevertheless, the struggles with nature are always interwoven with ideological
struggles. The inflated items thus often concern ideology indirectly. On the one

hand, they are often used to express the positive characters' revolutionary will and heroic spirit. On the other hand, it is under the inspiration and encouragement of the Party's and Mao's ideology or through the test of the political struggles that the positive characters become so powerful and all-conquering. For example,

> (14) *Women shi nan bu zhu de! gongshe sheyuan de <u>tie jian tou</u>, yong zi li geng sheng de <u>tie biandan</u>, yiding neng <u>dan qi gongshe de heshan</u>!*
> [Anyway, no difficulties can scare us! With our iron shoulders, our commune members can surely carry the mountains and rivers of the commune on the iron poles of self-reliance!] (J, p. 147)

> (15) *Ting Mao Zhuxi de hua, zou shehuizhuyi daolu de ren, yi gege dou shi tui bu dao, za bu bian, chui bu lan, qiao bu sui de xiangdangdang de tie da han.*
> [Those who do as Chairman Mao said, and take the socialist road, are every one a man of iron who can't be pushed over, pressed flat, hammered into mash, nor stricken to pieces.] (H, p. 504)

> (16) *. . . zai jieji douzheng, luxian douzheng de feng-huo zhong peiyang, zaojiu chulai de zhe yi dai nianqing ren, xin hong gutou ying, zhen shi <u>shang tian neng zhai xing, ru di neng qin long</u>!*
> [This generation of young people, who were tempered in the fire of the class and line struggles, have red hearts and hard bones; they really can go up to the sky to pluck stars, and go down into the earth to catch dragons!] (J, p. 229)

Usually, the exaggeration in rhetoric reflected in the inflated items consists of both magnification and minimization, i.e. it either magnifies the confidence and power of human beings and minimizes the might of nature, or it magnifies the spirit and power of heroes whilst minimizing the strength of enemies.

In many cases, such as examples (14) to (16) above, the inflated items are used to represent collective resolution and power. When used to describe individual characters' will and strength, the inflated expressions are often used to depict the main heroes. The descriptions of collective characters with inflated items mainly appear in the contexts of struggles with nature, but inflated expressions describing individual heroes are more often related to the context of political struggles. For example,

> (17) *Tamen kan zhe Gao Daquan shou li de banfu, <u>ju shang tian</u>, <u>luo xia di</u>, <u>yi dao dian shan</u>, <u>yi gu feng xiao</u>, shenshen de sha chuan jin shu gen li . . .*
> [They watched as the axe in Gao Daquan's hands, raised up to the sky then brought down to the ground, with lightning flashing and a gust of wind whistling, cut deeply into the tree root.] (D, p. 379)

> (18) *'Fang le haizi, you shi zhao wo!' Da Lao Jiang <u>sheng ru zhong</u>, <u>zhan ru</u>*

song, tingli zai guizi mianqian, <u>xiang yi zuo bu dao de gao shan</u>.
['Set free the child, I take responsibility for everything!' With his voice like bell and his posture like a pine, Old Jiang stood straight in front of the Japanese soldiers, like a solid and towering mountain.] (E, p. 11)

(19) *Qingke zhi zhong, ta sixu fanteng* . . . <u>*Yu mantian fengyu, tian ta di lie,*</u> <u>*shan beng shi qing*</u>, *ziji neng* <u>*zuo gang liang tie zhu, lei da bu fei, dian hong*</u> <u>*bu san, ji gen bu dong*</u>?
[In a trice, thoughts thronged his mind . . . In the boundless wind and rain, with the sky falling down, the earth subsiding, the mountains collapsing, and the rocks cracking, could I become so stable that I wouldn't move under the attack of lightning and thunderbolt, just like a steel roof beam or an iron pillar?] (J, p. 53)

(20) *Liu Wangchun de liang zhi yanjing, jiu* <u>*xiang liang ba li jian*</u>, *na muguang zhen yao* <u>*ba Li Mianfu de wuzang liufu she chuan*</u>.
[Liu Wangchun's two eyes were like two sharp swords, seemingly able to stab through Li Mianfu's vital internal organs.] (J, p. 277)

All the above inflated items are contextual ad hoc creations. In addition, there are a number of idiomatic phrases and expressions in Chinese vocabulary which have inflated meaning. Our investigation shows that such established inflated items also account for much in CR novels. For example,

(21) *Yanqian zhe ge nianqing ren yijing neng* <u>*ding tian li di*</u> . . .
[The young man in front of him has become indomitable (literally, 'towering from earth to sky') . . .] (J, p. 229)

(22) *Women* <u>*bai zhe bu nao*</u>, <u>*kui ran ru shan*</u>!
[We never yield in spite of hundreds of setbacks, but stand majestically like mountains!] (J, p. 388)

(23) *Zhe yi sheng, ru* <u>*qingtian pili*</u>, *zhe liang zhang, shi* <u>*wan jun leiting*</u>, *ba Shi Jigen da yun le*.
[The shout as a bolt from the blue, and the two slaps as thunderbolts, made Shi Jigen faint.] (G, p. 528)

Chapter 13

The Vocabulary Style in General Perspective

THE GENERAL STYLE OF CR NOVEL VOCABULARY

Above we have analysed twelve vocabulary categories of CR novel through which the stylistic characteristics of each category have been presented. Now we place the results concerning the density of the categories into a general perspective (see Table 19).

For the sake of generalization, the twelve categories may be stylistically grouped into A and B below:

A: Idioms, proverbs, *xiehouyu*, classical verses, bookish items, colloquial items, and dialectal items.

B: Vulgar items, ideological items, military items, meteorological items, and inflated items.

Group A (the first stylistic classification) may be taken as a lexicological classification which is based mainly on the form (including lexical source) of the items, and Group B (the second stylistic classification) a semantic classification which is based mainly on the meaning (including metaphorical meaning) of the items. In comparison with pre-CR novels, the density and distribution of the twelve vocabulary categories represent the lexical style of CR novels.

As shown in Table 19, the comprehensive distribution pattern is that the CR novels have a higher density of ideological items, idioms, *xiehouyu*, classical verses, bookish items, military items, meteorological items, and inflated items, and the pre-CR novels have higher density of vulgar items, proverbs, colloquial items, and dialectal items. It needs to be noted that for proverbs, the CR novels have a higher density of literary proverbs although they have a lower density of folk proverbs, which produces a lower density of the whole category. Next, for *xiehouyu*, because the quantitative distinction between the pre-CR novels and CR novels is blurred by some exceptional samples, the present statistical result cannot be taken as a generalized stylistic feature.

According to the above comprehensive pattern of distribution density, it may be reasonably concluded that in comparison with the pre-CR novels, the holistic vocabulary style of the CR novels is more bookish in form and more politicized in meaning.

Firstly, within the first stylistic classification, in addition to a higher rate of specific items under 'bookish', the CR novels have a higher density of idioms, literary proverbs and classical verses, which also share the stylistic characteristic of bookishness. On the one hand, the bookish style of literary proverbs and classical verses are naturally definite because they are quotations from classical literature. As to idioms, they are generally taken to be bookish because most of them also come from traditional literature. On the other hand, in addition to a lower density of specific items under 'colloquial', the CR novels have a lower rate of folk proverbs and dialectal items. The folk proverbs are established oral sayings and have evident colloquial style. The colloquial style of dialectal items is also distinctive because they are usually from local spoken language, some of which even lack suitable Chinese character transcripts. Therefore with regard to CR novel vocabulary, the higher density of specific bookish items, idioms, literary proverbs, and classic verses is one side of the holistic bookish style, and the lower density of specific colloquial items, folk proverbs and dialectal items is the complementary side of the bookishness.

Next, within the second stylistic classification, all of the categories are more densely distributed in the CR novels, with the exception of vulgar expressions. In CR novels the other four categories (ideological items, military items, meteorological items, and inflated items) are all politicized. Not restricted to the items under 'ideological', the metaphorical meaning of all the categories are generally related to politicized struggles and are usually used in contexts concerning ideology. As for vulgar expressions, which have a lower density in CR novels, their reduced distribution, as stated above, is related to an ideological principle in dealing with the characters' language, i.e. only the vulgar expressions spoken by positive characters have been reduced. Thus, the distribution of all the categories in the second stylistic classification indicates the more politicized style of CR novel vocabulary in comparison with that of pre-CR novels.

Apart from the politicized characteristic, the distributive pattern of the categories in the second stylistic classification (higher density of ideological, military, meteorological and inflated items, and lower density of vulgar expressions) indicates another feature which is consistent with the bookish style shown by the distribution of the categories in the first stylistic classification. Firstly, for the four categories with high density, the ideological items as a whole are bookish rather than colloquial because they are mainly from political documentation such as newspapers, political magazines and politicians' works. The military and meteorological items under discussion are figures of speech which are usually related to ideology. Compared to their literal usage, the metaphorical use of these items is more bookish in rhetoric. The inflated items also have a certain rhetorical bookish flavour. Secondly, vulgar expressions which have a low rate in CR novels are clearly colloquial. To sum up, politicization in meaning and bookishness in form are the unified general style of the CR novel vocabulary.

PERIOD STYLE AND AUTHORS' PERSONAL STYLES

The above generalized vocabulary style, based on the comprehensive distributions of the two stylistic classifications, i.e. bookish in form and politicized in meaning, may be regarded as the period style of the CR novels' vocabulary which novelists during the Cultural Revolution followed intentionally and/or unintentionally. But the period style cannot be shown uniformly in all CR novels because of different authors' individual or personal styles.

In the present investigation we found that more and larger distributive irregularities exist in individual pre-CR novels than in CR novels. The consequent conclusion could be that the authors' personal language styles are not as conspicuous in CR novels as in pre-CR novels. In other words, the period style predominates over the novelists' personal styles to a greater extent in CR novels.

Lastly, within CR novels the dissimilarities of the individual distributions in the first stylistic classification are larger than those in the second. According to the above definition, the first stylistic classification is based on the 'form' features and no direct relationship exists between its categories and ideology. But the second stylistic classification is based on the 'meaning' characteristics and its categories are generally related to ideology. Thus the fact that the first stylistic classification has larger dissimilarities in the individual distributions shows that the authors' personal language styles become more prominent in the distribution of the non-ideological items.

Conclusion

THE PRESENT STUDY IN PERSPECTIVE

The publication of one hundred and twenty-six novels in a ten-year period is a rather small number in a country as large as China. However, taking into account the political circumstances during the years of the Cultural Revolution, this figure is actually high because the average annual quantity was at a similar level to that of the pre-CR period. This study has concentrated on twenty-four CR agricultural novels, which occupy a prominent place among all CR novels.

Literary Characteristics

The first part of this study is literary analysis concentrating on the characterization of the novels' main heroes. It has analysed five aspects. The first is personal background, which covers the main heroes' age, sex, marital state, class origin, family background, education and military experience. In analysing these personal factors, this study has emphasized their significance in the overall characterization of the heroes.

The second aspect is physical qualities. By listing a number of stereotyped words and expressions with respect to the heroes' constitution, air, features, expression, manner, bearing, voice, etc., the analysis has stressed two points: Firstly, examining the way in which the authors describe the heroes' physical appearance, which from one angle shows the heroes' 'loftiness, greatness and perfection'; and secondly, analysing the exterior characteristics of the heroes as indicative of current aesthetic views on the physical portrait of idealized heroes.

The third aspect is ideological qualities, which are divided into the qualities of class and line struggles and the qualities of altruism and collectivism. In the case of the former, the analysis primarily concerns the heroes' political foresight and insight into the politicized campaigns in the countryside; in the case of the latter, the analysis has emphasized the heroes' thoughts and actions in serving the public or others' interests. In recognizing that ideological qualities are also important in the characterization of the main heroes of pre-CR novels, the analysis has accordingly emphasized the differences between the heroes in CR and pre-CR novels.

The fourth aspect of the characterization of heroes involves temperamental and behavioural qualities. The analysis concerns the heroes' feelings, manners and conduct which are primarily based on their temperamental and behavioural qualities rather than on pure ideological consciousness. Qualities such as generosity, honesty, modesty, level-headedness, reasonableness, politeness, and submissiveness, all commonly shared by the heroes, have been emphasized in this analysis. This aspect has also involved an analysis of the foundation of the values and standards shown in the characterization of the heroes with respect to temperament and behaviour. The part played by traditional Chinese conventions and norms in forming the foundation has been discussed.

The fifth and final aspect is prominence given to the heroes, which concerns the methods used by the authors to set off the heroes by following the 'three prominences' and other stock devices. In particular, the relationship between the heroes and other characters, as well as that between the heroes and natural surroundings, has been explored.

Some findings with respect to the literary characteristics of CR novels, for instance the fact that the main heroes' ideological qualities are emphasized in the characterization, are to be expected because they conform to generally recognized literary trends and policies. As to the expected characteristics, this analysis has examined both the ways in which the novels display such characteristics, and the extent to which the characteristics conform to expectations. This principle has also been pursued in the investigation into the linguistic characteristics of the CR novels. Other findings, however, were not expected and some even prove contrary to generally believed trends or facts about CR fiction. The following is a summary of some less predictable yet significant points.

1. It was expected that CR literature would bear little relation to pre-CR literature, since the latter was attacked during the Cultural Revolution. However, this study indicates that CR literature followed the same direction as pre-CR literature and carried through the pre-CR radical line. The theories attacked during the Cultural Revolution had been criticized in the pre-CR period, and many principles promoted in the CR period had been previously set forth in the pre-CR period.

2. Similarity was expected to exist in certain aspects of the main heroes. For instance, the heroes share similar ideological qualities because of the official unification of ideology, and the relationship between the heroes and other characters is patternized because it is based on the formulaic 'three prominences'. However, it was not expected that this similarity would also cover aspects such as the heroes' personal backgrounds, temperamental qualities, and physical qualities, given that there were no established or formulaic theories which would provide for such similarity. For example, portraits of physical qualities follow certain set characteristics and include a number of stereotyped laudatory words and expressions, which make the main heroes share a general resemblance.

3. During the Cultural Revolution, the overriding value in personal qualities was spiritual beauty, and the preference for physical beauty was attacked as bourgeois or petty bourgeois sentiment. However, this study shows that CR novelists set out to create a 'unity' of spiritual and physical beauty. So the main heroes of CR novels are generally portrayed as having physical or outward beauty.

4. It is widely known that traditional Chinese culture, especially that based on Confucianism, was attacked in the propaganda of the Cultural Revolution. However, temperamental and behavioural qualities such as kindness, righteousness, generosity, gentleness, honesty, loyalty, intelligence, reasonableness and politeness, consistently emphasized in the heroes' characters, all find reference in Confucian doctrines. This study has reached the tentative conclusion that the foundation of the heroes' temperamental and behavioural qualities is a combination of the current ideological principles and traditional orthodox Confucian moral, behavioural and temperamental norms.

5. For the CR agricultural novels, in view of the heroes' status as peasants, their low level of education, and their roles in class and line struggles, it was not expected that the CR novels would attach much importance to the heroes' 'artistic' qualities. Nevertheless, it is shown, for example, that the heroes tend to admire beautiful scenery, with such things as bright moonlight, beautiful flowers, and flowing water inspiring them to poetry, music and/or painting. These descriptions further indicate the idealistic nature of the portrayal of the heroes.

Linguistic Characteristics

The second part of this study is linguistic analysis focusing on lexical style. Statistical and comparative approaches to style have been employed for they have the support of objective and contrastive evidence. The analysis is based on ten sample novels (three pre-CR novels and seven CR novels). Twelve stylistic categories have been established for the analysis. They are vulgar expressions, ideological words and expressions, idioms, proverbs, *xiehouyu*, classical verse segments, 'bookish', 'colloquial', dialectal words, military items in metaphorical use, meteorological items in metaphorical use, and inflated items. Apart from the meteorological items and inflated items which are primarily analysed qualitatively, the other ten categories have been analysed quantitatively. In aiming for a high degree of precision, most of these categories have been counted exhaustively. In all cases of quantitative analysis, the investigation has presented the density and distribution of stylistic items, which are concerned with the commonly shared characteristics of vocabulary use, the relation between the common characteristics and the authors' individual characteristics of vocabulary use, and the similarities and differences of vocabulary use between the pre-CR novels and CR novels. In some cases, the analysis has presented the density and distribution of stylistic items according to narrators and different types of character, demonstrating further the significance of linguistic style in the literary characteristics. After the twelve categories of stylistic item were each investigated separately, a comprehensive analysis placing all the categories into a general framework was made so as to reach conclusions about the general or holistic lexical style of CR novels.

For expected stylistic characteristics, the analysis, based on statistics, has emphasized the extent to which the characteristics conform to expectations. For example, it is generally thought that the language of CR novels is strongly political in style. This judgement has been confirmed in this investigation by a high density of relevant stylistic items such as ideological words and expressions, military items in metaphorical use, meteorological items in metaphorical use, and inflated items. On the other hand, this study has presented a number of unexpected results. Some of these results concern the style of individual novelists and individual works. For instance, Hao Ran's CR novel *The Golden Road* is often criticized by Chinese and Western scholars for being excessively marked by ideological flavour. However, this study shows that from the linguo-stylistic point of view, this novel has the lowest density of ideological words and expressions of the CR novels sampled. The density along this dimension is even lower than that of Liu Qing's well-known pre-CR novel *The Builders*. Other unexpected results concern the general linguistic style of CR novels. Below is a summary of some significant unexpected stylistic characteristics commonly shared by CR novels.

1. It was expected that the intensification of the direction to serve workers, peasants, and soldiers would further promote the colloquial style of CR novels. But quite the contrary emerged. The language of CR novels has a lower rate of colloquial stylistic items, such as specific colloquial items and folk proverbs, in comparison with pre-CR novels. Moreover, since traditional Chinese literature was under attack during the Cultural Revolution, it was expected that bookish stylistic items derived from traditional literature, such as specific bookish items, idioms, literary proverbs and classical verses, would be less densely distributed in CR novels than in pre-CR novels. Yet according to this study, CR novels have a higher density of these bookish stylistic items than pre-CR novels. These distribution patterns indicate that CR novels generally have a stronger bookish language style than pre-CR novels.

2. In view of the fact that abusive words and other vulgar expressions were prevalent in denouncing opposed people or things during the Cultural Revolution, and in view of the fact that the major motifs of CR novels are class and line struggles, it was expected that CR novels would have a denser distribution of vulgar words and expressions. However, this study indicates that the rate of vulgar expressions in CR novels is only about fifty percent of that in pre-CR novels. Therefore, the language style of unofficial writings such as big-character posters and leaflets or oral slogans, which were replete with vulgar words and expressions, are not representative of the linguistic style of official CR publications. Generalizations that CR writings and speeches were full of vulgar expressions do not properly reflect this fact.

3. The campaign to popularize Modern Standard Chinese has been the government's fundamental language policy since 1956. It is generally thought by post-CR scholars in mainland China that the popularization of Modern Standard Chinese was impeded during the Cultural Revolution. However, this investigation has shown a trend towards decreasing dialectal items in CR novels. That means that if the frequency of dialectal items in CR novels can reflect the popularization of Modern Standard Chinese, the campaign was not 'impeded', but rather promoted during the decade.

Moreover, on the holistic level, although the relationship between general linguistic style and the authors' individual language style is less predictable, it is nevertheless important. In comparing CR with pre-CR novels, the general language style in the CR novels predominates over the novelists' personal language style to a greater extent. On the other hand, within the CR novels, the authors' individual language styles are more prominent in the distribution of the stylistic items as classified according to 'form' or lexicalogical features.

CR NOVELS AND CONTEMPORARY CHINESE LITERATURE

The Creation of CR Novels

In contemporary Chinese literature, one important role played by CR novels is that they tested the newly established literary theories and principles from the angle of fictional creation.

At the beginning of the Cultural Revolution, the authorities made efforts to cultivate their ideal literature and art while criticizing pre-CR literature and art. The model theatrical works represented the highest achievements of their effort. Based on these theatrical works, a set of new principles and regulations was established. Until the end of the Cultural Revolution, these principles and regulations were promoted in the literary and art world and to a great extent they shaped the current aesthetic views on literature and art.

Fiction was one of the most important fields in which to carry out the newly established principles and regulations due to the genre's suitability. The authors of CR novels were also highly conscious in their attitude towards the new literary and artistic theories and principles. Thus from the literary point of view, CR novels and their creation represent a particular literary trend in contemporary Chinese literature.

Wendy Larson pointed out, 'From the experiments of early realist writers up through the socialist realism of the post-Yan'an period, realism as fiction form attained the stolidity and power of a reified yet nonetheless revolutionary modern literary ideology.'[1] Realism was consistently promoted in the history of communist Chinese literature between the 1930s and the 1970s. In emphasizing specific political purposes or tasks at different stages, all important literary slogans were based on realism or included realism: 'national revolutionary realism', 'democratic realism', 'realism of the Three People's Principles', 'revolutionary realism', 'socialist realism'. The slogan of 2RR (2RR-2), which was exclusively promoted during the Cultural Revolution, also included realism. Actually, in the CR period, discussions about literary theories and criticism were generally still within the past theoretical frame of Socialist Realism, i.e. 'the theory of reflection, theory of typicality, the theory of truth and the theory of the relationship between world outlook and creative method'.[2] Moreover, taking into account factors regarding technique of expression, such as structure, narration, characterization and language, CR novels shared the basic style of previous novels which were accepted as works of realism.

Nevertheless, the realism represented in CR novels is different from the conventional understanding of realism, according to which artistic authenticity — the authenticity of representation in works — is significant.[3] However, authenticity in this sense was criticized in China in the years between the 1950s and 1970s. A set of symbolic formulations became popular in defining authenticity, including 'developing authenticity' and 'essential authenticity'. These formulations stemmed from the tenets of Socialist Realism.[4] Based on these formulations, the connotation of artistic authenticity tended towards increasing idealization. After revolutionary romanticism was officially juxtaposed with revolutionary realism, idealization was further justified and emphasized and reached its peak in the Cultural Revolution.

This study shows the idealization of life as described in CR novels. With respect to the characterization of the main heroes, the standards of 'loftiness, greatness, perfection and brilliance' epitomize this idealization. The heroes' heroic and revolutionary personal or family backgrounds, their handsome or beautiful appearance, their extraordinary political foresight and insight, their complete altruism, their well-cultivated manner and behaviour, their relationship with other characters etc., all embody this principle. The values reflected in the idealization are ideology and elements of traditional culture.

Apart from the principle of idealization, another general principle governing

CR novels can be drawn from this study, namely, 'standardization', which includes purification and unification with regard to both literary and linguistic aspects. With respect to the literary aspect, standardization is first of all reflected in the purification and unification of literary policies and theories. Radical theories and principles were promoted, but all challenging propositions were denounced. The model theatrical works were set as examples, and the experiences of their creation were established as formulaic principles. Secondly, fictional factors regarding content, such as time settings, motif types, subject matter categories, and character varieties, are all highly unified, i.e. they are generally related to modern workers, peasants and soldiers. Thirdly, factors concerning technique of expression including narration, structure and characterization follow the promoted formulaic patterns or principles. In characterization, for instance, the main heroes' personal background, ideological awareness, and behavioural qualities are all portrayed according to a set of established ideological and traditional didactic criteria. Even portraits of physical appearance follow certain set features and include a number of stereotyped words of praise, making the heroes share a handsome/beautiful resemblance. Moreover, the relationship between heroes and other characters was formularized into the fixed 'three prominences' and 'three foilings'.

As to the linguistic aspect, a variety of lexical distributive features in CR novel language reveals elements of the standardization. For example, the language of CR novels has a low rate of dialectal words and expressions, which indicates that it follows the direction of the popularization of Modern Standard Chinese, which is primarily concerned with overcoming dialectal elements. Next, CR novel language includes low rates of vulgar and colloquial elements but high rates of bookish and idiomatic elements. This suggests that CR novels tend towards purifying their language, i.e. decreasing casual and informal elements. Moreover, in contrast to pre-CR novels, the differences between authors' individual language styles are fewer among CR novels. This suggests a tendency towards unification of language style.

On the one hand, the above idealization and standardization reflect the authorities' efforts to create their 'not only ideologically correct, but also artistically advanced literature'. On the other hand, they reflect the strict control of the authorities over literature during the Cultural Revolution.[5] Furthermore, the idealization and standardization reflect the current aesthetic views on literature, which were in accordance with the fashion of the period of setting examples. During the Cultural Revolution, apart from collective models like Daqing in industry, Dazhai in agriculture, and the PLA in the country as a whole, numbers of individual examples were set in different professions and at different stages. Setting examples was intended to propagate their didactic effect. With respect to literature, its social didactic effect had consistently been promoted in China and had become an important part of literary aesthetic standards.[6] During the Cultural Revolution, literature's didactic effect was even further emphasized. The heroes and their lives as described in literary works were taken to be models of the people, and even negative characters were taken to be 'teachers by negative example' [*fanmian jiaoyuan*]. It is evident that idealization and standardization in literary creation intensified the didactic effect, i.e. by offering idealized and standardized models to readers.

However, CR novels were denounced after the Cultural Revolution, and the theories and slogans upon which the novels were based were also accordingly repudiated. This fact evidences the failure of CR fictional creation. Since the governing principles of CR fictional creation are idealization and standardization, the failure of CR fictional creation suggests that idealization and standardization are misleading principles for literature. It thus could be concluded that literary creation in the immediate post-CR period would take an inverse direction, i.e. supporting authenticity, individuality and originality.

CR Novels and Pre-CR Fiction

It is known that radical literary policies and theories held the dominant position in pre-CR literature. We may draw the relationship between CR novels and pre-CR fiction from several angles. Firstly, CR novels carried on the radical elements of pre-CR fiction. In accordance with changing political situations, and out of artistic awareness, literary intellectuals often challenged the radical tendency of the pre-CR period. The eight negative expressions listed in Jiang Qing's 'Forum Summary' are examples. Moreover, in the pre-CR period, as Joe C. Huang has pointed out, some writers tried to strike a balance between giving prominence to ideology and maintaining artistic authenticity, and this made their works 'not only first-class political novels but also brilliant artistic achievements'.[7] However, during the Cultural Revolution the authorities led by Jiang Qing charged that pre-CR literature was impaired by a revisionist line. With this, a general clean-up of all pre-CR views challenging the radical tendency was launched. This clean-up offered the authorities an opportunity to carry out more fully pre-CR radical theories and principles. Therefore, CR novels are a comprehensive expression of the pre-CR radical theories and principles in fictional creation.

Secondly, in many respects, the relationship between CR novels and pre-CR fiction is not only 'inheritance' but development. With respect to characterization of heroes, for instance, in view of the increasing tendency towards idealization in pre-CR fictional creation, Shao Quanlin proposed deepening realism. According to Shao, it was important to carefully portray not only the heroes but also the people in the middle, for the sake of the authenticity of realism. Moreover, heroes were also imperfect. Shao's proposal was criticized by the pre-CR radical line. Nevertheless, the criticism did not go so far as to officially promote 'perfect heroes'. So, neither were concrete theories on perfect heroes officially established, nor were writers claiming to intentionally create perfect heroes. However, during the Cultural Revolution portraying perfect heroes was openly declared as the primary task of socialist literature. A series of standards and formulations was established to implement this principle. Writers also claimed to follow the standards, principles and formulations conscientiously.

Lastly, the theoretical documents, principles and slogans governing pre-CR literature, such as Mao's 'Yan'an Talks' and the slogan 2RR, were still promoted as literary theoretical foundations in the CR period, although the pre-CR literary works were generally repudiated. That means that CR novels and pre-CR fiction share the same theorectical foundation but represent different understandings. With respect to 2RR for example, in fictional creation before the Cultural Revolution, Liu Qing's *The Builders* was an acknowledged work representing this creative method. Later, however, *The Builders* was attacked in the Cultural Revolution even though the 2RR method was further promoted. Evidently, then, the attack on the previous representative works, whilst promoting the creative method upon which these works were based, suggests the CR and pre-CR authorities' different interpretations of 2RR.

Therefore, CR literature epitomized and developed pre-CR radical literary policies and theories. CR novels carried forward pre-CR radical theories and principles in fictional creation.

CR Novels and Post-CR Fiction

Post-CR fiction here mainly refers to those works published between 1977 and 1987.[8] Although 'the political orientation of literature of the Gang-of-Four period and earlier continued to exert a strong influence' in the first two years after the Cultural Revolution, the change in post-CR literature started and gradually speeded up during the post-CR period.[9] The change in political climate after the Cultural Revolution was certainly important in bringing about a new trend in post-CR literature. Nevertheless, the repudiation of CR literature including CR novels played a significant role in leading to a change in the direction of fiction away from its former ways. This change of direction indicates that post-CR fictional creation followed a tendency in which novelists intentionally emphasized and intensified many elements which were antithetical to CR novel creation.

First of all, a new tendency developed towards the diversification of creative methods and styles. Leo Ou-fan Lee's following statement shows the cause and significance of a change of literary techniques.

> Given this general legacy of modern Chinese literature — its moral weight, ideological thrust, and its later appropriation by politics — it is most significant that, after the downfall of the Gang of Four, a number of writers . . . are beginning

to pay renewed attention to technique . . . And they labour conscientiously with technical innovations . . . In a sense, this new phenomenon can be viewed as a literary form of dissidence, of departing from and thereby challenging the long-established theory and practice of imaginative writing'.[10]

During the first stage of the post-CR period, the disapproval of CR literature with respect to creative methods and literary styles aroused the literary world's efforts at restoring the realism of pre-CR literature. Later, the repudiation of CR literature inspired people to re-examine pre-CR literature and to criticize the pre-CR tendency of unification of literary theories and policies. Consequently, realism's monopoly position in contemporary Chinese literature was undermined. A variety of collective and individual literary styles and creative methods came into being in post-CR literature. In 1987, Wang Meng, himself a writer and Minister of Culture from 1986 to 1989, described the diversity of literary methods and styles in post-CR fictional creation.

> . . . In 1980, people began to debate whether fiction in the stream-of-consciousness style [*yishiliu*] was understandable;[11] in 1983, people set off on a discussion about modernism [*xiandai-pai*]. However, in 1985, various new methods became fashionable. People discussed the formation of typical characters and the important role of human nature. The tradition of realism as writing truth was restored, the styles and methods such as fantasticality [*huangdan*], abnormality [*bianxing*], illusion [*xuni*], magic [*mohuan*] and psychoanalysis, came into vogue . . .'[12]

Michael D. Duke observed, 'Many writers began to experiment with nontraditional narrative forms including nonlinear plot lines or plotless narratives, multiple narrators, unreliable narrators and antiheroes, stream-of-consciousness, metafiction, and magic realism.'[13] Joseph S. M. Lau and Howard Goldblatt also commented, 'The Chinese writers of the post-Mao era have entered a brave new world of narrative possibilities that enables them to circumvent political taboos and illuminate the realities of China through forms and techniques as diverse as parable, farce, modernism, avant-gardism, and, more recently, magical realism.'[14]

Writers have consciously tried to develop and establish their individual literary style. Many popular writers (including some CR novelists), such as Wang Meng, Wang Zengqi, Zhang Xianliang, Jiang Zilong, Liu Xinwu, Chen Rong, Gu Hua, Zhang Kangkang, Zheng Wanlong, Zhang Jie, Jia Pingwa, Li Hangyu, Zong Pu, A Cheng, Wang Shuo, Han Shaogong, Mo Yan, Zhang Xinxin, Wang Anyi, Liu Suola, and Zhang Chengzhi, have demonstrated their rather consistent individual characteristics.[15] Based on individual styles, different schools formed and developed. For instance, according to critics in 1986, post-CR fiction may at least be classified into seven schools: fiction exploring social problems, fiction describing provincial cultures, fiction of feelings and images, fiction depicting town cultures, fiction with a 'queer flavour', native-soil fiction, and illogical fiction.[16] It is likely that the above unusual diversity of literary styles and methods is inversely related to the unusual unification of styles and methods of the CR period.

CR novels tend to describe modern workers, peasants and soldiers. Other categories of time-settings, subject matter or people, such as historical events and people, and contemporary intellectuals, were avoided. However, it is precisely these things that became popular in post-CR fiction. For example, it is widely known that post-CR novels on historical events and people are one of the representative achievements of post-CR fiction, while novels about contemporary intellectuals are also important. Other categories of subject matter which were ignored or avoided during the CR period but which became popular in the post-CR period, include overseas Chinese life, science,[17] knight-errantry, crime and hooliganism,[18] and secret societies. Furthermore, no contemporary tragic stories can be found in pre-CR and CR fiction because it was held that tragedies could not occur in socialist China. Yet 'scar fiction', which targets the tragedies in individual lives in contemporary China, is an important part of post-CR literature.

In CR novels, the main heroes are all characterized according to the standards of 'loftiness, greatness, perfection'. By contrast, in post-CR novels published after 1978, not only are these heroes absent, but even the less idealized pre-CR heroes are missing. Post-CR fiction tends to have non-heroic characters as its protagonists. In many cases, middle characters or even negative characters as defined during the pre-CR and CR periods become the main characters of post-CR fiction. For example, in scar fiction many protagonists are the 'rightists' of 1957 or the 'counter-revolutionaries' of the Cultural Revolution. In the novels describing people and events in history, most protagonists are old aristocrats, emperors, officials, scholars, landlords etc., all of whom had been condemned during the CR period.

In pre-CR novels, individual human nature is subordinate to class nature, as prescribed by ideology. Thus, despite pre-CR heroes' hesitations in dealing with conflicts between personal interests and collective or others' interests, it is always the case that the characters privilege the latter over the former. This principle is further developed in CR novels: Heroes wholeheartedly devote themselves to the Party's cause without regard to personal interest, and their personal delight, anger and sorrow are all related to the pursuit of Party policies and the public interest. However, in post-CR fiction, dimensions of human nature including personal feelings, individual interests, physiological desires, etc. are commonly seen. For instance, love and sex were banned in CR novels, but descriptions of love and sex are popular in post-CR fiction. According to Perry Link in 1983, 'Romantic love, perhaps because it was banned from the printed page for the decade 1966-76, became a hackneyed theme. Even stories whose main interest lay elsewhere often included a touch of melodramatic romance, almost as if a formula required it.'[19] Wang Meng, one of the writers promoting human nature, expressed reservations at the overt depictions of sexuality in post-CR fiction. He stated, '. . . It is certain that life as depicted in literature and art includes sexuality, and people's psychology includes their sexual desires and feelings. However, seeing that authors enthusiastically scramble [*qu zhi ruo wu* — literally, going after something like a flock of ducks] to describe them, I cannot help worrying that it is becoming rampant and may go beyond acceptable limits . . .'[20]

As to language style, CR novels show a tendency towards unification. Dominated by the general period style, authors' individual language styles are not conspicuously shown. However, post-CR fiction shows considerable diversification of individual language style. Leo Ou-fan Lee observed the trend towards experimentalism in post-CR fictional language, and stated, 'the use of language as style — the particular manner of linguistic expression evolved by the writer — did not enter into general discussion until after 1976'.[21] With regard to vocabulary, CR novels have a high density of ideological items, idioms, classical items, literary proverbs, bookish items, military items, meteorological items in metaphorical use, and inflated items, but a low density of vulgar items, folk proverbs, colloquial and dialectal items. These patterns of distribution indicate that the language in CR novels tends towards a formal, standard and plain style. By contrast, the language in post-CR fiction shows a trend towards relaxed, informal, substandard or non-standard, but sometimes abstruse and ambiguous style. The aforementioned stylistic items generally have a contrasting pattern of distribution in post-CR fiction. For example, CR novels tend to avoid vulgar expressions and dialectal items, thereby contributing to a more formal and standardized language, whilst post-CR novels show a marked increase in both of these categories. It seems fashionable for characters' speech to include abusive words, and for novels set in the countryside to use many local dialectal words and expressions. It is not surprising, however, that ideological expressions, one of the most densely distributed stylistic items in CR novels, are greatly reduced in post-CR novels. It should be noted that although the language of pre-CR novels has also an inverse distribution of the above categories of stylistic item, the contrast between pre-CR novels and CR novels is smaller than that between CR novels and post-CR novels.

Despite other factors, then, CR fiction has played a significant role in deciding the development of post-CR fiction. That is, the elements which are emphasized in CR fiction are weakened in post-CR fiction, and the elements which are ignored or avoided in CR fiction are subsequently intensified in post-CR fiction. According to this study, all of the main characteristics of CR novels are governed by the principles of idealization and standardization. Thus post-CR fiction clearly developed in a direction contrary to these two principles, i.e. it developed towards authenticity in representation and the diversification of content and form.

Tables

Table 1 Sample Novels

Group	Ref. code	Author and title	Publication year	Time setting	Geographical setting	Subject matter	Authorship
I Pre-CR novels	A	Zhou Libo, Great Changes in a Mountain Village (Vol. 1)	1958	1955–56	South-central		Professional
	B	Liu Qing, The Builders	1960	1953	West	Cooperative transformation	
	C	Hao Ran, The Sun Shines Bright (Vol. 1)	1964	1957	North		
	D	Hao Ran, The Golden Road (Vol. 1)	1972	1950–51			
II	E	Chen Rong, Evergreen				Opposition to quotas on household basis	Novice
	F	Lin Yu and Xie Shu, The Roaring Songhua River (Vol. 1)	1975	1962	Northeast		Two; one professional
CR novels	G	Zhu Jian, Qingshi Fort		1964	East	Socialist education	Novice
	H	The 'Three-in-one' Group of Baise Prefecture, Mountains Green after Rain	1976	1964–68	Southwest	Learning from Dazhai	'Three-in-one' group
	I	Tian Dongzhao, The Long Rainbow		1970	North		Novice
	J	Gu Hua, The Mountains and Rivers Roar		1972–73	South-central		Amateur novice

Table 2   Number of Chinese Characters in the Ten Novels

Novel ref.	Total no. recorded by publisher	No. calculated by author		Total no. (accuracy up to ±500)
		No. per line by line no. per page	No. per page by total page no.	
A	223,000	27 x 26	702 x 306	215,000
B	n/a	27 x 26	702 x 511	359,000
C	472,000	27 x 26	702 x 672	472,000
D	n/a	27 x 26	702 x 648	455,000
E	340,000	25 x 24	600 x 565	339,000
F	310,000	26 x 25	650 x 481	313,000
G	n/a	26 x 25	650 x 531	345,000
H	360,000	25 x 24	600 x 589	353,000
I	360,000	26 x 24	624 x 576	359,000
J	n/a	28 x 26	728 x 539	392,000

Table 3   The Density of Vulgar Expressions

3 – 1   The ten novels

Novel ref.	Total no. Chinese characters	Total vulgar exps.	No. vulgar exps. per 100,000 chas.
A	215,000	108	50.23
B	359,000	99	27.58
C	472,000	146	30.93
D	455,000	44	9.67
E	339,000	30	8.85
F	313,000	63	20.13
G	345,000	155	44.92
H	353,000	72	20.40
I	359,000	32	8.91
J	392,000	38	9.69

3 – 2   The two groups compared

Group ref.	Total no. Chinese characters	Total vulgar exps.	No. vulgar exps. per 100,000 chas.
I	1,046,000	353	33.75
II	2,556,000	434	16.98

Table 4 The Distribution of Vulgar Expressions over the Functional Varieties

4 – 1   The ten novels

Novel ref.	Total vulgar exps.	Generally uncouth		Expletive		Abuse		Humorous		Grammatical auxiliary	
		No.	%	No.	%	No.	%	No.	%	No.	%
A	108	25	23.1	2	1.9	62	57.4	18	16.7	1	0.9
B	99	17	17.2	9	9.0	67	67.7	4	4.0	2	2.0
C	146	38	26.0	8	5.5	75	51.4	12	8.2	13	8.9
D	44	16	36.4	5	11.4	19	43.2	1	2.3	3	6.8
E	30	9	30.0	0	0	16	53.3	1	3.3	4	13.3
F	63	30	47.6	5	7.9	20	31.7	4	6.3	4	6.3
G	155	58	37.4	6	3.9	87	56.1	1	0.6	3	1.9
H	72	32	44.4	3	4.2	36	50.0	1	1.4	0	0
I	32	13	40.6	2	6.3	15	46.9	2	6.3	0	0
J	38	11	28.9	0	0	20	52.6	6	15.8	1	2.6

4 – 2   The two groups compared

Group ref.	Total vulgar exps.	Generally uncouth		Expletive		Abuse		Humorous		Grammatical auxiliary	
		No.	%	No.	%	No.	%	No.	%	No.	%
I	353	80	22.7	19	5.4	204	57.8	34	9.6	16	4.5
II	434	167	38.5	21	4.8	213	49.1	16	3.7	15	3.5

Table 5 The Distribution of Vulgar Expressions by Sex

5 – 1   The ten novels

Novel ref.	Total vulgar exps.	Male		Female		Others		Narrator	
		No.	%	No.	%	No.	%	No.	%
A	108	64	59.3	42	38.9	2	1.9	0	0
B	99	80	80.8	13	13.1	2	2.0	4	4.0
C	146	101	69.2	43	29.5	1	0.7	1	0.7
D	44	37	84.1	4	9.1	0	0	3	6.8
E	30	13	43.3	16	53.3	0	0	1	3.3
F	63	49	77.8	8	12.7	2	3.2	4	6.3
G	155	94	60.6	49	31.6	4	2.6	8	5.2
H	72	42	58.3	20	27.8	2	2.8	8	11.1
I	32	15	46.9	14	43.8	2	6.3	1	3.1
J	38	27	71.1	6	15.8	2	5.3	3	7.9

5 – 2　The two groups compared

Group ref.	Total vulgar exps.	Male		Female		Others		Narrator	
		No.	%	No.	%	No.	%	No.	%
I	353	245	69.4	98	27.8	5	1.4	5	1.4
II	434	277	63.8	117	27.0	12	2.8	28	6.5

Table 6　The Distribution of Vulgar Expressions According to Type of Speaker

6 – 1　The ten novels

Novel ref.	Total vulgar exps.	Main hero		Main villain		Other positive characters		Backward elements		Other negative characters		Others	
		No.	%	No.	%	No.	%	No.	%	No.	%	No.	%
A	108	3	2.8	0	0	52	48.1	50	46.3	1	0.9	2	1.9
B	99	5	5.1	14	14.1	54	54.5	19	19.2	0	0	6	6.1
C	146	1	0.7	9	6.2	56	38.4	56	38.4	23	15.8	2	1.4
D	44	1	2.3	1	2.3	19	43.2	17	38.6	3	6.8	3	6.8
E	30	0	0	3	10.0	6	20.0	15	50.0	5	16.7	1	3.0
F	63	2	3.2	0	0	20	31.7	29	46.0	6	9.5	6	9.5
G	155	2	1.3	23	14.8	35	22.6	36	23.2	47	30.3	12	7.7
H	72	2	2.8	15	20.8	29	41.7	15	20.8	0	0	10	13.9
I	32	0	0	5	15.6	15	46.9	8	25.0	1	3.1	3	9.4
J	38	3	7.9	1	2.6	20	52.6	6	15.8	3	7.9	5	13.2

6 – 2　The two groups compared

Group ref.	Total vulgar exps.	Main hero		Main villain		Other positive characters		Backward elements		Other negative characters		Others	
		No.	%	No.	%	No.	%	No.	%	No.	%	No.	%
I	353	9	2.5	23	6.5	162	45.9	125	35.4	24	6.8	10	2.8
II	434	8	1.8	48	11.1	145	33.4	126	29.0	65	15.0	40	9.2

Table 7   The Distribution of Vulgar Expressions According to Targets of Abuse

7.1   Types of Character as Targets

7.1 – 1   The ten novels

Novel ref.	Total abuse exps.	Main hero		Main villain		Other positive characters		Backward elements		Other negative characters		Others	
		No.	%	No.	%	No.	%	No.	%	No.	%	No.	%
A	62	4	6.5	0	0	23	37.1	22	35.5	5	8.1	8	12.9
B	75	6	8.0	2	2.7	18	24.0	31	41.3	11	14.7	7	9.3
C	67	12	17.9	8	11.9	15	22.4	29	43.3	2	3.0	1	1.5
D	19	0	0	0	0	2	10.5	3	15.8	12	63.2	2	10.5
E	16	0	0	1	6.3	3	18.8	0	0	8	50.0	4	25.0
F	20	0	0	0	0	4	20.0	13	65.0	0	0	3	15.0
G	87	5	5.7	16	18.4	12	13.8	25	28.7	25	28.7	4	4.6
H	36	0	0	3	8.3	6	16.7	19	52.8	4	11.1	4	11.1
I	15	1	6.7	0	0	3	20.0	3	20.0	8	53.3	0	0
J	20	1	5.0	8	40.0	3	15.0	2	10.0	6	30.0	0	0

7.1 – 2   The two groups compared

Group ref.	Total abuse exps.	Main hero		Main villain		Other positive characters		Backward elements		Other negative characters		Others	
		No.	%	No.	%	No.	%	No.	%	No.	%	No.	%
I	204	22	10.8	10	4.9	56	27.5	82	40.2	18	8.8	16	7.8
II	213	7	3.3	28	13.1	33	15.5	65	30.5	63	29.6	17	8.0

7.2   Family Members as Targets

7.2 – 1   Family Members vs. Non-Family Members

7.2 – 1.1   The ten novels

Novel ref.	Total abuse exps.	Family members		Non-family members	
		No.	%	No.	%
A	62	32	51.6	30	48.4
B	67	10	14.9	57	85.1
C	75	12	16.0	63	84.0
D	19	1	5.3	18	94.7
E	16	10	62.5	6	37.5
F	20	10	50.0	10	50.0
G	87	20	23.0	67	77.0
H	36	14	39.0	22	61.1
I	15	0	0	15	100
J	20	0	0	20	100

7.2 – 1.2   The two groups compared

Group ref.	Total abuse exps.	Family members		Non-family members	
		No.	%	No.	%
I	204	54	26.5	150	73.5
II	213	55	25.8	158	74.2

7.2 – 2   Among Family Members

7.2 – 2.1   The ten novels

Novel ref.	Total abuse exps. by family members	Hubsands		Wives		Children	
		No.	%	No.	%	No.	%
A	32	0	0	14	43.8	18	56.2
B	10	0	0	0	0	10	100
C	12	4	33.3	0	0	8	66.7
D	1	0	0	0	0	1	100
E	10	0	0	0	0	10	100
F	10	1	10.0	3	30.0	6	60.0
G	20	16	80.0	4	20.0	0	0
H	14	11	78.6	1	7.1	2	14.3
I	0	0	0	0	0	0	0
J	0	0	0	0	0	0	0

7.2 – 2.2   The two groups compared

Group ref.	Total abuse exps. by family members	Husbands		Wives		Children	
		No.	%	No.	%	No.	%
I	54	4	7.4	14	25.9	36	66.7
II	55	28	50.9	8	14.5	19	34.5

Table 8   The Density of Ideological Expressions

8 – 1   The ten novels

Novel ref.	Total no. Chinese characters	Total ideological words	No. ideological words per 1,000 characters
A	215,000	604	2.81
B	359,000	2,183	6.08
C	472,000	1,683	3.57
D	455,000	2,094	4.60
E	339,000	3,084	9.10
F	313,000	1,865	5.96
G	345,000	2,353	6.82
H	353,000	3,206	9.08
I	359,000	2,729	7.60
J	392,000	3,150	8.04

8 – 2   The two groups compared

Group ref.	Total no. Chinese characters	Total ideological words	No. ideological words per 1,000 characters
I	1,046,000	4,470	4.27
II	2,556,000	18,480	7.23

Table 9   The Distribution of Ideological Expressions by Character

9 – 1.1   The ten novels

Novel ref.	Main hero				Main villain			
	Name	Total no. words	No. ideo. words	%	Name	Total no. words	No. ideo. words	%
A	Liu Yusheng	2,023	57	2.82	Gong Ziyuan	765	4	0.53
B	Liang Shengbao	5,948	167	2.81	Yao Shijie	2,761	69	2.50
C	Xiao Changchun	12,377	263	2.12	Ma Zhiyue	5,598	70	1.25
D	Gao Daquan	12,929	379	2.93	Feng Shaohuai	4,174	71	1.70
E	Jiang Chunwang	9,544	618	6.47	Jiang Yulin	3,797	45	1.19

9 – 1.1 (Continued)

Novel ref.	Main hero				Main villain			
	Name	Total no. words	No. ideo. words	%	Name	Total no. words	No. ideo. words	%
F	Zhao Guang'en	7,638	319	4.17	Jia Weimin	4,142	94	2.27
G	Lian Hua	20,720	731	3.53	Shi Jigen	4,802	67	1.40
H	Wei Gengtian	17,602	878	4.99	Wei Junping	5,938	56	0.94
I	Shi Caihong	17,586	780	4.44	Zhao Deming	6,394	163	2.55
J	Liu Wangchun	22,835	982	4.30	Long Youtian	6,985	136	1.95

9 – 1.2

Novel ref.	Old poor peasant				Young woman			
	Name	Total no. words	No. ideo. words	%	Name	Total no. words	No. ideo. words	%
A	Sheng Youting	3,137	27	0.86	Sheng Shujun	1,912	13	0.68
B	Liang Yongqing	2,132	25	1.17	Gaixia	1,644	20	1.20
C	Ma Laosi	3,301	31	0.94	Jiao Shuhong	6,184	62	1.00
D	Zhou Zhong	4,781	93	1.95	Zhou Liping	1,316	37	2.81
E	Jiang Yutian	1,032	40	3.88	Guiying	1,133	41	3.62
F	Liu Fu	704	13	1.85	Liu Yingzi	742	24	3.24
G	Geng Shan	3,136	94	3.00	Jing Chunhong	5,987	184	3.12
H	Zhao Yiliang	3,035	92	3.03	Li Guifen	1,043	20	1.92
I	Shi Fengyang	1,695	23	1.36	Shi Huying	2,227	65	2.92
J	Du-er Lao Xiong	2,813	95	3.38	Lu Bugu	1,724	73	4.23

9 – 2.1 The two groups compared

Group ref.	Main hero			Main villain		
	Total no. words	No. ideo. words	%	Total no. words	No. ideo. words	%
I	20,348	487	2.39	9,115	143	1.57
II	108,874	4,687	4.30	36,232	632	1.74

9 – 2.2

Group ref.	Old poor peasant			Young woman		
	Total no. words	No. ideo. words	%	Total no. words	No. ideo. words	%
I	8,572	83	0.97	9,739	95	0.98
II	17,196	450	2.62	14,082	444	3.15

Table 10 Eighty-two High-frequency Ideological Items

10 – 1 Occurrence of the Eighty-two High-frequency Ideological Items in the Ten Novels

Ideological Items	Time specific	Non-time specific	Meaning specific	Quasi-meaning specific	A	B	C	D	E	F	G	H	I	J
											Novel reference and frequency			
baochan dao hu	+	`	+	`	0	0	0	0	517	34	6	6	0	4
Dayuejin	+	`	+	`	0	0	0	0	4	10	2	2	0	7
dazibao	+	`	+	`	0	0	0	0	0	0	2	53	29	44
dangan	+	`	+	`	9	14	23	12	41	10	0	6	6	3
daolu	`	+	`	+	3	20	31	16	42	30	19	55	14	7
dizhu	`	+	+	`	10	20	48	67	51	64	37	36	23	15
dou	`	+	`	+	1	0	21	13	48	10	61	98	57	39
douzheng	`	+	`	+	2	27	46	48	148	70	170	95	88	139
fandang	`	+	+	`	0	0	0	0	10	0	28	5	0	1
fangeming	`	+	+	`	7	4	4	10	8	0	71	17	6	7
fangxiang	`	+	`	+	0	3	5	3	5	1	3	27	23	1
fubi	`	+	`	+	0	0	0	0	0	0	23	4	1	22
fumong	`	+	+	`	1	108	26	15	5	4	9	4	6	1
gaizao	`	+	`	+	3	19	2	8	6	20	16	9	2	20
geming	`	+	+	`	14	25	42	105	32	54	136	165	168	183
gongzuodui; gongzuozu	+	`	+	`	0	8	4	26	192	3	60	0	2	0
gongchandang; dang	`	+	+	`	34	281	151	168	180	108	221	113	89	122
gongchandangyuan; dangyuan	`	+	+	`	27	103	48	115	47	28	77	34	12	28
gongchanzhuyi	`	+	+	`	0	5	7	14	6	5	6	14	6	5
gongqingtuan; qingniantuan; tuan	`	+	+	`	19	8	9	4	8	7	1	0	0	6
gongqingtuanyuan; qingniantuanyuan; tuanyuan	`	+	+	`	2	51	4	20	26	5	3	0	0	8
guojia	`	+	`	+	3	38	42	54	6	35	16	31	42	31

10 – 1 (Continued)

Ideological Items	Time specific	Non-time specific	Meaning specific	Quasi-meaning specific	Novel reference and frequency									
					A	B	C	D	E	F	G	H	I	J
Guomindang	'	+	+	'	6	18	12	15	8	0	2	9	0	4
hezuohua	+	'	+	'	36	2	22	0	18	14	7	10	30	7
hongweibing	+	'	+	'	0	0	0	0	0	0	0	24	1	21
huzhuzu	+	'	+	'	14	186	3	54	5	13	1	3	1	3
jiti	'	+	'	+	2	28	18	5	60	42	14	32	103	13
jianku fendou	'	+	'	+	0	0	0	0	0	6	1	26	2	17
jieji	'	+	+	'	0	33	14	13	32	46	44	18	12	54
jieji diren	'	+	+	'	0	1	1	0	6	2	28	56	30	22
jieji douzheng	'	+	+	'	0	0	2	1	34	51	80	31	33	54
jiefang	'	+	+	'	14	83	8	12	29	17	21	25	29	35
jingshen	'	+	'	+	2	16	2	25	14	34	13	56	35	27
jiu shehui	'	+	+	'	3	23	13	35	11	7	11	4	17	6
juewu	'	+	'	+	0	27	6	4	21	2	5	4	11	2
lichang	'	+	'	+	0	10	11	2	14	5	2	3	4	9
luxian	'	+	'	+	0	10	8	1	47	2	14	45	68	117
luxian douzheng	'	+	+	'	0	0	0	0	6	0	5	3	2	14
Makesi-Lieningzhuyi; Ma-Liezhuyi; Ma-Lie	'	+	+	'	0	1	0	3	7	10	4	9	21	18
Mao Zedong; Mao Zhuxi	'	+	+	'	14	34	4	46	122	82	95	188	127	70
Mao Zedong Sixiang	'	+	+	'	0	0	0	3	2	11	3	10	18	9
minzhu	'	+	+	'	1	3	13	7	5	10	2	1	1	3
nongye xue Dazhai; (xue) Dazhai	+	'	+	'	0	0	0	0	0	0	6	205	234	69
nongye shengchan hezuoshe; nongye she	+	'	+	'	23	9	145	3	6	5	0	4	3	0
pipan	'	+	'	+	0	4	2	1	5	4	15	34	15	52
pin-gunong	'	+	+	'	0	78	8	26	2	22	0	3	0	1

10–1 (Continued)

Ideological Items	Time specific	Non-time specific	Meaning specific	Quasi-meaning specific	Novel reference and frequency									
					A	B	C	D	E	F	G	H	I	J
pinnong	'	+	+	'	21	47	61	21	46	3	28	10	14	27
pin-xiazhongnong	'	+	+	'	0	0	13	0	196	48	25	39	17	86
qingxiang	'	+	'	+	0	0	1	0	4	1	0	10	6	0
qunzhong	'	+	'	+	6	91	97	94	133	49	56	256	355	203
renmin gongshe; gongshe	+	'	+	'	0	0	0	0	48	14	9	4	6	12
ru she	+	'	+	'	66	5	35	0	6	7	0	2	4	0
shehuizhuyi	'	+	+	'	19	12	67	151	91	101	85	106	34	99
Shehuizhuyi Jiaoyu Yundong; Shejiao	+	'	+	'	0	0	0	0	0	0	23	2	0	0
shijieguan	'	+	'	+	0	0	0	1	6	7	2	4	5	14
sixiang	'	+	'	+	29	85	41	66	60	91	123	88	193	119
siyou-zhi	'	+	'	+	0	4	0	20	1	0	0	0	35	0
Siqing	+	'	+	'	0	0	0	0	0	0	6	15	0	3
tudi gaige; tugai	+	'	+	'	10	124	46	179	22	21	2	11	27	9
(weida) ningxiu	'	+	+	'	0	2	3	0	2	0	5	2	3	19
wuchanjieji	'	+	+	'	0	0	1	8	10	29	21	11	4	55
Wuchanjieji Wenhua Da Geming; Wenhua Da Geming; Wenge	+	'	+	'	0	0	0	0	0	0	0	85	72	219
xin shehui	'	+	+	'	3	17	9	23	3	5	0	0	1	0
xinsheng shiwu	+	'	+	'	0	0	0	0	0	0	0	1	17	26
xiuzhengzhuyi	'	+	+	'	0	0	0	0	5	9	3	20	12	60
xuanchuan	'	+	+	'	15	35	15	52	11	2	21	7	7	3
xuexi	'	+	'	+	3	14	5	25	75	28	66	94	68	29
yishixingtai	'	+	+	'	0	0	0	0	10	3	2	0	0	0
you (qing)	'	+	+	'	6	1	0	0	17	5	1	1	21	14

10 – 1 (Continued)

Ideological Items	Time specific	Non-time specific	Meaning specific	Quasi-meaning specific	Novel reference and frequency									
					A	B	C	D	E	F	G	H	I	J
yuanze	`	+	`	+	0	9	16	0	8	24	6	5	3	8
yundong	`	+	+	`	15	27	10	45	20	11	121	114	56	70
zhongnong; shangzhongnong; fuyu-zhongnong	`	+	+	`	10	141	143	29	39	44	0	5	7	4
zhengzhi	`	+	+	`	6	18	7	8	29	33	8	19	8	34
Zhongyang; Dang Zhongyang; Zhonggong Zhongyang	`	+	+	`	4	8	1	3	9	1	26	20	4	4
zaofan	`	+	+	`	0	0	0	0	0	0	0	21	4	15
zibenzhuyi	`	+	+	`	1	5	19	5	50	81	34	62	44	49
zichanjieji	`	+	+	`	0	2	4	0	11	37	12	18	2	43
zi li geng sheng	`	+	`	+	0	0	0	0	5	22	3	40	2	41
Zongluxian	+	`	+	`	0	18	5	0	2	0	1	2	0	1
zou zibenzhuyi daolu de dangquanpai; zouzipai	+	`	`	`	0	0	0	0	0	0	12	19	3	18
zuzhi	`	+	`	+	3	7	10	57	32	16	38	9	8	12
zuo (qing)	`	+	+	`	2	3	0	0	11	0	0	2	3	0

10 – 2 Distribution of the Eighty-two High-frequency Ideological Items According to Semantic Features

10 – 2.1 The ten novels

Novel ref.	Total frequency	Time specific		Non-time specific		Meaning specific		Quasi-meaning specific	
		No.	%	No.	%	No.	%	No.	%
A	469	158	33.69	311	66.31	412	87.85	57	12.15
B	1,974	366	18.54	1,608	81.46	1,562	79.13	412	20.87
C	1,424	283	19.87	1,141	80.13	1,060	74.44	364	25.56
D	1,741	274	15.74	1,467	84.26	1,298	74.55	443	25.45
E	2,804	861	30.71	1,943	69.29	2,064	73.61	740	26.39
F	1,582	131	8.28	1,451	91.72	1,083	68.46	499	31.54
G	2,067	137	6.63	1,930	93.37	1,401	67.78	666	32.22
H	2,664	454	17.04	2,210	82.96	1,639	61.52	1,025	38.48
I	2,423	435	17.95	1,988	82.05	1,184	48.87	1,239	51.13
J	2,598	446	17.17	2,152	82.83	1,676	64.51	922	35.49

10 – 2.2 The two groups compared

Group ref.	Total frequency	Time specific		Non-time specific		Meaning specific		Quasi-meaning specific	
		No.	%	No.	%	No.	%	No.	%
I	3,867	807	20.87	3,060	79.13	3,034	78.46	833	21.54
II	15,879	2,738	17.24	13,141	82.76	10,345	65.15	5,534	34.85

Table 11 Quotations from Mao

11 – 1 The ten novels

Novel ref.	No. quotations from Mao	No. characters of quotaions from Mao
A	3	34
B	2	238
C	0	0
D	7	348
E	11	648
F	12	474
G	19	835
H	32	487
I	26	589
J	27	1,175

11 – 2 The two groups compared

Group ref.	No. quotations from Mao		No. characters of quotaions from Mao	
	Total	Average	Total	Average
I	5	1.7	272	90.7
II	134	19.1	4,556	650.9

Table 12   The Density of Idioms, Proverbs, *Xiehouyu* and Classical Verse Segments

12 – 1   The ten novels

Novel ref.	Total no. Chinese characters	Idioms		Proverbs		Xiehouyu		Classical verses	
		No.	No. per 100,000 chas.	No.	No. per 100,000 chas.	No.	No. per 100,000 chas.	No.	No. per 100,000 chas.
A	215,000	308	143.26	106	49.30	10	4.65	2	0.93
B	359,000	395	110.03	40	11.14	1	0.28	3	0.84
C	472,000	763	161.65	118	25.00	25	5.30	2	0.42
D	455,000	990	217.58	89	19.56	19	4.18	5	1.10
E	339,000	662	195.28	81	23.89	13	3.83	4	1.18
F	313,000	666	212.78	58	18.53	29	9.27	7	2.24
G	345,000	691	201.45	60	17.39	15	4.34	4	1.16
H	353,000	825	233.71	211	59.77	73	20.68	6	1.70
I	359,000	570	158.77	41	11.42	8	2.23	2	0.58
J	392,000	1,313	334.95	77	19.64	9	2.30	3	0.77

12 – 2   The two groups compared

Group ref.	Total no. Chinese characters	Idioms		Proverbs		Xiehouyu		Classical verses	
		No.	No. per 100,000 chas.	No.	No. per 100,000 chas.	No.	No. per 100,000 chas.	No.	No. per 100,000 chas.
I	1,046,000	1,466	140.15	264	25.24	36	3.44	7	0.67
II	2,556,000	5,717	223.67	617	24.14	166	6.49	31	1.21

Table 13　The Distribution of Idioms in Narration/Description and Dialogue/ Monologue

13 – 1　The ten novels

Novel Ref.	Total Idioms	No. idioms in authors' narration/description		No. idioms in characters' dialogue/monologue	
		No.	%	No.	%
A	308	203	65.91	105	34.09
B	395	294	74.43	101	25.57
C	763	565	74.05	198	25.95
D	990	654	66.06	336	33.94
E	662	487	73.56	175	26.44
F	666	442	66.37	224	33.63
G	691	439	63.53	252	36.47
H	825	388	47.03	437	52.97
I	570	341	59.82	229	40.18
J	1,313	809	61.61	504	38.39

13 – 2　The two groups compared

Group Ref.	Total Idioms	No. idioms in authors' narration/description		No. idioms in characters' dialogue/monologue	
		No.	%	No.	%
I	1,466	1,062	72.44	404	27.56
II	5,717	3,560	62.27	2,157	37.73

Table 14　The Distribution of Idioms by Character

14 – 1.1　The ten novels

Novel ref.	Main hero				Main villain			
	Name	Total no. words	No. idioms	‰	Name	Total no. words	No. idioms	‰
A	Liu Yusheng	2,023	7	3.46	Gong Ziyuan	756	2	2.65
B	Liang Shengbao	5,948	16	2.68	Yao Shijie	2,761	6	2.17
C	Xiao Changchun	12,377	32	2.59	Ma Zhiyue	5,598	27	4.82
D	Gao Daquan	12,929	51	3.94	Feng Shaohuai	4,174	23	5.51
E	Jiang Chunwang	9,544	28	2.93	Jiang Yulin	3,797	12	3.16
F	Zhao Guang'en	7,638	32	4.19	Jia Weimin	4,142	18	4.35
G	Lian Hua	20,720	72	3.47	Shi Jigen	4,802	14	2.92
H	Wei Gengtian	17,602	103	5.85	Wei Junping	5,938	46	7.75
I	Shi Caihong	17,586	48	2.73	Zhao Deming	6,394	20	3.13
J	Liu Wangchun	22,835	149	6.53	Long Youtian	6,985	61	8.73

14 – 1.2

Novel ref.	Old poor peasant				Young woman			
	Name	Total no. words	No. idioms	‰	Name	Total no. words	No. idioms	‰
A	Sheng Youting	3,137	11	3.51	Sheng Shujun	1,912	2	1.05
B	Liang Yongqing	2,132	1	0.47	Gaixia	1,644	2	1.22
C	Ma Laosi	3,301	5	1.51	Jiao Shuhong	6,184	15	2.43
D	Zhou Zhong	4,781	19	3.97	Zhou Liping	1,316	8	6.08
E	Jiang Yutian	1,032	2	1.94	Guiying	1,133	1	0.88
F	Liu Fu	704	1	1.42	Liu Yingzi	742	3	4.04
G	Geng Shan	3,136	10	3.19	Jing Chunhong	5,987	18	3.01
H	Zhao Yiliang	3,035	10	3.29	Li Guifen	1,043	2	1.92
I	Shi Fengyang	1,695	2	1.18	Shi Huying	2,227	7	3.14
J	Du-er Lao Xiong	2,813	19	6.75	Lu Bugu	1,724	5	2.90

14 – 2.1   The two groups compared

Group ref.	Main hero			Main villain		
	Total no. words	No. idioms	‰	Total no. words	No. idioms	‰
I	20,348	55	2.70	9,115	33	3.62
II	108,874	483	4.44	36,232	194	5.35

14 – 2.2

Group ref.	Old poor peasant			Young woman		
	Total no. words	No. idioms	‰	Total no. words	No. idioms	‰
I	8,572	18	2.10	9,739	19	1.95
II	17,196	63	3.66	14,082	44	3.12

Table 15   Number of Chinese Characters in the Sample Pages of the Ten Novels

Novel ref.	Total no. Chinese characters	No. Chinese chas. in the sample pages	Explanation of sampling	Percentage
A	215,000	32,292	pages 2–3 in each chapter	15.02
B	359,000	42,120	pages 2–3 in each chapter	11.73
C	472,000	71,604	pages 2–3 in each chapter	15.17
D	455,000	63,180	page 2 in each chapter, page 3 in odd chapter	13.89
E	339,000	36,600	page 2 in each chapter	10.80
F	313,000	37,050	pages 2–4 in each chapter	11.84
G	345,000	36,400	pages 2–3 in each chapter	10.55
H	353,000	39,600	pages 2–3 in each chapter	11.22
I	359,000	37,440	pages 2–3 in each chapter	10.43
J	392,000	62,608	pages 2–3 in each chapter	15.97

Table 16   The Density of 'Bookish' and 'Colloquial'

16 – 1   The ten novels

Novel ref.	Total no. Chinese chas. in the sample pages	Bookish words No.	Bookish words No. per 1,000 chas.	Colloquial words No.	Colloquial words No. per 1,000 chas.
A	32,292	191	5.91	25	0.77
B	42,120	161	3.82	34	0.81
C	71,604	224	3.13	69	0.96
D	63,180	315	4.99	52	0.82
E	36,600	102	2.79	87	2.38
F	37,050	208	5.61	28	0.76
G	36,400	161	4.42	9	0.25
H	39,600	185	4.67	23	0.58
I	37,440	154	4.11	13	0.38
J	62,608	443	7.08	15	0.24

16 – 2   The two groups compared

Group ref.	Total no. Chinese chas. in the sample pages	Bookish words No.	Bookish words No. per 1,000 chas.	Colloquial words No.	Colloquial words No. per 1,000 chas.
I	146,016	576	3.94	128	0.88
II	312,878	1,568	5.01	227	0.73

Table 17 The Density of Dialectal Expressions

17 – 1 The ten novels

Novel ref.	Total no. Chinese characters in the sample pages	Total dialectal expressions in the sample pages	No. dialectal expressions per 1,000 characters
A	32,292	633	19.60
B	42,120	249	5.91
C	71,604	251	3.51
D	63,180	157	2.48
E	36,600	173	4.73
F	37,050	276	7.45
G	36,400	44	1.21
H	39,600	157	3.96
I	37,440	101	2.70
J	62,608	119	1.90

17 – 2 The two groups compared

Group ref.	Total no. Chinese characters in the sample pages	Total dialectal expressions in the sample pages	No. dialectal expressions per 1,000 characters
I	146,016	1,133	7.76
II	312,878	1,027	3.28

Table 18 The Density of Military Words and Expressions

18 – 1 The ten novels

Novel ref.	Total no. Chinese characters	Total military exps.	No. military exps. per 100,000 chas.
A	215,000	9	4.18
B	359,000	22	6.12
C	472,000	40	8.47
D	455,000	58	12.75
E	339,000	128	37.76
F	313,000	111	35.46
G	345,000	93	26.97
H	353,000	301	85.27
I	359,000	116	32.31
J	392,000	804	205.10

18 – 2   The two groups compared

Group ref.	Total no. Chinese characters	Total military exps.	No. military exps. per 100,000 chas.
I	1,046,000	71	6.79
II	2,556,000	1,611	63.03

Table 19   General Comparison of the Twelve Categories between the Two Groups

Stylistic categories	Comparison between the two groups ('+' indicates 'more'; '-' indicates 'fewer')	
	Group I	Group II
Vulgar items	+	-
Ideological items	-	+
Idioms	-	+
Proverbs	+ (literary -, folk +)	- (literay +, folk -)
Xiehouyu	-	+
Classical verses	-	+
Bookish items	-	+
Colloquial items	+	-
Dialectal items	+	-
Military items	-	+
Meteorological items	-	+
Inflated itmes	-	+

Table 20   Number of Words by the Main Heroes

20 – 1   The ten novels

Novel ref.	The main heroes' names	Total no. Chinese characters	No. words by the heroes	No. words by the heroes per 1,000 characters
A	Liu Yusheng	215,000	2,023	9.41
B	Liang Shengbao	359,000	5,948	16.57
C	Xiao Changchun	472,000	12,377	26.22
D	Gao Daquan	455,000	12,929	28.42
E	Jiang Chunwang	339,000	9,544	28.15
F	Zhao Guang'en	313,000	7,638	24.40
G	Lian Hua	345,000	20,720	60.06
H	Wei Gengtian	353,000	17,602	49.86
I	Shi Caihong	359,000	17,586	48.99
J	Liu Wangchun	392,000	22,835	58.25

20 – 2 The two groups compared

Group ref.	Total no. Chinese characters	No. words by the heroes	No. words by the heroes per 1,000 characters
I	1,046,000	20,348	19.45
II	2,556,000	108,854	42.59

Notes

INTRODUCTION

1. See Lowell Dittmer, *China's Continuous Revolution: The Post-Liberation Epoch 1949–1981* (Berkeley, 1987), pp. 77–8.
2. On the role played by Jiang Qing in deciding the literature and art of the Cultural Revolution, cf. Merle Goldman, *China's Intellectuals: Advise and Dissent* (Cambridge, Mass., 1981), Chapter 5, 'The Cultural Revolution', pp. 117–55.
3. See Hua-yuan Li Mowry, *Yang-pan Hsi: New Theater in China* (Berkeley, 1973), p. iii.
4. See 'Summary of the Forum on the Work in Literature and Art in the Armed Forces with which Comrade Lin Biao Entrusted Comrade Jiang Qing' ['Lin Biao Tongzhi weituo Jiang Qing Tongzhi zhaokai de budui wenyi gongzuo zuotanhui jiyao'], *Chinese Literature*, No. 9 (1967), pp. 32–3; and *Hongqi* [*Red Flag*], No. 9 (1967), p. 17.
5. Among studies on Chinese literature and art of the Cultural Revolution (official and unofficial) are D. W. Fokkema's 'Chinese Literature Under the Cultural Revolution', *Literature East and West*, 13 (1969), pp. 335–58, Hua-yuan Li Mowry's *Yang-pan Hsi: New Theater in China* (Berkeley, 1973), Bonnie S. McDougall's 'Poems, Poets, and Poetry 1976: An Exercise in the Typology of Modern Chinese Literature', *Contemporary China*, Vol. 2, No. 4 (Winter 1978), pp. 76–124, D. E. Pollard's 'The Short Story in the Cultural Revolution', *The China Quarterly*, No. 73 (1978), pp. 99–121, Leo Ou-fan

Lee's 'Dissent Literature from the Cultural Revolution', *Chinese Literature: Essays, Articles, Reviews*, 1 (1979), pp. 59–80, Paul Clark's 'Film-making in China: From the Cultural Revolution to 1981', *The China Quarterly*, No. 94 (1983), pp. 304–22, Perry Link's 'Hand-copied Entertainment Fiction from the Cultural Revolution', in Perry Link *et al.* (eds.), *Unofficial China: Popular Culture and Thought in the People's Republic* (Boulder, 1989), pp. 17–36, and Liu Dawen's '"Dixia xiaoshuo" de cangsang' ['Vicissitudes of "Underground Chinese Fiction"'], in Liu Dawen, *Zhongguo wenxue xinchao* [*The New Trends of Chinese Literature*] (Hong Kong, 1988), pp. 179–85.

6. Cf. Leo Ou-fan Lee, 'The Politics of Technique: Perspectives of Literary Dissidence in Contemporary Chinese Fiction', in Jeffrey C. Kinkley (ed.), *After Mao: Chinese Literature and Society 1978–1981*, p. 162.

7. See J. H. Miller, 'The Function of Rhetorical Study at the Present Time', *ADE* (Association of Departments of English) *Bulletin*, No. 62, pp. 10–8; also quoted in Barbara Couture (ed.), *Functional Approaches to Writing: Research Perspectives* (London, 1986), p. 3.

8. The statistics are based on the following materials: Meishi Tsai's *Contemporary Chinese Novels and Short Stories, 1949–1974: An Annotated Bibliography* (Cambridge, Mass., 1979), Kam Louie's and Louise Edwards's *Bibliography of English Translations and Critiques of Contemporary Chinese Fiction 1945–1992* (Taipei, 1993), Hans J. Hinrup's An *Index to 'Chinese Literature' 1951–1976* (London, 1978), Beijing Tushuguan Zhongwen Tongyi Bianmu Zu [the Cataloguing Group of Chinese Books of Beijing Library]'s *1974–1978 Zhongwen tushu yinshua kapian leiji lianhe mulu* [*A Joint Catalogue of Chinese Books between 1974 and 1978*] (Beijing, 1979), and the library catalogues of Beijing University, Beijing Normal University, Fudan University, Wuhan University, and Huazhong Normal University.

9. See Ershi Er Yuanxiao Bianxiezu [The Writing Group of Twenty-Two Universities], *Zhongguo dangdai wenxue shi* [*A History of Contemporary Chinese Literature*] (Fuzhou, 1985), Vol. 3, pp. 357–8.

10. See Guo Zhigang *et al.*, *Zhongguo dangdai wenxue shi chugao* [*A First Draft of the History of Contemporary Chinese Literature*] (Beijing, 1993), Vol. 2, p. 873.

11. See Jeffrey C. Kinkley, 'Chinese Crime Fiction and Its Formulas at the Turn of the 1980s', in Kinkley (ed.), *After Mao: Chinese Literature and Society 1978–1981* (Cambridge, 1985), pp. 89–90.

12. According to Rudolf G. Wagner, science fiction had certain development in China in the pre-CR period although it was mainly intended to serve science popularization and did not develop well. But this genre disappeared during the Cultural Revolution. See Rudolf G. Wagner, 'Lobby Literature: The Archeology and Present Functions of Science Fiction in China', in Jeffrey C. Kinkley (ed.), *After Mao: Chinese Literature and Society 1978–1981*, pp. 17–62.

13. Mao called upon the whole country to learn from the army in December

1963. On the background and development of the campaign of learning from the PLA, see Byung-joon Ahn, *Chinese Politics and the Revolution: Dynamics of Policy Progresses* (Seattle, 1976), Chapter 6, 'The Army's Emulation Campaigns', pp. 123–36.

14. See Yao Wenyuan, '«Zai Yan'an Wenyi Zuotanhui shang de jianghua» shi jinxing Wuchanjieji Wenhua Da Geming de geming gangling' ['"Talks at the Yan'an Conference on Literature and Art" is a Guiding Document for the Great Proletarian Cultural Revolution'], *Hongqi*, No. 9 (1967), p. 34.

15. It was claimed that Liu Shaoqi was the supporter of the policy of 'fixing farm output quotas for each household'. During the first CR period, 'the official explanation of the Cultural Revolution is that it was the final battle in a long-term struggle between two lines: the correct Maoist line, and the revisionist line upheld by "China's Khrushchev", the "No. 1 power holder in the party taking the capitalist road", head of state and heir apparent Liu Shaoqi'. See Roderick MacFarquhar, *The Origins of the Cultural Revolution* (New York, 1974), Vol. 1, p. 2. On the policy of 'quotas on household' and its relationship with the Cultural Revolution, cf. also Byung-joon Ahn, *Chinese Politics and the Revolution: Dynamics of Policy Progresses*, Chapter 4, 'The Adjustments and Their Legacies', pp. 48–88.

16. See Byung-joon Ahn, *Chinese Politics and the Revolution: Dynamics of Policy Progresses*, Chapter 5, 'The Party's Socialist Education Movement', pp. 89–123; Zhu Jian's CR novel *Qingshibao* [*Qingshi Fort*] (Nanjing, 1976), pp. 379–81.

17. See Zhang Tuosheng, 'Yi jiu qi wu nian de quanmian zhengdun' ['The Comprehensive Rectification in 1975'], in Tan Zongji, *Shi nian hou de pingshuo: "Wenhua Da Geming" shi lun ji* [*Comments after Ten Years: A Collection of Papers on the Cultural Revolution*] (Beijing, 1987), p. 120.

18. On the background and development of the campaign of learning from Dazhai in agriculture, see Byung-joon Ahn, *Chinese Politics and the Revolution: Dynamics of Policy Progresses*, Chapter 6, 'The Army's Emulation Campaigns', pp. 123–36.

19. See Bonnie S. McDougall, 'Poems, Poets, and Poetry 1976: An Exercise in the Typology of Modern Chinese Literature', in *Contemporary China*, Vol. 2, No. 4 (Winter 1978), p. 103.

20. Many of Hao Ran's writings have been translated into English, e.g. *The Golden Road* [*Jinguang da dao*], trans. by Carmen Hinton and Chris Gilmartin (Beijing, 1981); excerpts as 'The Stockman' from his pre-CR novel *Yanyang tian* [*The Sun Shines Bright*], *Chinese Literature*, 3 (Mar. 1972), pp. 3–48; excerpts from another CR novel *Xisha ernü* [*Sons and Daughters of Hsisha*], *Chinese Literature*, 10 (Oct. 1974), pp. 3–66; 'Moonlight in the Eastern Wall' ['Yue zhao dong qiang'], *Chinese Literature*, 11 (Nov. 1959), pp. 41–9; 'The Eve of Her Wedding' ['Xi–qi'], trans. by Gladys Yang, *Chinese Literature*, 6 (Jun. 1965), pp. 20–33; 'Aunt Hou's Courtyard' ['Tiemian wusi'], trans. by

Kate Sears, in Helen F. Siu (ed.), *Furrows—Peasants, Intellectuals, and the State: Stories and Histories From Modern China* (Stanford, 1990), pp. 147–55; *Caixia ji* [*Bright Clouds*] (a collection of short stories) (Beijing, 1974); and 'Huanle de hai' ['A Sea of Happiness'], *Chinese Literature*, 1 (Jan. 1975), pp. 3–52.

21. English translations of Zhang Jun's writings include 'Apricot Orchard', trans. by Chang Su, *Chinese Literature*, 2 (Feb. 1965), pp. 45–54, and 'Her House Has to Wait', trans. by Gladys Yang, *Chinese Literature*, 2 (Feb. 1965), pp. 61–70. His CR novel is *Qin long tu* [*Capturing the Dragon*] (Shijiazhuang, 1974).

22. English translations of Li Ruqing's fiction include *Island Militia Women* [*Haidao nü minbing*] (Beijing, 1975), and (with Li Ju-ch'ing) 'The Conch Horn Sounds', *Chinese Literature*, 5 (May 1971), pp. 98–100.

23. English translations of Zhang Kangkang's post-CR fiction include 'The Wasted Years' ['Kongbai'], trans. by Shen Zhen, *Chinese Literature*, 3 (March 1982), pp. 5–16, 'The Right to Love' ['Ai de quanli'], trans. by R.A. Roberts, in R.A. Roberts and Angela Knox (eds.), *One Half of the Sky* (London, 1987), pp. 51–81, 'Northern Lights' ['Beiji guang'], *Chinese Literature* (Winter, 1988), pp. 92–102, and (with Mei Jin) 'The Tolling of a Distant Bell' ['Youyuan zhong-sheng'], trans. by Daniel Bryant, in Michael S. Duke (ed.), *Contemporary Chinese Literature: An Anthology of Post-Mao Fiction and Poetry* (Armonk, 1984), pp. 98–108.

24. Many of Zheng Wanlong's post-CR writings have been translated into English, e.g. *Strange Tales from Strange Lands: Stories by Zheng Wanlong*, edited by Kam Louie (Ithaca, 1993); 'Clock' ['Zhong'], trans. by Jeanne Tai, in Jeanne Tai (ed.), *Spring Bamboo: A Collection of Contemporary Chinese Short Stories* (New York, 1989), pp. 3–18; and 'Mother Lode', trans. by Jeffrey C. Kinkley, in Michael S. Duke (ed.), *Worlds of Modern Chinese Fiction: Short Stories and Novellas from the People's Republic, Taiwan, and Hong Kong* (Armonk, 1991), pp. 319–28. Zheng Wanlong's CR novel is *Xiangshuiwan* [*Xiangshui Bend*] (Beijing, 1976).

25. Many of Chen Rong's (Shen Rong) post-CR writings have been translated into English, e.g. *At Middle Age* [*Ren dao zhongnian*] (a collection of English translations of her novellas) (Beijing, 1987), mostly translated by Gladys Yang; 'At Middle Age', also trans. by Margaret Decker, in Perry Link (ed.), *Roses and Thorns* (Berkeley, 1984), pp. 261–338; 'A Gift of Night Fragrance' ['Song ni yi zhi yelaixiang'], trans. by Gladys Yang, *Chinese Literature*, (Spring, 1989), pp. 3–56; and 'Classmates' ['Tongchuang'], trans. by Long Xu, in Long Xu (ed.), *Recent Fiction from China 1987–1988: Selected Stories and Novellas* (Lewiston, 1991), pp. 65–80.

26. Gu Hua's CR novel is *Shanchuan huxiao* [*The Mountains and Rivers Roar*] (Changsha, 1976). Many of his writings have been translated into English, e.g. *Pagoda Ridge and Other Stories* (a collection of English translations of

his novellas and short stories) (Beijing, 1985); *A Small Town Called Hibiscus*, trans. by Gladys Yang (Beijing, 1983); 'The Sieve' ['Shaizi'], trans. by Yu Fanqin, *Chinese Literature* (Summer, 1988), pp. 3–10. There are three different English translations for his novella 'Pa man qing teng de mu wu'. They are 'The Log Cabin Overgrown with Creepers', trans. by W. J. F. Jenner, *Chinese Literature*, 12 (Dec. 1982), pp. 5–35, and in the above *Pagoda Ridge and Other Stories*, pp. 147–85; 'The Ivied Cabin', trans. by Richard Belskey, in W. C. Chau (ed.), *Prize Winning Stories from China: 1980–1981* (Beijing, 1985), pp. 110–44; and 'The Ivy-Covered Cabin', trans. by Tam King-fai, in Helen F. Siu (ed.), *Furrows—Peasants, Intellectuals, and the State: Stories and Histories From Modern China*, pp. 181–206.

27. English translations of Mo Yingfeng's writings include 'The Roadside Inn', *Chinese Literature*, 12 (Dec. 1972), pp. 39–45, 'A Conversation Overheard at Night', *Chinese Literature*, 7 (Jul. 1973), pp. 3–9, and 'Moistened by Rain and Dew, Young Crops Grow Strong' ['Yu run miao zhuang'], *Chinese Literature*, 9 (Sept. 1969), pp. 79–86.

28. English translations of Li Huixin's writings include 'The Girl in the Mountains', *Chinese Literature*, 10 (Oct. 1973), pp. 30–8.

29. See Gu Hua, *Shanchuan huxiao*, p. 540.

30. See Perry Link, 'Fiction and the Reading Public in Guangzhou and Other Chinese Cities, 1979–1980', in Jeffrey C. Kinkley (ed.), *After Mao: Chinese Literature and Society 1978–1981*, p. 249.

31. See Perry Link, 'Introduction: On the Mechanics of the Control of Literature in China', in Link (ed.), *Stubborn Weeds: Popular and Controversial Chinese Literature after the Cultural Revolution* (London, 1983), p. 3–4.

32. See Jeffrey C. Kinkley, 'Introduction', in Kinkley (ed.), *After Mao: Chinese Literature and Society 1978–1981*, p. 10.

33. See Li Chi, 'Communist War Stories', in Cyril Birch's *Chinese Communist Literature* (New York, 1963), p. 141.

34. See Yao Wenyuan, '«Zai Yan'an Wenyi Zuotanhui shang de jianghua» shi jinxing Wuchanjieji Wenhua Da Geming de geming gangling', *Hongqi*, No. 9 (1967), p. 29.

35. See Editorial Department of *Red Flag*, 'The Compass for the Great Proletarian Cultural Revolution', *Chinese Literature*, No. 9 (1966), pp. 42–5.

36. See Bonnie S. McDougall, *Mao Zedong's 'Talks at the Yan'an Conference on Literature and Art': A Translation of the 1943 Text with Commentary* (Ann Arbor: Center for Chinese Studies, the University of Michigan, 1980), pp. 72–3.

37. See Shanghai Shi «Longjiang Song» Ju-zu [The Performing Group of *Song of Long River* of Shanghai], 'Yan zhe Mao Zhuxi wuchanjieji wenyi luxian qianjin' ['Advance along Chairman Mao's Proletarian Literary and Artistic Line'], *Hongqi*, No. 6 (1972), p. 23.

38. See Bonnie S. McDougall, *Mao Zedong's 'Talks at the Yan'an Conference on Literature and Art': A Translation of the 1943 Text with Commentary*, p. 70 and p. 95.

39. See Yu Yan, 'Geming de xianshizhuyi he geming de langmanzhuyi xiang jiehe wenti de taolun' ['The Discussion on the Combination of Revolutionary Realism and Revolutionary Romanticism'], *Wenxue Pinglun*, No. 2 (1959), p. 122.

40. See 'Summary of the Forum on the Work in Literature and Art in the Armed Forces with which Comrade Lin Biao Entrusted Comrade Jiang Qing', *Chinese Literature*, No. 9 (1967), pp. 35–6.

41. See Liu Zengjie, *Zhanhuo zhong de Mousi (19–20 shiji Zhongguo wenxue sichao shi, disi juan)* [*Moses in Flames of War (A History of Chinese Literary Trends in the 19th-20th Centuries, IV)*] (Kaifeng, 1992), p. 234.

42. See Ershi Er Yuanxiao Bianxiezu, *Zhongguo dangdai wenxue shi*, Vol. 1, p. 149.

43. See Herman Ermolaev, *Soviet Literary Theories 1917–1934: The Genesis of Socialist Realism* (New York, 1977), p. 197.

44. See Wang Yafu and Zhang Hengzhong, *Zhongguo xueshu jie dashi ji (1919–1985)* [*A Chronicle of Events in Chinese Academic Circles (1919–1985)*] (Shanghai, 1988), p. 187.

45. Ibid.

46. 'Gei Yan'an Lu Xun yishu wenxue yuan de tici' ['Dedication to the Lu Xun College of Literature and Art'] in *Mao Zedong wenyi sixiang taolunhui wenji* [*A Collection of Papers from the Symposium of Mao Zedong Literary Thought*] (Beijing: Renmin Wenxue Chubanshe, 1985), pp. 149–50.

47. See He Jingzhi, 'Mantan shi de geming langmanzhuyi' ['On the Revolutionary Romanticism of Poetry'], *Wenyi bao*, No. 9 (1958), p. 3.

48. See Zhou Yang, *Wo guo shehuizhuyi wenxue yishu de daolu* [*The Road of Literature and Art in China*] (Beijing, 1960), pp. 52–3.

49. See Peng Qihua, *Xianshizhuyi fansi yu tansuo* [*A Re-examination and Exploration of Realism*] (Wuhan, 1992), pp. 6–8.

50. See Zhou Yang, *Wo guo shehuizhuyi wenxue yishu de daolu*, pp. 42–3.

51. The argument originated in Stalin's comment of the 1930s: 'You must understand that if a writer frequently and honestly reflects the truth of life he cannot fail to arrive at Marxism'. See Herman Ermolaev, *Soviet Literary Theories 1917–1934: The Genesis of Socialist Realism*, p. 167.

52. See Zhu Zhai, 'Lixiang yu xianshi' ['The Ideal versus Realisty'], *Wenxue Pinglun*, No. 6 (1960), p. 13.

53. See Hu Jingzhi, 'Lixiang yu xianshi zai wenxue zhong de bianzheng jiehe' [The dialectical unity of the ideal and reality in literature], *Wenxue Pinglun*, No. 1 (1959), p. 96.

54. See *Zhou Yang wenji* [*Collected Works of Zhou Yang*] (Beijing, 1984), Vol. 1, p. 243.

55. See 'Summary of the Forum on the Work in Literature and Art in the Armed

Forces with which Comrade Lin Biao Entrusted Comrade Jiang Qing', *Hongqi*, No. 9 (1967), pp. 19–20.

56. See Jiang Qing, 'Wei renmin li xin gong' ['Make New Contributions to the People'], in Tianshan Chubanshe, *Jiang Qing guanyu Wenhua Da Geming de yanjiang ji* [*A Collection of Jiang Qing's Speeches on the Cultural Revolution*] (Aomen, 1971), pp. 53–5.

57. Quoted in a *Hongqi* editorial 'Weida de zhenli, ruili de wuqi' ['Great Truth, Sharp Weapon'], *Hongqi* (1967, 9), p. 21.

58. See Mao Zedong, 'Two Instructions Concerning Literature and Art', *Chinese Literature*, No. 9 (1967), pp. 11–2.

59. Ibid.

60. Yao Wenyuan's 'Ping Hai Rui baguan' ['Views on Hai Rui's Dismissal from Office'] was first published in *Wen Hui Bao* (10 Nov. 1965). Ref. Jack Gray, *Rebellions and Revolutions: China from the 1800s to the 1980s* (Oxford, 1990), pp. 326–50; and Jonathan D. Spence, *The Search for Modern China* (New York, 1990), p. 808.

61. See 'Summary of the Forum on the Work in Literature and Art in the Armed Forces with which Comrade Lin Biao Entrusted Comrade Jiang Qing', *Chinese Literature*, No. 9 (1967), p. 26.

62. On the persecution suffered by Chinese literary intellectuals during the Cultural Revolution, see Merle Goldman, *China's Intellectuals: Advise and Dissent*, pp. 132–3.

63. According to Merle Goldman, 'the Cultural Revolution's interpretation of May Fourth culture as well as the vehemence of the aspect of the campaign launched at the time of the Shanghai forum had more to do with the biases of Jiang Qing and the radical intellectuals than with Mao . . . Most of Europe's great nineteenth-century writers — Balzac, Zola, Gogol, Turgenev, Dostoevsky, Chekhov, and Tolstoy — were denounced because of the profound effect of their critical realism and Western humanism on the May Fourth intellectuals. Furthermore, their approach ran counter to the Cultural Revolution's emphasis on revolutionary romanticism and class struggle. They were accused of "glorifying" love, individualism, and alienation — values opposed to the spirit of self-sacrifice, collectivism, and ideological commitment which the revolution sought to instill.' See Merle Goldman, *China's Intellectuals: Advise and Dissent*, p. 126. In fact the key targets of foreign literature determined in the 'Forum Summary' were contemporary Soviet literature. Moreover, as regards the reason for denying foreign literature, according to our observation, the authorities seemed to be more ambitious, i.e. apart from the personal biases and ideological values, the authorities intentionally strove to create a brand new trend of literature and art by excluding the existing literary categories.

64. See Laifong Leung, *Morning Sun: Interviews with Chinese Writers of the Lost Generation* (Armonk, 1994), pp. 231–2.

65. See Larson and Wedell-Wedellsborg, 'Introduction', in their edited *Inside Out: Modernism and Postmodernism in Chinese Literary Culture* (Aarhus, 1993), p. 16. On foreign literature in China, see Marián Gálik, 'Foreign Literature in the People's Republic of China between 1970–1979', *Asian and African Studies*, 19 (1983), pp. 55–95.

66. In response to critics such as He Qifang and Lin Mohan against his views on literature and art, Hu Feng wrote his 'Dui wenyi wenti de yijian' ['Views on Literature and Art'] and sent it to the CCP Central Committee in April 1954. It was published as an appendix to *Wenyi Bao* No. 1–2 (1955) to be rebutted. A nationwide campaign against Hu Feng started in April 1955.

67. Quoted in Yi Qun, 'Tan Chen Yong de "zhenshi" lun' ['On Chen Yong's Theory of "Truthfulness"'], in Shanghai Wenyi Chubanshe (ed.), *Shehuizhuyi xianshizhuyi luwen ji* [*A Collection of Papers on Socialist Realism*] (Shanghai, 1959), Vol. 2, p. 295 and p. 298.

68. See Li Helin, 'Shi nian lai wenyi lilun he piping shang de yi ge xiao wenti' ['A Small Issue in Literary and Art Theory and Criticism of the Last Ten Years'], *Wenyi Bao*, No. 1 (1960), p. 41.

69. See Editorial Department of *Wenyi Bao*, 'Guanyu "xie zhongjian renwu" de cailiao' ['Materials on "Writing Middle Characters"'], *Wenyi Bao*, No. 8–9 (1964), p. 19.

70. See Editorial Department of *Wenyi Bao*, 'Ticai wenti' ['On subject matter'], *Wenyi Bao*, No. 3 (1961), pp. 2–6.

71. See Editorial Department of *Wenyi Bao*, 'Guanyu "xie zhongjian renwu" de cailiao', *Wenyi Bao*, No. 8–9 (1964), p. 17.

72. See Lin Wei *et al.*, *'Si-ren-bang' pipan* [*Critique of the 'Gang of Four'*] (Beijing, 1983), p. 372.

73. Ibid., p. 379

74. Ibid., pp. 372–3.

75. See the editorial, 'Wuchanjieji Wenhua Da Geming wansui' ['Long live the Great Proletarian Cultural Revolution'], *Hongqi*, No. 8 (1966), p. 7.

76. See *Zhou Yang wenji*, Vol. 2, p. 417.

77. Ibid., pp. 204–5.

78. Ibid., p. 252.

79. See Editorial Department of *Wenyi Bao*, 'Guanyu "xie zhongjian renwu" de cailiao', *Wenyi Bao*, No. 8–9 (1964), p. 17.

80. Ibid.

81. See Shanghai Jingju-tuan «Zhiqu Weihushan» Ju-zu [The Performing Group of *Taking Tiger Mountain by Strategy* of Shanghai Peking Opera Troupe], 'Nuli suzao wuchanjieji yingxiong renwu de guanghui xingxiang — Dui suzao Yang Zirong deng yingxiong xingxiang de yixie tihui' ['To Try Hard to Create Dazzlingly Brilliant Proletarian Heroic Images: Experiences of Creating the Heroic Images like Yang Zirong'], *Hongqi*, No. 11 (1969), pp. 62–3.

82. See Qian Haoliang, 'Suzao gaoda de wuchanjieji yingxiong xingxiang' ['To

Create Lofty and Great Proletarian Heroic Images'], *Hongqi*, No. 8 (1967), p. 68.

83. See Lin Wei *et al.*, *'Si-ren-bang' pipan*, pp. 389–90.
84. Ibid.
85. Ibid.
86. Quoted in Guo Zhigang *et al.*, *Zhongguo dangdai wenxue shi chugao*, Vol. 2, pp. 872–3.
87. See Bonnie S. McDougall, 'Poems, Poets, and Poetry 1976: An Exercise in the Typology of Modern Chinese Literature', *Contemporary China*, Vol. 2, No. 4 (Winter 1978), p. 99.
88. See Leo Ou-fan Lee, 'The Politics of Technique: Perspectives of Literary Dissidence in Contemporary Chinese Fiction', in Jeffrey C. Kinkley (ed.), *After Mao: Chinese Literature and Society 1978–1981*, p. 159.

INTRODUCTION TO PART I

1. Liu Qing's *The Builders* (Vol. 1) has two editions. The first was published before the Cultural Revolution, and the second during the Cultural Revolution. As to the differences between the two editions, see Yan Gang, *«Chuangye shi» yu xiaoshuo yishu* [*The Builders* and Fiction Art], (Shanghai, 1981). In this study, the analysis of this novel is based on the first edition.

CHAPTER 1: PERSONAL BACKGROUND

1. See *Chinese Literature*, No. 9 (1967), p. 37.
2. See Feng Yunan, *Yinshatan* [*Yinsha Beach*] (Tianjin, 1976), p. 60.
3. See Zhou Libo, *Shanxiang ju bian* [*Great Changes in a Mountain Village*] (Beijing, 1962), Vol. 1, p. 204.
4. See Bonnie S. McDougall, 'Poems, Poets, and Poetry 1976: An Exercise in the Typology of Modern Chinese Literature', *Contemporary China*, Vol. 2, No. 4 (Winter 1978), p. 100.
5. See Zhongguo Gongchandang Hunan Sheng Weiyuanhui Xiezuo Xiaozu, 'Chongfen fahui funü zai geming he jianshe zhong de zuoyong' ['Give Full Play to Women in the Revolution and Production'], *Hongqi*, No. 10 (1971), pp. 60–4.
6. See Chen Rong, *Wan nian qing*, p. 11.
7. See Zhu Jian, *Qingshibao*, p. 30.
8. See Feng Yunan, *Yinshatan*, p. 21.
9. See Chen Rong, *Wan nian qing*, p. 15.

10. Ibid.
11. See *Renmin Ribao, Hongqi, Jiefangjun Bao* (editorial), 'Renzhen xuexi liang tiao luxian douzheng de lishi' ['Study Seriously the History of Struggles between Two Lines'], *Hongqi*, No. 5 (1968), pp. 4–11. Among studies of the theory of continuous revolution in China, there are Stuart Schram's 'Mao Tse-tung and the Theory of Permanent Revolution', *The China Quarterly*, No. 46 (April-June 1971), pp. 221–45, John Bryan Starr, 'Conceptual Foundations of Mao Tse-tung's Theory of Continuous Revolution', *Asian Survey*, 11:6 (June 1971), pp. 610–28, and Lowell Dittmer, *China's Continuous Revolution: The Post-Liberation Epoch 1949–1981*. According to Dittmer, 'the attempt to "continue the revolution under the dictatorship of the proletariat" has dominated Chinese politics more than any single concern in the three decades since the founding of the People's Republic'. See Dittmer's book above, p. 1.
12. See Wang Dongman, *Zhanghe chun* [*Spring Comes to Zhang River*] (Taiyuan, 1976), p. 197.
13. Ibid.
14. Ibid., pp. 196–8.
15. See Zhu Jian, *Qingshibao*, p. 117.
16. See D. E. Pollard, 'The Short Story in the Cultural Revolution', *The China Quarterly*, No. 73 (1978), p. 104.
17. See *Hongqi*, No. 5 (1970), p. 43.
18. See Gu Hua, *Shanchuan huxiao*, p. 253.
19. See Tian Dongzhao, *Chang hong* [*The Long Rainbow*] (Taiyuan, 1976), Vol. 1, pp. 84–5.
20. See Wang Dongman, *Zhanghe chun*, p. 137.
21. See Zhang Xue, *Shan li ren* [*Mountain People*] (Jinan, 1976), p. 77.

CHAPTER 2: PHYSICAL QUALITIES

1. See Gu Hua, *Shanchuan huxiao*, p. 142.
2. See Wang Zhijun, *Nuli de nü'er* [*The Daughter of Slaves*] (Huhehaote, 1975), p. 5.
3. See Guangxi Zhuangzu Zizhiqu Baise Diqu San-jiehe Chuangzuo Zu, *Yu hou qingshan*, p. 11.
4. See Hao Ran, *Jinguang da dao*, Vol. 1, p. 579.
5. See Wang Zhijun, *Nuli de Nü'er*, p. 5.
6. See Ba Shan, 'Weihu he jiaqiang dang de tuanjie' ['Uphold and Enhance the Party Unity'], *Hongqi*, No. 7 (1973), pp. 9–14.
7. See Tian Dongzhao, *Chang hong*, Vol. 1, p. 226.
8. See Chen Rong, *Wan nian qing*, p. 273.

9. Ibid., p. 369.

10. See Gu Hua, *Shanchuan huxiao*, p. 502.

11. Ibid., p. 474.

12. See Chen Rong, *Wan nian qing*, p. 15.

13. See Wang Zhijun, *Nuli de nü'er*, p. 292.

14. See Wu Zuguang, 'Peking Opera and Its Great Master Mei Lanfang', in Wu Zuguang *et al.* (eds.), *Peking Opera and Mei Lanfang: A Guide to China's Traditional Theatre and the Art of Its Great Master* (Beijing, 1981), p. 11.

15. Ibid., pp. 6–7.

16. Ibid., p. 6.

17. See Huang Zuoling, 'Mei Lanfang, Stanislavsky, Brecht — A Study in Contrasts', in Wu Zuguang *et al.* (eds.), *Peking Opera and Mei Lanfang: A Guide to China's Traditional Theatre and the Art of Its Great Master*, pp. 28–9.

18. Ibid. p. 16.

19. See Tian Dongzhao, *Chang hong*, Vol. 1, p. 36.

20. Ibid., Vol. 2, p. 1129.

21. See Hao Ran, *Jinguang da dao*, Vol. 2, p. 265.

22. Ibid., p. 440.

23. See Walter Scott, *Ivanhoe* (London, 1897), p. 54.

24. Ibid., p. 212.

25. See Mikhail Sholokhov, English trans. by Robert Daglish, *Virgin Soil Upturned* (a novel in two books). Book 1, in Raduga Publishers, *Mikhail Sholokhov: Collected Works in Eight Volumes* (Vol. 6) (Moscow, 1984), pp. 55–6.

26. See Walter Scott, *Ivanhoe*, p. 220.

27. See Mikhail Sholokhov, English trans. by Robert Daglish, *Virgin Soil Upturned* (a novel in two books). Book 2, in Raduga Publishers, *Mikhail Sholokhov: Collected Works in Eight Volumes* (Vol. 7), p. 171.

28. Ibid., p. 25.

CHAPTER 3: IDEOLOGICAL QUALITIES

1. See Fudan Daxue Zhongwen Xi «Jinguang Da Dao» Pinglun Zu [The Commenting Group of *The Golden Road* at the Department of Chinese Language and Literature of Fudan University], *«Jinguang Da Dao» pingxi* [An Analysis of *The Golden Road*] (Shanghai, 1975), pp. 1–6.

2. See Liu Qing, *Chuangye shi*, Vol. 1, p. 231.

3. See Zhao Junxian, *Zhongguo dangdai xiaoshuo shi gao — Renwu xingxiang xilie lun* [A Draft of the History of Contemporary Chinese Fiction: On the Characterization] (Beijing, 1989), pp. 69–73.

4. See Yan Gang, *«Chuangye shi» yu xiaoshuo yishu*, pp. 77–8.

5. See Joe C. Huang, *Heroes and Villains in Communist China* (New York, 1973), pp. 246–7.

6. See T. A. Hsia, 'Heroes and Hero-Worship in Chinese Communist Fiction', in Cyril Birch (ed.), *Chinese Communist Literature* (New York, 1963), pp. 131–3.

7. See Hao Ran, *Jinguang da dao*, Vol. 1, p. 104.

8. See Tian Dongzhao, *Chang hong*, Vol. 1, p. 8.

9. Ibid., Vol. 2, p. 1008.

10. See Gu Hua, *Shanchuan huxiao*, p. 378.

11. Ibid., p. 379.

12. See Hao Ran, *Jinguang da dao*, Vol. 1, p. 489.

13. The three early articles of Mao [*lao san pian*] are 'Wei renmin fuwu' ['Serve the People'] (1944), 'Jinian Baiqiu'en' ['In Memory of Norman Bethune'] (1939) and 'Yu Gong yi shan' ['The Foolish Old Man Who Removed the Mountains'] (1945). All three articles may be found in Foreign Languages Press (ed.), *Selected Readings from the Works of Mao Tsetung* (Beijing, 1971).

14. See Mao Zedong, 'Wei renmin fuwu', in Foreign Languages Press (ed.), *Selected Readings from the Works of Mao Tsetung*, pp. 310–2.

15. See Mao Zedong, 'Jinian Baiqiu'en', in Foreign Languages Press (ed.), *Selected Readings from the Works of Mao Tsetung*, pp. 179–81.

16. See Joe C. Huang, *Heroes and Villains in Communist China*, p. 280.

17. See Liu Qing, *Chuangye shi*, Vol. 1, p. 488.

18. Ibid., p. 229.

19. Ibid., p. 229–30.

20. Ibid., p. 487.

21. See Zhou Libo, *Shanxiang ju bian*, Vol. 1, p. 131.

22. See Hao Ran, *Jinguang da dao*, Vol. 2, pp. 99–100.

23. Ibid., Vol. 1, p. 442.

24. Ibid., p. 570.

25. See Tian Dongzhao, *Chang hong*, Vol. 1, p. 200.

26. Ibid., pp. 200–1.

27. See Nikolai Ostrovsky, English trans. by R. Prokofieva, *How the Steel was Tempered* (2 vols.), 2nd English edition (Moscow, 1959), Vol. 2, pp. 284–5.

28. Ibid., p. 114.

29. Ibid., pp. 17–8.

30. Ibid., p. 288.

31. Ibid., pp. 283–5.

32. See Gleb Struve, *Russian Literature under Lenin and Stalin, 1917–1953* (Norman, 1971), p. 248.

33. See Mikhail Sholokhov, English trans. by Robert Daglish, *Quiet Flows the Don*, 2 vols. in this first unabridged English edition (the original in Russian consists of four volumes) (Moscow, 1988), Vol. 2, p. 738.

34. Zhou Libo, *Bao feng zhou yu* [*Hurricane*] (Beijing, 1952), 2 vols. The manuscript of this novel was completed in December 1948.

CHAPTER 4: TEMPERAMENTAL AND BEHAVIOURAL QUALITIES

1. See Hao Ran, *Jinguang da dao*, Vol. 1, p. 585.
2. Ibid., p. 593.
3. See Chen Rong, *Wan nian qing*, p. 276.
4. Ibid., p. 344.
5. See Hao Ran, *Jinguang da dao*, Vol. 1, p. 376.
6. Ibid., p. 227.
7. See Gu Hua, *Shanchuan huxiao*, p. 155.
8. See Chen Rong, *Wan nian qing*, pp. 236–8.
9. See Tian Dongzhao, *Chang hong*, Vol. 1, p. 560.
10. Ref. Lowell Dittmer and Chen Ruoxi, *Ethics and Rhetoric of the Chinese Cultural Revolution* (Berkeley, 1981), p. 22.
11. Ibid.
12. Ref. Hua-yuan Li Mowry, *Yang-pan Hsi: New Theater in China* (Berkeley, 1973), pp. 45–9.
13. See Gu Hua, *Shanchuan huxiao*, p. 350.
14. See Chen Rong, *Wan nian qing*, p. 7.
15. See Gu Hua, *Shanchuan huxiao*, p. 387.
16. See Chen Rong, *Wan nian qing*, p. 411.
17. See Hao Ran, *Jinguang da dao*, Vol. 1, p. 107.
18. See 'Lin Biao Tongzhi weituo Jiang Qing Tongzhi zhaokai de budui wenyi gongzuo zuotanhui jiyao', *Hongqi*, No. 9 (1967), p. 19.
19. See Chen Rong, *Wan nian qing*, p. 480.
20. Ibid., p. 412.
21. See Tian Dongzhao, *Chang hong*, Vol. 2, p. 708.
22. See Tang Jinhai *et al.* (eds.), *Mao Dun zhuan ji 1 — (2)* [*A Special Collection of Mao Dun*] (Fuzhou, 1983), p. 1249.
23. See Hao Ran, *Jinguang da dao*, Vol. 1, p. 234.
24. See Guangxi Zhuangzu Zizhiqu Baise Diqu San-jiehe Chuangzuo Zu, *Yu hou qingshan*, pp. 96–7.
25. See Chen Rong, *Wan nian qing*, pp. 319–20.
26. See Gu Hua, *Shanchuan huxiao*, p. 305.
27. See Chen Rong *Wan nian qing*, p. 320.
28. Ibid., p. 412.
29. See Tian Dongzhao, *Chang hong*, Vol. 2, p. 841.
30. See Bonnie S. McDougall, 'Poems, Poets, and Poetry 1976: An Exercise in

the Typology of Modern Chinese Literature', *Contemporary China*, Vol. 2, No. 4 (Winter 1978), pp. 106–7.

31. See Gu Hua, *Shanchuan huxiao*, p. 134.

32. Ibid., p. 304.

33. Ibid., p. 305.

34. See Alexander Welsh, 'Scott's Heroes', in D. D. Devlin (ed.), *Walter Scott: Modern Judgements* (Bristol, 1968), pp. 64–7.

35. See P. F. Fisher, 'Providence, Fate, and the Historical Imagination in Scott's *The Heart of Midlothian*', in D. D. Devlin (ed.), *Walter Scott: Modern Judgements*, pp. 104–7.

36. See Marian H. Cusac, *Narrative Structure in the Novels of Sir Walter Scott* (Paris, 1969), p. 67.

37. See Joseph E. Duncan, 'The Anti-Romantic in *Ivanhoe*', in D. D. Devlin (ed.), *Walter Scott: Modern Judgements*, pp. 146–7.

38. See Walter Scott, *Ivanhoe*, pp. 292–3.

39. See Mao Zedong, 'Jinian Baiqiu'en', in Foreign Languages Press (ed.), *Selected Readings from the Works of Mao Tsetung*, pp. 180–1.

40. See Tang Yijie, *Zhongguo chuantong wenhua zhong de Ru Dao Shi* [*Confucianism, Taoism and Buddhism in Traditional Chinese Culture*] (Beijing, 1988), pp. 55–77; Zhang Dainian, *Zhongguo gudian zhexue gainian fanchou yaolun* [*An Analysis of Concepts of Traditional Chinese Philosophy*] (Beijing, 1989), p. 170; and idem, *Wenhua yu zhexue* [*Culture versus Philosophy*] (Beijing, 1988), p. 73 and p. 321.

41. See William Edward Soothill, *The Analects of Confucius* (Yokohama, 1910), pp. 557–9.

42. Quoted in Zhang Dainian, *Wenhua yu zhexue*, p. 320.

43. See Ding Xuelei, 'Pipan Liu Shaoqi de fandong renxing-lun' ['Critique of Liu Shaoqi's Reactionary Theory of Human Nature'], *Hongqi*, No. 11 (1971), pp. 33–42.

44. See Merle Goldman, *China's Intellectuals: Advise and Dissent* (Cambridge, Mass., 1981), p. 166. Goldman further pointed out, 'This was not the first time that the denunciation of Confucianism and praise of Legalism were chosen as the medium for a political movement. The conflict between the Confucians and the Legalists had been treated as analogous to the present since the May Fourth movement . . .' Ibid., p. 167.

45. See John DeFrancis, *Annotated Quotations from Chairman Mao* (New Haven, 1975), p. 142.

46. See Hou Wailu *et al.*, *Zhongguo sixiang tongshi* [*A History of Chinese Thought*] (Beijing, 1957), Vol. 2, pp. 169–83.

47. See John DeFrancis, *Annotated Quotations from Chairman Mao*, p. 122.

48. Ibid., p. 115.

49. See William Edward Soothill, *The Analects of Confucius*, p. 587.

50. Quoted in Hou Wailu *et al.*, *Zhongguo sixiang tongshi*, p. 386.

51. See John DeFrancis, *Annotated Quotations from Chairman Mao*, p. 123.
52. See William Edward Soothill, *The Analects of Confucius*, p. 557.
53. Quoted in Zhang Dainian, *Zhongguo gudian zhexue gainian fanchou yaolun*, p. 170.
54. See John DeFrancis, *Annotated Quotations from Chairman Mao*, p. 78.
55. See William Edward Soothill, *The Analects of Confucius*, p. 567.
56. Ibid., pp. 397–9.
57. See John DeFrancis, *Annotated Quotations from Chairman Mao*, p. 142.
58. Quoted in Hou Wailu *et al.*, *Zhongguo sixiang tongshi*, p. 173.
59. See John DeFrancis, *Annotated Quotations from Chairman Mao*, p. 120.
60. See Yin Menglun, 'Cong «Lun yu» kan Kongzi de yuyan jiaoyu lun' ['On Confucian Thought of Language Education Indicated in *The Analects of Confucius*'], in Zhonghua Kongzi Yanjiusuo [The Institute for Kongzi in China] (ed.), *Kongzi yanjiu lunwen ji* [*Collected papers of research into Kongzi*] (Beijing, 1987), pp. 338–51.
61. Quoted in Beijing Daxue Zhongwen Xi, *Zhongguo xiaoshuo shi* [*A History of Chinese Fiction*] (Beijing, 1978), p. 212 and p. 222.
62. See Chao Yue, 'Lun Kongzi de meixue sixiang' ['On Confucian Aesthetic Thought'], in Zhonghua Kongzi Yanjiusuo (ed.), *Kongzi yanjiu lunwen ji*, p. 438.
63. See Joseph S. M. Lau and Howard Goldblatt, 'Introduction', in Lau and Goldblatt (eds.), *The Columbia Anthology of Modern Chinese Literature* (New York, 1995), p. xvi.
64. See Zhou Libo, *Shanxiang ju bian*, Vol. 1, p. 100.

CHAPTER 5: PROMINENCE GIVEN TO THE MAIN HEROES

1. See Lowell Dittmer and Chen Ruoxi, *Ethics and Rhetoric of the Chinese Cultural Revolution*, p. 76.
2. See Chen Rong, *Wan nian qing*, p. 94.
3. See Hao Ran, *Yanyang tian* [*The Sun Shines Bright*] (Beijing, 1964), Vol. 1, p. 531.
4. Ibid.
5. Cf. Fudan Daxue Zhongwen Xi «Jinguang Da Dao» Pinglun Zu, *«Jinguang Da Dao» pingxi*, p. 61.
6. In CR novels, a number of characters' names have symbolic meaning. For instance, in Hao Ran's *The Golden Road*, the name of the hero Gao Daquan is a homophonic for 'loftiness, greatness and perfection'; the name of the landlord Meng Fubi is a homophonic for 'craving restoration of the old order (such that he even dreams about it)'; the name of the landlord's son Qishan

is a changed form of the idiom *dong shan zai qi*, which means 'staging a comeback'.

7. See Hao Ran, *Jinguang da dao*, Vol. 1, p. 437.
8. Ibid., p. 539.
9. See Guangxi Zhuangzu Zizhiqu Baise Diqu San-jiehe Chuangzuo Zu, *Yu hou qingshan*, p. 337.
10. Ibid., p. 467.
11. See Hao Ran, *Jinguang da dao*, Vol. 1, pp. 345–6.
12. See Mikhail Sholokhov, English trans. by Robert Daglish, *Virgin Soil Upturned*, Book 1, pp. 54–5.
13. Ibid., Vol. 2, pp. 445–7.
14. See Tian Dongzhao, *Chang hong*, Vol. 1, p. 15.
15. See Hao Ran, *Jinguang da dao*, Vol. 1, p. 581.
16. Ibid., pp. 453–4.
17. See Guangxi Zhuangzu Zizhiqu Baise Diqu San-jiehe Chuangzuo Zu, *Yu hou qingshan*, p. 463.
18. See Tian Dongzhao, *Chang hong*, Vol. 2, p. 1087.
19. See Guangxi Zhuangzu Zizhiqu Baise Diqu San-jiehe Chuangzuo Zu, *Yu hou qingshan*, p. 270.
20. See Gu Hua, *Shanchuan huxiao*, pp. 371–2.
21. See Mikhail Sholokhov, English trans. by Robert Daglish, *Virgin Soil Upturned*, Book 1, pp. 54–5.
22. See Hao Ran, *Jinguang da dao*, Vol. 2, pp. 585–6.
23. Ibid.
24. See Tian Dongzhao, *Chang hong*, Vol. 2, p. 844.
25. Ibid.
26. Ibid., p. 848.
27. See Hao Ran, *Jinguang da dao*, Vol. 2, pp. 440–1.
28. See Guangxi Zhuangzu Zizhiqu Baise Diqu San-jiehe Chuangzuo Zu, *Yu hou qingshan*, pp. 221–2.
29. See Tian Dongzhao, *Chang hong*, Vol. 2, pp. 858–9.
30. See Gu Hua, *Shanchuan huxiao*, p. 293.
31. Ibid., p. 294.
32. Ibid.
33. See Lin Yu *et al.*, *Paoxiao de Songhuajiang* [*The Roaring Songhua River*] (Ha'erbin, 1975), Vol. 1, pp. 158–9.
34. See Chen Rong, *Wan nian qing*, pp. 539–40.
35. See Hao Ran, *Jinguang da dao*, Vol. 1, p. 566.
36. See Guangxi Zhuangzu Zizhiqu Baise Diqu San-jiehe Chuangzuo Zu, *Yu hou qingshan*, p. 330.
37. See Sun Feng, *Wan shan hong* [*Mountains Emblazoned with Crimson*] (Wuhu, 1976), p. 138.
38. See Gu Hua, *Shanchuan huxiao*, p. 160.

39. See Fudan Daxue Zhongwen Xi «Jinguang Da Dao» Pinglun Zu, *«Jinguang Da Dao» pingxi*, pp. 24–5.

INTRODUCTION TO PART II

1. See Ferdinand de Saussure, English trans. by W. Baskin, *Course in General Linguistics* (New York, 1959), p. 13; and G. N. Leech & M. H. Short, *Style in Fiction* (London, 1992), pp. 10–1, and p. 38.

2. See Leech and Short, *Style in Fiction*, pp. 10–40; and also ref. Raymond S. W. Hsü, *The Style of Lu Hsün: Vocabulary and Usage* (Hong Kong, 1979), pp. 12–5.

3. See John Spencer and Michael J. Gregory, 'An Approach to the Study of Style', in N. E. Enkvist *et al.*, *Linguistics and Style* (London, 1964), pp. 66–83; Stephen Ullmann, *Language and Style* (Oxford, 1964), pp. 132–53; and Hsü, *The Style of Lu Hsün: Vocabulary and Usage*, p. 14.

4. The fact that the style of speech and writing during the period was mainly criticized as being full of politicized, stereotyped and empty words and expressions proves from one angle the prominence of the period's vocabulary style. See Wang Boxi, '"Si-ren-bang" de wenfeng jiqi yingxiang' ['The Writing Style of the "Gang of Four" and Its Influence'], *Zhongguo Yuwen* (1978, 1), pp. 55–9; and Lowell Dittmer and Chen Ruoxi, *Ethics and Rhetoric of the Chinese Cultural Revolution* (Berkeley, 1981), pp. 43–6.

5. See Leech and Short, *Style in Fiction*, pp. 42–71; Werner Winter, 'Style as Dialects', in Lubomír Dolezel and Richard W. Bailey (eds.), *Statistics and Style*, pp. 3–9; and Dolezel, 'A Framework for the Statistical Analysis of Style', ibid., pp. 10–23.

6. See Leech and Short, *Style in Fiction*, pp. 51–4; and Spencer and Gregory, 'An Approach to the Study of Style', in N. E. Enkvist *et al.*, *Linguistics and style*, pp. 59–105; and M.A.K. Halliday, 'Descriptive Linguistics in Literary Studies', in Donald C. Freeman, *Linguistics and Literary Style* (New York, 1970), p. 68.

7. Among the CR agriculture novels, the following three are taken to be the best ones by post-CR critics: Ke Fei's *Chun chao ji*, Hao Ran's *Jinguang da dao*, and Chen Rong's *Wan nian qing*. See Guo Zhigang *et al.*, *Zhongguo dangdai wenxue shi chugao* (Beijing, 1993), Vol. 2, pp. 878–9.

8. The diversity of Chinese dialects is so great that some scholars think that 'the Chinese dialectal complex is in many ways analogous to the Romance language family in Europe'. See Jerry Norman, *Chinese* (New York, 1988), p. 187.

9. See 'Introduction to the Work' ['Neirong shuoming'] by the publisher, in Gao Zhongwu, *Kongque gao fei* (Beijing, 1976), verso.

10. The term 'set expression' denotes a group of words standing in a fixed association. Examples include restricted collocations, idioms, catch phrases, proverbs, aphorisms, and other stereotyped forms. See David Crystal, *An Encyclopaedic Dictionary of Language and Languages* (Oxford, 1992).

11. Owing to a lack of consensus on word classification by usage in Chinese, the present one is based on several views with some modifications. See Li Xingjian and Liu Shuxin, *Zenyang shiyong ciyu* [*How to Use Words and Expressions*] (Tianjin, 1975), p. 100; Zhang Zhigong *et al.*, *Xiandai Hanyu* [*Modern Chinese*] (Beijing, 1982), pp. 136–42; Zhang Jing *et al.*, *Xiandai Hanyu* [*Modern Chinese*] (Beijing, 1988), pp. 166–79); and Zhang Yunfei *et al.*, *Xiandai Yingyu cihuixue gailun* [*An Introduction to Modern English Lexicology*] (Beijing, 1987), pp. 14–30.

12. See Zhang Yufei, *Xiandai Yingyu cihuixue gailun*, p. 18.

13. See Jerry Norman, *Chinese*, pp. 155–6; Yuen Ren Chao, *A Grammar of Spoken Chinese* (Berkeley, 1968), pp. 136–93; and Charles N. Li and Sandra A. Thompson, *Mandarin Chinese: A Functional Reference Grammar* (Berkeley, 1981), pp. 10–5.

14. The most popular dictionary of Modern Standard Chinese in China. In addition to the lexical items of the Modern Standard Chinese, it includes dialectal, old, literary, and some other items in common use. The items with typical stylistic identity are labelled, such as 'colloquial', 'bookish', 'dialectal', and 'swearing'. Compiled by Zhongguo Shehui Kexueyuan Yuyan Yanjiusuo. Beijing, 1983 (2nd ed.).

15. See Jerry Norman, *Chinese*, p. 155.

16. The most popular small-sized dictionary of Chinese idioms in China. Its over 3,000 items are sufficient to cover the idioms used in the sample novels. Compiled by Beijing Daxue Zhongwen Xi 1955 Ji Yuyan Ban Tongxue. Beijing, 1981 (4th ed.).

17. A popular *xiehouyu* dictionary with more than 2,000 items. But it cannot cover all the items appearing in the ten novels because *xiehouyu* often relates to local dialectal vocabulary. The special structure of *xiehouyu*, however, makes them easy to be distinguished from other categories. Compiled by Wen Duanzheng *et al.* Beijing, 1984.

18. The most comprehensive dictionary of Chinese proverbs. But it includes a few of four syllabic items which are comprised in *A Small Dictionary of Chinese Idioms*, such as *da cao jing she* [beat the grass and startle the snakes] (p. 84), *li ling zhi hun* [be purblind owing to one's lust for profits] (p. 210), *shui dao qu cheng* [something achieved when conditions are ripe] (p. 400), *zuo zei xin xu* [have a guilty conscience] (p. 633). In order to keep consistency, I put such items under idioms. Compiled by Meng Shoujie *et al.* Beijing, 1990.

19. The only special dictionary-like reference I have found about colloquialisms. The over 1,000 items, however, are based on Beijing Colloquial vocabulary.

Therefore, I only use this book as a complementary reference of *A Modern Chinese Dictionary*. Compiled by Zhang Jihua. Beijing, 1988.

20. A popular reference book in China about Chinese dialectal words. But it is insufficient to cover all the items appearing in the novels because of the diversity of Chinese dialectal vocabulary. It is complemented by use of *A Modern Chinese Dictionary*; intuition is also involved. Compiled by Beijing Daxue Zhongguo Yuyan Wenxue Xi Yuyanxue Jiaoyanshi. Beijing, 1964.

21. Although the best available source, I cannot follow this work unconditionally, because there are some obviously non-military words and expressions included. For example, *zhengzhi luxian* [political line] (p. 37), *Zhongguo Gongchandang* [the Chinese Communist Party] (p. 103), *fan-geming fenzi* [a counterrevolutionary] (p. 109), *qunzhong* [the masses] (p. 346). Compiled by Joseph D. Lowe. Boulder, 1977.

22. The only dictionary-like book about ideological vocabulary I can get. But there are two problems. At first, some items can be surely excluded from 'political phrases', such as *yan zhe wu zui, wen zhe zu jie* [blame not the speaker but be warned by his words] (p. 503), *yeyu xuexiao* [sparetime school] (p. 505). Secondly, most items in the glossary are phrases. In order to achieve the greatest precision in counting, I lay down the rule to take words and word-like phrases as the counting unit. Therefore, in this glossary, *wuchanjieji zhuanzheng xia jixu geming de lilun* [the theory of continuing the revolution under the dictatorship of the proletariat] is one item, but I count *wuchanjieji* [the proletariat] *zhuanzheng* [dictatorship] and *geming* [revolution] respectively, and they become three stylistic items. The book can thus mainly be used to offer a political word range. Intuition is involved. Compiled by Lau Yee-fui *et al.* (Hong Kong, 1977).

23. 'Monologue' here refers to a character's talking to himself or thinking. But sometimes the distinction between characters' monologue and narrator's narration is obscured. In order to avoid inconsistency, it is ruled that either of the following situations is used as formal mark to identify monologue: (1) with quotation marks; (2) without quotation marks, but with leading words like *xiang* [think], *shuo* [say] etc. followed by a colon or comma.

CHAPTER 6: VULGAR EXPRESSIONS

1. See Lars-Gunnar Andersson and Peter Trudgill, *Bad Language* (London, 1992), pp. 14–7, 53–89.
2. Ibid., p. 55.
3. See Chen Yuan, *Yuyan yu shehui shenghuo* [*Language versus Social Life*] (Hong Kong, 1979), p. 57 and 60.
4. Lars-Gunnar Andersson and Peter Trudgill classify 'swearing' into four

functional varieties: expletive, abusive, humorous, and auxiliary. See *Bad Language*, p. 61. On the basis of their classification, I have categorized vulgar expressions into five types and defined them according to the actual situation in Chinese.

5. See Zhou Libo, *Shanxiang ju bian*, Vol. 1, pp. 169–82.

6. See Hao Ran, *Yanyang tian* (Beijing, 1964), Vol. 1, pp. 183–4, p. 252.

7. See Zhou Libo, *Shanxiang ju bian*, Vol. 1, pp. 145–7, p. 150, pp. 151–3, p. 157.

8. No *lan-pi-gou* can be found in references. It may be an incorrect form of *lai-pi-gou*.

CHAPTER 7: IDEOLOGICAL EXPRESSIONS

1. The two idioms '*zi li geng sheng*' and '*jianku fendou*' have no literal ideological meaning. In CR novels, however, they generally have a positive ideological colour concerning Mao's line (see the example in F, p. 82). In the novels about learning from Dazhai, they become more politicized, being specifically taken to be the spirit and road of Dazhai (see the examples in H, p. 373, and in J, p. 266).

2. I sampled three paragraphs from each of the ten novels, and calculated the average ratio between ideological items and the total words (rather than characters) which form the ideological contexts. The result is 1:7.74.

3. Liu Qing's *The Builders* has been acknowledged by orthodox mainland Chinese critics as 'an epic about the cooperative transformation of agriculture in China'. See Yan Gang, «*Chuangye shi*» *yu xiaoshuo yishu* [*The Builders and Fiction Art*] (Shanghai, 1981), pp. 16–50; Ershi Er Yuanxiao Bianxiezu, *Zhongguo dangdai wenxue shi* [*A History of Contemporary Chinese Literature*] (Fuzhou, 1982), Vol. 2, p. 153; and Guo Zhigang *et al.*, *Zhongguo dangdai wenxue shi chugao*, Vol. 1, p. 350.

4. According to those criticisms, *The Sun Shines Bright* was rather seriously influenced by the current politics, especially the intensification of class struggle, and *The Golden Road* is a highly politicized novel. See Guo Zhigang *et al.*, *Zhongguo dangdai wenxue shi chugao*, Vol. 1, pp. 224–9; and Ershi Er Yuanxiao Bianxiezu, *Zhongguo dangdai wenxue shi*, Vol. 2, p. 206, and Vol. 3, pp. 42–3.

5. In this analysis, I put the ideological items in proportion to the quantity of word units.

6. The pre-CR novel *Yanyang tian* by Hao Ran is an exception. As the most influential pre-CR novel approved by the authorities during the Cultural Revolution, it obviously has some characteristics of CR novels, such as giving prominence to the main hero and intensifying the conflict between the hero and the main villain. In the novel, the total numbers of words by

the main hero Xiao Changchun and the main villain Ma Zhiyue are so large that they are on the middle level of CR novels.

7. See Gu Hua, *Shanchuan huxiao*, pp. 420–6.
8. Here only some Non-time Specific items are taken into consideration, because Time Specific items mainly related to special time or campaigns, which cannot be reasonably compared. For example, the Time Specific item *baochan dao hu* appeared 517 times in Chen Rong's *Wan nian qing*, but not once in the three pre-CR novels and Hao Ran's *Jinguang da dao*.
9. According to Lowell Dittmer, 'Mao's prestige among the masses was artificially enhanced during the early 1960s via a publicity blitz, promoted most actively by the People's Liberation Army (PLA) . . . It was in fact here that the "personality cult" was born . . . The apparent efficacy of the cult . . . may in part be attributed to the simplification, exaggeration, and endless repetition of Maoist slogans . . . During the Cultural Revolution itself, the cult was taken to extreme lengths . . .' See Dittmer, *China's Continuous Revolution: The Post-Liberation Epoch 1949–1981* (Berkeley, 1987), p. 79.
10. See Xie Zuozhu, 'Yongyuan zhuazhu jieji douzheng zhe ge gang' ['Grip the Key Link of Class Struggle forever'], *Hongqi*, No. 3–4 (1969), pp. 27–30; and 'Zhongguo Gongchandang zhangcheng' ['The Constitution of the Chinese Communist Party'] adopted by Zhongguo Gongchandang Dijiu Ci Quanguo Daibiao Dahui on the 14th of April in 1969, ibid., 1969, 5, pp. 34–8.
11. Being non-time specific, all items indicating class status appear in both pre-CR and CR novels except 'pin-xiazhongnong' which is the combination of 'pinnong' and 'xiazhongnong', and does not appear in the novels whose time-setting is before 1957. So we cannot find it in samples A, B, and D.
12. See the editorial by *Renmin Ribao*, *Hongqi* and *Jiefangjun Bao*, 'Renzhen xuexi liang tiao luxian douzheng de lishi' ['Study Seriously the History of Struggles between Two Lines'], *Hongqi*, No. 5 (1968), pp. 4–11; and Zhongguo Gongchandang Xiyang Xian Dazhai Gongshe Weiyuanhui, 'Luxian douzheng yao niannian jiang yueyue jiang tiantian jiang' ['The Line Struggle Must Be Stressed Yearly, Monthly and Daily'], *Hongqi*, No. 12 (1971), pp. 29–32.
13. As the first novel published after the launch of the Cultural Revolution in 1966, it was highly praised by the authorities. Shortly after, it was overshadowed by Hao Ran's *Jinguang da dao*, the second CR novel. See Guo Zhigang *et al.*, *Zhongguo dangdai wenxue shi chugao*, Vol. 2, p. 877.
14. Among the CR novels, *Hongnan zuozhan shi*, the first novel published during the Cultural Revolution, is taken to be the most politicized by post-CR commentators. See Ershi Er Yuanxiao Bianxiezu, *Zhongguo dangdai wenxue shi*, Vol. 3, pp. 41–2; and Guo Zhigang *et al.*, *Zhongguo dangdai wenxue shi chugao*, Vol. 2, p. 877.

CHAPTER 8: IDIOMS, PROVERBS, *XIEHOUYU*, AND CLASSICAL VERSES

1. See Huang Borong and Liao Xudong, *Xiandai Hanyu* [*Modern Chinese*] (Lanzhou, 1983), Vol. 1, pp. 268–9; and Shi Shi, *Hanyu chengyu yanjiu* [*A Study of Chinese Idioms*] (Chengdu, 1979), pp. 381–9.

2. See Shi Shi, *Hanyu chengyu yanjiu*, pp. 130–2; and Ma Guofan, *Chengyu* [*Idioms*] (Huhehaote, 1978), pp. 89–90.

3. See Ma Guofan, *Chengyu*, pp. 42–6; Shi Shi, *Hanyu chengyu yanjiu*, pp. 158–61; and Wang Xijie, *Hanyu xiucixue* [*Chinese Rhetoric*] (Beijing, 1985), pp. 178–9.

4. See Shi Shi, *Hanyu chengyu yanjiu*, pp. 26–49, 180–202; Ma Guofan, *Chengyu*, pp. 28–38, and pp. 96–127.

5. See Wang Boxi, '"Si-ren-bang" de wenfeng jiqi yingxiang', *Zhongguo Yuwen*, No. 1 (1978), pp. 55–9; and Lowell Dittmer and Chen Ruoxi, *Ethics and Rhetoric of the Chinese Cultural Revolution*, p. 45.

6. See Shi Shi, *Hanyu chengyu yanjiu*, p. 123, pp. 203–4, pp. 368–70; and Wang Xijie, *Hanyu xiucixue*, pp. 100–3.

7. In their *Ethics and Rhetoric of the Chinese Cultural Revolution*, Lowell Dittmer and Chen Ruoxi also pointed out the prevalence of antithesis in the Cultural Revolution, but their illustration focuses on ideological content rather than rhetorical style. See pp. 14–7.

8. See Ma Guofan, *Chengyu*, pp. 214–7.

9. The other novels by Liu Qing that I have investigated concerning proverbs and *xiehouyu* include *Zhong gu ji* [*The Story of Planting*] (2nd ed., Beijing, 1958) and *Tong qiang tie bi* [*Wall of Bronze*] (2nd ed., Beijing, 1958).

10. For the principle of authorship of 'three-in-one' or 'tri-unification' ['*san jiehe*'], see Hua-yuan Li Mowry, *Yang-pan Hsi: New Theater in China* (Berkeley, 1973), pp. 17–8, and pp. 25–9.

11. See Wang Qin, *Yanyu xiehouyu gailun* [*Introduction to Proverbs and Xiehouyu*] (Changsha, 1980), pp. 74–86, and Yang Lan, '*Fangyan*' ['*Dialect*'], in «Gongan Xianzhi» Bianzuan Weiyuanhui, *Gongan xianzhi* [*The Annals of Gongan County*] (Shanghai, 1990), pp. 590–610.

12. Ref. Wang Qin, *Yanyu xiehouyu gailun*, p. 178.

13. As far as I know, this is the most popular dictionary collecting well-known lines of classical poetry. In addition to interpretation, each item has detailed notes about time (dynasty), author, title, and style. Compiled by Lü Ziyang. Beijing, 1986.

14. In 1954, Mao launched a campaign criticizing Hu Shi's and Yu Pingbo's research methodology in *Hong lou meng*. From then on, the novel has been the most uniformly praised of all the classical novels by Chinese authorities. The quotations from the novel during the Cultural Revolution were usually

verse lines describing the negative characters' internal strife and tragic fates rather than love and pleasure.

CHAPTER 9: 'BOOKISH' AND 'COLLOQUIAL'

1. See Huang Borong and Liao Xudong, *Xiandai Hanyu*, Vol. 2, p. 503; Zhang Zhigong, *Xiandai Hanyu*, Vol. 3, p. 35.
2. See Huang Borong and Liao Xudong, *Xiandai Hanyu*, Vol. 1, pp. 257–63; Zhang Zhigong, *Xiandai Hanyu*, Vol. 1, pp. 142–50.
3. Zhang Jihua's *Changyong kouyu yuhui* may not be strictly counted as a typical reference book on the colloquialisms of Modern Standard Chinese, because it includes some Beijing dialectal items which have not entered the vocabulary of Modern Standard Chinese, such as *shuapiao* [show off], *lengkeke* [be in a trance], and *bukengbuha* [keep silent].
4. In 'Fanli' ['Guide to the Use of the Dictionary'], it is stated that the label '*shu*' [bookish] relates to '*wenyan ci*' [classical literary words], but the range is obviously different from the classical literary words defined in other linguistic works. For instance, in both Huang's *Xiandai Hanyu* and Zhang's *Xiandai Hanyu*, classical literary items include so-called 'historical words' such as *junzhu* [monarch], *tianming* [destiny], *diwang* [emperor], *chengxiang* [prime minister (in ancient time)]. But most of such historical words are not labelled bookish in *Xiandai Hanyu Cidian*. Actually, by surveying the items labelled bookish, we have reason to think that the classification in the dictionary is mainly based on the level of stylistic colour rather than word source.
5. See Yang Shuzhong, *Duoyici tongyici fanyici* [*Polyseme, Synonym and Antonym*] (Beijing, 1983), pp. 40–1.
6. It is true that a number of colloquial words (most are nouns) are suffixed with '-*er*', such as '*diaomenr*' [pitch] (F, p. 462), '*dahuor*' [you all] (E, 116), and '*biziyanr*' [nostril] (C, p. 27). However, not all words with this suffix can be regarded as colloquial items although they are often used in spoken language. For example, '*dir*' [land] (E, p. 222), '*far*' [method] (C, p. 559), '*shenqir*' [expression, air] (F, p. 461), '*ziwer*' [taste] (F, p. 218). Moreover, retroflex suffixation is mainly based on the northen dialect sound system, and addition of '*er*' is related to place-setting and/or authors' own dialects. Of the ten novels, only four include retroflex suffication. They are Hao Ran's *The Sun Shines Bright* and *The Golden Road*, Chen Rong's *Evergreen*, and Lin Yu's *The Roaring Songhua River*, which are all written by northern writers and are set in the North. Retroflex suffixation may result in different change in actual pronounciation, but the writing practice in all cases is to add 'r' in *pinyin*, and to add '*er*' in characters. See Ping-cheng T'ung and D. E.

Pollard, *Colloquial Chinese* (London, 1982), p. 9; Huang Borong, *Xiandai Hanyu*, pp. 107–9.

CHAPTER 10: DIALECTAL EXPRESSIONS

1. There exits some inconsistency about the definition of the vocabulary of Modern Standard Chinese. Some scholars define it as being based on Northern dialect which covers a vast region. See Li Xingjian, *Putonghua he fangyan* [*Modern Standard Chinese and Dialects*] (Shanghai, 1985), pp. 24–7; Huang Borong, *Xiandai Hanyu*, Vol. 1, pp. 12–3. Some others state that it is based on Beijing dialect which covers a small district. See Jerry Norman, *Chinese*, pp. 136–7; T'ung and D. E. Pollard, *Colloquial Chinese*, p. 1. However, it is agreed by all that the vocabulary of the standard language has incoporated a lot of dialectal (Northern and other dialects) words and phrases. Large numbers of items labelled dialectal in *Xiandai Hanyu cidian* have been accepted or are being accepted into Modern Standard Chinese.

2. In 1951, the government noted that 'Correct use of language was politically significant in all walks of life under the leadership of the Communist Party', and called people 'to use the language correctly, and to struggle for the purity of the language'. In October of 1955, the norm of Modern Standard Chinese was set, and then the government initiated the campaign to popularize the standard language. As the basic language policy of the government, it was written into the Constitution. See Li Xingjian, *Putonghua he fangyan*, pp. 24–9, p. 109.

3. Ibid., pp. 43–4, p. 110.

4. There is a wide range of opinion on the main purpose and the basic spirit of the Cultural Revolution. See for example Gargi Dutt and V. P. Dutt, *China's Cultural Revolution* (Bombay, 1970), pp. 1–2, pp. 13–4, pp. 24–5; Lowell Dittmer and Chen Ruoxi, *Ethics and Rhetoric of the Chinese Cultural Revolution*, pp. 1–11; Lowell Dittmer, *China's Continuous Revolution: The Post-Liberation Epoch 1949–1981*, pp. 91–3. Nevertheless, seeking unity in all things or making all things uniform was noteworthy. This was reflected in a series of intensified campaigns during the period, such as calling people to learn from the PLA to unify behaviour, and encouraging people to struggle against the revisionist and bourgeois line to unify ideology and leadership. Moreover, during this period the authorities set a number of examples for emulation in all walks of life, designed to seek unity. For the counted campaigns and relevant significance, see Gargi Dutt and V. P. Dutt, *China's Cultural Revolution*, pp. 18–67, pp. 78–9; Anita Chan, *Chidren of Mao: Personality Development and Political Activism in the Red Guard Generation* (Seattle, 1985), pp. 124–84; H. C. Chuang, *The Great Proletarian Cultural*

Revolution: A Terminological Study (Berkeley, 1967), pp. 27–38.

5.   We can find quite a few general criticisms concerning stereotyped ['*taohua*'] style of language use during the Cultural Revolution although these criticisms are not specifically related to language in fiction. The manifestation of the style was to repeat words and expressions from official newspapers, magazines, and other propaganda documents. This parroting fashion is itself an aspect of uniformity. Under the impact of the stereotyped style and the spirit of unity, CR novelists might be inclined to use standardized language elements rather than diversified local items.

6.   From the 1940s to the 1970s, it was common for Chinese authors to go down to observe real life. According to Wendy Larson, 'Leftist efforts to make certain that writers "immerse themselves in life" were initiated in the 1930s and took concrete form in Maoist literary policy'. See Wendy Larson, *Literary Authority and the Modern Chinese Writer: Ambivalence and Autobiography* (Durham, 1991), p. 158. In 1942 Mao proposed that writers should have a good knowledge of those whom they described, including their language. See Mao Zedong, 'Talks at the Yenan Forum on Literature and Art', in Foreign Languages Press (ed.), *Selected Readings from the Works of Mao Tsetung* (Beijing, 1971), p. 254. In the 1950s, in response to calls from the authorities, some professional novelists settled in the countryside. Liu Qing and Zhou Libo were representative of this trend. See Ershi Er Yuanxiao Bianxiezu, *Zhongguo dangdai wenxue shi*, Vol. 1, pp. 113–5, Vol. 2, pp. 148–52.

CHAPTER 11: MILITARY WORDS AND EXPRESSIONS

1.   It is generally recognized that using metaphors is a characteristic phenomenon in the rhetoric during the first CR period. Although CR novels were produced during the second CR period, their language also includes large numbers of metaphors. Yet, the dimensions are different. For example, the rhetoric of the first period stressed violent action relative to that of the second period.

2.   See T. A. Hsia, *Metaphor, Myth, Ritual and the People's Commune* (Berkeley, 1961), pp. 1–15.

3.   See H. C. Chuang, *The Great Proletarian Cultutal Revolution: A Terminological Study*, pp. 44–5.

CHAPTER 12: METEOROLOGICAL VOCABULARY AND INFLATED EXPRESSIONS

1. According to *A Modern Chinese Dictionary* [*Xiandai Hanyu cidian*], *dongfeng* indicates 'revolutionary forces', and *chunfeng* indicates 'pleasant countenance'.

CONCLUSION

1. See Wendy Larson, 'Literary Modernism and Nationalism in Post-Mao China', in Wendy Larson and Anne Wedell-Wedellsborg (eds.), *Inside Out: Modernism and Postmodernism in Chinese Literary Culture* (Aarhus, 1993), pp. 184–5. Following Larson's example, I am here 'consciously suppressing the obviously different formal characteristics and epistemological underpinnings of critical realism, socialist realism, revolutionary realism', and so on, because 'they all constitute "realism" within Chinese literary discourse'. Cf. the above book, p. 195.
2. See Peng Qihua, *Xianshizhuyi fansi yu tansuo* [*A Re-examination and Exploration of Realism*] (Wuhan, 1992), p. 256.
3. Even the conventional understanding of realism in China did not have the same implications as that of Western cultural usage. As Marston Anderson has shown, 'Realism was not primarily endorsed by Chinese thinkers for what Westerners associate most closely with it, its mimetic pretense, that is the simple desire to capture the real world in language . . . Instead realism was embraced because it seemed to meet Chinese needs in the urgent present undertaking of cultural transformation by offering a new model of creative generativity and literary reception.' See Marston Anderson, *The Limits of Realism: Chinese Fiction in the Revolutionary Period* (Berkeley, 1990), p. 37.
4. Cf. Herman Ermolaev, *Soviet Literary Theories 1917–1934: The Genesis of Socialist Realism* (New York, 1977), pp. 196–8. Wendy Larson also has a comment relative to the 'authenticity' of Socialist Realism: 'When modernist and critical realist writers fight against the "falsity" of socialist realism in the late 1970s and demand "truth" in their own works, their stance is only partially a claim that the socialist realism form in itself promotes falsity; as I have tried to show in this paper, it also is a struggle against the pretense to morality and nationality that those favoring socialist realism assert.' See Wendy Larson, 'Literary Modernism and Nationalism in Post-Mao China', in Wendy Larson and Anne Wedell-Wedellsborg (eds.), *Inside Out: Modernism and Postmodernism in Chinese Literary Culture*, p. 195.
5. On literary control in contemporary China, see Perry Link, 'Introduction: On the Mechanics of the Control of Literature in China', in Link (ed.),

Stubborn Weeds: Popular and Controversial Chinese Literature after the Cultural Revolution (London, 1983), pp. 1–28.

6. To emphasize the didactic effect of literature in the Chinese tradition is evidenced in Confucius's comment on the *Shi jing* [*Book of Poetry*]. Confucius held that poetry served the fundamental purpose of transmitting cultural values. The didactic effect was also stressed by the sixth-century literary critic Liu Xie. He argued that emotion and principle were interwoven in a fine piece of literature (See Liu Hsieh, *The Literary Mind and the Carving of Dragons*, Taipei, 1975, pp. 246–7). The eleventh-century philosopher Zhou Dunyi proposed *wen yi zai Dao* [writing as a vehicle of the Way]. During the May Fourth era social values of literature were firmly advocated by intellectuals of the New Literature campaign. Since the Yan'an period, didactic principles of Marxist criticism had been intensified, according to which literary text should serve 'as an illustration of the tenets of social ideology'. Cf. Marston Anderson, *The Limits of Realism: Chinese Fiction in the Revolutionary Period*, p. 4).

7. See Joe C. Huang, *Heroes and Villains in Communist China* (New York, 1973), p. 26.

8. I establish the scope of post-CR fiction under discussion within the first decade after the Cultural Revolution because the CR period was ten years. Furthermore, many materials about post-CR fiction I have got are within the ten years.

9. Cf. Kam Louie, 'Love Stories: The Meaning of Love and Marriage in China', in Jeffrey C. Kinkley (ed.), *After Mao: Chinese Literature and Society 1978– 1981* (Cambridge, Mass., 1985), p. 66.

10. See Leo Ou-fan Lee, 'The Politics of Technique: Perspectives of Literary Dissidence in Contemporary Chinese Fiction', in Jeffrey C. Kinkley (ed.), *After Mao: Chinese Literature and Society 1978–1981*, p. 161.

11. With only stream of consciousness taken into account, the opposition between CR and post-CR fiction is evident. As Elly Hagenaar has shown, 'The fact that stream of consciousness appeared in literature in the course of the 1980s is significant, as it marks a fundamental change with respect to the preceding period. The change amounts to an "inward turn" in literature: that is, the prevalent form of realism in fiction, involving depiction of literary characters through their actions, was replaced by characterisation through descriptions of consciousness.' See Elly Hagenaar, *Stream of Consciousness and Free Indirect Discourse in Modern Chinese Literature* (Leiden, 1992), p. 1.

12. See Wang Meng, 'Xu — Yangyang daguan, congcong shi nian' ['A Spectacular Sight in the Last Ten Years'], in Song Yaoliang, *Shi nian wenxue zhu chao* [*The Main Trends of Literature in the Last Ten Years*] (Shanghai, 1988), pp. 5–6.

13. See Michael S. Duke, 'Introduction', in Duke (ed.), *Worlds of Modern Chinese*

Fiction: Short Stories and Novellas from the People's Republic, Taiwan, and Hong Kong (Armonk, N.Y., 1991), p. x.

14. See Joseph S. M. Lau and Howard Goldblatt, 'Introduction', in Lau and Goldblatt (eds.), *The Columbia Anthology of Modern Chinese Literature* (New York, 1995), p. xv.

15. Many writings of these writers have been translated into English. Cf. Kam Louie and Louise Edwards (eds.), *Bibliography of English Translations and Critiques of Contemporary Chinese Fiction 1945–1992* (Taipei, 1993).

16. The classification of these seven schools is quoted in Liu Dawen's 'Duoyuan-hua de wenxue xinchao' ['Varied New Literary Trends'], in Liu Dawen, *Zhongguo wenxue xinchao* (Hong Kong, 1988), pp. 41–51.

17. On the booming science fiction in post-CR China, see Rudolf G. Wagner, 'Lobby Literature: The Archeology and Present Functions of Science Fiction in China', in Jeffrey C. Kinkley (ed.), *After Mao: Chinese Literature and Society 1978–1981*, pp. 17–62.

18. On crime fiction in post-CR China, see Jeffrey C. Kinkley, 'Chinese Crime Fiction and Its Formulas at the Turn of the 1980s', in Kinkley (ed.), *After Mao: Chinese Literature and Society 1978–1981*, pp. 89–132.

19. See Perry Link, 'Introduction: On the Mechanics of the Control of Literature in China', in Link (ed.), *Stubborn Weeds: Popular and Controversial Chinese Literature after the Cultural Revolution*, p. 25.

20. See Wang Meng, 'Xu — Yangyang daguan, congcong shi nian', in Song Yaoliang, *Shi nian wenxue zhu chao*, p. 8.

21. See Leo Ou-fan Lee, 'The Politics of Technique: Perspectives of Literary Dissidence in Contemporary Chinese Fiction', in Jeffrey C. Kinkley (ed.), *After Mao: Chinese Literature and Society 1978–1981*, p. 162.

Select Bibliography

Ahn, Byung-joon (1976). *Chinese Politics and the Revolution: Dynamics of Policy Progresses*. Seattle: University of Washington Press.

Anderson, Marston (1990). *The Limits of Realism: Chinese Fiction in the Revolutionary Period*. Berkeley: University of California Press.

Andersson, Lars-Gunnar and Trudgill, Peter (1992). *Bad Language*. London: Penguin Books.

Beijing Daxue Zhongguo Yuyan Wenxue Xi Yuyanxue Jiaoyan-shi [The Teaching and Research Section of Chinese Department of Beijing University] (1964). *Hanyu fangyan cihui* [*A Word List of Chinese Dialects*]. Beijing: Wenzi Gaige Chubanshe.

Beijing Daxue Zhongwen Xi [Chinese Department of Beijing University] (1978). *Zhongguo xiaoshuo shi* [*A History of Chinese Fiction*]. Beijing: Renmin Wenxue Chubanshe.

Beijing Daxue Zhongwen Xi 1955 Ji Yuyan Ban Tongxue [The Linguistics Class (1955) of the Chinese Department of Beijing University] (1981). *Hanyu chengyu xiao cidian* [*A Small Dictionary of Chinese Idioms*]. 4th rev. ed. Beijing: Shangwu Yinshuguan.

Beijing Tushuguan Zhongwen Tongyi Bianmu Zu [the Cataloguing Group of Chinese Books of Beijing Library] (1979). *1974–1978 Zhongwen tushu yinshua kapian leiji lianhe mulu* [*A Joint Catalogue of Chinese Books between 1974 and 1978*]. Beijing: Shumu Wenxian Chubanshe.

Birch, Cyril (ed.) (1963). *Chinese Communist Literature*. New York: Frederick A. Praeger.

Chan, Anita (1985). *Children of Mao: Personality Development and Political Activism in the Red Guard Generation*. Seattle: University of Washington Press.

Chao, Yue (1987). 'Lun Kongzi de meixue sixiang' ['On Confucian Aesthetic Thought']. In Zhonghua Kongzi Yanjiusuo (ed.), *Kongzi yanjiu lunwen ji*, pp. 435–46.

Chao, Yuen Ren (1968). *A Grammar of Spoken Chinese*. Berkeley: University of California Press.

Chen (Shen), Rong (1975). *Wan nian qing* [*Evergreen*]. Beijing: Renmin Wenxue Chubanshe.

—— (1987). *At Middle Age* [*Ren dao zhongnian*] (English ed.). Beijing: Chinese Literature.

Chen, Yuan (1979). *Yuyan yu shehui shenghuo* [*Language versus Social Life*]. Hong Kong: Shenghuo Dushu Xinzhi Sanlian Shudian.

Chuang, H. C. (1967). *The Great Proletarian Cultural Revolution: A Terminological Study*. Berkeley: Centre for Chinese Studies, University of California.

Clark, Paul (1983). 'Film-making in China: From the Cultural Revolution to 1981', *The China Quarterly*, No. 94 (1983), pp. 304–22.

Couture, Barbara (ed.) (1986). *Functional Approaches to Writing: Research Perspectives*. London: Frances Pinter.

Crystal, David (1992). *An Encyclopaedic Dictionary of Language and Languages*. Oxford: Basil Blackwell.

Cusac, Marian H. (1969). *Narrative Structure in the Novels of Sir Walter Scott*. Paris: Mouton.

DeFrancis, John (1975). *Annotated Quotations from Chairman Mao*. New Haven: Yale University Press.

Devlin, D. D. (ed.) (1968). *Walter Scott: Modern Judgements*. Bristol: Macmillan.

Dittmer, Lowell (1987). *China's Continuous Revolution: The Post-Liberation Epoch 1949–1981*. Berkeley: University of California Press.

Dittmer, Lowell and Chen, Ruoxi (1981). *Ethics and Rhetoric of the Chinese Cultural Revolution*. Berkeley: Centre for Chinese Studies, University of California.

Dolezel, Lubomír (1969). 'A Framework for the Statistical Analysis of Style'. In Dolezel, L. and Bailey, R. W. (eds.), *Statistics and Style* (New York: American Elsevier Publishing Company, 1969), pp. 10–25.

Dolezel, Lubomír and Bailey, Richard W. (eds.) (1969). *Statistics and Style*. New York: American Elsevier Publishing Company.

Duke, Michael S. (ed.) (1984). *Contemporary Chinese Literature: An Anthology of Post-Mao Fiction and Poetry*. Armonk, N.Y.: M.E. Sharp.

—— (ed.) (1991). *Worlds of Modern Chinese Fiction: Short Stories and Novellas from the People's Republic, Taiwan, and Hong Kong*. Armonk, N.Y.: M.E. Sharpe.

Dutt, Gargi and Dutt, V. P. (1970). *China's Cultural Revolution*, Bombay: Asia

Publishing House, 1970.

Eberstein, Bernd (1988–1990). *A Selective Guide to Chinese Literature 1900–1949*. 4 vols. Leiden: E. J. Brill.

Editorial Department of *Red Flag* (1966). 'The Compass for the Great Proletarian Cultural Revolution', *Chinese Literature*, No. 9 (1966), pp. 42–5.

Editorial Department of *Wenyi Bao*, 'Ticai wenti' ['On subject matter'], *Wenyi Bao*, No. 3 (1961), pp. 2–6.

———— (1964). 'Guanyu "xie zhongjian renwu" de cailiao' ['Materials on "Writing Middle Characters"'], *Wenyi Bao*, No. 8–9 (1964), pp. 15–20.

Enkvist, N. E., Spencer, J., and Gregory, M. J. (1964). *Linguistics and Style*. London: Oxford University Press.

Ermolaev, Herman (1977). *Soviet Literary Theories 1917–1934: The Genesis of Socialist Realism*. New York: Octagon Books.

Ershi Er Yuanxiao Bianxiezu [The Writing Group of Twenty-Two Universities] (1982–1985). *Zhongguo dangdai wenxue shi* [*A History of Contemporary Chinese Literature*]. 3 vols. Fuzhou: Fujian Renmin Chubanshe.

Feng, Yunan (1976). *Yinshatan* [*Yinsha Beach*]. Tianjin: Tianjin Renmin Chubanshe.

Fokkema, D. W. (1969). 'Chinese Literature Under the Cultural Revolution', *Literature East and West*, 13 (1969), pp. 335–58.

Foreign Languages Press (ed.) (1971). *Selected Readings from the Works of Mao Tsetung* (English ed.). Beijing: Foreign Languages Press.

Freeman, Donald C. (1970). *Linguistics and Literary Style*. New York: Holt, Rinehart and Winston.

Fudan Daxue Zhongwen Xi «Jinguang Da Dao» Pinglun Zu [The Commenting Group of *The Golden Road* at the Department of Chinese Language and Literature of Fudan University] (1975). *«Jinguang da dao» pingxi* [*An Analysis of The Golden Road*]. Shanghai: Shanghai Renmin Chubanshe.

Gálik, Marián (1983). 'Foreign Literature in the People's Republic of China between 1970–1979', *Asian and African Studies*, 19 (1983), pp. 55–95.

Gao, Yunlan (1956). *Xiao cheng chunqiu* [*Stories in a Small City*]. Beijing: Zuojia Chubanshe.

Goldman, Merle (1981). *China's Intellectuals: Advise and Dissent*. Cambridge, Mass.: Harvard University Press.

Gray, Jack (1990). *Rebellions and Revolutions: China from the 1800s to the 1980s*. Oxford: Oxford University Press.

Gu, Hua (1976). *Shanchuan huxiao* [*The Mountains and Rivers Roar*]. Changsha: Hunan Renmin Chubanshe.

———— (1981). *Furongzhen* [*Furong Town*]. Beijing: Renmin Wenxue Chubanshe. Trans. by Gladys Yang as *A Small Town Called Hibiscus*. Beijing: Chinese Literature, 1983.

Guangxi Zhuangzu Zizhiqu Baise Diqu San-jiehe Chuangzuo Zu [The 'Three-in-one' Group of the Baise Prefecture of Guangxi Zhuang Autonomous

Region] (1976). *Yu hou qingshan* [*Mountains Green after Rain*]. Beijing: Renmin Wexue Chubanshe.

Gunn, Edward (1991). *Rewriting Chinese: Style and Innovation in Twentieth-Century Chinese Prose*. Stanford: Stanford University Press.

Guo, Zhigang et al.(1993). *Zhongguo dangdai wenxue shi chugao* [*A First Draft of the History of Contemporary Chinese Literature*] (a textbook for institutions of higher learning). 2nd ed., 2 vols. Beijing: Renmin Wenxue Chubanshe.

Hagenaar, Elly (1992). *Stream of Consciousness and Free Indirect Discourse in Modern Chinese Literature*. Leiden: Centre of Non-Western Studies, Leiden University).

Halliday, M.A.K. (1964). 'Descriptive Linguistics in Literary Studies'. In Donald C. Freeman, *Linguistics and Literary Style* (New York: Holt, Rinehart and Winston, 1970), pp. 57–72.

Hao, Ran (1964–66). *Yanyang tian* [*The Sun Shines Bright*]. Vol. 1, 1st ed., Beijing: Zuojia Chubanshe, 1964; Vol. 2 and 3, 1st ed., Beijing: Renmin Wenxue Chubanshe, 1966. English Excerpts as 'The Stockman', *Chinese Literature*, 3 (Mar. 1972), pp. 3–48.

——— (1972–74). *Jinguang da dao* [*The Golden Road*]. Vol. 1, 1st ed., 1972; Vol. 2, 1st ed., 1974. Beijing: Renmin Wenxue Chubanshe. Trans. by Carmen Hinton and Chris Gilmartin. Beijing: Foreign Languages Press, 1981. Fourteen chapters of this novel were published as 'The Bright Road' in *Chinese Literature*, 9 (September 1975), pp. 4–66; 10 (October 1975), pp. 4–59. The first nine chapters appeared as 'The First Step' in *Chinese Literature*, 1 (January 1973), pp. 4–62.

He, Zhi (1956). 'Xianshizhuyi — guangkuo de daolu' ['Realism: the Broad Path'], *Renmin Wenxue*, No. 9 (1956), pp. 1–13.

Hinrup, Hans J. (ed.) (1978). *An Index to 'Chinese Literature' 1951–1976*. London: Curzon Press.

Hongqi (editorial). 'Weida de zhenli, ruili de wuqi' ['Great Truth, Sharp Weapon'], *Hongqi*, No. 9 (1967), pp. 21–3.

Hou, Wailu et al. (1957) *Zhongguo sixiang tongshi* [*A History of Chinese Thought*]. 6 vols. Beijing: Renmin Chubanshe.

Hsia, C. T. (1971). *A History of Modern Chinese Fiction*. New Haven: Yale University Press.

Hsia, T. A. (1961). *Metaphor, Myth, Ritual and the People's Commune*. Berkeley: Centre for Chinese Studies, University of California.

——— (1963). 'Heroes and Hero-Worship in Chinese Communist Fiction'. In Cyril Birch (ed.), *Chinese Communist Literature* (New York: Frederick A. Praeger, 1963), pp. 113–38.

Hsü, Raymond S. W. (1979). *The Style of Lu Hsün: Vocabulary and Usage*. Hong Kong: Centre of Asian Studies, University of Hong Kong.

Hu, Feng (1955). 'Dui wenyi wenti de yijian' ['Views on Literature and Art']. As an appendix to *Wenyi Bao* No. 1–2 (1955).

Hu, Jingzhi (1959). 'Lixiang yu xianshi zai wenxue zhong de bianzheng jiehe' [The dialectical unity of the ideal and reality in literature], *Wenxue Pinglun*, No. 1 (1959), pp. 84–96.

Huang, Borong and Liao, Xudong (1983). *Xiandai Hanyu* [Modern Chinese]. 2 vols., Lanzhou: Gansu Renmin Chubanshe.

Huang, Joe C. (1973). *Heroes and Villains in Communist China*. New York: Pica Press.

Jiang, Qing (1967). 'Wei renmin li xin gong' ['Make New Contributions to the People']. In Tianshan Chubanshe, *Jiang Qing guanyu Wenhua Da Geming de yanjiang ji* [A Collection of Jiang Qing's Speeches on the Cultural Revolution] (Aomen, 1971), pp. 45–61.

Ke, Fei (1974). *Chun chao ji* [Swift is the Spring Tide]. 2 vols. Shanghai: Shanghai Renmin Chubanshe.

Kinkley, Jeffrey C. (ed.) (1985). *After Mao: Chinese Literature and Society 1978–1981*. Cambridge, Mass.: Harvard University Press.

———— (1985). 'Introduction'. In Jeffrey C. Kinkley (ed.), *After Mao: Chinese Literature and Society 1978–1981*, pp. 1–14.

———— (1985). 'Chinese Crime Fiction and Its Formulas at the Turn of the 1980s'. In Jeffrey C. Kinkley (ed.), *After Mao: Chinese Literature and Society 1978–1981*, pp. 89–132.

Larson, Wendy (1991). *Literary Authority and the Modern Chinese Writer: Ambivalence and Autobiography*. Durham: Duke University Press.

———— (1993). 'Literary Modernism and Nationalism in Post-Mao China', in Wendy Larson and Anne Wedell-Wedellsborg (eds.), *Inside Out: Modernism and Postmodernism in Chinese Literary Culture*, pp. 172–97.

Larson, Wendy and Wedell-Wedellsborg, Anne (eds.) (1993). *Inside Out: Modernism and Postmodernism in Chinese Literary Culture*. Aarhus: Aarhus University Press.

Lau, Joseph S. M. and Goldblatt, Howard (eds.) (1995). *The Columbia Anthology of Modern Chinese Literature*. New York: Columbia University Press.

———— (1995). 'Introduction', in Joseph S. M. Lau and Howard Goldblatt (eds.), *The Columbia Anthology of Modern Chinese Literature*, pp. xv–xxiii.

Lau, Yee-fui *et al.* (1977). *Glossary of Chinese Political Phrases*. Hong Kong: Union Research Institute.

Lee, Leo Ou-fan (1979). 'Dissent Literature from the Cultural Revolution', *Chinese Literature: Essays, Articles, Reviews*, 1 (1979), pp. 59–80.

———— (ed.) (1985). *Lu Xun and His Legacy*. Berkeley: University of California Press.

———— (1985). 'The Politics of Technique: Perspectives of Literary Dissidence in Contemporary Chinese Fiction'. In Jeffrey C. Kinkley (ed.), *After Mao: Chinese Literature and Society 1978–1981*, pp. 159–90.

Lee, Yee (1983). *The New Realism: Writings from China after the Cultural Revolution*. New York: Hippocrene Books.

Leech, Geoffrey N. and Short, Michael H. (1992). *Style in Fiction*. London: Longman.

Leung, Laifong (1994). *Morning Sun: Interviews with Chinese Writers of the Lost Generation*. Armonk: M. E. Sharpe.

Li, Charles N. and Thompson, Sandra A. (1981). *Mandarin Chinese: A Functional Reference Grammar*. Berkeley: University of California Press.

Li, Chi (1963). 'Communist War Stories'. In Cyril Birch, *Chinese Communist Literature* (New York: Frederick A. Praeger, 1963), pp. 139–57.

Li, Helin (1960). 'Shi nian lai wenyi lilun he piping shang de yi ge xiao wenti' ['A Small Issue in Literary and Art Theory and Criticism of the Last Ten Years'], *Wenyi Bao* (1960, 1), pp. 38–42.

Li, Huixin (1976). *Lancangjiang pan* [*Beside the Lancang River*]. Beijing: Renmin Wenxue Chubanshe.

Li, Ruqing (1975). *Island Militia Women* [*Haidao nü minbing*] (English ed.). Beijing: Foreign Languages Press.

——— (1976). *Wan shan hong bian* [*Mountains in Red*] (Vol. 1). Beijing: Renmin Wenxue Chubanshe.

Li, Xingjian (1985). *Putonghua he fangyan* [*Modern Standard Chinese and Dialects*]. Shanghai: Shanghai Jiaoyu Chubanshe.

Li, Xingjian and Liu, Shuxin (1975). *Zenyang shiyong ciyu* [*How to Use Words and Expressions*]. Tianjin: Tianjin Renmin Chubanshe.

Li, Yunde (1972–76). *Feiteng de qun shan* [*Seething Mountains*]. 3 vols. Beijing: Renmin Wenxue Chubanshe.

'Lin Biao Tongzhi weituo Jiang Qing Tongzhi zhaokai de budui wenyi gongzuo zuotanhui jiyao' ['Summary of the Forum on the Work in Literature and Art in the Armed Forces with which Comrade Lin Biao Entrusted Comrade Jiang Qing'], *Hongqi* (1967), No. 9, pp. 11–20.

Lin, Wei *et al.* (ed.) (1983). *'Si-ren-bang' pipan* [*Critique of the 'Gang of Four'*]. Beijing: Zhongguo Shehui Kexue Chubanshe.

Lin, Yu (1957). *Zhai shang fengyan* [*Beacons on the border*]. Wuhan: Changjiang Wenyi Chubanshe.

——— (1958). *Yan fei sai-bei* [*The Wild Swans Fly North*]. Beijing: Zuojia Chubanshe.

——— and Xie, Shu (1975). *Paoxiao de Songhuajiang* [*The Roaring Songhua River*]. 2 vols. Ha'erbin: Heilongjiang Renmin Chubanshe.

Link, Perry (ed.) (1983). *Stubborn Weeds: Popular and Controversial Chinese Literature after the Cultural Revolution*. London: Blond & Briggs.

——— 'Introduction: On the Mechanics of the Control of Literature in China', in Perry Link (ed.), *Stubborn Weeds: Popular and Controversial Chinese Literature after the Cultural Revolution*, pp. 1–28.

——— (ed.) (1984). *Roses and Thorns*. Berkeley: University of California Press.

——— (1985). 'Fiction and the Reading Public in Guangzhou and Other Chinese Cities, 1979–1980'. In Jeffrey C. Kinkley (ed.), *After Mao: Chinese*

Literature and Society 1978–1981 (Cambridge, Mass.: Harvard University Press, 1985), pp. 221–76.

———— (1989). 'Hand-copied Entertainment Fiction from the Cultural Revolution'. In Link, Perry *et al.* (eds.), *Unofficial China: Popular Culture and Thought in the People's Republic*, pp. 17–36.

Link, Perry *et al.* (eds.) (1989). *Unofficial China: Popular Culture and Thought in the People's Republic*. Boulder: Westview Press.

Liu, Dawen (1982) '"Dixia xiaoshuo" de cangsang' ['Vicissitudes of "Underground Chinese Fiction"'], *Dangdai Wenyi* [*Contemporary Literature and Art*], No. 8 (1982).

———— (1987). 'Duoyuan-hua de wenxue xinchao' ['Varied New Literary Trends']. In Liu Dawen, *Zhongguo wenxue xinchao*, pp. 41–51.

———— (1988). *Zhongguo wenxue xinchao* [*The New Trends of Chinese Literature*]. Hong Kong: Dangdai Wenyi Chubanshe.

Liu, Hsieh (Liu Xie) (1975). *The Literary Mind and the Carving of Dragons*. Trans. by Vincent Yu-chung Shih. Taipei: Chung Hwa Book Company.

Liu, Qing (1958). *Zhong gu ji* [*The Story of Planting*]. 2nd ed., Beijing: Renmin Wenxue Chubanshe.

———— (1958, 1976). *Tong qiang tie bi* [*Wall of Bronze*]. 2nd ed., 1958; 3rd ed., 1976. Beijing: Renmin Wenxue Chubanshe. Trans. by Sidney Shapiro. Beijing: Foreign Languages Press, 1954, 1982.

———— (1960, 1977). *Chuangye shi* [*The Builders*] (Vol. 1). 1st ed., 1960; 2nd ed., 1977. Beijing: Zhongguo Qingnian Chubanshe. Trans. by Sidney Shapiro as *Builders of a New Life*. Beijing: Foreign Languages Press, 1964, 1977. Excerpts trans. as 'The Builders' in *Chinese Literature*, 10 (Oct. 1960), pp. 72–162; 11 (Nov. 1960), pp. 59–142; 12 (Dec. 1960), pp. 88–179; 1 (Jan. 1978), pp. 3–51. Excerpts also trans. by William B. Crawford, in Kai-yu Hsu (ed.), *Literature of the People's Republic of China*. Bloomington: Indiana University Press, 1980, pp. 450–62.

Liu, Zengjie (1992). *Zhanhuo zhong de Mousi (19–20 shiji Zhongguo wenxue sichao shi, disi juan)* [*Moses in Flames of War (A History of Chinese Literary Trends in 19th-20th Centuries, IV)*]. Kaifeng: Henan Daxue Chubanshe.

Louie, Kam (1985). 'Love Stories: The Meaning of Love and Marriage in China'. In Jeffrey C. Kinkley (ed.), *After Mao: Chinese Literature and Society 1978–1981* (Cambridge, Mass.: Harvard University Press, 1985), pp. 63–88.

———— (1989). *Between Fact and Fiction: Essays on Post-Mao Chinese Literature and Society*. Broadway, New South Wales: Wild Peony.

Louie, Kam and Louise Edwards (eds.) (1993). *Bibliography of English Translations and Critiques of Contemporary Chinese Fiction 1945–1992*. Taipei: Center for Chinese Studies.

Lowe, Joseph D. (1977). *A Dictionary of Military Terms: Chinese-English and English-Chinese* [*Han-Ying Ying-Han jun-yu cidian*]. Boulder, Colorado: Westview Press.

Lü, Ziyang (1986). *Lidai shici ming ju cidian* [*A Dictionary of Well-known Lines of Classical Poetry Through the Dynasties*]. Beijing: Zuojia Chubanshe.

Ma, Guofan (1978). *Chengyu* [*Idioms*]. Huhehaote: Nei Menggu Renmin Chubanshe.

MacFarquhar, Roderick (1974–83). *The Origins of the Cultural Revolution*. 2 vols. New York: Columbia University Press.

Mao, Zedong (1942). 'Talks at the Yenan Forum on Literature and Art'. In Foreign Languages Press (ed.), *Selected Readings from the Works of Mao Tsetung* (Beijing: Foreign Languages Press, 1971), pp. 250–86.

——— (1963–64), 'Two Instructions Concerning Literature and Art'. *Chinese Literature*, No. 9 (1967), pp. 11–2.

McDougall, Bonnie S. (1978). 'Poems, Poets, and Poetry 1976: An Exercise in the Typology of Modern Chinese Literature', *Contemporary China*, Vol. 2, No. 4 (Winter 1978), pp. 76–124.

——— (1980). *Mao Zedong's 'Talks at the Yan'an Conference on Literature and Art': A Translation of the 1943 Text with Commentary*. Ann Arbor: Center for Chinese Studies, the University of Michigan.

——— (ed.) (1984). *Popular Chinese Literature and Performing Arts in the People's Republic of China 1949–1979*. Berkeley: University of California Press.

——— (1988). 'Breaking Through: Literature and the Arts in China, 1976–1986', *Copenhagen Papers in East and Southeast Asian Studies*, No. 1 (1988), pp. 35–65.

——— (1991). 'Problems and Possibilities in Translating Contemporary Chinese Literature', *The Australian Journal of Chinese Affairs*, Issue 25 (1991), pp. 37–67.

Meng, Shoujie *et al.* (1990). *Hanyu yanyu cidian* [*A Dictionary of Chinese Proverbs*]. Beijing: Beijing Daxue Chubanshe.

Miller, J. H. 'The Function of Rhetorical Study at the Present Time', *ADE* (Association of Departments of English) *Bulletin*, No. 62, pp. 10–8.

Mowry, Hua-yuan Li (1973). *Yang-pan Hsi: New Theater in China*. Berkeley: Centre for Chinese Studies, University of California.

Norman, Jerry (1988). *Chinese*. New York: Cambridge University Press.

Ostrovsky, Nikolai, (English trans.) R. Prokofieva (1959). *How the Steel was Tempered*. 2nd English edition; 2 vols. Moscow: Foreign Languages Publishing House.

Ouyang, Shan (1959). *San jia xiang* [*Three Families in a Lane*]. Guangzhou: Guangdong Renmin Chubanshe.

Peng, Qihua (1992). *Xianshizhuyi fansi yu tansuo* [*A Re-examination and Exploration of Realism*]. Wuhan: Wuhan Daxue Chubanshe.

Pollard, D. E. (1978). 'The Short Story in the Cultural Revolution', *The China Quarterly*, No. 73 (1978), pp. 99–121.

Qi, Wende (1973). 'Yan zhe wei gong-nong-bing fuwu de fangxiang jixu qianji — Xuexi «Zai Yan'an Wenyi Zuotanhui shang de jianghua»' ['Continue to

Advance in the Direction of Serving Workers, Peasants and Soldiers: A Study of "Talks at the Yan'an Conference on Literature and Art"'], *Hongqi*, No. 6 (1973), pp. 36–40.

Qian, Haoliang (1967). 'Suzao gaoda de wuchanjieji yingxiong xingxiang' ['To Create Lofty and Great Proletarian Heroic Images'], *Hongqi*, No. 8 (1967), pp. 66–70.

Qiu, Lan (1988). *Zhongguo dangdai wenxue shi lüe* [*A Brief History of Contemporary Chinese Literature*]. Beijing: Gaodeng Jiaoyu Chubanshe.

Renmin Wenxue Chubanshe Bianjibu [The Editorial Department of the People's Literature Press] (ed.) (1978).'*Yinmou wenyi*' *pipan* [*Critique of 'Conspiratorial Literature and Art*']. Beijing: Renmin Wenxue Chubanshe.

Saussure, F. de, (English trans.) W. Baskin (1959). *Course in General Linguistics*. New York: McGraw-Hill.

Schram, Stuart (1971). 'Mao Tse-tung and the Theory of Permanent Revolution', *The China Quarterly*, No. 46 (April-June 1971), pp. 221–45.

Shanghai Jingju-tuan «Zhiqu Weihushan» Ju-zu [The Performing Group of *Taking Tiger Mountain by Strategy* of Shanghai Peking Opera Troupe] (1969). 'Nuli suzao wuchanjieji yingxiong renwu de guanghui xingxiang — Dui suzao Yang Zirong deng yingxiong xingxiang de yixie tihui' ['To Try Hard to Create Dazzlingly Brilliant Proletarian Heroic Images: Experiences of Creating the Heroic Images like Yang Zirong'], *Hongqi*, No. 11 (1969), pp. 62–71.

Shanghai Shi «Longjiang Song» Ju-zu [The Performing Group of *Song of Long River* of Shanghai] (1972). 'Yan zhe Mao Zhuxi wuchanjieji wenyi luxian qianjin' ['Advance along Chairman Mao's Proletarian Literary and Artistic Line'], *Hongqi*, No. 6 (1972), pp. 14–23.

Shanghai Wenyi Chubanshe (1959). *Shehuizhuyi xianshizhuyi luwen ji* [*A Collection of Papers on Socialist Realism*]. 2 vols., Shanghai: Shanghai Wenyi Chubanshe.

Shanghai Xian «Hongnan zuozhan shi» Xiezuo Zu [The Writing Group of *Battle Chronicles of Hongnan* of Shanghai County] (1972). *Hongnan zuozhan shi* [*Battle Chronicles of Hongnan*]. Shanghai: Shanghai Renmin Chubanshe.

Shi, Shi (1979). *Hanyu chengyu yanjiu* [*A Study of Chinese Idioms*]. Chengdu: Sichuan Renmin Chubanshe.

Sholokhov, Mikhail, (English trans.) Robert Daglish (1984). *Virgin Soil Upturned* (a novel in two books). Book 1 is included in *Mikhail Sholokhov: Collected Works in Eight Volumes* (Vol. 6), and book 2 in Vol. 7. Moscow: Raduga Publishers.

———— First unabridged separate English edition (1988). *Quiet Flows the Don*. The original in Russian consists of four volumes. 2 vols. in this English edition. Moscow: Raduga Publishers.

Siu, Helen F. (ed.) (1990). *Furrows—Peasants, Intellectuals, and the State: Stories and Histories From Modern China*. Stanford: Stanford University Press.

Song, Yaoliang (1988). *Shi nian wexue zhu chao* [*The Main Trends of Literature in* the Last Ten Years]. Shanghai: Shanghai Wenyi Chubanshe.

Soothill, William Edward (1910). *The Analects of Confucius*. Yokohama: The Fukuin Printing Company.

Spence, Jonathan D. (1990) *The Search for Modern China*. New York: W. W. Norton & Company.

Spencer, John and Gregory, Michael J. (1964). 'An Approach to the Study of Style'. In Enkvist, N. E. *et al*, *Linguistics and Style* (London: Oxford University Press, 1964), pp. 59–109.

Starr, John Bryan (1971). 'Conceptual Foundations of Mao Tse-tung's Theory of Continuous Revolution', *Asian Survey*, 11:6 (June 1971), pp. 610–28.

Struve, Gleb (1971). *Russian Literature under Lenin and Stalin, 1917–1953*. Norman: University of Oklahoma Press.

'Summary of the Forum on the Work in Literature and Art in the Armed Forces with which Comrade Lin Biao Entrusted Comrade Jiang Qing', *Chinese Literature*, No. 9 (1967), pp. 23–38.

Sun, Feng (1976). *Wan shan hong* [*Mountains Emblazoned with Crimson*]. Wuhu: Anhui Renmin Chubanshe.

Tai, Jeanne (ed.) (1989). *Spring Bamboo: A Collection of Contemporary Chinese Short Stories*. New York: Random House.

Tan, Zongji *et al*. (1987). *Shi nian hou de pingshuo: "Wenhua Da Geming" shi lun ji* [*Comments after Ten Years: A Collection of Papers on the Cultural Revolution*]. Beijing: Zhong-gong Dangshi Ziliao Chubanshe.

Tang, Jinhai *et al*. (eds.) (1983). *Mao Dun zhuan ji 1 — (2)* [*A Special Collection of Mao Dun*]. Fuzhou: Fujian Renmin Chubanshe.

Tang, Yijie (1988). *Zhongguo chuantong wenhua zhong de Ru Dao Shi* [*Confucianism, Taoism and Buddhism in Traditional Chinese Culture*]. Beijing: Zhongguo Heping Chubanshe.

Tian, Dongzhao (1976). *Chang hong* [*The Long Rainbow*]. 2 vols. Taiyuan: Shanxi Renmin Chubanshe.

Tianshan Chubanshe (ed.) (1971). *Jiang Qing guanyu Wenhua Da Geming de yanjiang ji* [*A Collection of Jiang Qing's Speeches on the Cultural Revolution*]. Aomen [Macao]: Tianshan Chubanshe.

Tsai, Meishi (1979). *Contemporary Chinese Novels and Short Stories, 1949–1974: An Annotated Bibliography*. Cambridge, Mass.: Council on East Asian Studies, Harvard University.

T'ung, Ping-cheng and Pollard, D. E. (1982). *Colloquial Chinese*. London: Routledge & Kegan Paul.

Ullmann, Stephen (1964). *Language and Style*. Oxford: Basil Blackwell.

Wagner, Rudolf G. (1985). 'Lobby Literature: The Archeology and Present Functions of Science Fiction in China'. In Jeffrey C. Kinkley (ed.), *After Mao: Chinese Literature and Society 1978–1981* (Cambridge, Mass.: Harvard University Press, 1985), pp. 17–62.

Wang, Boxi (1978). '"Si-ren-bang" de wenfeng jiqi yingxiang' ['The Writing

Style of the "Gang of Four" and Its Influence'], *Zhongguo Yuwen* [*Chinese Linguistics*], No. 1 (1978), pp. 55–9.

Wang, Dongman (1976). *Zhanghe chun* [*Spring Comes to Zhang River*]. Taiyuan: Shanxi Renmin Chubanshe.

Wang, Lei (1974). *Jianhe lang* [*Waves on the Jian River*]. Shanghai: Shanghai Renmin Chubanshe.

Wang, Meng (1988). 'Xu — Yangyang daguan, congcong shi nian' ['A Spectacular Sight in the Last Ten Years']. In Song Yaoliang, *Shi nian wenxue zhu chao* (Shanghai: Shanghai Wenyi Chubanshe, 1988), pp. 5–9.

Wang, Phyllis and Gibbs, Donald A. (eds.) (1991). *Readers' Guide to China's Literary Gazette, 1949–1966*. Berkeley: Centre for Chinese Studies, Institute of East Asian Studies, University of California.

Wang, Qin (1980). *Yanyu xiehouyu gailun* [*Introduction to Proverbs and Xiehouyu*]. Changsha: Hunan Renmin Chubanshe.

Wang, Xijie (1983). *Hanyu xiucixue* [*Chinese Rhetoric*]. Beijing: Beijing Chubanshe.

Wang, Yafu and Zhang, Hengzhong (1988). *Zhongguo xueshu jie dashi ji (1919–1985)* [*A Chronicle of Events in Chinese Academic Circles (1919–1985)*]. Shanghai: Shanghai Shehui Kexueyuan Chubanshe.

Wang, Zhijun (1975). *Nuli de nü'er* [*The Daughter of Slaves*]. Huhehaote: Nei Menggu Renmin Chubanshe.

Wen, Duanzheng *et al.* (1984). *Xiehouyu cidian* [*A Dictionary of Xiehouyu*]. Beijing: Beijing Chubanshe.

Winter, Werner (1969). 'Style as Dialects'. In Dolezel, L. and Bailey, R. W. (eds.), *Statistics and Style* (New York: American Elsevier Publishing Company, 1969), pp. 3–9.

Wu, Han (1961). *Hai Rui baguan* [*Hai Rui's Dismissal from Office*]. Beijing: Beijing Chubanshe.

Wu, Zuguang *et al.* (eds.) (1981). *Peking Opera and Mei Lanfang: A Guide to China's Traditional Theatre and the Art of Its Great Master*. Beijing: New World Press.

Xu, Long (ed.) (1991). *Recent Fiction from China 1987–1988: Selected Stories and Novellas*. Lewiston: The Edwin Mellen Press.

Yan, Gang (1981). *«Chuangye shi» yu xiaoshuo yishu* [*The Builders and Fiction Art*]. Shanghai: Shanghai Wenyi Chubanshe.

Yang, Lan (1996). 'Socialist Realism' v 'Revolutionary Realism plus Revolutionary Romanticism'. In Hilary Chung (ed.), *In the Party Spirit: Socialist Realism and Literary Practice in the Soviet Union, East Germany and China*, pp. 88–105. Amsterdam: Rodopi, 1996.

——— (1996). 'Military Style in the Language of the PRC Novels during the Cultural Revolution'. *Macrolinguistics*, No. 6–7, 1996, pp. 113–24.

——— (1997). 'The Language of Chinese Fiction of the Cultural Revolution: A Style of Anti-vulgarity'. *Leeds East Asia Papers*, No. 52, 1997, pp. 1–25.

———— *et al.* (1994). *Zhonghua xiao baikequanshu: Yuyan wenzi* [*The Concise Encyclopaedia of China: Language and Characters*]. Chengdu: Sichuan Cishu Chubanshe and Sichuan Jiaoyu Chubanshe, 1994.

Yang, Mo (1958). *Qingchun zhi ge* [*Song of Youth*]. Beijing: Zuojia Chubanshe.

Yang, Shuzhong (1983). *Duoyici tongyici fanyici* [*Polyseme, Synonym and Antonym*]. 1st ed., 1972; 2nd ed., 1983. Beijing: Beijing Chubanshe.

Yao, Wenyuan (1967). '«Zai Yan'an Wenyi Zuotanhui shang de jianghua» shi jinxing Wuchanjieji Wenhua Da Geming de geming gangling' ['"Talks at the Yan'an Conference on Literature and Art" is a Guiding Document for the Great Proletarian Cultural Revolution'], *Hongqi*, No. 9 (1967), pp. 29–35.

Yao, Xueyin (1963). *Li Zicheng* (Vol. 1). Beijing: Zhongguo Qingnian Chubanshe.

Ye, Xin (1978). *Yan Ying* [*Stone Falcon*]. Shanghai: Shanghai Renmin Chubanshe.

Yi, Qun (1958). 'Tan Chen Yong de "zhenshi" lun' ['On Chen Yong's Theory of "Truthfulness"']. In Shanghai Wenyi Chubanshe (ed.), *Shehuizhuyi xianshizhuyi luwen ji* (Shanghai: Shanghai Wenyi Chubanshe, 1958), pp. 294–305.

———— (1963). *Lun wuchanjieji geming wenyi de fazhan fangxiang* [*On the Direction of the Development of Proletarian Literature and Art*]. Shanghai: Shanghai Wenyi Chubanshe.

Yin, Menglun (1987). 'Cong «Lun yu» kan Kongzi de yuyan jiaoyu lun' ['On Confucian Thought of Language Education Indicated in *The Analects of Confucius*']. In Zhonghua Kongzi Yanjiusuo (ed.), *Kongzi yanjiu lunwen ji* (Beijing: Jiaoyu Kexue Chubanshe, 1987), pp. 338–51.

Yu, Yan (1959). 'Geming de xianshizhuyi he geming de langmanzhuyi xiang jiehe wenti de taolun' ['The Discussion on the Combination of Revolutionary Realism and Revolutionary Romanticism'], *Wenxue Pinglun*, No. 2 (1959), p. 122.

Yue, Daiyun (1988). *Intellectuals in Chinese Fiction*. Berkeley: Center for Chinese Studies, University of California.

Zhang, Dainian (1988). *Wenhua yu zhexue* [*Culture versus Philosophy*]. Beijing: Jiaoyu Kexue Chubanshe.

———— (1989). *Zhongguo gudian zhexue gainian fanchou yaolun* [*An Analysis of Concepts of Traditional Chinese Philosophy*]. Beijing: Zhongguo Shehui Kexue Chubanshe.

Zhang, Jihua (1988). *Changyong kouyu yuhui* [*Colloquial Vocabulary in Common Use*]. Beijing: Yanshan Chubanshe.

Zhang, Jing *et al.* (1988). *Xiandai Hanyu* [*Modern Chinese*]. Beijing: Gaodeng Jiaoyu Chubanshe.

Zhang, Kangkang (1975). *Fenjie xian* [*Demarcation*]. Shanghai: Shanghai Renmin Chubanshe.

Zhang, Tuosheng (1987). 'Yi jiu qi wu nian de quanmian zhengdun' ['The Comprehensive Rectification in 1975']. In Tan Zongji, *Shi nian hou de* pingshuo: "Wenhua Da Geming" shi lun ji (Beijing: Zhong-gong Dangshi Ziliao Chubanshe, 1987), pp. 102–40.

Zhang, Xue (1976). Shan li ren [Mountain People]. Jinan: Shandong Renmin Chubanshe.

Zhang, Yunfei (1987). Xiandai Yingyu cihuixue gailun [An Introduction to Modern English Lexicology]. Beijing: Beijing Shifan Daxue Chubanshe.

Zhang, Zhigong et al. (1982). Xiandai Hanyu [Modern Chinese]. 3 vols. Beijing: Renmin Jiaoyu Chubanshe.

Zhao, Junxian (1989). Zhongguo dangdai xiaoshuo shi gao — Renwu xingxiang xilie lun [A Draft of the History of Contemporary Chinese Fiction: On the Characterization]. Beijing: Renmin Wenxue Chubanshe.

Zheng, Yuanhan (1989). Yanyu fengge-xue [Stylistics of Language]. Wuhan: Hubei Jiaoyu Chubanshe.

Zhongguo Gongchandang Dijiu Ci Quanguo Daibiao Dahui [The Ninth National Congress of the Communist Party of China] (1969). 'Zhongguo Gongchandang zhangcheng' ['The Constitution of the Chinese Communist Party'], Hongqi, No. 5 (1969), pp. 34–8.

Zhongguo Shehui Kexueyuan Yuyan Yanjiusuo [The Language Research Institute of Chinese Academy of Social Science] (1983). Xiandai Hanyu cidian [A Modern Chinese Dictionary]. 2nd rev. ed. Beijing: Shangwu Yinshuguan.

Zhonghua Kongzi Yanjiusuo [The Institute for Kongzi in China] (ed.) (1987). Kongzi yanjiu lunwen ji [Collected papers of research into Kongzi]. Beijing: Jiaoyu Kexue Chubanshe.

Zhou, Jiajun (1975). Shan feng [Mountain Wind]. Shanghai: Shanghai Renmin Chubanshe.

Zhou, Libo (1952). Bao feng zhou yu [Hurricane]. 2 vols. Beijing: Renmin Wenxue Chubanshe. Trans. by Meng-hsiung Hsu. Beijing: Foreign Languages Press, 1955.

—— (1962). Shanxiang ju bian [Great Changes in a Mountain Village]. 2 vols. Beijing: Zuojia Chubanshe. Vol. 1, trans. by Derek Bryan. Beijing: Foreign Languages Press, 1961. Excepts published as 'Great Changes in the Mountain Life', Chinese Literature, 10 (Oct. 1959), pp. 5–49. Excerpts trans. by Donald A. Gibbs, in Kai-yu Hsu (ed.), Literature of the People's Republic of China. Bloomington: Indiana University Press, 1980, pp. 242–56.

Zhou, Yang (1949). 'Xin de renmin de wenyi' ['The New Literature and Art of the People']. In Zhou Yang wenji, Vol. 1 (Beijing: Renmin Wenxue Chubanshe, 1984), pp. 512–35.

—— (1958). 'Xin minge kaituo le shige de xin daolu' ['New Folk Songs have Opened a New Path for Poetry']. Hongqi, No. 1 (1958), pp. 33–8.

—— (1960). Wo guo shehuizhuyi wenxue yishu de daolu [The Road of Literature and Art in China]. Beijing: Renmin Wenxue Chubanshe.

—— (1984). Zhou Yang wenji [Collected Works of Zhou Yang]. Vols. 1 and 2. Beijing: Renmin Wenxue Chubanshe.

Zhu, Jian (1976). *Qingshibao* [*Qingshi Fort*]. Nanjing: Jiangsu Renmin Chubanshe.

Zhu, Zhai (1960). 'Lixiang yu xianshi' ['The Ideal versus Reality'], *Wenxue Pinglun*, No. 6 (1960), pp. 9–13.

Appendix 1: The 24 CR Agricultural Novels

Bi, Fang and Zhong, Tao (1974). *Qian chong lang* [*Billows and Waves*]. Beijing: Renmin Wenxue Chubanshe. 684 pp.

Chen, Dabin (1975). *Benteng de Dongliuhe* [*The Surging Dongliu River*]. Tianjin: Tianjin Renmin Chubanshe. 363 pp.

Chen (Shen), Rong (1975). *Wan nian qing* [*Evergreen*]. Beijing: Renmin Wenxue Chubanshe. 565 pp.

Cheng, Xianzhang (1976). *Zhangtianhe* [*Zhangtian River*]. Guangzhou: Guangdong Renmin Chubanshe. 336 pp.

Feng, Yunan (1976). *Yinshatan* [*Yinsha Beach*]. Tianjin: Tianjin Renmin Chubanshe. 565 pp.

Gao, Zhongwu (1976). *Kongque gao fei* [*The Peacock Flies High*]. Beijing: Renmin Wenxue Chubanshe. 678 pp.

Gu, Hua (1976). *Shanchuan huxiao* [*The Mountains and Rivers Roar*]. Changsha: Hunan Renmin Chubanshe. 539 pp.

Guangxi Zhuangzu Zizhiqu Baise Diqu San-jiehe Chuangzuo Zu [The 'Three-in-one' Group of the Baise Prefecture of Guangxi Zhuang Autonomous Region] (1976). *Yu hou qingshan* [*Mountains Green after Rain*]. Beijing: Renmin Wexue Chubanshe. 589 pp.

Hao, Ran (1972–74). *Jinguang da dao* [*The Golden Road*]. Vol. 1, 1st ed., 1972, 648 pp.; Vol. 2, 1st ed., 1974, 688 pp. Beijing: Renmin Wenxue Chubanshe.

Heilongjiang Sheng Shuangcheng Xian Geming Weiyuanhui, Zhongguo Renmin Jiefangjun Jing Zi 801 Budui Lianhe Chuangzuo Zu' [The Collaborative Writing Group of the Revolutionary Committee of Shuangcheng County in Heilongjiang Province and the PLA 801 Unit under the Beijing Command] (Wang Zhongyu, Chen Genxi and Xie Shu did the actural writing) (1975). *Jing lei* [*Violent Thunder*]. 2 vols. Tianjin: Tianjin Renmin Chubanshe. 911 pp.

Jiashan Xian Geweihui Chuangzuozu [The Writing Group of the Revolutionary Committee of Jiashan County] (1975). *Cui ling zhaoxia* [*Dawn over Emerald Ridge*]. Hefei: Anhui Renmin Chubanshe. 214 pp.

Ke, Fei (1974). *Chun chao ji* [*Swift is the Spring Tide*]. 2 vols. Shanghai: Shanghai Renmin Chubanshe. 1108 pp.

Lin, Yu and Xie, Shu (1975). *Paoxiao de Songhuajiang* [*The Roaring Songhua River*]. 2 vols. Ha'erbin: Heilongjiang Renmin Chubanshe. 1046 pp.

Shanghai Xian «Hongnan zuozhan shi» Xiezuo Zu [The Writing Group of *Battle Chronicles of Hongnan* of Shanghai County] (1972). *Hongnan zuozhan shi* [*Battle Chronicles of Hongnan*]. Shanghai: Shanghai Renmin Chubanshe. 584 pp.

Shao, Chuang (1974). *Baizhangling* [*Baizhang Ridge*]. Hangzhou: Zhejiang Renmin Chubanshe. 354 pp.

Sun, Feng (1976). *Wan shan hong* [*Mountains Emblazoned with Crimson*]. Wuhu: Anhui Renmin Chubanshe. 495 pp.

Tian, Dongzhao (1976). *Chang hong* [*The Long Rainbow*]. 2 vols. Taiyuan: Shanxi Renmin Chubanshe. 1131 pp.

Tuerdi, Keyoumu, (Chinese trans.) Ma Junmin and Liu Fajun (1975). *Kezile shan xia* [*At the Foot of the Kezile Mountain*]. Wulumuqi: Xinjiang Renmin Chubanshe. 309 pp.

Wang, Dongman (1976). *Zhanghe chun* [*Spring Comes to Zhang River*]. Taiyuan: Shanxi Renmin Chubanshe. 725 pp.

Wang, Zhijun (1975). *Nuli de nü'er* [*The Daughter of Slaves*]. Huhehaote: Nei Menggu Renmin Chubanshe. 304 pp.

Yang, Chuntian (1976). *Jumanghe* [*The Jumang River*]. Huhehaote: Nei Menggu Renmin Chubanshe. 358 pp.

Zhang, Xue (1976). *Shan li ren* [*Mountain People*]. Jinan: Shandong Renmin Chubanshe. 308 pp.

Zheng, Wanlong (1976). *Xiangshuiwan* [*Xiangshui Bend*]. Beijing: Beijing Renmin Chubanshe. 544 pp.

Zhu, Jian (1976). *Qingshibao* [*Qingshi Fort*]. Nanjing: Jiangsu Renmin Chubanshe. 531 pp.

Appendix 2: Annotated Bibliography of Novels of the Cultural Revolution

This bibliography includes all CR novels with a length of over 200 pages except for a few for which we lack certain information regarding authorship, publisher, page number or content.

Bai, Wei (1976). *Shaonian hong hua bing* [*Youthful Red Painters*]. Taiyuan: Shanxi Renmin Chubanshe. 235 pp.

— This novel is set during the Cultural Revolution. A group of children headed by a juvenile heroine make propaganda in a village through painting. Seeing that some people attempt to spread anti-revolutionary cultural elements in the village, the children unite to carry out class struggle with their paintings. They finally expose a hidden class enemy and educate the backward villagers.

Beijing Shi Tong Xian San-jiehe Chuangzuo Zu [The 'Three-in-one' Writing Group of Tong County, Beijing City] (1976). *Chenguang qu* [*A Song of Dawn*]. Beijing: Renmin Wenxue Chubanshe. 590 pp.

— This novel describes a group of school-leavers who go to live and work in the countryside. They strive to turn wasteland to farmland by moving sand. They also oppose the spontaneous capitalist forces both in cities and in the countryside.

Bi, Fang and Zhong, Tao (1974). *Qian chong lang* [*Billows and Waves*]. Beijing: Renmin Wenxue Chubanshe. 684 pp.

— Set in a village in north-east China between 1965 and 1966, this novel describes the development of agricultural mechanization in the village.

The Party secretary of the village leads a group of people in assembling parts of used machines into a tractor. The theme of the story is promotion of self-reliance in agricultural mechanization in the countryside.

Bian, Zizheng (1976). *Zaolin Cun* [*Zaolin Village*]. Hefei: Anhui Renmin Chubanshe. 273 pp.

— This novel describes a group of juveniles participating in class struggle and collective labour in the village. The novel indicates that the promoted 'three revolutionary movements' (of class struggle, the struggle for production and scientific experiment) are a great school for children's education and growth.

Cai, Weicai (1975). *Jifeng* [*The Gale*]. Wuhan: Hubei Renmin Chubanshe. 234 pp.

— Set in the south of Hebei Plain in the late stages of the Sino-Japanese War, this novel describes a unit of the district army guided by the Party. The unit plays a major role in fighting against a plan of the Japanese army and its puppet government, according to which a large number of labourers are forced to work for them.

Cai, Zhenxing (1976). *Ji zhan changkong* [*The Great Battle of the Skies*]. Shanghai: Shanghai Renmin Chubanshe. 238 pp.

— A novel for children. In summer of 1962 a national defence project is under construction. A unit of the Kuomintang airforce attempts to bomb the construction site. An air unit of the PLA meets the enemy in the sky. A fiery battle is presented in the novel. The enemy is finally routed and the defence project is safe.

Chang, Zheng (1974). *Zhongliu dizhu* [*The Mainstay*]. Shijiazhuang: Hebei Renmin Chubanshe. 434 pp.

— Mao issued a directive in 1963: 'We must re-harness the Hai River'. The construction of the whole project lasted several years. This novel describes the people of a county in the Hai River valley, who work hard to contribute to the project. The coordination between different fronts in the construction is emphasized.

Chen, Dabin (1975). *Benteng de Dongliuhe* [*The Surging Dongliu River*]. Tianjin: Tianjin Renmin Chubanshe. 363 pp.

— This novel is set in a village to the north of the Huai River in 1953. The villagers firmly carry out collectivization and fight capitalist ideology, class enemies, and natural disasters.

Chen (Shen), Rong (1975). *Wan nian qing* [*Evergreen*]. Beijing: Renmin Wenxue Chubanshe. 565 pp.

— This novel is set in a village in north China in the early 1960s. A county official comes down to the village to carry out a policy of fixing household output quotas. His ideas and actions are opposed by the Party secretary of the village and his followers, who firmly uphold the previous system of collective production. Finally an official instruction from the supreme level proves that the county official is wrong.

Cheng, Jian (1975). *San tan Hongyudong* [*Exploring Thrice the Hongyu Cave*]. 2 vols. Shanghai: Shanghai Renmin Chubanshe. 934 pp.

— A novel for children. It describes a geological prospecting team looking for a water source for a big project for war-readiness in a mountain area. The project cannot be carried out until the problem of shortage of water is solved. The geological prospecting team overcomes various difficulties and finds a good water source. Class and ideological struggles are also presented.

Cheng, Shuzhen (1975). *Gangtie juren* [*The Steel Giants*].

Cheng, Xianzhang (1976). *Zhangtianhe* [*Zhangtian River*]. Guangzhou: Guangdong Renmin Chubanshe. 336 pp.

— A novel about the campaign of learning from Dazhai. The story is set in a village of Guangdong province. Under the leadership of the village Party branch, the villagers start to build a great irrigation works on the Zhangtian River. The project is completed through the support of the county Party secretary who comes down to the village to gain practical experience.

Ding, Mao and Wang, Lin (1976). *Xique Cun de haizi* [*The Children of Xique Village*]. Huhehaote: Nei Menggu Renmin Chubanshe. 206 pp.

— A novel set in a mountain village. In his autumn holiday from school a juvenile hero takes part in labour in the village piggery. He works hard in order to make a contribution to the campaign of learning from Dazhai. During this time he detects a class enemy's sabotage acts.

Ding, Yingchuan (1975). *'04' hao chanpin* [*No. '04' Products*]. Xi'an: Shaanxi Renmin Chubanshe. 383 pp.

— This novel is set on the industrial front in 1971. It centres on the production of a particular product in a factory. The main hero and his followers dare to think and act in technical innovation and experimentation, and fulfil state assignments well. They also avert sabotage by class enemies and spies.

Du, Jun (1975). *Zhiqi ge* [*A Song of Aspirations*]. Guangzhou: Guangdong Renmin Chubanshe. 402 pp.

— This novel is written by a worker. Set in the early 1960s, it presents a story on the industrial front. A big chemical plant is under construction in the coastal region of the South China Sea. The process of construction is interwoven with class and line struggles. The workers' altruism and self-reliance are emphasized.

Feng, Yunan (1976). *Yinshatan* [*Yinsha Beach*]. Tianjin: Tianjin Renmin Chubanshe. 565 pp.

— A novel about learning from Dazhai in the countryside. Refusing to accept a position in the city, a demobilized PLA soldier comes back to his native place and determines to transform a sandy beach into arable land. He becomes the Party secretary of the village. His ideas and actions encounter opposition from hidden class enemies and a backward colleague. However, he achieves his goal after a series of struggles.

Fu, Zikui (1976). *Lan-tian zhi* [*The Will in the Blue Sky*]. Wuhan: Hubei Renmin Chubanshe. 535 pp.

— This novel describes a group of PLA soldiers. They first go to join the Korean War, and then come back to China to train in aircraft combat. Finally they go back to fight bravely as soldiers of the air force. The novel indicates the importance of the PLA traditions established in the Yan'an period.

Gao, Zhongwu (1976). *Kongque gao fei* [*The Peacock Flies High*]. Beijing: Renmin Wenxue Chubanshe. 678 pp.

This novel is set among the Dai ethnic minorities. The people are organized by the Party to carry out collectivization. Although the campaign is opposed by the former rich locals and other enemies, the novel's tone is rather relaxed. Some critics comment on the local flavour of the novel's description of the Dai people's lives.

Gong, Cheng (1975). *Hongshikou* [*Hongshi Gateway*]. Beijing: Renmin Wexue Chubanshe. 538 pp.

— This novel is set in a mine in 1972. Before an important new project goes into operation, hidden enemy agents attempt to sabotage it. Public security men detect their activities and crush their conspiracy.

Gu, Hua (1976). *Shanchuan huxiao* [*The Mountains and Rivers Roar*]. Changsha: Hunan Renmin Chubanshe. 539 pp.

— A novel about learning from Dazhai in agriculture. It is set in a mountainous area of Hunan Province during the Cultural Revolution. The main hero, a newly appointed young Party secretary of a commune, leads people to build a big irrigation works. The project was originally planned by previous leaders to be completed in three years, but the hero proposes to finish it within six months. He and his followers struggle with conservative cadres, class enemies and capitalist-roaders, and accomplish the project ahead of the new schedule.

Gu, Junchi (1976). *Qingshaonian hu po shao* [*Youthful Sentries on the Lake*]. Nanjing: Jiangsu Renmin Chubanshe. 231 pp.

— This novel reflects class struggle in a wharf. An underground transport group tries to expand its business and struggles against the collective ownership, but its activities are exposed by the attack of the positive group.

Guan, Jianxun (1976). *Yun yan* [*The Swallow through Cloud*]. Beijing: Renmin Wenxue Chubanshe. 522 pp.

— This novel describes a school-leaver settling in the countryside. Responding to Mao's call, the heroine willingly experiences the difficulties and hardships of the countryside.

Guangxi Zhuangzu Zizhiqu Baise Diqu San-jiehe Chuangzuo Zu [The 'Three-in-one' Group of the Baise Prefecture of Guangxi Zhuang Autonomous Region] (1976). *Yu hou qingshan [Mountains Green after Rain]*. Beijing: Renmin Wexue Chubanshe. 589 pp.

— This novel is set in a mountain village in south China between 1965 and 1966. Led by the main hero, the villagers carry out the campaign of learning from Dazhai. They start to build an irrigation works which is opposed by the Party secretary of the commune. Just as the conflict between the hero and the secretary becomes fierce, the Cultural Revolution starts. The commune secretary is criticized for opposing the campaign of learning from Dazhai, and the hero wins the struggle.

Guo, Chengqing (1975). *Dadao ji [The Broadsword]*. 3 vols. Beijing: Renmin Wexue Chubanshe. 1740 pp.

— One of the longest novels produced in the CR period. The main story is set during the Sino-Japanese War. A unit of the Eighth Route Army employs guerrilla warfare to fight the enemy bravely. The novel is intended to indicate the importance of the close relationship between army and the masses in winning a great war.

Guo, Xianhong (1973). *Zhengtu [Long Trek]*. 2 vols. Shanghai: Shanghai Renmin Chubanshe. 737 pp.

— A novel about school-leavers. Set in the Cultural Revolution, it depicts a group of Shanghai school-leavers who go to live and work on a farm in Heilongjiang province. In addition to working hard with local people to increase grain production, they carry out struggles against hidden enemies.

Hang, Tao (1974). *Jiang shui taotao [The River Water Surges]*. Shanghai: Shanghai Renmin Chubanshe. 271 pp.

— This novel is set soon after the foundation of the People's Republic. A fleet of dredgers sails to Nanjing from Shanghai to aid in defending an embankment and dealing with a breach. The novel shows the crew's heroism, inspired by the policy of the Party's Second Plenary Session of the Seventh Party Congress.

Hao, Ran (1972–74). *Jinguang da dao [The Golden Road]*. Vol. 1, 1st ed., 1972, 648 pp.; Vol. 2, 1st ed., 1974, 688 pp. Beijing: Renmin Wenxue Chubanshe.

— A novel about agricultural collectivization. Set in a village of Hebei province soon after the Land Reform, it centres on how the main hero leads villagers to take the road of collectivization. An official of the county government and some of his subordinates attempt to carry out a policy of developing individual property. By means of his awareness of and sensitivity to ideology, the hero opposes this policy and organizes villagers to form mutual aid teams and then a cooperative.

—— (1974). *Xi-sha ernü [Daughters and Sons of the Xi-sha Archipelagos]*. 2 vols.; Vol. 1, 349 pp. Beijing: Beijing Renmin Chubanshe.

— This novel is about the 1974 armed clash in the Xi-sha Archipelagos between China and the then South Vietnam. It depicts how local Chinese residents exploit and develop the archipelagos under the leadership of the Party, and then how Chinese troops and the local people fight for the archipelagos. The author's intention to explore some new ideas is evident in the form of this novel. For instance, the attempt to produce poetic flavour in the novel's language.

Heilongjiang Sheng Shuangcheng Xian Geming Weiyuanhui, Zhongguo Renmin Jiefangjun Jing Zi 801 Budui Lianhe Chuangzuo Zu' [The Collaborative Writing Group of the Revolutionary Committee of Shuangcheng County in Heilongjiang Province and the PLA 801 Unit under the Beijing Command] (Wang Zhongyu, Chen Genxi and Xie Shu did the actual writing) (1975). *Jing lei* [*Violent Thunder*]. 2 vols. Tianjin: Tianjin Renmin Chubanshe. 911 pp.

— The longest CR novel describing the Movement of Socialist Education (1963–66). The story is set in a village in north China. The main hero, an ex-serviceman, leads his followers to carry out struggle against class enemies and new-born bourgeois elements within the Party's organizations at the grass-roots level.

«Hong hua» Chuangzuo zu (Zhang, Xiangwu did the actual writing) (1976). *Hong hua* [*Red Flowers*]. Shenyang: Liaoning Renmin Chubanshe. 216 pp.

— A novel about school-leavers. A group of Beijing school-leavers go to live and work in a prairie to be re-educated by local poor and lower-middle herdsmen. Supported by the herdsmen, they practise scientific experiments and cultivate a new type of fine-breed cows in the campaign of learning from Dazhai.

Hu, Yinqiang (1976). *Qianxi* [*The Eve*].

Hu, Zhengyan (1976). *Jimingshan xia* [*Below the Jiming Mountain*]. Beijing: Renmin Wenxue Chubanshe. 286 pp.

— A novel set on the eve of the campaign in which the PLA forced its way across the Yangtze River. A juvenile hero takes an important directive from the front headquarters to a guerrilla unit. The brave and resourceful hero experiences a series of dangerous events before reaching his destination. Towards the end of the novel, the guerrilla unit follows the directive and greatly contributes to the campaign by collaborating with the PLA regular troops.

Ji, Yanhua (1973). *Yanminghu pan* [*By the Yanming Lake*]. Changchun: Jilin Renmin Chubanshe. 411 pp.

— The cooperative medical programme with the barefoot doctor system is one of the so-called socialist new 'things' [*shehuizhuyi xinsheng shiwu*] in the countryside during the CR period. This novel describes a school-leaver becoming a barefoot doctor in the countryside. Her brother, a professional surgeon, comes to help her. The assiduous and altruistic youth does very well and is warmly supported by the villagers.

Jiashan Xian Geweihui Chuangzuozu [The Writing Group of the Revolutionary

Committee of Jiashan County] (1975). *Cui ling zhaoxia* [*Dawn over Emerald Ridge*]. Hefei: Anhui Renmin Chubanshe. 214 pp.

— This novel is set in a village in the east of Anhui province between 1969 and 1970. After coming back from Dazhai for a visit, the heroine leads the villagers to build a reservoir. One of her colleagues, a hidden class enemy, plots to frustrate her plan, but fails.

Jin, Anfu (1976). *Huoyan* [*The Flame*]. Tianjin: Tianjin Renmin Chubanshe. 298 pp.

Jin, Qingyu (1976). *Yingxiong de xiangtu* [*The Hero's Land*]. Guiyang: Guizhou Renmin Chubanshe. 520 pp.

— A novel about the Sino-Japanese War. Set in south-west Shandong province in 1941, this novel describes a guerrilla detachment fighting Japanese troops. The Japanese army and traitorous troops launch mopping-up operations, and the local people suffer greatly. Supported by Eighth Route Army troops, the guerrilla detachment attacks the enemy bravely.

Ke, Fei (1974). *Chun chao ji* [*Swift is the Spring Tide*]. 2 vols. Shanghai: Shanghai Renmin Chubanshe. 1108 pp.

— These two volumes are part of a projected series planned by the author in the 1950s. An ex-serviceman, the main hero, comes back to his native place to lead the villagers in consolidating the agricultural producers' cooperatives. There are considerable tensions between the hero and local spontaneous capitalist forces, manipulated by one of his former friends.

Ke, Yang (1976). *Nongnu ji* [*Serfs' Halberds*]. Tianjin: Tianjin Renmin Chubanshe. 529 pp.

— This novel is about the suppression of the Tibetan rebellion in 1959. The novel describes the rebellion's background, covering the support of foreign forces and the leadership of the Tibetan local government and upper circles. The story centres on the suppression in a district in which suzerains and their followers respond to the rebellion.

—— and Ge, Ji (1973). *Lian xin suo* [*Twin-heart Lock*]. Taiyuan: Shanxi Renmin Chubanshe. 374 pp.

— A cavalry unit of the New Fourth Army approaches the Communist areas under a Korean captain. As they approach a village, Japanese troops begin to loot. A village woman yields her own baby to the enemy's atrocities instead of the new-born baby of the Korean captain and his wife. Later the Korean couple name their surviving baby after the woman's dead baby. A silver twin-heart lock is made to represent the friendship between the two peoples.

Li, Fan and Chi, Songnian (1976). *Kuangbiao qu* [*A Song of Hurricane*] (Vol. 1). Shenyang: Liaoning Renmin Chubanshe. 536 pp.

Li, Fengzhu (1974). *Baowei Maliangshan* [*Defending Maliang Mountain*]. Shenyang: Liaoning Renmin Chubanshe. 373 pp.

— This novel is about the Korean War, describing a unit of the Chinese

People's Volunteers which fights in defence of its position under the coordination of the local North Korean people.

Li, Huixin (1976). *Lancangjiang pan* [*Beside the Lancang River*]. Beijing: Renmin Wenxue Chubanshe. 534 pp.

— A novel about professional doctors. A group of medical workers come down to the countryside to serve peasants. Their action is welcomed by the people in the countryside. The novel also indicates that the professional intellectuals learn a lot through 're-education' by the poor and lower-middle peasants.

Li, Liangjie and Yu, Yunquan (1974). *Jiaoliang* [*Rivalry*]. Shanghai: Shanghai Renmin Chubanshe. 463 pp.

— A novel set on the industrial front. A new factory Party secretary comes to an assembly shop which is producing a special machine for national defence. He organizes the workers to criticize capitalist practices. A number of accidents happen such as strange posters being put up and drafts discovered to be missing. The workers do not succeed in manufacturing the machine until the exposure of the hidden enemy.

Li, Mingxing (1975). *Hong liu gungun* [*A Red Torrent Surges Forward*]. Zhengzhou: Henan Renmin Chubanshe. 428 pp.

Li, Rongde and Wang, Ying (1975). *Dayanshan* [*The Dayan Mountain*]. Beijing: Beijing Renmin Chubanshe. 415 pp.

— A novel about the Sino-Japanese War. A unit of the Eighth Route Army raids a city occupied by the Japanese army, and seizes some machines of an arsenal. After moving the machines into the Dayan Mountain Base, the unit lures in the enemy and wins a battle.

Li, Ruqing (1976). *Wan shan hong bian* [*Mountains in Red*] (Vol. 1). Beijing: Renmin Wenxue Chubanshe. 613 pp.

— This novel is set in the Second Civil War (1927–37). A Red Army unit follows Mao's idea of establishing bases in the countryside and comes to a mountain area in south China. It overcomes various difficulties, defeating both open and hidden enemies and expanding its force.

Li, Xueshi (1972). *Kuangshan fengyun* [*Storm over the Mine*]. Shanghai: Shanghai Renmin Chubanshe. 231 pp.

— A novel concerning the Sino-Japanese War. After a worker in a Japanese-occupied coal mine is arrested by the occupiers, his wife takes their son and escapes the mine. Having heard that her husband is dead, the wife returns to her own town. The son joins the mine and helps the anti-Japanese activities of other children. A CCP member comes to organize guerrilla teams and the boy finally joins the Eighth Route Army.

Li, Yunde (1972-76). *Feiteng de qun shan* [*Seething Mountains*]. 3 vols. Beijing: Renmin Wenxue Chubanshe. Vol. 1 (1972), 470 pp; Vol. 2 (1973), 339 pp; Vol. 3 (1976), 619 pp.

— One of the longest CR novels (the first edition of Vol. 1 was printed in 1966). The story is set in north-east China between 1948 and 1953. When the PLA liberates a mine in 1948, the factories of the mining area have been destroyed. Under the leadership of the Party the factories are successfully restored, and develop well. In the process the officers and workers experience a series of class and line struggles.

—— (1975). *Tan bao ji* [*A Record of Treasures Exploration*]. Shenyang: Liaoning Renmin Chubanshe. 238 pp.

— The students of a middle school in Liaoning province go to the mountains to look for mineral deposits in their summer holiday. The novel focuses on a group of the students who make achievements both in defeating sabotage of the class enemy and in finding deposits.

Lin, Yu and Xie, Shu (1975). *Paoxiao de Songhuajiang* [*The Roaring Songhua River*]. 2 vols. Ha'erbin: Heilongjiang Renmin Chubanshe. 1046 pp.

— A novel about line struggle in the countryside. It is set in a village of north-east China in the early 1960s. The plot of this novel is complex. The main hero, an old man, leads the villagers to struggle against local class enemies and the upper bourgeois elements headed by a county official who is a hidden enemy agent.

Liu, Huaizhang (1975). *Jiliu* [*Turbulent Current*]. Shijiazhuang: Hebei Renmin Chubanshe. 294 pp.

— This novel is about the reconstruction of the Hai River, a response to Mao's directive made in 1963: We must re-harness the Hai River. It concerns a key project of the whole construction, demonstrating the combined effort of workers and peasants and their spirit of self-reliance.

Liu, Yanlin (1973). *Dongfeng haodang* [*The East Wind Blows with Mighty Power*]. Beijing: Renmin Wenxue Chubanshe. 478 pp.

— This novel is set in a pharmaceutical factory in Beijing, with the theme of promoting the Charter of the Anshan Iron and Steel Company. The positive core confronts manifold opposition and struggle. The hidden enemy who has sabotaged the laboratory and equipment is finally exposed. The incident offers a lesson for backward cadres and workers, and brings about an advance in production.

Liu, Yunpeng (1976). *Liuhetun fenghuo* [*The Beacon at Liuhe Village*]. Huhehaote: Nei Menggu Renmin Chubanshe. 464 pp.

— A novel about the Sino-Japanese War. In the war a unit of the Eighth Route Army comes to the plain of central Hebei to found bases against the Japanese army and Chinese traitors. The novel emphasizes the cruelty of the Japanese army and the brave struggles of the Chinese people under the Party.

Lu, Zhiluo (1975). *Lu* [*The Road*]. Changsha: Hunan Renmin Chubanshe. 351 pp.

— A novel about railway construction. It describes a militia company building a section of railway through mountains. Centring on a key project at a dangerous and difficult place, it emphasizes the hardship of the project and the altruism of the people on the construction site.

Ma, Chun (1973-75). *Longtan chunse* [*Spring on Dragon Beach*]. 2 vols., Vol. 1, 1973, pp. 1–296; Vol. 2, 1975, pp. 297–690. Tianjin: Tianjin Renmin Chubanshe.

    — A novel about the reconstruction of the Hai River. Mao issued a directive in 1963: 'We must re-harness the Hai River'. The two volumes of this novel cover different construction sites. The novel shows the combined effort of workers and peasants.

Min, Guoku (1975). *Fengyundao* [*The Island of Wind and Clouds*]. Shenyang: Liaoning Renmin Chubanshe. 406 pp.

    — Set in 1962, this novel describes a squad of the PLA navy. A group of army men assigned by the Kuomingtang slip into Fengyundao and attempt to coordinate with local hidden agents to carry out sabotage. They are caught by the navy squad and local militiamen.

Mo, Yingfeng (1976). *Xiao bing chuang da shan* [*Young Soldiers Brave a Journey to Great Mountains*]. Shanghai: Shanghai Renmin Chubanshe. 582 pp.

    — A group of juveniles go into remote mountains to gather medicinal herbs. They work in order to help the village barefoot doctor and support the cooperative medicine programme. Although a series of dangerous events caused by precipices and jungles are depicted, class struggle is presented as the main storyline.

Mu, Chongguang (1975). *Fenghuo* [*Beacons*]. Jinan: Shandong Renmin Chubanshe. 488 pp.

    — This novel is set in the initial stages of the Sino-Japanese War. The Party attempts to build bases against the Japanese army in the mountainous area of Jiaodong. Party representatives show heroism through experiencing various trials and hardships in mobilizing and organizing the masses.

Mu, Fu (1974). *Fengyu Xinghua Cun* [*Upheaval in Xinghua Village*]. Guangzhou: Guangdong Renmin Chubanshe. 210 pp.

    — A novel about the cooperative medical programme in the countryside. It depicts how the heroine, a barefoot doctor, contributes to the newly established CR medical programme in a fishing village. When she is away for treatment, a phoney doctor attempts to impair the rural medical programme and almost causes the death of a sick girl. Upon returning, the heroine saves the girl and solidifies the medical system.

Nan, Shao (1972). *Niutianyang* [*Niutianyang*]. Shanghai: Shanghai Renmin Chubanshe. 380 pp.

    — The novel is set in a coastal region of Guangdong province. As early as 1957, the local government and people try to transform the salty coast but fail. In summer 1962, a PLA division is engaged in the project in response to the campaign of 'Production and Preparing for War'. The novel specially depicts a company's work in building piers and filling in arable fields. The story is interwoven with sabotage by enemy agents and raids by

Kuomintang troops. The PLA division's work is so successful that its later production is abundant enough to aid foreign countries.

Nantong Shi «Fuxiao de haojiao» Chuangzuo Zu [The Writing Group of *The Bugle Call before Dawn*, Nantong City] (1975). *Fuxiao de haojiao* [*The Bugle Call before Dawn*]. Nanjing: Jiangsu Renmin Chubanshe. 462 pp.

— This novel is set in central Jiangsu during the Third Civil War (1945–49). A printing house guided by the Party prints a large amount of the Party's newspapers and other propaganda materials. The work plays an important role in supporting the PLA's fighting.

Qu, Xingqi (1976). *Famu-ren zhuan* [*A Story of Lumber-men*]. 2 vols. Beijing: Renmin Wenxue Chubanshe. 803 pp.

— This novel describes line struggle in thè forestry industry. It aims to glorify the principles established in the Charter of the Anshan Iron and Steel Company, such as keeping politics firmly in command, strengthening Party leadership, reforming irrational and outdated rules and regulations, and going all out with technical innovation and revolution.

Ran, Huaizhou (1974). *Jianshe-zhe* [*The Builders*]. Tianjin: Tianjin Renmin Chubanshe. 534 pp.

— A novel set on the industrial front. The cadres and workers in an iron works in north China put politics in command and carry out a series of class and line struggles. The novel indicates that revolution is the prerequisite for development of production in an enterprise.

Shan, Meng (1975). *Caihong qu* [*Rainbow Song*]. Guangzhou: Guangdong Renmin Chubanshe. 228 pp.

— In 1962 the workers and cadres of a factory of agricultural machinery engage in technical innovation. They successfully design and produce a kind of long-distance sprayer.

Shan, Xuepeng (1975). *Bohai yuge* [*Fishermen's Songs in the Bo Sea*]. Beijing: Renmin Wenxue Chubanshe. 341 pp.

— A novel about fishing. Under the leadership of the main hero who is an old fisherman and the Party secretary, the fishermen in a fishing village near the Bo Sea break with conventional ways and explore new methods of fishing. Sabotage by class enemies and interference by conservative cadres are overcome, and a great advance in production is brought about.

Shang, Gong (1976). *Dou xiong* [*Struggling against the Bear*]. Shanghai: Shanghai Renmin Chubanshe. 330 pp.

— A novel of anti-espionage. The detectives of a security bureau detect and catch agents of the Soviet Union with the help of local people. The novel also describes the inner contradictions between the personnel within the security bureau.

Shanghai Shi Zaochuan Gongsi Wenyi Chuangzuozu [The writing Group of Shanghai Shipbuilding Company] (1975). *Da hai pu lu* [*Paving the Way to the Sea*].

Shanghai Xian «Hongnan zuozhan shi» Xiezuo Zu [The Writing Group of *Battle Chronicles of Hongnan* of Shanghai County] (1972). *Hongnan zuozhan shi* [*Battle Chronicles of Hongnan*]. Shanghai: Shanghai Renmin Chubanshe. 584 pp.

— This was the first novel published during the Cultural Revolution. Set in the countryside near Shanghai, it is about agricultural collectivization, which is interwoven with the main theme of serious class and line struggles. The ideological flavour of this novel is generally acknowledged.

Shao, Chuang (1974). *Baizhangling* [*Baizhang Ridge*]. Hangzhou: Zhejiang Renmin Chubanshe. 354 pp.

— Set between 1964 and 1965, this novel describes the villagers of Baizhangling Brigade as they build a reservoir in the mountains in response to Mao's call to learn from Dazhai.

Shen, Shungen (1974). *Shui xia jianbing* [*Underwater Vanguards*]. Beijing: Beijing Renmin Chubanshe. 419 pp.

— A team of PLA navy soldiers is assigned to assist in building a hydropower station. They collaborate with the workers, cadres and technical staff at the construction site, brave severe cold and swift currents, catch hidden enemies, and accomplish their mission.

Shi, Wenju (1973). *Zhandi hong ying* [*Red Tassels on the Battleground*]. Beijing: Renmin Wenxue Chubanshe. 252 pp.

— This novel depicts how a shepherd-boy enslaved by a landlord becomes a PLA soldier. Fearing the landlord's persecution, the juvenile hero and other boys escape to a mountain cave but return with the PLA. He becomes captain of the Young Pioneers of the village. Later, he is captured by enemy, but escapes through a tunnel and returns to the village. He joins the PLA towards the end of the novel.

Song, Zhenguo (1976). *Cha shan chun* [*Spring Comes to the Tea Mountains*]. Wuhu: Anhui Renmin Chubanshe. 256 pp.

— A group of school-leavers go to live and work in a mountain area in the south of the Yangtze River. With the help of the local poor and lower-middle peasants, they reclaim wasteland to plant tea.

Sun, Feng (1976). *Wan shan hong* [*Mountains Emblazoned with Crimson*]. Wuhu: Anhui Renmin Chubanshe. 495 pp.

— This novel is labelled as a trial edition. It is set in a village in Anhui province in 1957. A group of people including class enemies and new-born bourgeois elements attempt to disband an agricultural producers' cooperative and develop capitalism. The young Youth League secretary organizes other villagers to attack the group through a series of activities including the performing arts.

Sun, Jiayu (1976). *Zhanhuo cui chun* [*Flames of War Bring in the Spring*]. Nanjing: Jiangsu Renmin Chubanshe. 484 pp.

— A novel about the Korean War. Set in the middle of the war, it centres on the story of a regiment of the Chinese People's Volunteers. The novel presents a series of fierce fights between this regiment and its rival, an American regiment, showing their combat effectiveness.

Tian, Dongzhao (1976). *Chang hong* [*The Long Rainbow*]. 2 vols. Taiyuan: Shanxi Renmin Chubanshe. 1131 pp.

— Set in a village in the Cultural Revolution, this novel is about learning from Dazhai. Dissatisfied with the previous progress of the village in the campaign of learning from Dazhai, the heroine is determined to lead the villagers to get going and go all out. They start to build an irrigation works. Manipulated by a hidden enemy, a number of people including the heroine's colleagues and superiors oppose the project. After a series of events concerning class and line struggle, the project is successfully completed.

Tong, Bian (1975). *Xin lai de xiao Shizhu* [*The Newcomer Xiao Shizhu*]. Beijing: Renmin Wenxue Chubanshe. 314 pp.

— The unique CR novel set on the sporting front. This novel depicts a sporting juvenile. Cultivated by the Party, the hero overcomes various difficulties and achieves success, displaying unusual vigour and courage.

Tuerdi, Keyoumu, (Chinese trans.) Ma Junmin and Liu Fajun (1975). *Kezile shan xia* [*At the Foot of the Kezile Mountain*]. Wulumuqi: Xinjiang Renmin Chubanshe. 309 pp.

— The original of this novel is written by a Uighur novelist. Set in south Xinjiang in the Cultural Revolution, the novel describes Uighur peasants diverting snow water from the top of mountains for irrigation of foothills in the Campaign of Learning from Dazhai. The project is interwoven with class and line struggles.

Wang, Dong (1975). *Caoyuan mingzhu* [*A Bright Pearl in the Prairie*]. Shenyang: Liaoning Renmin Chubanshe. 344 pp.

Wang, Dongman (1976). *Zhanghe chun* [*Spring Comes to Zhang River*]. Taiyuan: Shanxi Renmin Chubanshe. 725 pp.

— Set in a mountain village in the early 1960s, this agricultural novel is about the opposition to quotas on household basis. Giving up the opportunity to study or work in the city, the heroine willingly works in the countryside and becomes the Party secretary of the village. She withstands pressure from upper levels and leads the villagers in consolidating and developing the collective economy.

Wang, Jingzhong (1976). *Wan li zhan-qi hong* [*A Vast Land of Red Fighting Flags*]. Wuhan: Hubei Remin Chubanshe. 419 pp.

— The novel is based on the deeds of a company of the PLA. The company experiences the Sino-Japanese War, the Civil War (1945–49), and the Korean War. It is known for its bravery and altruism in fighting. Huang Jiguang, a historical figure who died in the attempt to block enemy's embrasure in the Korean War, belongs to this company.

Wang, Lan (1974). *Longze* [*The Dragon Swamp*]. Shenyang: Liaoning Renmin Chubanshe. 203 pp.

— A group of Mongolian children play an active role in production and class struggle of their native place.

Wang, Lei (1974). *Jianhe lang* [*Waves on the Jian River*]. Shanghai: Shanghai Renmin Chubanshe.

— A novel describing the life of a group of school-leavers in the countryside. Willing to accept 're-education' through poor and lower-middle peasants, the school-leavers actively participate in local revolution and production. The novel aims to indicate that the countryside is a proper place for the growth and development of the school-leavers.

Wang, Shige (1976). *Huo wang* [*A Net of Fire*]. Beijing: Jiefangjun Wenyi Chubanshe. 344 pp.

— A novel concerning the Korean War. A regiment of anti-aircraft gunners of the Chinese People's Volunteers fights skilfully and bravely on the Korean battleground. In spite of its inferior military equipment, the regiment defeats a powerful American air unit.

Wang, Shimei (1975). *Tie xuanfeng* [*Mighty Whirlwind*] (Vol. 1). Beijing: Renmin Wenxue Chubanshe. 491 pp.

— This novel describes a group of Beijing school-leavers going to live and work on a large prairie. They actively take part in local revolution and production, and establish close friendships with local poor and lower-middle herdsmen.

Wang, Xiaoying (1975). *Hong Yan* [*Hong Yan*]. Shanghai: Shanghai Renmin Chubanshe. 205 pp.

— A novel for juveniles. A group of school-leavers led by the heroine Hong Yan go to live and work on a tea plantation in a mountainous area. They identify with the local peasants and play active roles in the revolution and production of the plantation.

Wang, Zhijun (1975). *Nuli de nü'er* [*The Daughter of Slaves*]. Huhehaote: Nei Menggu Renmin Chubanshe. 304 pp.

— Set in a district practising both agriculture and animal husbandry in the Cultural Revolution, this novel is about learning from Dazhai. The story concerns the construction of irrigation works, improvement of the production environment, and struggles against the class enemy.

Wu, Yanke (1976). *Hu shang xiao Balu* [*The Little Eighth Route Army Men on the Lake*]. Jinan: Shandong Renmin Chubanshe. 380 pp.

— Set in the Sino-Japanese War, this novel describes a troop of the Eighth Route Army mobilizing fishermen to fight Japanese troops and traitors to China. It portrays a juvenile who is tempered in the fights and becomes a brave soldier under the guidance of the Party.

Xi'an Tielu Fen-ju Gongren Chuangzuo Zu [The Workers Writing Group of Xi'an Railway Division] (1976). *Qidi chang ming* [*Long Blast of the Siren*]. Xi'an: Shaanxi Renmin Chubanshe. 626 pp.

— Set in the Great Leap Forward (1958–59), this novel describes the activities of railway workers in revolution and production. The workers work hard with altruistic spirit to solve the problems posed by great quantities of material and limited transport facilities.

Xiang, Chun (1975). *Mei cheng nuhuo* [*Flames of Fury in the Coal City*]. Jinan: Shandong Renmin Chubanshe. 880 pp.

— This novel is set in a coal mine in the Sino-Japanese War. The workers are organized by the Party to struggle against Japanese occupiers. The novel is intended to portray heroes, showing their dignity, bravery and wisdom in front of the powerful enemies.

Xu, Chunyun (1976). *Huohong Shiliu Cun* [*Fiery Shiliu Village*]. Hefei: Anhui Renmin Chubanshe. 284 pp.

— Set in the early period of the People's Republic when the project of reconstructing the Huai River was being undertaken. Headed by a juvenile hero, the Children's Corps of a village try to support the project. The children dare to struggle against the evil class enemy. Again and again they trace and expose the enemy's acts of sabotage, and contribute to the process of the construction.

Xu, Tesheng (1976). *Biansai feng xiao* [*The Wind Whistles around the Frontier Fortress*]. Beijing: Jiefangjun Wenyi Chubanshe. 411 pp.

— This novel is set in a frontier area in Xinjiang. A number of soldiers of the production corps and the local herdsmen unite to oppose the enemy. Having excluded the interference of wrong ideology and line and smashed enemy agents' sabotage acts, they successfully reach the frontier posts and intensify the defence.

«Yanhe zai zhaohuan» Xiezuo zu [The Writing Group of *The Yan River is Beckoning*] (1976). *Yanhe zai zhaohuan* [*The Yan River is Beckoning*]. Beijing: Renmin Wenxue Chubanshe. 424 pp.

— This novel describes a group of school-leavers coming to live and work in Yan'an. With enthusiasm for carrying out the Red Army's revolutionary tradition, they work hard in the mountain area. They also participate in local class struggle and try to develop scientific farming.

Yang, Chuntian (1976). *Jumanghe* [*The Jumang River*]. Huhehaote: Nei Menggu Renmin Chubanshe. 358 pp.

— This novel is set in a mountain area in early 1962. Led by the main hero, the peasants build an irrigation works. Class and line struggle is emphasized above the labour at the construction site.

Yang, Xiao (1973). *Hongyu* [*Hongyu*]. Beijing: Renmin Wenxue Chubanshe. 270 pp.

— A novel about the cooperative medical programme in the countryside. Supported by the village Party secretary, Hongyu, a mountain village youth, becomes a barefoot doctor of the village. He always puts villagers' health before his own interests. He overcomes various difficulties in the process of improving his professional skills and collecting herbal medicines. In spite of malicious slander and other obstacles, he gains the support of the villagers.

Zhang, Changgong (1973). *Qingchun* [*Youth*]. Hulanhaote: Nei Menggu Renmin Chubanshe. 375 pp.

— This is a unique CR novel in diary form. It records the story of a group of school-leavers from Beijing, Tianjin and Shanghai who join a PLA production unit in the Inner Mongolian area during the Cultural Revolution. Class and ideological struggle and production are related.

—— (1974). *Gebi hua* [*Flowers of the Gobi*]. Shanghai: Shanghai Renmin Chubanshe. 266 pp.

— Set in a desert area of Inner Mongolia, this novel depicts a girl who plays an important role in transforming the desert into an oasis. She serves in the work team as a cook, and exposes a hidden reactionary, who happens to be a co-op chief. A living spring is found towards the end of the novel.

—— and Zheng, Shiqian (1975). *Bian cheng fengxue* [*Wind and Snow in the Frontier City*]. Beijing: Renmin Wenxue Chubanshe. 658 pp.

— This novel is set in a city on the border of northern China during the Third Civil War (1945–49). A group of traders work for the Communist Party and struggle against the local authorities and Kuomintang agents. They finally control leadership on the commercial front, then control the grain trade, and offer military supplies to the PLA.

Zhang, Enru (1974). *Wangyunfeng* [*Wangyun Peak*]. Ha'erbin: Heilongjiang Renmin Chubanshe. 475 pp.

— A novel about the Korean War. With the help of local Northern Korean people, a group of sentries at an observation post of the Chinese People's Volunteers keep watch on the movements of American fighters and collect information on a mountain.

Zhang, Feng (1974). *Jiao lin ernü* [*Sons and Daughters of the Rubber Plantation*]. Guangzhou: Guangdong Renmin Chubanshe. 343 pp.

— Set in a PLA-operated plantation in 1962, this novel centres on a newly established production team. More specifically, it depicts the heroine and her 13-member women's production team. The mobilization of the PLA for the impending attack by Kuomintang troops and the corresponding military exercises are also emphasized.

Zhang, Jianguo (1976). *Xia man Longwan* [*Pink Clouds Envelop Dragon Bend*]. Beijing: Renmin Wenxue Chubanshe. 303 pp.

— This novel describes a school-leaver becoming a responsible and skilled keeper of a village's marten farm. It also includes struggle against class enemies and the wrong line.

Zhang, Jun (1974). *Qin long tu* [*Capturing the Dragon*] (Vol. 1). Shijiazhuang: Hebei Renmin Chubanshe. 634 pp.

— A novel about reconstruction of the Hai River. Several CR novels describe this famous irrigation project. The novel recounts the combined efforts of workers, peasants and soldiers. Class struggle, line struggle and ideological struggle are interwoven with the construction.

Zhang, Kangkang (1975). *Fenjie xian* [*Demarcation*]. Shanghai: Shanghai Renmin Chubanshe. 462 pp.

— Set in the Cultural Revolution (around 1973), this novel describes a group of school-leavers going to live and work on a state farm in Heilongjiang province. After the farm is flooded, the school-leavers and other workers oppose the line represented by the head of a working team from the upper level. They overcome natural disasters and achieve a harvest.

Zhang, Xue (1976). *Shan li ren* [*Mountain People*]. Jinan: Shandong Renmin Chubanshe. 308 pp.

— A novel about learning from Dazhai in the countryside. It is set in a mountain village with serious shortage of water. Inspired by the spirit of Dazhai people, the villagers start to transform the natural environment. They experience various hardships, smash class enemy sabotage, and then succeed in their project.

Zhaorigebatu (1974). *Tieqi* [*The Cavalry*]. Huhehaote: Nei Menggu Renmin Chubanshe. 324 pp.

— This novel is set on a prairie of Inner Mongolia during the Civil War (1945–49). A company of PLA cavalry soldiers collaborate with an infantry unit to fight Kuomintang troops. They successfully enlist the support of the local Mongolian people in their military actions.

Zheng, Jiazhen (1972). *Jiang pan zhaoyang* [*Morning Sun by the River*]. Shanghai: Shanghai Renmin Chubanshe. 695 pp.

— Set in a state farm in north-east China in 1963, this novel describes how positive characters develop production on the farm. The story concerns a series of activities in production such as harvesting and mechanization. The contradiction between the positive core and the hidden reactionaries is also prominent.

Zheng, Wanlong (1976). *Xiangshuiwan* [*Xiangshui Bend*]. Beijing: Beijing Renmin Chubanshe. 544 pp.

— This novel is set in a mountain village in 1962. After suffering three successive years of drought, some villagers have lost confidence in finding a solution to the problem. But the Party secretary of the village and his followers insist on seeking sources of water and then achieve their goal. The process is interwoven with their struggle against class enemy and the line of individual farming.

Zheng, Zhi (1972). *Ji zhan wuming chuan* [*Fiery Battle at the Nameless River*]. Beijing: Renmin Wenxue Chubanshe. 442 pp.

— A novel about the Korean War. A company of the Chinese People's Volunteers fight American troops in defending a bridge on a river. The bridge has strategic significance for supplying the front. The soldiers' bravery and spirit of self-sacrifice are accentuated.

Zhou, Jiajun (1975). *Shanfeng* [*Mountain Wind*]. Shanghai: Shanghai Renmin Chubanshe. 341 pp.

    — A group of school-leavers from Shanghai go to live and work on a farm. In response to Mao's call to learn from Dazhai, the school-leavers are led by the heroine to open up the wasteland on a mountain. They oppose the ideology of a local cadre, overcome various difficulties, and ultimately attain their goal.

Zhou, Liangsi (1972). *Fei xue ying chun* [*Whirling Snow Brings in the Spring*]. 2 vols. Shanghai: Shanghai Renmin Chubanshe. 692 pp.

    — A novel about miners. It describes class struggle and production at an iron mine after the onset of the Cultural Revolution. The mining project is not completed until the main hero and his followers succeed in exposing the hidden enemy.

Zhou, Xiao (1974). *Xiadao* [*Pink Cloud Island*]. Beijing: Jiefangjun Wenyi Chubanshe. 386 pp.

    — This novel is set on an island near southern China in 1962. When Kuomintang troops decide to launch an offensive against mainland China, the PLA and native fishermen on the island are engaged in the defence of the coastline. Military secrets of the PLA leak out to the enemy. In investigating this case, the leader of the garrison and his men capture the spies, unearth collaborators on the island, and wipe out an armed force.

Zhou, Zhentian (1976). *Douzheng zai jixu* [*The Struggle Continues*]. Shijiazhuang: Hebei Renmin Chubanshe. 292 pp.

    — A novel of anti-espionage. The story is set in 1970. Mainland Chinese detectives detect and catch some Kuomintang agents who attempt to steal the blueprint of an arsenal and to sabotage the production of the factory. One of the agents has hidden himself for many years.

Zhu, Jian (1976). *Qingshibao* [*Qingshi Fort*]. Nanjing: Jiangsu Renmin Chubanshe. 531 pp.

    — A novel about the Socialist Education Movement (1963–66). The story is set in a village in north Jiangsu. Manipulated by hidden class enemies, the negative elements in the village run wild and sabotage the collective ownership. The main hero, a demobilized PLA soldier, comes back to his native place, organizes an attack against the negative side and wins the struggle.

«Zuan Tian-feng» San-jiehe Chuangzuo Zu [The 'Three-in-one' Writing Group of *Going Deep into Towering Mountains*] (Xi Zhi did the actual writing) (1975). *Zuan tian feng* [*Going Deep into Towering Mountains*]. Beijing: Renmin Wenxue Chubanshe. 401 pp.

    — This novel describes a unit of the PLA railway engineering corps. The officers and soldiers work hard amid difficulties, continuing the tradition of the Red Army. They build a big steel bridge in a mountainous area where the Red Army passed by on the Long March.

Glossary

This glossary is alphabetically arranged, in Western-style letter-based alphabetical order rather than Hanyu Pinyin syllabic alphabetical order. It contains the Chinese words and expressions, except some common items, appearing in the text, notes and bibliography. The whole titles of literary works are generally listed. The glossary basically takes words and set expressions as items, but in cases of stylistic items, it takes the stylistic unit as a glossary item, which might be a word, a phrase, a clause or a sentence.

ai qian dao de　挨千刀的
ai sheng tan qi　唉聲嘆氣
airen　愛人
Anhui　安徽
anlewo　安樂窩
ao xue song　傲雪松
ba　把
ba gen zha　把根扎
Ba Jie Shi Zhong Quanhui gongbao
　　八屆十中全會公報
ba jin chuan duo　把緊船舵
ba xian guo hai, ge xian qi neng
　　八仙過海，各顯其能
ba xian guo hai, ge xian shen tong
　　八仙過海，各顯神通

bai　百
Bai Erxian　白二仙
Bai Juyi　白居易
Bai mao nü　白毛女
Bai Wei　白蔚
bai zhe bu nao　百折不撓
baijie　白潔
baijun　白軍
baikequanshu　百科全書
Baise　百色
baitou lang　白頭浪
Baizhangling　百丈嶺
ban　班
ban ren gao　半人高
banfa　辦法

banfu 板斧

bang 傍

bang kan 幫刊

bantian 半天

bantian lei 半天雷

banye chi huanggua — bu zhi touwei
半夜吃黃瓜 — 不知頭尾

Bao feng zhou yu 暴風驟雨

bao-fengyu 暴風雨

baolei 堡壘

baowei 保衛

Baowei Maliangshan 保衛馬良山

baoyuan 抱怨

Bei Dao 北島

beihou 背後

Beijing Shi 北京市

Benteng de Dongliuhe 奔騰的東流河

bi 臂

bi 屄

Bi Fang 畢方

bi ta zui wai 鼻塌嘴歪

Bi yun tian, huanghua di, xifeng
jin, bei yan nan fei 碧雲天，黃
花地，西風緊，北雁南飛

Bian cheng fengxue 邊城風雪

Bian Zizheng 邊子正

bianjibu 編輯部

bianmu zu 編目組

bianpao qi ming 鞭炮齊鳴

Biansai feng xiao 邊塞鳳嘯

bianxiezu 編寫組

bianxing 變形

bianzheng 辯證

bianzuan 編纂

biaoqing 表情

bing 冰

biziyanr 鼻子眼儿

bodong 波動

Bohai yuge 渤海漁歌

bolan zhuangkuo 波瀾壯闊

bu bei bu su 不卑不俗

bu si huigai 不思悔改

Bu xi de langchao 不息的浪潮

bu zheng zhi feng 不正之風

buguan 不管

bukengbuha 不吭不哈

buli 不利

bushu 部署

butong 不同

buxing 步行

Cai Weicai 蔡維才

Cai Zhenxing 蔡振興

Caihong qu 彩虹曲

Caixia ji 彩霞集

cangcui yu di 蒼翠欲滴

canguan 參觀

canmoubu 參謀部

canzhan 參戰

cao 肏

Cao Xueqin 曹雪芹

Caoyuan mingzhu 草原明珠

cha 差

Cha shan chun 茶山春

chailang 豺狼

Chang hong 長虹

'Chang ting song bie' 長亭送別

Chang Zheng 長正

changpian xiaoshuo 長篇小說

changqing guo mu 常青果木

changqing rong 常青榕

Changsha 長沙

changyong 常用

Chao Yue 晁樾

chao-jieji 超階級

chaoshishi 潮濕濕

chaoshui 潮水

che 撤

che qi chang mianxian 扯起長棉線

chedi 徹底

Chen Dabin 陳大斌

Chen Dachun 陳大春

Chen Qingshan 陳慶山

Chen Xianjin 陳先晉

Chen Yong 陳涌

Chen Yuan 陳原

Cheng Jian 程建

cheng ren zhi mei　成人之美
Cheng Shuzhen　程樹榛
Cheng Xianzhang　程賢章
Chenguang qu　晨光曲
chengxiang　丞相
chengyu　成語
chengzhang　成長
chentu　塵土
chezhi　撤職
chi　痴
chi de qi　吃得起
Chi Songnian　遲松年
chifan　吃飯
chong　衝
chong de shang　衝得上
chong shangqu　衝上去
chongfen　充分
chongfeng　沖鋒
chongfeng chu zhen　沖鋒出陣
chongman　充滿
chongsha　衝殺
chongshuachongshua　沖刷沖刷
chu jing shang qing　觸景傷情
chu jing sheng qing　觸景生情
chuan lai　傳來
chuang　闖
chuang dong　窗洞
Chuangye shi　創業史
chuangzao　創造
chuangzuo　創作
chuangzuo zu　創作組
Chuanshanlang　穿山狼
chuanshengtong　傳聲筒
chuantong　傳統
chuanyue　穿越
chubanshe　出版社
chugao　初稿
chui　錘
chui bu lan　錘不爛
chuifeng zhuangdan　吹風壯膽
Chun chao ji　春潮急
chunfeng　春風
chunfeng qing fu　春風輕拂

chunlei gungun　春雷滾動
chunshui　春水
chunyiangran　春意盎然
chusheng　畜牲
chushi bu li　出師不利
chuyuan　出院
ci　詞
ci qiong li qu　詞窮理屈
cidao　刺刀
cidian　詞典
cihui　詞匯
cihuixue　詞匯學
Cong Weixi　從維熙
congcong　匆匆
congcongrongrong　從從容容
congkan　叢刊
conglai　從來
conglin　叢林
Cui ling zhao xia　翠嶺朝霞
cun kou　村口
cunzai　存在
cuoshi　措施
da　搭
da cao jing she　打草驚蛇
da chi yi jing　大吃一惊
da dianhua　打電話
da feng da lang　大風大浪
da gong wu si　大公無私
Da hai pu lu　大海鋪路
Da Jingya　大金牙
Da Lao Jiang　大老江
Da niao zhengce — zheng zhi yan, bi
　　zhi ya　打鳥政策 — 睜隻眼，閉
　　隻眼
da piao　大瓢
da shou da jiao　大手大腳
da touzhen　打頭陣
dachui ban　大錘班
Dadao ji　大刀記
dadui　大隊
daduizhang　大隊長
dahui　大會
daibiao　代表

dailing 帶領

daitouren 帶頭人

dajia 大家

dajiahuor 大家伙儿

dajun 大軍

dalaocu 大老粗

dan 擔

dang 當

dang 黨

dang-nei 黨內

dangan 單干

dangdai 當代

dangyang 蕩漾

dangzhong 當中

danwei 單位

dao da yi pa 倒打一耙

daodi 到底

daolu 道路

daoluan 搗亂

daoshan huohai 刀山火海

daoshou 到手

dapao 大炮

Daqing 大慶

daxiao 大笑

daxue 大學

Dayanshan 大雁山

daye 大爺

dayuan 大院

Dayuejin 大躍進

Dazhai 大寨

dazhang 打仗

dazhangfu 大丈夫

dazibao 大字報

daziran 大自然

Deng Daniu 鄧大牛

Deng Dianju 鄧殿舉

Deng Jiukuan 鄧久寬

Deng Xiumei 鄧秀梅

di qiang wo ruo 敵強我弱

di xiu fan 帝修反

dian hong bu san 電轟不散

dian shan lei ming 電閃雷鳴

diao 屌

diaobao 碉堡

diaodong 調動

diaomenr 調門儿

diba 堤壩

didi 底底

difang 地方

ding 頂

Ding Mao 丁茂

ding tian li di 頂天立地

Ding Yingchuan 丁盈川

dinggang 頂剛

diqu 地區

dir 地儿

diren 敵人

diwang 帝王

diwei 地位

Dixia xiaoshuo de cangsang 地下小説
的滄桑

dizhu 地主

dong 凍

Dong Liang 董良

Dong Lingyun 董淩雲

dongfeng 東風

Dongfeng haodang 東風浩蕩

dongren 動人

dongyuan 動員

dou 抖

dou jun yan bi 陡峻岩壁

Dou xiong 鬥熊

douzheng 鬥爭

Douzheng zai jixu 鬥爭在繼續

du 堵

du duan zhuan xing 獨斷專行

Du Jun 杜峻

duan xian zhiyuan 斷線紙鳶

duanpian xiaoshuo 短篇小説

Du-er Lao Xiong 獨耳老熊

dui'ou 對偶

duixiang 對象

duo 多

duo feng duo yu 多風多雨

duoshao 多少

duoyici 多義詞

duozan　多咱
dushu　讀書
e　屙
e lang　惡浪
e xuanfeng　惡旋風
eguo　惡果
er　兒
erqie　而且
fadong　發動
fahui　發揮
Famu-ren zhuan　伐木人傳
fan xing　繁星
fan-geming　反革命
fanbaifanbaiyan　翻白翻白眼
fanchen　反襯
fanchou　範疇
fandong　反動
fan'er　反而
fang　方（言）
fangpi　放屁
fangyan　方言
fanji　反擊
fanli　凡例
fanmian　反面
fanshen　反身
fanshen zhang　翻身仗
fansi　凡是
fantian　翻天
fanxiu fangxiu　反修防修
fanyici　反義詞
Fanyou　反右
far　法兒
Fei li wu shi, fei li wu ting, fei li wu
　yan, fei li wu dong　非禮勿視，
　非禮勿聽，非禮勿言，非禮勿動
Fei xue ying chun　飛雪迎春
feiji　飛機
Feiteng de qunshan　沸騰的群山
feiyang bahu　飛揚跋扈
fen bu gu shen　奮不顧身
fen lu jin bing　分路進兵
fenbian　分辯

fenfa tuqiang　奮發圖強
feng　風
feng bo lang li　風波浪里
feng chui yu da　風吹雨打
Feng Menglong　馮夢龍
feng pozi　瘋婆子
Feng Shaohuai　馮少懷
Feng Yunan　馮育楠
fengbo　風波
fengbu　縫補
fengfenglanglang　風風浪浪
fengge　風格
fenggexue　風格學
Fenghuo　烽火
fenglang　風浪
Fengyu Xinghua Cun　風雨杏花村
Fengyundao　風雲島
Fenjie xian　分界線
fenju　分局
fenming　分明
fentou　分頭
fu　幅
Fu Zikui　傅子奎
Fugui bu neng yin, pinjian bu neng yi,
　weiwu bu neng qu, ci zhi wei
　dazhangfu　富貴不能淫，貧賤
　不能移，威武不能屈，此之謂
　大丈夫
funong　富農
funü　婦女
'Fuqin'　父親
furen　夫人
Furongzhen　芙蓉鎮
fuwu　服務
Fuxiao de haojiao　拂曉的號角
fuyu biaoqing　富于表情
fuyuzhongnong　富裕中農
fuza　複雜
Gaixia　改霞
gailun　概論
gainian　概念
gan jiao　敢教
ganbaba　干巴巴

ganbu　干部
gandao　感到
gang　綱
gang liang tie zhu　鋼樑鐵柱
gangcai　剛才
gangling　綱領
Gangtie juren　綱鐵巨人
gangwei　崗位
gangyi　剛毅
gankuai　趕快
ganqing　敢情
ganxin　甘心
Gao Daquan　高大全
Gao Erlin　高二林
gao fei yuan zou　高飛遠走
Gao Jinfeng　高金鳳
Gao Lisong　高立松
gao shan　高山
Gao Yunlan　高雲覽
Gao Zhongwu　高中午
gaochang　高唱
gaoda　高大
gaoxing　高興
gaoxinhe　搞信河
Ge Ji　戈基
Ge ren zi sao men qian xue, bu guan ta ren wa shang shuang　各人自掃門前雪，不管他人瓦上霜
Gebi hua　戈壁花
gebo　胳膊
geming　革命
geming-zhe　革命者
gemingjia　革命家
Geng Jiaquan　耿嘉全
Geng Shan　耿山
gengu wei you　亙古未有
geren　個人
gesheng zhenzhen　歌聲陣陣
geweihui　革委會
gong　公
gong　恭
Gong Cheng　龔成
Gong Ziyuan　龔子元

gong-nong-bing　工農兵
Gong'an　公安
gongchandang　共產黨
gongchanzhuyi　共產主義
gongdi　工地
gongqingtuan　共青團
gongren　工人
gongshe　公社
gongtong　共同
gongzuo　工作
gou　狗
gou dongxi　狗東西
gou ji tiao qiang　狗急跳牆
gou ri de　狗日的
gouqiang　狗嗆
gu bu ke cui　固不可摧
Gu Hua　古華
Gu Junchi　顧駿翅
gu qian gu hou　顧前顧後
Gu Xinmin　谷新民
guafeng　刮風
Guan Hanqing　關漢卿
Guan Jianxun　管建勛
guang he re　光和熱
guangcai zhao ren　光彩照人
guangda　廣大
Guangdong　廣東
guanghui　光輝
guangkuo　廣闊
guangming　光明
guangming zhengda　光明正大
Guangxi　廣西
Guangzhou　廣州
guanmo　觀摩
guanyu　關於
guanzhi　管制
guashuai　掛帥
gudian　古典
gui-sunzi　龜孫子
gui-zaizi　鬼崽子
Guiyang　貴陽
Guiying　桂英
Guizhou　貴州

guizi 鬼子

gunainai 姑奶奶

guniang 姑娘

guniang-jia 姑娘家

Guo Chengqing 郭澄清

Guo Moruo 郭沫若

Guo Xianhong 郭先紅

Guo Zhigang 郭志剛

guo-neiwai 國內外

guojia 國家

guonian 過年

guoqu 過去

guren 古人

gutou ying 骨頭硬

guyi 故意

guyuci 古語詞

Ha'erbin 哈爾濱

hai qun zhi ma 害群之馬

Hai Rui ba guan 海瑞罷官

Haigang 海港

haipa 害怕

haishi 還是

haizi 孩子

han 函

han xin ru ku 含辛茹苦

Hang Tao 杭濤

hanhou 憨厚

Hanyu 漢語

hao bu li ji, zhuanmen li ren 毫不利己，專門利人

hao da xi gong 好大喜功

Hao feng pinjie li, song wo shang qingyun 好風憑借力，送我上青雲

hao huo 好貨

Hao Ran 浩然

haobi 好比

haochu 好處

haohan 好漢

haohaodangdang 浩浩蕩蕩

haokan 好看

haoling 號令

haoqing 豪情

haoshi 好事

He Fei 賀非

he shan shan rang lu, ji shui shui zhi liu 喝山山讓路，擊水水止流

He Zhi 何直

hedeng 何等

hefa 合法

Hefei 合肥

hei li tou hong 黑里透紅

Heilongjiang 黑龍江

Heluxiaofu 赫魯曉夫

Henan 河南

hengheng 哼哼

heshan 河山

hezuohua 合作化

Hong deng ji 紅燈記

Hong hua 紅花

Hong liu gungun 紅流滾滾

Hong lou meng 紅樓夢

Hong Yan 洪雁

hongliang 洪亮

Hongnan zuozhan shi 虹南作戰史

Hongqi 紅旗

hongqi zhaozhan 紅旗招展

Hongse niangzijun 紅色娘子軍

hongse tiandi 紅色天地

Hongshikou 紅石口

hongtuo 烘托

Hongweibing 紅衛兵

Hongyu 紅雨

hongzhaji 轟炸機

hongzhong ban de 洪鐘般的

Hou Laowu 侯老五

Hou Wailu 侯外廬

houjin 後進

houqinbing 後勤兵

Hu Feng 胡風

Hu Jingzhi 胡經之

Hu shang xiao Balu 胡上小八路

hu shuo ba dao 胡說八道

Hu Yinqiang 胡尹強

Hu Zhengyan 胡正言

huan xin zhuang 換新裝

Huang Borong　黃伯榮
huang gou-zi　黃狗子
Huang Guang　黃光
Huang Runsheng　黃潤生
Huang Xiuzhen　黃秀珍
Huang Zuolin　黃佐臨
huangdan　荒誕
huangkong　惶恐
Huanle de hai　歡樂的海
Hubei　湖北
Huhehaote　呼和浩特
huhuan　呼喚
hui　惠
hui　誨
hui chui shangzhen　揮錘上陣
hui ren bu juan　誨人不倦
huichang　會場
huizi　揮子
Hulala, si dasha qing, han linlin,
　hunshen fa jin　忽喇喇，似大廈
　傾，汗淋淋，渾身發喋
Hulanhaote　呼蘭浩特
Hunan　湖南
hundan　渾蛋
Huo wang　火網
huohai daoshan　火海刀山
huoli　火力
Huoyan　火焰
huzhuzu　互助組
ji feng baoyu　疾風暴雨
ji feng zhou yu　急風驟雨
ji gen bu dong　基根不動
Ji Yanhua　紀延華
Ji zhan changkong　激戰長空
Ji zhan wuming chuan　激戰無名川
Jia Weimin　賈為民
jian　劍
jian bu ke cui　堅不可摧
jian shimian　見世面
jian tian　見天
jianbang-zi　肩膀子
Jiang-bu-zhu　將不住
Jiang Chunwang　江春旺

Jiang Hongyun　江鴻運
Jiang pan zhaoyang　江畔朝陽
Jiang Qing　江青
Jiang shui taotao　江水滔滔
Jiang Yulin　江玉林
Jiang Yutian　江雨田
Jiang Zilong　蔣子龍
jiangjun　將軍
jianglai　將來
jiangnan　江南
Jiangsu　江蘇
Jianhe lang　劍河浪
jianjue　堅決
jiankang　健康
jianku fendou　艱苦奮斗
jianshe　建設
Jianshe-zhe　建設者
jianzao　建造
jiao　交
Jiao lin ernü　膠林兒女
jiao ma bu jue　叫罵不絕
Jiao Shuhong　焦淑紅
jiao'ao　驕傲
jiaobu　腳步
jiaodao　教導
jiaohua　狡猾
jiaojian　矯健
Jiaoliang　較量
jiaoyan-shi　教研室
jiaoyu　教育
jiaoyuan　教員
jiaozi　餃子
Jiashan Xian　嘉山縣
jiba　雞巴
jiben　基本
jicheng　繼承
jie jiao　戒驕
jie zao　戒躁
jiebai　潔白
jiefangjun　解放軍
Jiefangjun Bao　解放軍報
jiehe　結合
jieji　階級

jieji-xing　階級性

jiejidouzheng　階級鬥爭

jiejieshishi　結結實實

jieshou zai-jiaoyu　接受再教育

jifeng　疾風

Jifeng　疾風

jiguan　機關

jiji feng yin　寂寂封音

jijing　寂靜

jili　極力

Jiliu　激流

Jimingshan xia　雞鳴山下

jin　斤

Jin Anfu　金安福

jin luo mi gu　緊鑼密鼓

Jin Qingyu　晉慶玉

Jin Zhu　金柱

Jinan　濟南

jincan　進餐

jing　靜

jing bu qi　經不起

Jing Chunhong　景春紅

jing dong bu diao　經冬不凋

jing er wu shi　敬而無失

jing fengyu　經風雨

jing tao hai lang　惊濤駭浪

jingju　京劇

jingju-tuan　京劇團

jingong　進攻

jingshen　精神

jingshen huanfa　精神煥發

Jinguang da dao　金光大道

jingyan　經驗

jingzi　鏡子

jinhuai tanbai　襟懷坦白

jinian　紀念

jinjin　僅僅

jinjunling　進軍令

jinr　今儿

jinshen　謹慎

jintian　今天

jinxing　進行

jinzi　金子

jiongjiong you shen　炯炯有神

jiqi　及其

jiti　集體

jiu　舊

jiu jing　久經

jiu jing zhengzhan　久經征戰

jiufen　糾紛

jiuji　救濟

jiujing　究竟

jiushi　就是

jixu　繼續

jiyao　紀要

jiyu　給與

jiyuan hen shen　積怨很深

jizhu　記住

ju shang tian　舉上天

ju-zu　劇組

jue yi si zhan　決一死戰

juede　覺得

juedui　絕對

juejing　倔勁

juewu　覺悟

Jumanghe　巨蟒河

junmei　俊美

junxiu　俊秀

jun-yu　軍語

junzhu　君主

junzi　君子

Junzi yu qi yan, wu suo gou er yi yi
　　君子于其言，無所苟而已矣

kai xin yu　開新宇

kaige　凱歌

kaikuo　開闊

kaipi　開闢

kang　炕

kangli　伉儷

kanlai　看來

kaoyan　考驗

kapian　卡片

Ke Fei　克非

ke ji feng gong　克己奉公

ke ji fu li　克己復禮

Ke Yang　克揚

keguan guilü　客觀規律

kengqiang youli　鏗鏘有力

kexue　科學

kexueyuan　科學院

Kezile shan xia　克孜勒山下

kong　空

konghe　恐嚇

Kongque gao fei　孔雀高飛

Kongzi　孔子

kouhao　口號

Kousanxian　摳三縣

kouwei　口味

kouyu　口語

ku yu qi feng　苦雨淒風

kuaibanr　快板儿

kuan　寬

kuan jian kuo bei　寬肩闊背

Kuangbiao qu　狂飆曲

kuangfeng da zuo　狂風大作

Kuangshan fengyun　礦山風雲

kuangye　曠野

kui ran ru shan　巋然如山

kun shou you dou　困獸猶斗

kuo　闊

lachelache　拉扯拉扯

lai-tian　來天

laibuji　來不及

laipigou　癩皮狗

lalatata　邋邋遢遢

lan bu weijin　藍布圍巾

Lan-tian zhi　藍天志

Lancangjiang pan　瀾滄江畔

lang　浪

lang xin gou fei　狼心狗肺

langbei bukan　狼狽不堪

lao　老

lao dongxi　老東西

lao jiang xin bing　老將新兵

lao san pian　老三篇

Lao wu lao, yi ji ren zhi lao　老吾老，
　　以及人之老

lao yi bei　老一輩

lao-di　老弟

lao-mei　老妹

laodong　勞動

laoniang　老娘

laopo　老婆

laotianye　老天爺

laotouzi　老頭子

Laozi　老子

le shan bu juan　樂善不倦

le tou bao yan　勒頭暴眼

lei　雷

lei da bu fei　雷打不飛

leiji　累積

leiming ban de　雷鳴般的

lengbufang　冷不防

lengfeng　冷風

li　禮

Li Bai　李白

Li Bao'an　李保安

Li Fan　李凡

Li Fengzhu　李豐祝

Li Fugui　李富貴

Li Guifen　李桂芬

Li Hangyu　李杭育

Li He　李賀

Li Helin　李何林

Li Huixin　李惠薪

li jian　利劍

li jing pan dao　離經叛道

Li Ke　李克

Li Kuanding　李寬定

Li Liangjie　李良傑

li ling zhi hun　利令智昏

Li Mingxing　李明性

li qu ci qiong　理屈詞窮

Li Rongde　李榮德

Li Ruqing　黎汝清

Li Shangyin　李商隱

Li Shen　李紳

Li Xiaojun　李小俊

Li Xingjian　李行健

Li Xueshi　李學詩

Li Yinlan　李銀蘭

Li Yunde　李雲德

Li Zhiyao　栗志遙

Li Zicheng　李自成

Lian Chunshan　廉春山

Lian Hua　廉華

Lian xin suo　連心鎖

Liang Haishan　梁海山

liang jun duilei　兩軍對壘

liang mian san dao　兩面三刀

Liang San　梁三

Liang Shengbao　梁生寶

Liang Yongqing　梁永清

liang zhang　兩仗

liangshi　糧食

lianhe　聯合

lianpang　臉龐

lianxu　連續

liao xian pian　聊閑篇

Liao Xudong　廖序東

Liaoning　遼寧

lichang　立場

lidai　歷代

liji　立即

liliang　力量

lilun　理論

lin　淋

Lin Biao　林彪

Lin Wei　林葦

lin wei bu ju　臨危不懼

Lin Yu　林予

Ling si hao chanpin　'04' 號產品

lingdao　領導

lingxian　領先

lingxiu　領袖

lingyun zhi　凌雲志

lishi　歷史

Liu Dawen　劉達文

Liu Fu　劉福

Liu Hai　劉海

Liu Huaizhang　劉懷章

Liu Qing　柳青

Liu Shaoqi　劉少奇

Liu Shuxin　劉叔新

Liu Suola　劉索拉

Liu Wan　劉萬

Liu Wangchun　柳旺春

Liu Xiang　劉祥

Liu Xie　劉勰

Liu Xinwu　劉心武

Liu Yanlin　劉彥林

Liu Yingzi　劉英子

Liu Yunpeng　劉雲鵬

Liu Zengjie　劉增杰

Liu Zongyuan　柳宗元

liuda　溜達

Liuhetun fenghuo　柳河屯烽火

liushen　留神

liushui juanjuan　流水涓涓

lixiang　理想

lixiangzhuyi　理想主義

Long Youtian　龍友田

longlong　隆隆

Longse　龍澤

Lontan chunse　龍灘春色

Longwang Ye　龍王爺

longzhao　籠罩

Lu　路

Lu Bugu　魯布谷

Lu Junyi　盧俊義

Lu Linhan　魯林漢

Lu Xun　魯迅

Lu Zhiluo　魯之洛

lü　屢

lü fan cuowu　屢犯錯誤

Lü Ruifen　呂瑞芬

Lü Ziyang　呂自揚

luan qi ba zao　亂七八糟

lüe hou　略厚

lun　論

lunwen ji　論文集

Lunyu　論語

luo xia di　落下地

Luo Xuguang　羅旭光

Luo Yin　羅寅

luogu zhen tian　鑼鼓震天

luohua liushui　落花流水

luoluo dafang　落落大方

lüshi　律詩
luxian　路線
ma　媽
Ma Chun　馬春
Ma Guofan　馬國凡
Ma Laosi　馬老四
Ma Lianfu　馬連福
Ma Liben　馬立本
Ma Zhiyue　馬之悦
Ma-Liezhuyi　馬列主義
Mai Qing　麥青
Makesizhuyi　馬克思主義
mama　媽媽
man yan you lü　滿眼油綠
manman　滿滿
mantian　漫天
mantian feng xue　漫天風雪
mao　毛
Mao Dun　茅盾
mao niao　貓尿
Mao Zedong　毛澤東
Mao Zedong Sixiang　毛澤東思想
Mao Zhuxi　毛主席
maodun　矛盾
maomaoyu　毛毛雨
maozi　帽子
mei　美
Mei cheng nuhuo　煤城怒火
Mei Lanfang　梅蘭芳
mei lian　沒臉
meili　美麗
meipo　媒婆
meixue　美學
meiyou　沒有
meizi　妹子
Meng Fubi　孟復璧
meng po meng dao　猛潑猛倒
Meng Qishan　孟起山
Meng Shoujie　孟守杰
meng-hu pai　猛虎排
mengmenglonglong　朦朦朧朧
mengya　萌芽
mi wu nong yun　密霧濃雲

mianqian　面前
mianxie　棉鞋
mianyan　綿延
Min Guoku　閔國庫
Ming　明
mingliang　明亮
mingtang　名堂
mo bu guanxin　莫不關心
mo bu zuo sheng　莫不作聲
Mo dengxian, bai le shaonian tou,
　　kong bei qie　莫等閑，白了少
　　年頭，空悲切
Mo Yan　莫言
Mo Yingfeng　莫應豐
mohuan　魔幻
moluo　沒落
Mousi　繆斯
mu　畝
Mu Chongguang　牟崇光
Mu Fu　牧夫
Mu Guiying　穆桂英
mubiao　目標
muguang　目光
mulu　目錄
musong　目送
na gu-zi　那股子
nage　哪個
nainai　奶奶
namen　哪門
namen　納悶
nan　難
nan bing nü jiang　男兵女將
Nan nü shou shou bu qin　男女授受
　　不親
Nan Shao　南哨
nan zun nü bei　男尊女卑
nanguai　難怪
Nanjing　南京
nannü　男女
Nantong Shi　南通市
nanzihan　男子漢
nao　鬧
naodai　腦袋

naozi　腦子

naxie　哪些

nayang　哪樣

Nei Menggu　內蒙古

niang　娘

niangmen　娘們

niangzijun　娘子軍

Niannian you ru lin zhen ri, xinxin chang si guo qiao shi　念念有如臨陣日，心心常似過橋時

nianqing　年輕

nianqing ren　年輕人

niao　鳥

niu gui she shen　牛鬼蛇神

Niutianyang　牛田洋

Nong Liji　農力吉

nong mei da yan　濃眉大眼

nong yun mi bu　濃雲密布

nongcun　農村

Nongnu ji　農奴戟

nongye xue Dazhai　農業學大寨

nuli　努力

Nuli de nü'er　奴隸的女兒

Nuo fan cuo baba — jiao cheng yi tuan　糯飯搓粑粑 — 攪成一團

nüren-jia　女人家

Ouyang Shan　歐陽山

paichi daji　排斥打擊

pao-sa　拋撒

paohong　炮轟

paohuo　炮火

paosheng　炮聲

Paoxiao de Songhuajiang　咆哮的松花江

peichen　陪襯

peiyang　培養

Peng Qihua　彭啟華

pianpian　偏偏

piantan si ji　偏袒私己

piaoliang　漂亮

piaopiao yu xian　飄飄欲仙

piguyan　屁股眼

pili　霹靂

pili ban de　霹靂般的

pin-xiazhongnong　貧下中農

ping　評

pinglun　評論

pinglunzu　評論組

pingshuo　評說

pingxi　評析

pinnong　貧農

pipan　批判

piping　批評

po　頗

po jiu li xin　破舊立新

popo　婆婆

poyi　婆姨

pu　鋪

pubian　普遍

pudian　鋪墊

pushi　樸實

putonghua　普通話

qi shou ba jiao　七手八腳

Qi Wende　戚文德

qi you ci li　豈有此理

qi yun　起雲

qia si　恰似

qian　牽

Qian chong lang　千重浪

Qian Haoliang　錢浩亮

qian jun wan ma　千軍萬馬

qian pa lang hou pa hu　前怕狼後怕虎

'Qian shi tiao'　前十條

qiangjian youli　強健有力

qiangsheng　槍聲

qianjin　前進

qianmian　前面

qianqianwanwan　千千萬萬

qianwan　千萬

Qianxi　前夕

qianxu　謙虛

qianxun　謙遜

qiao bu sui　敲不碎

qiao yan ling se　巧言令色

Qidi chang ming　汽笛長鳴

qie kan　且看

qieyi　愜意

qifeng　淒風

qin　親

Qin long tu　擒龍圖

Qin Zhaoyang　秦兆陽

Qing　清

Qingchun　青春

Qingchun zhi ge　青春之歌

qinghui　清輝

qingjing　清靜

qingke　頃刻

qinglang　晴朗

qingmie　輕蔑

Qingming　清明

qingnian　青年

Qingshaonian hu po shao　青少年護
　泊哨

Qingshibao　青石堡

qingsu　傾訴

qingtian pili　晴天霹靂

qingxiangxing　傾向性

qingxu　情緒

Qingyun　晴雲

qingzhan　請戰

qinjing　欽敬

qinna　擒拿

Qingzhushe　青竹蛇

qinzi　親自

qiong ze si bian　窮則思變

qiongqiong jie li　煢煢孑立

qishi　其實

Qiu Lan　邱嵐

qixi　奇襲

Qixi Bahutuan　奇襲白虎團

qizi　妻子

qu　曲

Qu Xingqi　屈興岐

qu zhi ruo wu　趨之若鶩

quanguo　全國

quanmian　全面

que　卻

qunzhong　群眾

quzi　曲子

Ran Huaizhou　冉懷舟

rang　讓

ren　仁

ren mian shou xin　人面獸心

renhe　任何

renliu　人流

renmin　人民

renmin gongshe　人民公社

Renping fenglang qi, wen zuo diaoyu
　chuan　任憑風浪起，穩坐釣魚
　船

renshi　認識

renwu　人物

renxing　人性

renzhen　認真

ri　日

ri biao ye zhang　日標夜長

rouhe　柔和

rounen　柔嫩

ru dao shi　儒道釋

ru ku han xin　茹苦含辛

ru niao shou san　如鳥獸散

Ru you Zhougong zhi cai zhi mei, shi
　jiao qie lin, qiyu bu zu guan ye yi
　如有周公之才之美，使驕且
　吝，其余不足觀也矣

ruci　如此

Ruixue zhao fengnian　瑞雪兆豐年

rujin　如今

sa　仁

sa　酒

sai　塞

San jia xiang　三家巷

san peichen　三陪襯

San tan Hongyudong　三探紅魚洞

san tuchu　三突出

san yan liang yu　三言兩語

san-jiehe　三結合

sanbu　散步

Sang Cheng　桑誠

Sanguo yanyi　三國演義

sao can yun　掃殘雲

saoshe 掃射

saozi 嫂子

secai 色彩

sha 傻

sha 啥

Shaanxi 陝西

Shajiabang 沙家浜

shan 閃

shan beng shi qing 山崩石傾

Shan feng 山風

Shan li ren 山里人

Shan Meng 山萌

Shan Xuepeng 單學鵬

shan yu yu lai feng man lou 山雨欲
來風滿樓

Shanchuan huxiao 山川呼嘯

Shandong 山東

shang 上

shang daoshan 上刀山

Shang Gong 尚弓

shang tian neng zhai xing, ru di neng
qin long 上天能摘星，入地能
擒龍

shanggan 傷感

Shanghai 上海

Shanghai Xian 上海縣

shangqie 尚且

shangtou 上頭

shangwu 晌午

shanhe yi xin 山河一新

Shanxi 山西

Shanxiang ju bian 山鄉巨變

shanying 山鷹

Shao Chuang 紹闖

Shao Quanlin 邵荃麟

shaohuopo 燒火婆

Shaonian hong hua bing 少年紅
畫兵

she chuan 射穿

Shede yi shen gua, gan ba huangdi la
xia ma 捨得一身剮，敢把皇帝
拉下馬

shehui 社會

shehuizhuyi 社會主義

Shehuizhuyi Jiaoyu Yundong 社會主
義教育運動

Shen Shungen 沈順根

shen wei 神威

shen yu yan 慎于言

shencai yiyi 神采奕奕

sheng ru zhong 聲如鍾

Sheng Shujun 盛淑君

Sheng Youting 盛佑亭

shenghuo 生活

shengji bobo 生機勃勃

shengli 勝利

shengqi bobo 生氣勃勃

shengqi huhu 生氣虎虎

shengshi haoda 聲勢浩大

shenqi 神氣

shenqir 神氣ル

shense 神色

Shenyang 沈陽

shenzhi 甚至

sheyuan 社員

shi 詩

shi 使

shi 史

shi 是

Shi Caihong 石彩虹

Shi Changqing 石長慶

Shi Fengyang 石鳳陽

Shi Huying 石虎英

Shi Jigen 史繼根

Shi Laifu 石來富

Shi Shi 史釋

Shi Weniu 石文駒

shi you ba jiu 十有八九

Shi Zhuang 石莊

shici 詩詞

shidai 時代

shide 似的

shifen 十分

shihou 時候

shiji 世紀

Shijiazhuang 石家莊

shijie　世界

shijing　使勁

shike　時刻

'Shiliu tiao'　十六條

shiqi　實其

shishi　誓師

shishi hui　誓師會

shiwu　失誤

shi-zi　勢子

shou de qi　受得起

shou de zhu　守得住

Shou e wu ru se yu　首惡無如色欲

shouwan　手腕

shu　恕

shu gen　樹根

Shu Ting　舒婷

shuang　霜

shuanglang　爽朗

shui dao qu cheng　水到渠成

Shui hu zhuan　水滸傳

Shui xia jianbing　水下尖兵

shui zhang chuan gao　水漲船高

Shuijinggong　水晶宮

shuimian　水面

shuji　書記

shumianyu　書面語

shumu　書目

shunxi jian　瞬息間

shuo qu fangpi　説蛆放屁

si bu ming mu　死不瞑目

si lu jingbing　四路精兵

si shi ba jie　四時八詳

si ye bu ming mu　死也不瞑目

si-ren-bang　四人幫

sichao　思潮

sihai　四海

siling　司令

silu　思路

simian　四面

Siqing　四清

sixiang　思想

sixin　死心

sixu fanteng　思緒翻騰

Song　宋

Song Jiang　宋江

Song Yaoliang　宋耀良

Song Zhenguo　宋振國

songtao huxiao　松濤呼嘯

suanji　算計

sui　碎

suidao　隧道

suihe　隨和

Sun Feng　孫颯

Sun Jiayu　孫家玉

Sun Jingrui　孫景瑞

Sun Qizhi　孫其智

suo zuo suo wei　所作所為

suoyi　所以

suzao　塑造

ta ma de　他媽的

ta niang de　他娘的

ta shang zhengtu　踏上征途

Tai Zai　泰崽

taidu　態度

Taishan ya ding bu wanyao　泰山壓
　　頂不彎腰

Taiyuan　太原

Tan bao ji　探寶記

Tan Zongji　譚宗級

Tang　唐

Tang Jinhai　唐金海

Tang Qun　唐群

Tang Yijie　湯一介

tangke　堂客

tanran ziruo　坦然自若

tansuo　探索

tanxu　談敘

tao　濤

tao　套

taolun　討論

taotao da lang　滔滔大浪

texing　特性

ti　悌

Tian Dongzhao　田東照

Tian Guifa　田貴發

tian ta di lie　天塌地裂

Tiananmen 天安門

Tianjin 天津

tianmen 天門

tianming 天命

tianqi 天氣

tianxia wei gong 天下為公

tiaozhan 挑戰

ticai 題材

tie da han 鐵打漢

tie jian tou 鐵肩頭

tie jiandan 鐵肩擔

Tie xuanfeng 鐵旋風

tie-guniang 鐵姑娘

Tie-mian wusi 鐵面無私

tiehanzi 鐵漢子

tielu 鐵路

Tieqi 鐵騎

tigao 提高

tihui 體會

ting er zou xian 鋌而走險

ting xiang 挺象

tingli 挺立

titi zhaozhao 蹄蹄爪爪

tong 通

Tong Bian 童邊

tong ling ban de 銅鈴般的

tong pian 通篇

Tong qiang tie bi 銅牆鐵壁

Tong Xian 通縣

tongshi 通史

tongtong yu guan 童童玉冠

tongxue 同學

tongyi 統一

tongyici 同義詞

tongzhi 同志

tou sha 頭紗

tou shang zhang jiao, shen shang zhang ci 頭上長角，身上長刺

toubu 頭部

toufa 頭髮

toutou 頭頭

toutounaonao 頭頭腦腦

tuanjie 團結

Tuerdi Keyoumu 圖爾迪·柯尤木

Tugai 土改

tuhua 圖畫

tui bu dao 推不倒

tujidui 突擊隊

tuqiu 土丘

turan 突然

tushu 圖書

tushuguan 圖書館

tuxi 圖希

waibiao 外表

waifeng 歪風

wailai ci 外來詞

wan hun wan yu 晚婚晚育

wan jun leiting 萬鈞雷霆

wan li changcheng 萬里長城

Wan li zhanqi hong 萬里戰旗紅

Wan nian qing 萬年青

Wan shan hong 萬山紅

Wan shan hong bian 萬山紅遍

Wang Anyi 王安憶

Wang Boxi 王伯熙

Wang Dong 王棟

Wang Dongman 王東滿

Wang Huaishan 王懷善

Wang Jingzhong 王精忠

Wang Lan 王蘭

Wang Lei 汪雷

Wang Lei 王磊

Wang Lin 王琳

Wang Meng 王蒙

Wang Qin 王勤

Wang Shifu 王實甫

Wang Shige 王世閣

Wang Shimei 王士美

Wang Shuo 王朔

Wang Wei 王微

Wang Xiaomei 王小梅

Wang Xiaoying 王小鷹

Wang Xijie 王希杰

Wang Ying 王穎

Wang Youqing 王友清

Wang Zengqi 汪曾祺

Wang Zhihuan　王之渙

wangba　王八

wangba-dan　王八蛋

wangji　忘記

wangsheng　旺盛

Wangyunfeng　望雲峰

wanmei　完美

wanshang　晚上

wansui　萬歲

wei bo bu xing　微波不興

Wei Chaoben　韋朝本

Wei Gengtian　韋耿田

Wei Junping　韋君平

wei renmin fuwu　為人民服務

weibing　衛兵

weida　偉大

weile　為了

weimiao　微妙

weisheng　尾聲

weituo　委托

weixiao　微笑

weiyan　威嚴

weiyuanhui　委員會

Wen Duanzheng　溫端正

wen liang gong jian rang　溫良恭儉讓

wen yi zai Dao　文以載道

wen zhe zu jie　聞者足戒

wen zhi binbin　文質彬彬

wenfeng　文風

wenhua　文化

wenhua zhan　文化站

wenji　文集

wenjian　穩健

wenshou　瘟收

wenti　問題

wenwendangdang　穩穩當當

wenxian　文獻

wenxue　文學

wenyan　文言

wenyan ci　文言詞

wenyi　文藝

Wenyi Bao　文藝報

wenzi　文字

wenzi gaige　文字改革

women　我們

wu　霧

Wu Han　吳玲

wu yan shi　五言詩

Wu Yanke　五廷科

wu zhong ren　五種人

Wu Zuguang　吳祖光

wucai binfen　五彩繽紛

wuchanjieji　無產階級

Wuchanjieji Wenhua Da Geming　無產階級文化大革命

wudong　舞動

wugui-wangba　烏龜王八

Wuhan　武漢

Wuhu　蕪湖

Wulan Tuoya　烏蘭托婭

Wulingshan xia　武陵山下

wuqi　武器

wuzang liufu　五臟六腑

xi　系

xi lang qian chong　細浪千重

Xi qi　喜期

Xi-sha ernü　西沙兒女

Xi xiang ji　西廂記

Xi Zhi　奚直

Xia man Longwan　霞漢龍灣

xia you guo　下油鍋

Xiadao　霞島

xiagui　下詭

xiahu　嚇唬

xian　顯

Xi'an　西安

xian yuanxing　現原形

xiandai　現代

xiandai xi　現代戲

xiandai-pai　現代派

Xiang　湘

Xiang Chun　向春

Xiang Liangao　項連高

xiang'an wushi　相安無事

xiangdangdang　響當當

Xiangshuiwan 響水灣

xiangying 響應

xianjin 先進

xianshi 現實

xianshizhuyi 現實主義

xianwei 縣委

xianzai 現在

xianzhi 縣誌

xiao 小

xiao 孝

Xiao bing chuang da shan 小兵闖大刪

Xiao Changchun 蕭長春

Xiao cheng chunjiu 小城春秋

xiao duzi 小犢子

Xiao Lin 蕭林

Xiao Long 小龍

xiaohua 笑話

xiaojiang 小將

xiaolong jingji 小農經濟

xiaosheng 笑聲

xiaoshuo 小説

xiaoxi 消息

xiaoyan 硝煙

xiaozu 小組

xiashuo 瞎説

xiazi 瞎子

xibalan 稀巴爛

xie feng 邪風

Xie Shu 謝樹

Xie Zuozhu 謝作柱

xiehouyu 歇後語

xielu 邪路

Xi'er 喜兒

xieyi 寫意

xiezi 楔子

xifu 媳婦

xihuan 喜歡

xili 洗禮

xili 犀利

xin 新

xin 信

xin dang-jia 新當家

xin hong 心紅

Xin Jianshe 新建設

Xin lai de xiao Shizhu 新來的小石柱

xin you ling xi yi dian tong 心有靈犀一點通

xin zhong you shu 心中有數

xingfu 幸福

xingshi 形勢

xingxiang 形象

xingying xiangdiao 形影相吊

xingzhi bobo 興致勃勃

xinli 心里

xinling 心靈

xinsheng shiwu 新生事物

xinshi nongmin 新式農民

xinxian jidang 心弦激蕩

xinxue 心血

xiong you cheng zhu 胸有成竹

xiongjiujiu 雄赳赳

Xique Cun de haizi 喜鵲村的孩子

xishua 洗刷

xitu 希圖

xiu bing ba zhan 休兵罷戰

xiu diqiu 繡地球

xiucixue 修辭學

xiuxi 休息

xiuzhengzhuyi 修正主義

xiwen 檄文

xu 序

Xu Tesheng 許特生

Xu Xing 徐星

xuanbu 宣布

xuanchuandui 宣傳隊

xuandu 選讀

xuanlan 絢爛

xuanzhan 宣戰

xue 雪

xue 學

Xue Baochai 薛寶釵

xue er bu yan 學而不厭

xuetong-lun 血統論

xuni 虛擬

xutan 敘談

xuwei 虛偽
yadao 壓倒
yagenr 壓根儿
Yan'an 延安
Yan fei sai bei 雁飛塞北
Yan Gang 閻綱
yan guo liu sheng, ren guo liu ming
　　雁過留聲，人過留名
Yan ying 岩鷹
yan zhe wu zui 言者無罪
yanchu 演出
yandong 嚴冬
Yang Bailao 楊白勞
Yang Chuntian 楊春田
Yang Daqun 楊大群
Yang Lan 楊嵐
Yang Mo 楊沫
Yang Shuzhong 楊書中
Yang Xiao 楊嘯
yangban xi 樣板戲
yangxiang 洋相
yangyang daguan 洋洋大觀
Yanhe zai zhaohuan 廷河在召喚
yanhu 掩護
yanjiang 演講
yanjing 眼睛
yanjiu 研究
yanjiusuo 研究所
yanjun 嚴峻
Yanminghu pan 雁鳴湖畔
yanqian 眼前
yanshuang linlie 嚴霜凜冽
Yanyang tian 艷陽天
yanyu 言語
yanyu 諺語
yanzhong 嚴重
Yao 瑤
Yao Shijie 姚士傑
Yao Wenyuan 姚文元
Yao Xueyin 姚雪垠
yaofeng 妖風
yaolun 要論
yaoyue 邀約

yayan 雅言
Ye Xin 葉辛
yemen 爺們
yeye 爺爺
yeyu xuexiao 業余學校
yeyu zuozhe 業余作者
yi 義
yi chu ji fa 一觸即發
yi dao dian shan 一道電閃
yi gu feng xiao 一股風嘯
yi gugu 一股股
yi pian laosao 一篇牢騷
yi qing er chu 一清二楚
yi qiong er bai 一窮二白
Yi Qun 以群
yi sheng bu keng 一聲不吭
yi tiao xian shang bang de liang zhi
　　mazha, shui ye pao bu diao 一條
　　線上綁的兩隻螞蚱，誰也跑
　　不掉
yi tong/zhen laosao 一通/陣牢騷
yi wen san bu zhi 一問三不知
yi zhong ben 乙種本
yiban 一般
yibeizi 一輩子
yidianr 一點儿
yijian 意見
yijian fenfen 意見紛紛
yijing 已經
yijing 意境
yilu 一路
Yin Menglun 殷孟倫
yinchang 吟唱
ying feng 迎風
yinggai 應該
yingjun 英俊
yingrao 縈繞
yingxiang 影響
yingxiong 英雄
Yingxiong de xiangtu 英雄的鄉土
yingzhan 應戰
yingzhao 映照
yingzi 影子

yinmou　陰謀

Yinshatan　銀沙灘

yinshua　印刷

yinyong　吟詠

yirong　遺容

yishiliu　意識流

yishixingtai　意識形態

yishu　藝術

yiwei　以為

yong　勇

yongshi　勇士

yongyuan　永遠

you bao pipa ban zhe mian　猶抱琵琶半遮面

you li zou bian tianxia　有理走遍天下

youqi　尤其

youran er sheng　油然而生

yu　雨

yu　遇

Yu hou qingshan　雨後青山

yu jia zhi zui, he huan wu ci　欲加之罪，何患無詞

Yu Laonian　余老蔫

yu ren gong er you li　與人恭而有禮

Yu Si　余四

yu wu lun ci　語無倫次

Yu Xiazi　雨瞎子

Yu Yan　于言

Yu Yunquan　俞雲泉

yu zhong bu tong　與眾不同

Yuan　元

yuan shan　遠山

yuan yu shenghuo, gao yu shenghuo　源于生活，高于生活

yuan zou gao fei　遠走高飛

yuanxiao　院校

yuanze　原則

Yue Fei　岳飛

Yue yi hua ying dong, yi shi yu ren lai　月移花影動，疑是玉人來

Yue Yong　岳勇

Yue zhao dong qiang　月照東牆

yuefa　越發

yuekan　月刊

yuhui　語匯

yun　雲

yun　暈

yun liang che dui　運糧車隊

Yun yan　雲燕

yundong　運動

yuwen　語文

yuyan　語言

yuyanxue　語言學

za　砸

za bu bian　砸不扁

zan bu jue kou　贊不絕口

zan kou bu jue　贊口不絕

zanshang　贊賞

zao qiang beng de　遭槍崩的

zaofan pai　造反派

zaofan you li　造反有理

zaojiu　造就

Zaolin Cum　棗林村

zaori　早日

zengjin　增進

zenme ban　怎麼辦

zeze you sheng　嘖嘖有聲

zha　炸

zha diao　炸掉

zhagu　扎古

Zhai shang fengyan　寨上烽煙

zhan　沾

zhan ding jie tie　斬釘截鐵

zhan ding qie tie　斬釘切鐵

zhan qian gu hou　瞻前顧後

zhan ru song　站如松

zhan shuang chi　展雙翅

zhan tian dou zai　戰天斗災

zhanchang　戰場

Zhandi hong ying　戰地紅纓

zhandou　戰斗

zhang　仗

Zhang Changgong　張長工

Zhang Chengzhi　張承志

Zhang Chunqiao　張春橋

Zhang Enru　張恩儒

Zhang Fei　張飛

Zhang Feng　張楓

Zhang Guizhen　張桂貞

Zhang Hang (/Xing)　張行

Zhang Jianguo　張建國

Zhang Jie　張潔

Zhang Jihua　張繼華

Zhang Jinfa　張金發

Zhang Jing　張靜

Zhang Jun　張峻

Zhang Kangkang　張抗抗

Zhang Tuosheng　張沱生

Zhang Xiangwu　張向午

Zhang Xianliang　張賢亮

Zhang Xinxin　張辛欣

Zhang Xue　張雪

Zhang Yunfei　張韻斐

Zhang Zhigong　張志公

zhangcheng　章程

Zhanghe chun　漳河春

Zhangtianhe　樟田河

zhangu　戰鼓

zhanhao　戰壕

Zhanhuo cui chun　戰火催春

zhanshi　戰士

zhanxian　戰線

zhanyang　瞻仰

zhanyou　戰友

zhao　罩

Zhao Deming　趙德明

Zhao Guang'en　趙光恩

Zhao Junxian　趙俊賢

Zhao Tie　趙鐵

Zhao Yiliang　趙義良

zhaoji　著急

zhaokai　召開

zhaopai　招牌

zhaoqi pengbo　朝氣蓬勃

Zhaorigebatu　照日閣巴圖

Zhaoxia　朝霞

zhaoyaojing　照妖鏡

zhaoying　照應

zhayan　眨眼

zhe　這

zhege　這個

zheme　這麼

zhen　鎮

zhendi　陣地

zhenfen buyi　振奮不已

zheng　爭

Zheng Jiazhen　鄭加真

Zheng Shiqian　鄭士謙

Zheng Suzhi　鄭素芝

Zheng Wanlong　鄭萬隆

Zheng Yuanhan　鄭遠漢

Zheng Zhi　鄭直

zhengdun　整頓

zhengfu　征服

zhengge　整個

zhenggui budui　正規部隊

zhengmian　正面

zhengqi lian　爭氣連

zhengshi　正是

Zhengtu　征途

zhengzheng yinghan　錚錚硬漢

zhengzhi　政治

Zhengzhou　鄭州

zhenshi　真實

zhenshi xing　真實性

zhentian　震天

zhenzheng　真正

zheteng　折騰

zhexie　這些

zhexue　哲學

zheyang　這樣

zhi　志

zhi　智

Zhi qu Weihushan　智取威虎山

zhi shan zhi shui　治山治水

Zhi zhi wei zhi zhi, bu zhi wei bu zhi, shi zhi ye　知之為知之，不知為不知，是知也

zhihui-bu　指揮部

zhijie liaodang　直接了當

Zhiqi ge　志氣歌

zhishi qingnian　知識青年
zhiyuan　志願
zhong　忠
Zhong gu ji　種谷記
Zhong Tao　鍾濤
Zhonghua　中華
zhongjian renwu　中間人物
Zhongliu dizhu　中流砥柱
zhongnong　中農
zhongpian xiaoshuo　中篇小説
Zhongwen　中文
Zhongyang　中央
Zhou Bo　周勃
Zhou Dunyi　周敦頤
Zhou Enlai　周恩來
Zhou Gucheng　周谷城
Zhou Jiajun　周家峻
Zhou Liangsi　周良思
Zhou Libo　周立波
Zhou Liping　周麗萍
Zhou Xiao　周肖
Zhou Yang　周揚
Zhou Zhentian　周振天
zhu chao　主潮
Zhu Jian　朱劍
Zhu Qingyu　朱慶余
Zhu Tiehan　朱鐵漢
Zhu Xi　朱熹
zhu Zhou wei nüe　助紂為虐

Zhuang　壯
zhuangzhuangshishi　壯壯實實
Zhuangzu　壯族
zhuanyou　轉悠
zhuazhu　抓住
zhun　準
zhunbei　準備
zhuozhuang　茁壯
zhurengong　主人公
zhuyao　主要
zhuzuo　著作
zi li geng sheng　自力更生
zi xing qi shi　自行其是
zi yan zi yu　自言自語
zibenzhuyi　資本主義
ziran zaihai　自然災害
ziweir　滋味儿
zizhiqu　自治區
Zong Pu　宗璞
Zongluxian　毅路線
zongxiang　縱向
zouzipai　走資派
Zuan Tian-feng　鑽天峰
zuichun　嘴唇
zuo zei xin xu　作賊心虛
zuor　昨儿
zuotanhui　座談會
zuoyong　作用
zuzhi　組織
zuzong　祖宗

Index

In this index, a span of numbers, e.g. 3–4, 38–41, indicates a continuous discussion over two pages or more. *Passim* is used for a cluster of references in close but not necessarily consecutive sequence. Countable items are listed in singular form.